IF BEALE STREET COULD TALK

If Beale Street Could Talk

MUSIC, COMMUNITY, CULTURE

ROBERT CANTWELL

UNIVERSITY OF ILLINOIS PRESS URBANA & CHICAGO

Manufactured in the United States of America
1 2 3 4 5 C P 5 4 3 2 1
This book is printed on acid-free paper.

Library of Congress
Cataloging-in-Publication Data
Cantwell, Robert
If Beale Street could talk : music,
community, culture / Robert Cantwell
p. cm.
Includes bibliographical references and index.
ISBN 978-0-252-03362-9 (cloth : alk. paper)
ISBN 978-0-252-07566-7 (pbk. : alk. paper)
1. Music—Social aspects—United States.
2. Folklore—United States.
3. Ethnomusicology—United States.
I. Title
ML3917.U6C36 2008
780—dc22 2008027206

For Archie Green

CONTENTS

ACKNOWLEDGMENTS

Six of these twelve essays first appeared, in somewhat different form, in the following publications:

"Fanfare for the Little Guy," in Robert Santelli and Emily Davidson, eds., *Hard Travelin': The Life and Legacy of Woody Guthrie*. Hanover, N.H.: Wesleyan University Press, 1999. Pp. 153–69.

"Feasts of Unnaming: Folk Festivals and the Representation of Folklife," in Robert Baron and Nicholas R. Spitzer, eds., *Public Folklore*. Washington, D.C.: Smithsonian Institution Press, 1992. Pp. 263–305.

"Folklore's Pathetic Fallacy," in *Journal of American Folklore*, volume 114, number 451 (Winter 2001): 56–67.

"*Habitus*, Ethnomimesis: A Note on *The Logic of Practice*," in *Journal of Folklore Research*, volume 36, numbers 2–3 (May-December 1999): 219–34.

"The Invisible Science: A Note on Language, Causality, and Calculation," in *The New England Review*, volume 16, number 1 (Winter 1994): 129–40.

"White City Elegy: Modern and Postmodern at the World's Fair," in Townsend Ludington, ed., *A Modern Mosaic: Art and Modernism in the United States*. Chapel Hill: University of North Carolina Press, 2000. Pp. 12–46.

INTRODUCTION

FOLKLIFE AS REAL LIFE

These essays address three distinct but closely conjoined domains of human life—music, festivity, and culture—in which persons, families, and communities take pleasure, find fulfillment, and secure identity and social inclusion. They reflect a period in the very recent past in which one might think fruitfully about these subjects and understand them in relation to the changing memberships, affiliations, and attachments wrought by a new and powerful commercial civilization that until quite recently we called "postmodernity" but that we recognize now as a new form of global capitalism then in the early stages of formation. What the essays will I hope have ultimately to teach will be the perennial but sometimes neglected truth that we share, as a society, a collective life that far transcends even our most urgent concerns as persons, families, and communities, and that nothing can be written or spoken that does not in some sense reflect what that larger membership enables and disables, permits and prohibits, demands and discourages.

The essays throughout make implicitly the familiar claim that we are social animals. But they carry this truism beyond the social-constructionist framework in which we typically find it, where social power is immanent and all-determining, into human social interaction itself, which though it must occur in the context of social institutions and in some relation to social power, nevertheless has a subtle and I daresay a natural life of its own—a process of imitation, communication, and representation I call "ethnomimesis."[1]

"Mimesis," or imitation, says Aristotle, is a form of learning: "this," it affirms, "is that." In classical thought mimesis is normally associated with the Homeric poems, the tragic drama, and, in neoclassicism, with art more generally; *ethno*mimesis is the social form of mimesis that shapes us as social beings and as personalities. It transpires at a level well below formal and informal practices, prevailing authority, and powerful institutions through, if you will, a God-given sensory and imaginative capability by which we perceive, imitate, interpret, fashion, and figure-forth and reproduce our social selves by means of sensory cues mostly inaccessible to empirical observation but unceasingly at work in social interactions of all sorts. From minute changes in the iris of the eye, to the galvanic response of the skin, the musculature of the face and limbs, and many other effects and functions including language and its many nuances, we are, as bodies, rich bearers of social, emotional, and personal information, and preternaturally sensitive readers and interpreters of that information; indeed we would do well to think of the entire sensory apparatus, adaptively speaking, less as a window to the world than as a channel from one human being to another, a complex network of cultural communication within which our very perceptions of the real are formed. While the formal practices, protocols, habits, and customs of day-to-day social interaction unfold unerringly to our social awareness, ethnomimesis, at a far deeper level, is writing its own social script, one that will carry us in unanticipated directions and that is the creative engine of social and cultural change, as it springs on the one hand from the immediate contact of people with their circumstances and on the other from their natural and inescapable communication with one another.

At certain stages in their history the attitudes and practices of a particular social group may vividly betray its adaptations to the concrete conditions of existence—scarcity of resources, say, or repressive laws, a particular natural environment, or prevailing kinds of labor, or even such wholesale transformations as migration or war; but ethnomimesis, so long as the community as such persists, particularly in face-to-face interactions, will sustain those attitudes and practices well after the originally formative conditions have expired, often in ways that either marvelously promote the economic and cultural well-being of the group in new historical conditions or just as inexplicably disable it. In recognition of these processes, some conservative groups such as the Amish may seek actually to perpetuate in a material as well as a customary sense the originally formative circumstances; others may seek ways in new historical conditions to adapt its traditional attitudes, habits, practices and so on, so far as possible accommodating culture to circumstance, or, at last, to adjust to circumstance in new and innovative ways that ethnomimesis registers and distributes.

Ethnomimesis, then, provides for both continuity and change. What for one generation were the ideas, attitudes, and practices springing from immediate and pressing material need—say practical survival skills and individual self-reliance—may become for the next an ideology of independence for which it struggles to find a place in a context of interdependence, consumerism, and perhaps affluence; what for one generation was an ideologically motivated and self-consciously alternative way of life—strict religious observance, perhaps, or some form of political activism—may become for its children, surprisingly to parents, simply what may be taken for granted, or what must be fiercely resisted and ultimately rebelled against. Ethnomimesis, in other words, is the process by which we create culture's tacit understandings, what Pierre Bourdieu calls *habitus,* the "durably installed generative principle of regulated improvisations"[2] or "social alchemy" out of which the knowledges that underlie the possibility of culture come into being.

In a sense "ethnomimesis," the concept and the process, has lain at the heart of folklore and folklore studies from the days of Johann Gottfried von Herder and William John Thoms. As an academic discipline, folklore has found itself hampered by an epistemological predicament arising from the difficulty of locating and defining the folk process in any but a negative and exclusionary sense: folklore—forms of communication, expression, practice, craft, art, and the imaginative in the broadest senses—was something that happened outside the boundaries or below the level of "official," hegemonic, or "disciplinary" institutions, techniques, and discourses and hence often, or so it appeared, typically amongst poor, underprivileged, "backward" or subordinate people who by virtue of that condition enjoyed possession, almost invariably, of some cultural artifact, narrative, song, idea, or practice whose origins either lay in some former time and superannuated way of life or had sprung directly from the conditions of their own subordinate status. Therein lay the fascination and the mystery of folklore: it seemed to "preserve" old-fashioned ways, often it seemed of breathtaking antiquity; it evidenced the persistence of traditional cultures, or the growth of new "oral," informal, or face-to-face cultures, in the midst of contemporary life and often in spite of it; it affirmed the vitality of culture in various sequestered or enclaved groups such as children, racial and ethnic minorities, workers and peasants, and became potentially a means of championing the dignity, the value, and the rights of such groups and of raising cultural and political consciousness on their behalf.

Moreover, folklore always transpired in telling contradistinction to the inexorably modernizing ways of life that seemed to have displaced it: oral traditions in the midst of widespread literacy, handicraft skills in the midst of industrial production, oppositional lores in the midst of technical, corporate, and political systems that would seem to have appropriated, in postmodernity, virtually the whole of culture to themselves. Hence always "folklore" needed to be understood and defined in terms of these contradistinctions: it was what *wasn't* taught in schools, transmitted in manuals or textbooks, enforced by the corporations or the political, technical, or cultural authority—though it might be carried along the very channels in which these hegemonies moved. What was said or sung on the playground or the assembly line, what was negotiated in the flea market under the canopy of the shopping mall, what revised or improved upon, by custom, the manual, schedule, or text, what might be transmitted via e-mail or a fax machine, in between invoices, memos, and reports: that was folklore. Seldom taught, as Bess Hawes remarked, but often learned. Folklore was what it wasn't. But what *was* it?

My own traffic with ethnomimesis began with the ballad wars, an old scholarly debate left over from the nineteenth-century into which I looked when, undertaking a study of bluegrass music, I needed to acquaint myself with a field in which I had considerable interest but no training. There the question was how the "traditional ballad," so called from the great ballad compendia of Francis James Child and George Lyman Kittredge, was learned and transmitted, especially in light of the ballads' conventional or formulaic elements on the one hand and their many variations over time on the other. Were there printed or written texts, sometimes called "ballets," or broadsides, that were passed down either literally as texts or else memorized, emulated, learned, remembered and misremembered? Or was there some sort of "collective composition" at work, in which real conclaves of ballad singers exchanged their songs, freely borrowing, improvising, and recombining the traditional elements? Or could the ballad be compared to the oral-formulaic epic that Milman Parry and Albert Lord had studied in Yugoslavia—a traditional fund of fixed verbal and narrative structures from which the ballad singer drew in a performative process at once rule-driven and extemporaneous that reproduced old ballads, variations upon them, as well as composing new ones? Or was composition more strictly literary, though governed by the same set of formulaic elements?

The answer, of course, was all of the above; but at a deeper level the ballad, like other oral-formulaic forms, in whatever medium or by whatever process it came into existence, depended upon the operation of a mimetic imagination that incorporated, remembered, imitated, and in some way reproduced or represented what it heard or read, and either by inscription or improvisation reproduced in a form that like all folk forms was conspicuously both original and traditional at the same time as it belonged to a particular moment, a particular performance, a particular performer, and a particular set of circumstances. It could be at once traditional and original, individually and collectively composed, aural and literary.

Also suggestive was a conversation I had with Alan Lomax in the late 1970s concerning a kinesic study in which he was engaged, recording conversations between people of several different cultural groups on film. By slowing the film down to a few frames per second, he reported, one could detect the subtlest gestures of conversation passing back and forth between the participants in a kind of unconscious dance in which each speaker imitated, at a level otherwise imperceptible, the other's gestures, movements, and facial expressions; speakers reported, moreover, their feeling that they had been in best communication with one another when this unconscious mimicry had been established. I never saw the films nor heard of anyone else repeating the experiment; but being "in sync" or "in touch" seemed intuitively true to me, and moreover it echoed, remarkably, the argument I had encountered many years earlier in Eric Havelock's superb discussion of the classical idea of "mimesis" in his *Preface to Plato.*[3] Havelock maintains that in the Platonic tradition "mimesis" means not only the imitation, impersonation, representation or "figuring-forth" of the heroic characters and their speeches by the poet, or their dramatization in the poetic performance, but the subconscious responses of the poet's audience through which the poet inspired its deep identification or empathy with the material. "The ears transmitted messages to the nervous system as a whole," Havelock writes, "and thus limbs, lips, and throat might perform slightly, and the nervous system in general would be sympathetically engaged with what he was hearing."[4] In an oral tradition, Havelock argues, audiences to poetry and drama reanimated in their bodies, at the same time as they suppressed the actual outward repetition, the words, actions, and emotions of the characters as the poet embodied them—much as spectators at sporting events can be seen to be physically moved by the action on the field. And not necessarily suppressed!

I cannot claim to have consciously and deliberately applied Havelock's idea when I went to study the Smithsonian's Festival of American Folklife in the mid 1980s. But it is plain in retrospect that the theory of ethnomimesis, insofar as it *is* a theory, was a way of explaining to myself the indescribably various, complex, and elusive social interactions on the National Mall, the thing that made it go—"figuring forth," communicating, imparting to the senses and to the feelings the innumerable forms of culture- and community-making that the festival brought together on the Mall.

Having resurrected the idea of mimesis in connection with the Smithsonian's Festival of American Folklife, albeit with a prefix attached, I cannot help but be gratified to find in the science pages of the *New York Times* more than a decade later a kind of neurobiological confirmation of ethnomimesis in what are called "mirror neurons"—cells that, according to *New York Times* science writer Sandra Blakeslee, "specialize in carrying out and understanding not just the actions of others but their intentions, the social meaning of their behavior and their emotions." Mirror neurons, reports neuroscientist Dr. Giacomo Rozzolatti, "allow us to grasp the minds of others not through conceptual reasoning but through direct simulation. By feeling, not thinking."

Distributed through several regions of the brain, mirror neurons respond to "chains of actions linked to intentions," such as kicking a ball or drinking a glass of water, *simulating* the action in the observer's own brain while inhibiting an actual repetition of it, and reading the intentions of the actor. One's understanding of the action proceeds from a "template" in the observer's brain based on her own actions and intentions; we are, in other words, more thoroughly even than the poets could have conceived, what we perceive. This mirroring process includes emotions—observing others' expressions of emotion, we literally feel, neurologically, what others are feeling. Neither Plato nor Aristotle had heard of "mirror neurons," but had discovered them nevertheless.

Mirror neurons, Blakeslee continues, quoting Patricia Greenfield, a UCLA psychologist, "provide a powerful biological foundation for the evolution of culture, each generation teaching the next by social sharing, imitation, and observation." Certain studies suggest that autism and related abridgments of the ability to read others' feelings, Greenfield says, may represent inadequate mirror cell function. And, perhaps most importantly for us, mirror neurons seem to work best in face-to-face interactions, of which "virtual reality and videos are but shadowy substitutes."[5]

No wonder "postmodernity" strikes us as unreal.

Most of us are blessed with a seismically responsive ethnomimetic system, operating always below the level of the outward flow of events and relations, registering attitudes and feelings, forming attachments and breaking them, issuing vital communications, adopting the forms that will help to shape us as persons and to represent those forms to others, particularly in the erotic field, where ethnomimesis performs its principal work. Indeed, we could not be social beings at all without such a capacity. From ethnomimesis comes art.

There are certain areas of expressive or otherwise purposeful collective activity, however, that direct the ethnomimetic power towards the accomplishment of specific cooperative tasks—and one of these, most instructive for me, was ensemble music, especially an improvisatory form like jazz or bluegrass. This is the context in which, both as a student of bluegrass music and jazz and as an amateur musician (emphasis on *amateur*), I became aware of the ethnomimetic process as a factor in musical performance. My testimony will add nothing to the vast consensus among jazz and other improvisatory ensemble musicians that such groups are held together by a mysterious interresponsivity that virtually transforms an aggregate of individual players into a single organism, capable of darting with the direction of the music this way and that as instantaneously as a pair of swallows, according to prompts of which probably no technical device could even so much as detect the existence.

A glance of the eye, a bend of the elbow, perhaps a shift in posture, carried of course like gleams of light on the stream of the music—by these signals musicians find themselves turning a corner, pursuing a path, opening a door almost in the moment before they know they are doing these things. We find the same split-second micrometer precise coordination in actors and dancers, sports teams, in teams of workers cooperating to place a beam or raise a roof, and I suspect would find it too, had we adequate instruments, in marital quarrels, psychological consultations, classroom discussions, and corporate board meetings. But it is far from confined to these activities. Rather, it is paradigmatic for human social behavior as a whole, and though not always controlled by it, it nevertheless transpires under the buzz and the patter, outside the scripts and stage directions, and usually brings desired, though not always expected, outcomes—think of the man and woman, total strangers, who arrive separately at a party, are never to be found in the same conversational group, and yet, well before the evening has ended, may be observed leaving the party together. This is the ground and the matrix of culture, and what sustains, outside of formal roles, institutional structures, and hegemonic power, the cultural process.

Lest ethnomimesis strike us as uniformly benign, however, we ought to consider its role in a society in which vast swaths of experience come to us, in fact, in represented or mediated form, the "virtual," televisual, digital, and audial processes that distinguish our period. Everyone is familiar with what would be merely crass were it not so insidious, the relentless intrusion of sounds and images—processed rock, golden oldies, classical "lite," and the like, as well as regular radio and television programming—into stores, restaurants, offices, elevators, and even rest rooms, the more easily I suppose to separate us from our dollar, from our own thoughts, and from the possibility of any connection with another person. Given the acknowledged power of music to cast its spell over the contours of experience, to arouse the memory of life's epochs and turning points, to set the commonplace vibrating with the tremors of ideality, why do we tolerate this impertinence, this constant distraction, this erosion of attention, by an interest transparently not our own? Has public space become so forbidding, the marketplace so aridly impersonal, the inward tendency of our own hearts so inimical to the business system that we must hourly be subjected to music, tranquilizing or agitating as the case may be, or to the television news or sporting events, in order that our complicity be sustained at all?

It is I suppose inevitable that we should become accustomed to all of this, to embrace it as appropriate and natural or even to anticipate and to need it, to feel deprived were the constant stream of public sounds and images suddenly to be cut off. We are naturally responsive, naturally communicative, naturally imitative creatures; inevitably a broadly mediated society will not only captivate us with sounds and images but, through ethnomimesis, shape us to its own forms—into people who begin to resemble and to adopt the images, ideas, speech, and actions, more properly the sheen of celebrity itself, of television actors, rock and hip-hop stars, fashion models and other commercial and popular figures, not excluding the characters in violent and salacious cartoons and video games. This of course is nothing new. What is different is the sheer scope, penetration, and ubiquity of mediated experience, which as it materially *replaces* real social experience undermines the foundations of ethnomimesis itself.

Such technical intrusions upon social life not only erode but may ultimately appropriate attention itself. Every technical innovation, from email to iPods, hand-held DVD players, and television cell phones, while offering a new channel of connection to others, simultaneously severs that connection, abolishing as it creates. From the street corner, the café, the pub, the front porch and even their own parlor and table, people disappear, having withdrawn into their cocoon of e-mail, iPod, cell phone, Blackberry, or Bluetooth. The very household, as a social scene, gives way to an aggregate of independent cells. Formerly public or quasi-public places such as airport lounges and luggage retrieval areas, retail floors and hotel lobbies, restaurants and bars, professional offices, schoolrooms and libraries, and even, with the Jumbotron, huge outdoor amphitheaters and indoor arenas, succumb to the well-nigh irresistible claim of the television image, where even in the context of public sociality private fantasy displaces shared experience; everywhere televisions, computers, DVD players, and cell phones displace both face-to-face conversation on the one hand and the ruminative, introspective inward life on the other. By a sinister kind of recursion, social life begins to look and sound like a hip sit-com, political discourse like the evening news, love and intimacy like an interactive blog. Experience itself, finally, with "reality TV," is fully appropriated, as if reality could be lived *only* on television, and this only as a pseudo-tribalist struggle for survival. And while atmospheric pollution and global warming are slowly carrying off the environment itself, images of natural beauty pacify us from computer screens and ceiling monitors.

Like capital itself, the proliferating field of mediated experience abridges, subtracts, reduces, and ultimately substitutes itself for an abiding social reality, all of it, of course, for direct or indirect commercial advantage, converting us into isolated and atomized consumers of a "culture," if such it can be called, of the social and political "irreality" that is the outcome of these inherently corrupting and stupefying processes. It is again, always the representation, the work of art, that acts reflexively in culture to circulate, distribute, and reinforce its forms, to make them available for use, contemplation, and change; but when capital drives the audial and televisual stream into every corner of lived experience, especially social experience, subverting and supplanting it, then ethnomimesis has been directed against itself, sickening the cultural body like an auto-immune disease. We need, I think, a "real-life" movement, capable of breaking the enchantment of electronic communication, marvelous as it may be in its place, and, at a higher level, of repudiating the commercially mediated experience in favor of immediate, not to say intimate, face-to-face interaction, a socially grounded cultural life, and, it follows morally and ethically, an ecologically sound cultural and natural environment. Our communications devices should facilitate, not replace, social life. Only, I say, *dis*connect.

. . . .

These essays move from privacy to society, from solitude to sociability, to social critique and finally, in a concluding essay, to social theory. I begin in my own record collection, devoting my attention to a few old records of jazz and blues, and to Harry Smith's *Anthology of American Folk Music,* an obscure but influential recorded anthology of forgotten "race" and "hillbilly" recordings of the 1920s conceived in 1952 by visionary artist, beatnik, and filmmaker Harry Smith. The aim here is to understand, introspectively, with material summoned from various memories, associations, and ideas, and in the context of recording itself, how these sounds acquire meaning. But the real subject, with all the idiosyncrasies of my own listening admitted, is attention itself, which the concluding two essays take up with reference to what we inherit, cognitively, from the intellectual revolutions of the seventeenth century, when a peculiarly modern form of attention, arising from calculation and quantity, displaced older symbolic modes of contemplation and threw the shadow of superstition and error over the essentially poetic and figurative intellectual forms it displaced—a displacement all folklorists in some way reiterate in their encounter with the folk.

The second section takes me out of my study to three festive events, actual and imaginary—first to the various folk festivals of the postwar "folk revival" period, and several that preceded them, to the World's Columbian Exhibition, one of the nineteenth century's great festivals of industrial capitalism, and finally, in Joyce's story "The Dead," to a local observance, the Misses Morkan's annual dance, where through the incremental, if temporary, dismantling of nephew Gabriel Conroy's various personal and cultural affectations we discover, harrowingly and unexpectedly, how profound are the stakes for identity and even for personality in the processes of festivity.

The third section of essays considers social differentiation from a greater distance, situating themselves at the frontier between races, classes, and peoples, between concentrations of cultural capital and rarifications of it, the frontier at which, where, implicitly, all essays on the subject of folklore are written, in an attempt to understand the theoretical implications for the understanding of culture of the idea of folklore itself. For we would not be contemplating the cultural "other" at all were it not for the social boundaries between us—boundaries that in this section define cultural staging areas, frames of reference, and modes of apprehension.

Some of these essays, therefore, are straightforwardly about art as it is embedded in the lives of particular peoples, times, and places, how we may through art recover meaning from them as well as about them. Hence the tendency here is towards the *experience* of art, that is, a phenomenological tendency, one that subordinates formal and historical questions to this primary concern. Of necessity then, I am forced back upon my own experience, in the conviction that, should culture be collective in the sense I claim it is, so that none of us can experience art in a way that does not in some way reflect the experience of others, my own experience may help to enrich that of my readers, even if their own readings and listenings may diverge from my own. I cannot prescribe a way to listen to "Canal Street Blues" or to contemplate Clarence Carter's painting "Jane Reed and Dora Hunt"; but I can hope that an account of my experience of these works may suggest the pattern, if not the specific substance, of another's.

Other essays take up the phenomenological problem in a more theoretical vein, considering the cultural and epistemological questions arising from the interpretative process—how, in the case of music, the character of the medium itself, and its social place, influences our perception of it, how we conceive, through representations, of "folk," "folklore," and "folk culture," and whether these putative social facts have any real existence in the world apart from the historical, social, racial, and other barriers that inform and deform our perception of them. They ask, too, what the nature of that culture, supposing it to have more than a merely speculative existence, might be—and, finally, whether the nature of culture itself, as Romantic thought from Rousseau and Wordsworth to Jurgen Habermas and Clifford Geertz, from the Social Contract and "The Solitary Reaper" to the Public Sphere and the Balinese Cockfight, has consistently affirmed, might not reveal itself more plainly at the quotidian or "everyday," or the folk or vernacular, level, than in the infinitely complicated networks of modern global society.

Underlying these approaches is what seems the inescapable fact, most fully explored in "The Parallax Effect," that whatever the ontological status of "folk" culture we cannot know or even perceive it apart from certain frameworks and modes of representation, whether a digital recording, a museum festival, a photograph or a painting, in which its special quality becomes evident through distinction and difference. So inseparable from the act of framing is folk culture that it would seem to be directly an effect of it, as if "folk" culture were actually an aspect or a feature of the modern or bourgeois imagination so peculiarly interested in it.

Though these essays do not spring uniformly from nor with unerring consistency address themselves to the issues and problems associated with the study of vernacular music and folklore, nor with any fidelity or consistency adopt the analytical methods of folklorists and ethnographers, they belong nevertheless to the conversations of folklorists and their fellow-travelers in literature, history, and the social sciences, that scholarly community most interested in vernacular or "roots" musics, in festive occasions, customs and celebrations, and in questions surrounding the idea of culture as such. Hence the critical eye, or as the case may be, the ear, tends to look backward historically, towards "vernacular" or traditional cultures, but with less attention paid to the cultures themselves than to their representation, and how their representation, whether theatrical and dramatic, as in the folk festivals, or literary, as in Joyce's story "The Dead," or in the form of recorded music, summons a relation otherwise prohibited by class, race, or history. The one apparent exception to this rule, because it explores the magnificent but transitory "White City" erected in Chicago at the World's Columbian Exhibition of 1893 by the great industrialists of the era, is "White City Elegy"—an essay that, by attempting to understand the Exposition as the ordinary visitor might have experienced it, and by comparison with some of the theme-parks and fairs of our own time, argues that the White City's imperial vision was eroded, quite literally, by its own materiality, and so was instead infused with the elegiac mood of a passing age and touched with a deep ambivalence about the system poised to succeed it. To do so requires that one measure the experience against what might plausibly have been the resources of the provincial nineteenth-century imagination on the one hand and on the other those of one passingly familiar with the traditions of the sublime in landscape painting as well as with Disneyland, the Bonaventure Hotel, and the behavior of plaster of Paris in the heat and humidity of a Chicago summer. This is the procedure throughout: one that attempts to take seriously not only the historicity of art but also its inevitably present, immediate, and urgent character.

More precisely, then, these essays in different ways themselves arise from "the parallax effect"—the curious and interesting way in which vernacular or "folk" culture, reveals itself fully only in that crowded epistemological zone where "epochs, technologies, polities, and the outlooks attached to them" converge and interact. The ethnomimetic process may arise within the dominant culture and as a response to it, or coax emergent cultures out of residual ones, or be itself one of the generative engines of emergent cultural forms, even as capital appropriates them; the point is that it is only by a kind of "parallax," or through intersecting cultural perspectives, that ethnomimesis as such commands an inference as to its existence, and is always meaningful in terms of that intersection. These essays work most, then, where the "folk" or vernacular culture, in some expressive mode, becomes audible to us, as in recordings of blues music, for example, in "Harvest of Illth"; or where on behalf of one or another political or cultural interest it is displayed, performed, or otherwise represented, as in "Feasts of Unnaming"; or where, as in the case of a traditional celebration such as the Misses Morkan's annual dance or at the White City in 1893, it percolates upwards from the deeps of the imaginative life to disrupt the pretensions and postures of economic and cultural power.

Power, of course, is always at issue in that intersection between the vernacular and the polite or the learned, the unencumbered ethnomimetic process and the infinitely ramified institutions, structures, and practices of twenty-first-century global civilization. Some of these essays, then, look closely at the cultural intersection itself—technically, as in "The Magic Eight-Ball," where digital succeeds analog recording in the Smithsonian's re-release of *The Folkways Anthology of American Folk Music,* or epistemologically, in "The Invisible Science," which attempts to engage consciousness itself at that point roughly in the seventeenth century in which a "scientific" revolution, and the Enlightenment that followed it, threw the entire medieval synthesis into the realm of the poetic, as against the scientific, by appropriating the underlying principle of music, the calculation of quantities, to the aim of attaching a symbolic account of the world to the actual machinery of nature. "Fanfare for the Little Guy," like "Harvest of Illth," maps the cultural intersection as a boundary between races and peoples, and hence as a site of contest and oppression, while two musical essays, "If Beale Street Could Talk" and "Darkling I Listen," listen self-consciously across that boundary, calling upon literary and historical resources to find the ways in which vernacular music may speak meaningfully to auditors far removed from it socially and historically.

And yet strictly speaking ethnomimesis is never really "unencumbered," for the very reason that it never reveals itself except in certain conjunctive moments. As the late Alan Dundes proclaimed, folklore is what the folklorist says it is—and that is because the act of naming makes available for thinking about what its unnamed aspect stalks under camouflage in the welter of Being. Hence in identifying and naming "folklore" we are never free from all of those meanings the very act of naming implies: first, of course, the thing itself, as a type of culture; second, the discipline or, better, the "profession" of folklore, also called "folklore," from which the act of naming proceeds, and finally "folklore" as, in effect, "that which is or has been said," that is, the "merely" folkloric, which like hearsay, rumor, tale, and lie, all in themselves both folklore and folkloric, are usually set in contradiction to truth and fact. That truth and fact upon closer examination may prove to be exceptionally subtle forms of hearsay, rumor, tale, or lie only points to the epistemological black hole that folklore in all its senses always implies.

The folklorist's manner of speaking always already supplies the terms in which folklore reveals itself. Unlike the anthropologist, who in the early days of the discipline was searching out the most pristinely isolated forest tribe, the folklorist is not interested in isolation; he or she is interested in relation—its character, its structure, its meaning, its cultural, social, and political functioning. It is in the interstices between communities, cultures, and peoples that folklife flourishes, and in the noetically rarified or vacant nooks and crannies into which the eye and ear of cultural and social power have not wholly penetrated, or to which they are from time to time inaudible and invisible—whether it is a passing exchange between strangers in an elevator, a rhyming game on the sidewalks of an urban wasteland abandoned by postwar industry, or a ballad sung in a remote section of the western North Carolina mountains.

"Remote" but never insular. Enchanted, at first, by the possibility of an unbroken tradition, an archaic custom, or a unique and original story, tale, ritual, or practice, the folklorist may become nervously proprietary about her collaborators, lest their genius lose its luster by contact with ethnographers, impresarios, academic monographs, museum galleries, craft cooperatives, and retail catalogues; but she soon discovers that her collaborators, at the same time as they are adorning their bodies with tattoos, embossing the spent brass shells of Israeli cannon with elaborate Persian designs, deejaying at the local hip-hop club, or building roadside shrines to auto-accident victims, are also attending school, or pulling down a salary, voting, paying automobile insurance, watching television, and maybe exchanging messages on MySpace. And it is in this apparent tension, she realizes, that the meaning of "folk culture" or ethnomimesis lies: for it is here that the shrine-builder or the rap singer acquires that keen edge of imaginative self-awareness through which ethnomimesis becomes a resource simultaneously of identity and resistance; a capacity that not only preserves them, in their culturally and usually economically shifting and uncertain position, against total cultural effacement, but through which they may alter the hues and renavigate the routes of the dominant culture itself.

. . . .

Thirty years ago we learned from the feminists that the personal was political. We are learning now that the political is the personal, in a sense that our generation, having been largely protected against most of the public calamities that marked the first half of the last century, could never have conceived—and that these two formulations, each of them irresistibly true in its own way, are joined by a still more compelling, if temporarily forgotten, principle, which is that the *political* is political; that personhood and citizenship, the private and the public life, are interdependent and mutually sustaining.

Some of us shaped by the experiences of the 1960s threw our lot into active politics. But many of us were content to cultivate our own garden, satisfied that our withdrawal from the political field was compensated by the implicitly political character of our personal and professional lives, including our socially progressive and environmental orientation; we remained confident that the voice of the opposition, the ideals of equality and democracy, the guarantees of our founding documents, the independence of the press, would remain securely in place while we turned our attention, during the four decades that elapsed from the defeat of Barry Goldwater in 1964 to the election of George W. Bush in 2000, to the elaboration of private life.

But by the 1980s it was plain that a cultural and political sea change was underway in America. The academic world was calling upon coruscating European ideas derived from Marx and Heidegger, from the Tel Quel Group, the Frankfurt School, Gramsci the Italian Marxist, and the French historian Foucault, to comprehend the bafflingly novel "postmodern" cultural situation, apparently but not obviously a development of "late capitalism," even to the extent of calling into question the very substantiality of truth claims and their validity, which had come to seem only another reflex of a mysterious power that was robbing us of our history and our selfhood and substituting spurious cultural "simulacra," or imitations without originals, between us and our collective life. This was ethnomimesis ungrounded, the "society of the spectacle." At once glamorous and appalling, late capitalism, however conceived, had seemed by its unprecedented expansion into the cultural field to have eroded those formerly secure foundations of bourgeois sensibility such as the aesthetic, the historical, the psychological, the scientific, even of subjectivity itself, in which the very possibility of both political effectivity and personal authenticity had been anchored.

What I once called "corporate totalitarianism," thinking of the spectacular diffusion of commercialism throughout the cultural sphere in the 1980s, seems finally to have achieved the cultural and political dominance only intimated twenty years ago. We found ourselves in 2006 under a political regime that was "postmodern" with a vengeance—by its own admission officially set against the "reality-based community"[6] in favor of a dream of driving forward the historical process according to the social agenda of the religious right, the economic agenda of the coal, oil, and gas producers, and the foreign-policy agenda of the imperialist wing of the neoconservative movement. For scholars and intellectuals not immediately engaged in politics, such a situation is at best distracting; at worst it is a kind of consuming obsession sadly incompatible with the disinterested work of criticism and scholarship, especially in the humanities, where against its backdrop music, festivity, and culture, especially folk culture, can seem remote or even irrelevant. In this political climate, one may perhaps be forgiven for wondering whether it is really pertinent or responsible to indulge oneself in such engaging topics as the *Folkways Anthology of American Folk Music* or the World's Columbian Exposition or the "dustbowl balladeer" Woody Guthrie, however much they may in some ultimate sense continue to matter. In this environment, indeed, it is difficult to think about anything other than the political turn of events, scarcely imaginable in our lifetimes, that cannot but arouse a feeling of individual and collective helplessness in the face of a development so long in the making that to undo it would require, it seems, that we somehow turn back the historical clock and do what we so myopically failed to do when it was imperative that we do it.

More important for us, from the cultural viewpoint, are the broader historical, demographic, social, and cultural causes behind the "Republican Revolution," which probably include the decline of metropolitan life and the proliferation of post-suburban residential and commercial spaces, the community-destroying triumph of the automobile, the shrinkage of the middle-class, the diffusion of personal privacy and corporate appropriation of the household, the proliferation of cable television channels, the transformation from an industrial to a service economy, and of course globalization itself, with its attendant effects upon corporate organization, capital and information flows, the labor supply, the distribution of wealth, the security of employment, wages, the environment, and so on; these are some of the forces that, as the postmodern theorists have maintained, opened hitherto unexploited areas of cultural life to the depredations of capital and brought about what Foucault famously called "the death of the subject."

What can be the place, at this juncture, of a collection of essays on music, festivity, and vernacular culture, which with two exceptions—both of which concern themselves with themes of darkness and obscurity—were written in the comparatively peaceful and prosperous decade before September 11, 2001? It may be that the elections to come will substantially alter the balance of power, and that the political horizon will brighten; but it is unlikely that the systemic causes behind our situation such as the influence of political money, the fragmentation and weakening of the press, or the corporatization of governance will correct themselves overnight. We can hope, perhaps, for at least a mitigation of the worst abuses, should a practical politics in a liberal tradition, which is after all the tradition of our founding documents, find its voice and reenter the political arena; but we can never again forget what European intellectuals of the last century learned the hard way, under despotism, totalitarianism, and war, that we can never again take for granted the integrity and the continuity of the political process as such, nor suppose that we may freely inquire into questions of art and culture, even when our work is "implicitly" or even explicitly political, at the expense of our responsibilities as citizens, upon which all the rest depends.

The aim of tyranny is always to undermine or to appropriate the ethnomimetic process—to uproot us from our grounding in the actuality of our own experience, to sever the social connections by which we share that experience and ratify it, to substitute its reality for our own so that historical change may follow the direction most favorable to the further aggrandizement of its own power. Hence our obligation as citizens demands that we carry our cultural capacity into the political realm—that we become a *political* community as much as we are an intellectual, cultural, or a socioeconomic one. Only through active citizenship can we break the spell of the simulacrum and expose the Man Behind the Curtain, who from a penthouse suite at the top floor of a Houston trophy building or a conference room in the West Wing, and on behalf of his stockholders, his campaign contributors, his lobbyists, and his political constituency has been manufacturing our reality for us.

It isn't enough to contribute to the right organizations, to read the right magazines and newspapers, to subscribe to the right blogs and listserves, to attach the right stickers to our auto bumpers, or even to embrace progressive practices in our household ecologies or our personal lives. We must achieve what the activist right-wing has achieved in the last forty years: a real political culture, grounded in face-to-face interactions extending from precincts, districts, localities, and regions across a national network of meetings, panels, boards, offices, seats, coalitions, constituencies, agencies, and institutions whose totality constitutes the substantive life of the political.

That uncanny power, unexpected and undetected, that as of this writing prevails in all the branches of government, whose influence is daily more apparent in education, entertainment, the media, commerce, science, and other institutions of life, is the power of ethnomimesis: and we have only ethnomimesis, the power of culture, to resist and ultimately to prevail over it.

And, should we succeed in this endeavor—though it will not be overnight, or even very soon—we will have discovered that music, family, and the culture of daily life migrate again to the heart of our concerns, at once the root and the flower of our renascent citizenship.

part I

DARKLING I LISTEN

1 IF BEALE STREET COULD TALK

A REFLECTION ON MUSICAL MEANING

The imaginative lives of my class and generation—an early baby boomer, middle class, college educated—have been perpetually riven by the conflicting claims of, on the one hand, high cultural opportunities and prerogatives connected with education and the professions, and on the other the powerful but often ungovernable and obscure promise of what has been called at various times folk, ethnic, traditional, "vernacular," or roots music: blues, rockabilly and rock-and-roll, old-time music and bluegrass, and by various revivals of these musics in commercial and intellectual culture. For me the rift began quite early—perhaps with Diana Washington's "Long John Blues," a hokum blues about of all things a *dentist,* full of sexual innuendo, which my half-brother, my elder by fifteen years and something of a bohemian, used to play on his phonograph when I was five or six years old.

In the period following the Second World War, and especially since the days of the "folk revival" of the early 1960s, these vernacular or "roots" musics, as well as various derivatives, imitations, traces, and revivals of them, have been more consistently present to us, through electronic reproduction, than perhaps any other cultural text save corporate advertising, providing a continuous accompaniment to quotidian life at home, in our automobiles, often in the workplace, on the street and, with the advent of the remarkable Apple iPod, potentially anywhere, everywhere, and always. For many people, particularly young people, great swaths of ordinary life, public and private, may be said to have been lived in accompaniment to music.

Hence "roots" music in many of our lives is vitally present and immediate, a kind of compass point in the construction of our social location and personal identities, even modes of life, and in the formation of political communities and political consciousness, no matter how apparently remote from them in time and place that music may be; it is pervasive in our consumer culture, in its derivative if not in its literal and authentic forms; and, as we all know intuitively, it is a very rich and powerful bearer of meaning. It is hardly trivial, but politically, morally, and emotionally compelling and perhaps still capable, as much of global popular culture is not, of offering resistance, in a way that is at once less than ideological and more than political, to the ongoing concentration, integration, and centralization of social power, even as commercial power especially endlessly appropriates and simulates it. That it is regularly converted into a form of advertising, assimilated into the fashion system, and deployed by transcontinental megacorporations either for colonizing new markets or for inventing new consumer wants testifies to its residual oppositionality even in these contexts. I confess I'm a little set back when a radio ad for Circuit City comes on, with, until the last refrain, some thoroughly engaging rhythm-and-blues instrumental—but the fact remains that ethnic, traditional, and vernacular musics mostly remain obdurately "other," even though as artifacts of marginal or enclaved cultures they necessarily partake of, but turn to their own purposes, the forms, the materials, and the practices of commercial culture. And therein lies a clue, if not quite the key, to why the music fascinates us.

For students and critics of roots music, the problem of reconciling the twin endowments of life in a consumer culture on the one hand, in which all but the most isolated and parochial people mostly all share, and of intimate experience with local, regional, and traditional cultures on the other, has become a creative opportunity, opening access to the prerogatives, privileges, and the aspirations associated with an achieved class standing, more or less expensive educations, and perhaps most significantly, the destinies their parents, following the lead of postwar consumer society, designed for them. Folklorists and ethnomusicologists of the postwar generation have discovered ways of attaching the apparatus of social scientific enquiry to the closely personal interests arising from class, ethnicity, region, or some other provincializing factor sublimated as an element of professional as well as social and cultural identity.

But the empiricizing and objectifying effect of this approach, with its methods derived from historiography, ethnography, linguistics, and musicology, dissolves the foundations of any true criticism in an ethical or hermeneutic sense, as these rely less upon a specific methodological posture than upon a kind of subtext of cultural insiderness—precisely what inspired the scientific interest to begin with. The painstaking, almost Talmudic minuteness with which folklorists, ethnomusicologists, discographers, and the like have traced the careers of traditional, early commercial, and other vernacular musicians, as well as of all the accompanists, managers, promoters, publicists, publishers, artist and repertoire men, and especially the radio stations and recording companies that were the engines of the hillbilly, race, and ethnic music industries, while deeply gratifying to the enthusiast, does not accomplish the first aim of a true criticism, which is to recover meaning, nor the last, which is to pass judgment.

How does one *describe* a musical effect? How do combinations of musical effects make music meaningful? To what extent does that meaning consist, as in any of the other arts, in a specific relationship between the music and the world outside of it? Close musicological analysis, undertaken either through the paradigms of a modified or supplemented European music theory or with devices of measurement and denotation newly fashioned for a particularly resistant but central issue such as blues phrasing, raise the level of musicological description substantially—but with the effect, sometimes, of turning dramatic, palpable, morally, emotionally, and intellectually charged performances into static, denatured empirical "data." Histories, ethnographies, massive discographical, biographical, or musicological studies, class-based social analyses, semiotic or phenomenological approaches all bring us into the near precincts of a coal-mining song or a Hank Williams ballad—but rarely do they lay hold of them the way the brilliant formulations of a jazz critic such as Andre Hodier, or of certain classical master-teachers whom I've observed at work, who, with an unbounded field of figurative language available to them, especially metaphors derived from tactility, have been able to put the character, the quality, and the power of musical sounds into words.

It was only recently that the impulse at work here was simply to validate roots music as a subject of serious study: to call down the blessing of a powerful educational establishment and of prestigious academic and cultural institutions upon the content, the history, and the energy of what a generation ago was mostly regarded, except by a few enthusiasts and bohemians on the political left, as something low, common, or primitive. That impulse arose quite appropriately I think out of the defensive hypothesis that blues or bluegrass or Klezmer or old-time music warranted serious scholarly and critical attention. But it arose, too, out of the listener's own sense, however outwardly absurd, of his or her own marginality, on the plane at which personal and professional domains overlap; for to legitimate our music was of course to legitimate ourselves. In our own time the study of vernacular music has become part of a much broader political project in the academy towards racial, ethnic, and cultural inclusiveness, and beyond that, of expanding the pedagogical repertoire—not only of introducing new "texts," but in weakening the dominance of textual metaphors and of textuality itself so that teaching and learning may be conducted in ways appropriate to the modes of appreciation belonging to cultures for whom "text" is not even a conceptual category. One cannot even think, now, about "teaching" traditional musics without cassette tapes, videos, compact discs, DVDs, and MP3s.

But in this last lies a paradox and a problem. To succeed in this project we've got to do more than traffic in the ephemera of pop culture, mire ourselves in the epistemological conundrums of ethnographic description, or rehearse by now tediously familiar and thoroughly tendentious ideological commonplaces, such as that roots musics are "counter hegemonic" or, on the other side, that they are commercially "invented." We've got to get at the ways in which vernacular music generates meaning, and open our discourse to the possibility of articulating that meaning. The problem of referentiality, in music criticism, is exactly the reverse of what it has been in literary theory. What theory only comparatively recently claims to have accomplished, the abolition of the referent, western music claims to have accomplished several centuries ago—a quite illusory claim in both instances. But the theoretical claim of music's self-consistency, while it has given us a formal music theory, has severely narrowed our understanding of the symbolic, symptomatic, pragmatic, and material connections of music to society, history, and culture.

Still deeper and as yet untheorized disconnections have arisen, I think, from the emergence of the infinitely capacious digital medium, which I take here simply as one of the agents of a wider global culture that like an explosive depth-charge has floated the killed artifacts of cultural expression to the historical surface where they have meaning only in relation to other artifacts in the total info-commodity system. Today's students of music, like our students of literature, suffer from a musical species of "damaged literacy," in Leon Botstein's phrase[1]—that is, a merely mechanical decoding facility that lacks a cultural context sufficiently rich to transform imaginatively letters into literature, musical sounds into music. Our students have access to virtually every kind of music ever recorded, or that is being performed on the planet; but the affective participation, the cultural recognitions, the immediate historical alignment that vitalizes music is often lost to them—a consequence of the ongoing technological, material, and economic decoupling of music from the social and historical contexts in which all music evolves, even including the new global musics arising in response to this novel situation, accompanied by the historical deterioration of those contexts under pressure of globalization. It is precisely an awareness of this predicament that compels many young people to reground music in their own communities and often in their own musicianship, so that being "in a band" or at least associating with one has become one of the authenticating rituals of adolescence: with the unsurprising result that the vocalities and instrumental techniques of young indie bands more and more faithfully capture the lifeworlds of the communities that produced them.

To recover and restore the deeper cultural connections may be a philosophical or an anthropological project, a historical or a musicological or critical one, or some other kind of enterprise; but whatever the discourse in which we place it, it seems to me to involve the problem of signs, is essentially imaginative, relies fundamentally upon metaphor, and is at bottom a literary, or at least a verbal, problem. More perhaps even than literature, music is profoundly and unshakably situated, socially, culturally, and historically, far more than can be evident in any text-based tradition, as our western European music is; its affective force, though not strictly semantic or even semiotic, arises out of the very patterning of its own material carriers that sound at once mimetically absorbs and discharges.

Hence the phenomenon of musical meaning is a problem fascinating to writers, because it asks them to speak about, and for, and through, to deploy a useful phrase from the late Northrop Frye, who was speaking of poetry, "a human productive power which in itself does not speak"—an introspective, almost intuitive, hermeneutic project, bound up with historical and material forces it at once shapes and is shaped by in ways that are psychologically and metaphysically inaccessible. Blues and jazz, as signs, metaphors, and as subjects, run continuously through African American literature from Frederick Douglass to Langston Hughes and Zora Neale Hurston, Ralph Ellison to James Baldwin, Amira Baraka to Toni Morrison; Houston Baker's *Blues, Ideology, and Afro-American Literature: A Vernacular Theory,* drawing heavily upon European literary theory, has become one of the masterworks of African American literary criticism. That many a writer or poet has secretly harbored a passion, and sometimes a considerable talent for, as well as a literary interest in, the jazz horn or blues piano, the old-time fiddle or banjo or song, is too well known really to require demonstration. From time to time that interest surfaces as a literary subject matter, as in say, the work of Ralph Ellison, James Dickey, and more recently Charles Frazier, author of the remarkable *Cold Mountain,* probably the only novel that attempts to embody as narrative what could be called an old-time music imaginary, appropriately picaresque and romantic; more typically, though, the writer with equal discretion nurtures and protects it as a principal element in the vitality of his or her creative work. Lee Smith, a highly successful North Carolina novelist, has published a fictional history of country music, a very colorful and convincing one, called *Devil's Dream,* drawing to good effect upon her childhood in western Virginia as well as upon the real-life careers of the Carter Family and various country and rockabilly stars.

Music can only make the sound of itself; but musical sounds—consonance and dissonance, rhythm and tempo, harmony and melody, timbre and tone color, texture, articulation, intensity, modality, and pitch—are, first, signifiers of concrete and specific human actions in a well-defined syntactic and semantic field, and all give rise to effects of sensation, emotion, movement, change, and so on that have direct and immediate psychological consequences, within particular cultural milieus, of these sounds, but that are not peculiar to them. When we discover that these effects are the same ones that might otherwise arise from contact with the objective world, particularly the world of our own interiority—a discovery keenly and transitively aesthetic—which we can do because by convention music does not emanate from that world, we become competent listeners to music. As I wrote in my book on bluegrass,[2] every act of hearing is essentially imaginative, an emergent erosion of the sensorium that in a kind of aesthetic emergency we seek to repair with material from the substantial world of touch and sight, as well as the insubstantial world of memory and desire, in short, a moment of cultural creation, of "reading."

That music listening involves this sort of remedial activity I think is evidenced by the fact that when we are deprived of it, as by a music video, we feel either as if we had been robbed of something or that some important work, somewhat impertinently, has been accomplished for us, however well or badly. Where vernacular music is concerned, I would go a step further and say that every musical sound commands an inference into the realm of human action, with its sensory, moral, emotional, and intellectual gradients, and in so commanding directs us into the worlds, social, historical, and personal, in which it both has its life and communicates its life to us. This is the creative process that permits the passage of music from one social milieu into another, where it is reread and recreated from the resources belonging to its new community of listeners—who, if the shoe fits, will wear it. That is why the "associations" that form around different musical kinds, and the attempts by cultural producers to supply them and shape them, are centrally involved in the power of the music to work the effects peculiar to it. They are the very heart of the matter.

Music is an organization of time: but here we are interested in the vitality and materiality of time, its immanence in conscious, organic, mechanical, and objective physical processes, musical and nonmusical, that constitute the phenomenality of time: what lend it substance, quality, extension, duration, and boundary, and that, most importantly, join it to history in all its aspects. It is essential to historicize any "text," for history is precisely what is missing in texts; but music historicizes itself, albeit obscurely, and the interpretation of music, which most of us seem to do quite handily without special training, involves our participation in that history. A musical analysis, then, suggests itself, again, as a semiotic and literary problem: articulating the musical process both for what it produces and what has produced it.

By way of analogy: baseball, like music, also produces and reproduces time; but to understand it in the way we would like to understand music means to take it not simply as an unfolding record of innings, of hits, runs, errors, and at-bats, but in its vital materiality: in terms of and in relation to such matters as social class, race and ethnicity, language, especially figurative language, the body, urban and rural spaces and the representation of them, individual personalities and narratives spun around them, grassy fields and summer afternoons, the wider sociopolitical and historical setting, and so on—all the embedded and associated factors that clearly situate the game in its cultural history, making it both a carrier and a producer of that history. Without these factors, baseball or any other sport would be a pretty arid affair; nor does the game, in its actual playing, merely "symbolize" these factors. Rather it embodies, materializes, animates, and drives them—the game is a cultural engine, as much of its history as about it, at once determining and determined by it. It is a beginning to understanding baseball to understand the difference between Babe Ruth, a home-run hitter at the close of a period of entrepreneurial industrial expansion and consolidation, and Ted Williams, home-run hitter in a period of bureaucratization and ever more exact and extensive social engineering; between Ebbetts Field, as Peter Rutkoff has argued,[3] as a theater for the affirmation of diverse emergent working-class ethnic identities, and Giants Stadium, as a theater for the flexion of corporate, monetary, and political muscle. What we are really interested in, in any case, is the player—and where musical meaning is at issue, it is the activity of the player, conceived *as* an activity, that is at stake.

It is the player, in music, who "leaps" from one note to the other, or "chooses" one note at the expense of another, or who delivers a note in a particular way, actions and choices in which musical meaning originates. That the "player" may be neither composer nor performer but a kind of fiction, like an implied narrator, whom we infer from the music, speaks to the interplay between player and listener in the genesis of musical meaning. All the processes enacted in music—the movement from note to note, the embodied note itself, exhaustively partaking of, indeed identical to the instrument or voice that produces it, the execution of pulses and beats, the swim into, upon, or over the rhythmic wave, the musical and poetic narrative itself, finally, of course, the sentient and corporal presence of the musician—import from history the significance proper to them in their own sphere to fashion out of these elements a parallel time that is as much an artifact of its "time" as a literary text and that, like a literary text, it reproduces. Producing its own kind of temporality, then, but a temporality superimposed upon and embedded in real time, assimilating it, and coloring it with its own history. Music throws its spell over lived experience, frames the phenomenal world, to represent or to read it; but at the same time the world returns to music to bring it to completion. Hence music produces both its own and our time: it is, in a sense, life, more life than life itself, not because it substitutes for life, but because it charges life, one might say orders it, with musical energy. Perhaps this is why young people cannot separate themselves from their iPods.

Music, then, is the confluence of many temporalities, organized, or, as the case may be, shattered and dispersed, by the musical process itself, which includes its presentation in and through a particular set of social, cultural, and mechanical practices. With its instrumentality music absorbs and projects its history as an element in its own metrical, rhythmic, and tonal medium, at the same time as significances from the surrounding lifeworld flow into it to mark each of its actions, gestures, and aspects, each in turn playing against and playing out of themselves in that strange sense of competing or convergent temporalities by which music transfixes experience just as it inhabits the body of experience.

A trailing double helix of twin cornets—King Oliver and Louis Armstrong—cruise the after-midnight pavements of "Canal Street Blues," as Honore Dutrey's trombone shines like a headlight on their wet, crawling surfaces, threading its way with the other instruments through a kind of tumult, where an apparent multitude of independent tracks weave themselves into a pattern as mobile and as regulated as a streetcar line. The interaction carries us to an open place, a kind of pedestrian intersection, defined by a regimentation of the instruments around the beat, where the voice of Johnny Dodds's clarinet, full of conviction, emerges from the congestion to make a beseeching, melancholy, ardent speech to which no one seems to be listening; now gradually many presences converge upon the spot, collectively seizing upon the restless wandering movements of the piece to forge out of it a kind of law, order, and purpose, arresting its directed linear forces in a web of intersecting melodic lines firmly anchored in a beat emphatically voiced by piano, banjo, and drums.

Thus far, impressionistically, the dynamic structure of "Canal Street Blues," recorded by King Oliver's Creole Jazz Band on April 6, 1923, in Richmond, Indiana. These impressions, then, cannot but have been shaped by the many transformations through which the play—rather the mechanically reproduced acoustic impression of the play—has passed from that day in Richmond to the day in 1979 upon which, on a stereo in the parlor of my semi-detached bungalow in Whipton Village, Devon, England, I first heard "Canal Street Blues." By that juncture, "Canal Street Blues" had become an artifact of a movement of collectors, discophiles, aficionados, historians, and technical engineers who rescued the rare old Gennett recording from what Brian Rust's sleeve notes call "the mists of over half a century" to reissue it on a long-playing vinyl record album with eighteen contemporaneous tunes by the same band on a British jazz label, VJM "Vintage Series," for me to unearth, a week or so earlier, from the dusty bins of a London record shop hidden in one of the narrow lanes of Soho.[4] All this properly belongs, I maintain, to its musical meaning, and that is why I report it.

"Canal Street Blues" comes to me, then, already richly constructed out of a highbrow aficionado's jazz culture with which, through literature and music, I have casually and somewhat disingenuously sought to identify myself since college days, a process of identification and affiliation in which trade in records, and visits to record shops, have proved imperative. It comes to me, moreover, not only through "the mists of over half a century," but through the disorientation I have experienced in my first weeks in England, where, living alone at the end of a residential street at the eastern edge of an unfamiliar and somewhat forbidding provincial city, I have experienced episodes of acute homesickness; indeed merely to listen to "Canal Street Blues" now has been a kind of victory, the result of long negotiations with a local electronics dealer whom I patronized in a kind of desperation to buy a stereo system I cannot afford, hoping to assuage my loneliness with the sounds of the two albums I bought on my last excursion to London—the only music, apart from the BBC's fine programs of American jazz, blues, and show music—I have to listen to.

Already culturally endorsed and ratified, then, and even, in a sense, appropriated by the new culture in which I find myself; but out of "the mists of over half a century" emerge for me half-formed shapes, resolving and dissolving images of places and times residing both represented and real at the deepest levels of my memory and reaching still further into an imaginary past whose transecting influences and formidable powers, deriving I suspect from the technics of the industrial age, form the elusive architecture of my own origins.

I was born in Chicago. I have a dim recollection of, or of hearing about, the old Lincoln Gardens on Thirty-first Street, where King Oliver used to play—and where, I think, my mother, as a teenager, and my father, though they hadn't met one another at that point, used to go dancing; at least I know that "Canal Street Blues," or music like it, was something familiar to them; that it used to make them pause at my bedroom door when, as I child, I played on my record player my little collection by a Dixieland band called the "Firehouse Five Plus Two." Hence that vanished world is vaguely present to me not only from my parents' few enigmatic and fragmentary suggestions about it but also from the many pictorial and dramatic representations of the world of urban jazz long abroad in books, magazines, plays, and films. Indeed, it could be said that the periodization of that epoch has been mostly accomplished in Hollywood, primarily in gangster films. Moreover, the old sad southwest side of Chicago, with its gray tenements under a gray sky, the broad relentless avenues, still unfolds in memory as an image drifting past a car window on somnolent summer afternoons and bitter cold winter days.

And as for Canal Street, we've all been there. I say this in a metaphorical sense. That its historical location may have been in New Orleans, not Chicago, is of no moment. For me, "Canal Street Blues" speaks of those childhood locales, and of my own promised life somehow associated with them through the lives of my parents; listening to it, while as my sense of identity dissolves in a foreign, unfathomed place, I by a kind of ritual of origins must rehearse, discovering in what Rust calls the recording's "pale impression" a ground in which to reroot myself.

Subjective, personal, even, perhaps, idiosyncratic, these associations; but they are no more fanciful, no more arbitrary, than any of the resources that we must bring to any representation, which is a triangulation of many different orders of signification, historical, cultural, social, and ideological, in order to make it "real," that is, to discover the means of our own conscious performance or playing of it. One can say, I think, at the very least, that "Canal Street Blues" captures a quality of urban American public space in the 1920s, both imparting to it and absorbing from it the characteristic juxtaposition in jazz of multifarious complex processes with isolated, solitary, perhaps lonely or alienated voices. In any case, we know intuitively it is not about hayricks, peasant workers, or sheep meadows. There is a reed instrument, the clarinet—but it sounds more like a taxi horn than a shepherd's pipe. Had the piece been called, perhaps, "Low-Down Brokenhearted Blues," another story might present itself; but I suspect the setting, or the flickering transparencies of it, might make itself known nevertheless. We might be looking out the window at a nocturnal scene, and not walking through it on worn soles and with a heavy step—but the music would situate us roughly at the same time and place.

Other listeners certainly would construct "Canal Street Blues" from different psychic and cultural material, but I think along structurally similar lines, and, perhaps, with more actual agreement upon the dynamic and symbolic "content" of the piece than my own account might by itself suggest—the sort of agreement, in fact, that can often be achieved through dialogue. "Canal Street Blues," in any case, and music like it, while producing its own imaginary time, also produces segments of as-yet-until-then still uninvented personal narrative and in a concrete sense produced my "time" in England, to which it remains permanently connected in my memory. This power, of music to "bring back" our times, but more, to create them, is not, again, some ancillary or secondary effect; it is just what music is about. Music must consume time, incorporating it with its own body, in order to live. In spite of that association, however, "Canal Street Blues" remains for me immune to penetration by the imagery and feeling-tone of that period of my life. *Associate* it with Exeter I might; but I *interpret* it according to its own lights. The convergence of these two processes, and the effort of imagination to reconcile them, just as it might reconcile the warring terms of a metaphor by discovering common elements, suggests I think interesting parallels between musical and linguistic meaning.

In fact one can make a very strong beginning in the understanding of vernacular music (and quite probably orchestral music as well) by refusing to think of it as music at all. The formal boundary between music and non-music so fundamental in the European classical tradition, while certainly one of the enabling gestures of any musical practice, in vernacular music is a boundary made to be crossed. When Bill Monroe plays the mandolin, to cite an instance with which I am tolerably familiar, he exhibits an extraordinary *musical* gift; but part of the meaning of his playing is that it registers, through his particular way of negotiating melody and of producing rhythm, the response of the instrument to his touch, which his style is designed to set forth with a tightly circumscribed range of nonmusical sounds such as buzz, rasp, and various kinds of percussiveness, various virtues and powers that far transcend the domain of music, carrying Monroe's performance, supported by banjo, fiddle, guitar, and bass, into a landscape of fence posts, outbuildings, highways, landscapes, and a passing horizon of mountains, valleys, and hills. These elements, coupled with Monroe's penchant for pentatonism, plagal modes, flatted tones, and the like, and a poetic compounded of nineteenth-century sentimental themes, southeastern and western place names, and autobiographical narratives, define the specific musical imaginary we now associate with the term "bluegrass."

Before we get into a few more musical examples, then, and at the risk of dislocating my argument, I want to mention one example from my own experience in which writing seems really to have approached the phenomenal reality, the "lifeworld," of a vernacular musical form—Nolan Porterfield's biography of "the singing brakeman," Jimmie Rodgers, the popular and pioneering country crooner of the 1920s from Meridian, Mississippi.[5] Porterfield is a novelist, and with a novelist's interest in places and in people surveys the entire folk culture of turn-of-the-century Mississippi: the circuses, tent shows, minstrel shows, and mountebanks, medicine show doctors, the petite bourgeois parlor culture, symbolized by the upright piano, shaped by women's volunteer organizations and the clergy, the railroad and especially the close interaction of the races on the railroad, the record business and the radio, the exotic infusions of jazz and Hawaiian music and the shifts in the cultural landscape towards a new urban synthesis that they indicated . . . and in its totality Porterfield succeeds somehow in bodying forth what, when we hear Jimmie Rodgers, we feel we are hearing.

There is of course a simple and unproblematic explanation for this, which is simply that Porterfield's biography is a literary account of the small-town southern regional culture that we in the North have for certain interesting and complex cultural and historical reasons long romanticized, idealized, and stereotyped, one that has been richly explored in, say, Faulkner, Welty, McCullers, Capote, and Harper Lee, among others, the culture that Rodgers's music, especially in the revivalist context in which we mostly encounter it, evokes and embodies, and to which we respond for roughly similar reasons. Certainly that is so. But it is interesting to consider, too, the more radical suggestion that Rodgers's music, his singing voice especially, somehow takes the impression of the textures, the contours, the colors, the tempos, the forms, shapes, and structures of its cultural moment—that it is a kind of auditory CAT-scan of culture as it is actually lived and experienced, a picture that it returns and returns again to its own cultural milieu with a gratifying superabundant redundancy, a neurological footprint of the times in which by listening we can live again.

I have talked to many musicians who feel intuitively that this is the case. I have read two or three psychological studies that suggest as much—in synesthetic linkages, say, between the perception of space, the contour of a melody, the character of a harmonic interval, or between certain colors and textures on the one hand and certain pitches or harmonic relationships on the other. Even with their undeniably physiological basis, however, most of these linkages appear to be, mysteriously, cultural. Bill Monroe used to insist that his mandolin compositions such as "Crossing the Cumberlands" or "Roanoake," were "about" the landscape around certain places he had traveled, and that the tunes somehow captured what he called "the lay of the land" as he observed it from the window of his bus. What shall we say, then, of the human voice itself, so freighted with memory, feeling, imagination, and experience?

To the West African traditional musician, these notions are entirely fitting and self-evident; the purpose of music, he might say, is to capture the soul or the spirit of the moment; to figure forth in sound the quality of an occasion, so that the community may be brought more decisively into participation in it, a kind of elaborate ideophone attached to the total gestalt or "feel" of the moment not by convention but by an undiscoverable neurological resonance between certain audial sensations, as cultural signs, and the gestalt or "feeling-tone" of a time and place. John Coltrane's compositions such as "Central Park West" or "A Night in Tunisia" would I think to a sympathetic listener suggest that he approached music in a similar spirit, and if I'm not mistaken the mimetic connection between these pieces and their imagined referents is vivid and precise. Coltrane in a sense creates Central Park West as surely as Thomas Cole created the Hudson River Valley.

And to this chorus of anecdotal evidence I'd like to add my own personal testimony. I grew up in the late forties and fifties in the Calumet, a heavily industrialized region of railroad yards, oil refineries, and steel mills that line the southern shore of Lake Michigan between South Chicago and Gary, Indiana. This area was heavily settled by migrating southerners, black and white, after the First World War, who followed the route of the old Rock Island and Illinois Central Lines from Arkansas, Mississippi, Alabama, western Kentucky, and Tennessee. Nick Lemann's *The Promised Land* documents this migration and assigns it, I think, its proper evaluation as one of the major cultural developments of the twentieth century—connecting it, I think accurately, to the rock-and-roll revolution and all the social upheavals that followed, as the black folk culture of the Mississippi Delta region established itself in a city that, until some time in the mid 1950s, was the industrial, commercial, and cultural capital of the American heartland.[6]

The uptempo, improvisatory piano blues called boogie-woogie followed the railroads from Mississippi in the south and Kansas City on the west to Chicago and enjoyed a period of popularity there in the late 1940s; it was one of the earliest responses of rural black barrelhouse and blues pianists to the new urban industrial environment: and for me the music is written all over with the texture, the color, the mood, the entire phenomenological message of the Calumet. If boogie could talk, it would say, I believe, "Calumet"—taking the Calumet here, of course, as emblematic of the many regions in the middle South and the urban North where railroads, steel, and oil converged at mid-century to create a mighty industrial landscape that for the many displaced provincial people driven there by economic necessity is a strange, plangent, restless dream that fairly cries out for absorption and catharsis in art. The Calumet and regions like it, around Memphis, in southern Michigan and northern Ohio, haven't given rise to many novelists or poets; but folk musics "about" the rural-to-urban migration are rife; would you be surprised to learn that Bill Monroe came from Rosine, Kentucky, in 1929 to Whiting, Indiana, in the heart of the Calumet, where he wrestled fifty-gallon oil drums nine hours a day in the Sinclair Oil refinery?

As a child I heard a good deal of country music on the radio—the National Barn Dance and such; but the only authentic traditional black music I heard was on the car radio, on Sunday mornings, when my father, who was an old-fashioned country doctor, and worked mostly in the black communities of Robbins, Dixmoor, Markham, and Harvey, where we lived, used to take me around on his round of house calls. We'd tune the radio into the far right-hand side of the AM dial, where black church services were being broadcast locally from the Baptist and Pentecostal congregations of the South Side.

Imagine my surprise, then, when, now nearly half a century later, I discover that the boogie-woogie, and the Chicago blues after it, was growing up only a few miles, literally, from where I lived, out of migrations of certain traditional musicians from the areas around Clarksdale, Mississippi, from people whose sons and daughters were my schoolmates and friends. I remain convinced that those men (and they were mostly men), working within a rural and parochial folk tradition, were discovering ways to record their experiences—not in a descriptive or programmatic way, but ideophonically—in the new urban environment, and that their music, in a language we understand but can't articulate, now stands permanently for that fundamental social, psychological, and cultural transformation. Hence it is particularly portentous to reflect, as Lemann has, on the fact that the Delta blues tradition, as it gathered force in Chicago, became, as it leaped the social gap between black and white, one of the motive forces of the massive cultural revolution we now associate with the appearance of Elvis Presley and rockabilly music.

Robert Palmer in *Deep Blues* observes that the Hausa word "buga" and Mandingo "bug" mean "to beat," as in beating a drum. "Booger Rooger," in black idiom before 1917, meant what it means today—to "boogie down": a wild celebration.[7] Boogie is obviously a blues in jump or uptempo dance rhythm: a jitterbug, with origins in lumber and turpentine camps, levees, and the oil fields of Texas, Oklahoma, and Missouri. The form is midwestern, and seems to have grown up around the Rock Island and Illinois Central railroad lines and centers. But its formative period was in Chicago in the 1930s through a seminal pianist named James Blythe. Blythe moved to Chicago from Louisville in 1916 and became the house pianist at Paramount Records, leading blues bands and contributing solo recordings. At night he formed with Lewis and Ammons, both Chicagoans, a local blues band that played at rent parties and bars. This group also included at different times, Jimmy Yancey, Clarence "Pine Top" Smith, who had recorded the first "boogie-woogie" in 1928, both from Alabama, Texan Hershel Thomas, "Cripple" Clarence Lofton, and J. H. "Mr. Freddie" Shayne.[8]

I've suggested that boogie is not programmatic or descriptive, but "ideophonic." Nevertheless it is worth considering what boogie-woogie has to do with the railroad. The shape, tempo, and texture of life in the Calumet, beginning at around the turn of the century when the major steel companies of Akron and Youngstown located on the southern shore of Lake Michigan, the iron ore mines in Ohio having given out and the Mesabi range now opening up, is entirely a phenomenon of the railroad. A landscape of mute titanic monoliths—storage tanks, refineries, rolling mills, iron furnaces, forging plants, grain elevators, paint and chemical factories, electrical generating stations, and so on—grew up there because on the flat cinder-strewn plain around Lake Calumet is where the railroad tracks from north, south, east, and west all converged with Great Lakes shipping. I grew up in this world, a world of railroad switch yards and crossings, long lines of red boxcars, gondola and tank cars sitting idle or rumbling over the intersection of the tracks with a highway, strange squat and elevated tanks, eyeless sun-blanched buildings, overhead wires, meandering service roads, wastelands of blackened ground or shallow ponds of ghastly brackish water, and of the night sounds of distant foundry hammers and railroad whistles.

Boogie woogie piano seems to absorb these energies: the deep, powerful, propulsive, regular thrust of a steam-driven piston, the myriad mechanical motions and auxiliary sounds of their transformation into kinetic energy, the rolling of wheels—boogie seems to be a kind of musical locomotive. But it is an engine whose sounds also carry the meaning and promise of the steam locomotive in the setting of the south-to-north, rural to urban migration. The music has drive, and forward movement, and a power that is more than mechanical; it is explosive. But it also carries a poignant sense of distant places both behind and ahead, promising a kind of deliverance from the past and at the same moment ephemeralizing the memory so that it becomes, as the miles pass behind us, ever more shining and idyllic. Meade Lux Lewis's "Honky Tonk Train Boogie"[9] is of course "about" a train—so much so that the famous triplet interlude, considered a ritual of passage for boogie pianists, is called "crossing the trestle."

Boogie woogie is a profoundly romantic, duplicitous, ambivalent music. Its very essence, I feel, is its micrometer-precise and technologically sophisticated coordination, like a steel mill, of high pitches and low, the former suggesting sharpness, fineness, lightness, ephemerality, smallness, and above all remoteness or distance, and the latter ponderous weight, mass, power, darkness, and even, perhaps things sinister or unnatural. Structurally speaking, there is no middle register in boogie-woogie: which is where the human voice lives. It is a music that fully exploits the piano's mechanical analysis of sound, calls attention to its technologically determined range, uniformity, and ductility, and incorporates the mechanical character of the piano structurally and semantically into itself. In the blues tradition, piano was already imbued with meanings belonging to the venues in which, in folk cultures, we are likely to find the piano: not the front parlor, but the tavern, the brothel, the honky-tonk. From the time that ragtime pianists in

New Orleans began the banjo imitations that became ragtime, the piano, as boogie drifted up from Clarksdale and Memphis, was an urban instrument, and associated with urban nocturnal festive life.

The emotional ambivalence and tension of boogie-woogie arises directly from its particular use of the instrument's technical resources. Ambivalence, a kind of mitosis or doubleness, goes to the very heart of the music, as anyone who has ever tried to play boogie understands. The player must almost literally divide the mind, and not merely the attention, in two, for in real boogie neither the left not the right hand parts is rote or automatic. In the right hand we hear melodic improvisations that come directly out of blues guitar and ragtime banjo playing, working in the well-known blues tetrachordal scale, with its "neutral" or ambiguous thirds and sevenths, which it produces by striking black and white keys together or in very quick alternation or succession. But, if the right hand is an instrumental "voice," it is a voice, again, uprooted, airy, distant, almost deprived of substance—all the conventional harmonic changes, with their two departures from home, one tentative, one decisive, are there, as are the many melodic variations; but they are disembodied, elusive, miniature, like toys.

If we look for the ground of the music, we find it of course in the bass: but the bass is something somehow not entirely in the human scale. It is almost too inexorable, too forceful: exhilarating and exciting, but something that drives rather than something driven, a sign that the tempo and pattern of life has now fallen under the sway of immense and not entirely benign social and technological forces that, while they expand immensely the range of human aptitude and possibility, also throw a dark, lowering presence over the field in which human freedom may move.

One of the most fascinating things about the boogie, which seems to have been a new direction in an old traditional music designed in response to radically changed conditions of living, is what jazz historians and musicologists have consistently noted: that of all the African American forms to that date, it was the most thoroughly "African." Like West African traditional music, it was based on counter-rhythms forged from the characteristically African annealing of rhythm and melody. In West African music, rhythm is not a temporal foundation upon which to erect an architecture of notes, but the very thing produced, by a formulaic improvisatory, and social process mostly alien to the Western classical tradition. The heart or kernel of every note in West African music is a percussive attack; every arrangement of notes is either a particular motif in which variations of pitch enunciate and guarantee the independence of a particular rhythm, "tunes on drums"—or the melodic terrain of a particular rhythmic utterance. West African music is a dialogue among counter-rhythms interacting at a site defined by a master beat; the coordination of independent rhythms is secured by the basic principle of threes and twos: typically accentual groupings of three, or triplet divisions of the beat, in duple meter, or, more infrequently, the other way around—duple time set over against triple meters, which we hear abundantly in reggae.

At the same time, though, boogie-woogie in a sense eviscerates or decapitates the blues, by assimilating all of its patterns into an environment of rhythmic quantities as regularized and rationalized as a large-scale industrial plant, impersonally setting us in motion across a landscape of transient and distant features that are out of reach before we can so much as identify, much less contemplate, them. West African traditional music, again, in its elaborate layering of drum rhythms and its characteristically leader-and-chorus patterns of song, is pervasively and fundamentally social. Both boogie and blues preserve this dimension in the interactions of singer and instrument, or of the pianist's two hands; but the urbanization of the blues, in the context of black folk culture, required the discovery of a distinctly urban voice—either one projected into an instrument that could imitate the physical forces of intelligent speech or in an altogether new blues vocality.

Birmingham blues pianist Walter Roland's little humoresque "House Lady Blues"[10] seems to capture a moment in the evolution of blues, in 1933, at which the old intimacy between the singer and his instrument had not been rent by the boogie pianist's drive, in the 1940s, towards the conquest of acoustic space with production-line counter-rhythms and telegraphic right-hand riffs. Roland's marvelous blues is tripartite: there is his youthful, delicate, vulnerable singing voice, every tone touched, at the same time as it complains and appeals, with a gentle irony directed against itself. There is the trembling vibrato and feather-light touch of his right hand, which virtually transforms the piano into another voice, one that plays the responsorial part in the leader-chorus interplay: listen to the little weir of tone he makes in the tonic-to-subdominant change in the first instrumental break: we hardly know when the change occurs—only that it has, because we find ourselves there, as if we'd gone over rapids in a skiff. Finally, there's his uncomplicated four-stroke bass, durable, strong enough to support the traffic across it, but not, like Lewis's Honky-Tonk Train or Ammon's Midnight Express,[11] a juggernaut, bent on running you down.

Roland, then, sounds like what he was, a musician shaped by the urban South before the Second World War, where labor, production, and trade hadn't yet assumed the more thoroughly rationalized, industrialized, and commercial forms, nor the social deracination, of the modern factory city, whose pianistic textures and vocalities have not yet been projected into and distorted by instruments suggestive of new forms of social organization and technical power.

This is precisely what I think happens in Bill Doggett's famous rhythm-and-blues instrumental "Honky Tonk,"[12] one of the major landmarks on the audial landscape of the 1950s. Doggett began as a rhythm-and-blues bandleader, and took up the Hammond organ in the 1940s when it was introduced as a swing instrument. He was an arranger for the Ink Spots and a member of Louis Jordan's orchestra. "Honky Tonk" is of much later date, 1956, but more than any other popular rhythm-and-blues instrumental it expresses with passionate earnestness and intensity the loneliness, anguish, and, ultimately, a kind of musical cathexsis in the struggle to discover ways of being human in an utterly strange, vast, and alienating industrial environment: indeed, the tune was improvised during one of the band's tours at a stop in industrial Findlay, Ohio.

The basic structure of "Honky Tonk" is very characteristically African American: an easygoing repetitive blues riff on an electric bass guitar, a regular offbeat accent or "backbeat," an undercurrent of guitar and organ chords providing the connective tissue, and of course Clifford Scott's speechifying saxophone. I think it is apparent that the saxophone in "Honky Tonk" is talking—or, more precisely, that it is doing everything speech does *except* talk. It is almost as if, were we granted a more exact auditory perception, the words might actually become intelligible to us. In fact, the entire performance seems one part of a dialogue, between lovers perhaps, for which the other instruments provide an occasion and a setting. We can hear the phrases, clauses, and sentences, the contours and cadences, even, I think, whole paragraphs, as it were, though we are hearing of course only the propulsions and intonations of speech, without the words themselves, which give to "Honky Tonk" the quality of an intimately consultative communication, one that seems to reflect or speculate, to comment on itself, makes an assertion (I am following here the actual unfolding of the tune), turns the assertion over and restates it, elaborates and amplifies it, and in its conclusion, like its forbears in jazz, brings its message home in the assenting participation, vocally and instrumentally, of the entire band. The tune ends with everyone in agreement, as if the band were finally persuaded that, after all, Scott has it right, whatever it is.

I am not talking about "text" in any sense, but a mimesis of the aural and physiological performance of speech so typical in African American music, jazz especially, in which meaningful hand and head gestures are strongly indicated, and may even be in some sense a physically displaced part of the horn player's performance. Horns are inherently instruments of enunciation, declamation, and alarm; they actually displace the laryngeal function to the lips and extend articulation through the hands—unlike chordophones, which model the resonant human thorax and are in effect independent presences, like dolls, or reeds such as clarinets and oboes, "pastoral" instruments because they further displace the laryngeal vibration to a fibrous, woody structure quite literally derived from marsh grasses. If horns may be said to speak out of the relation between self and society, reeds speak out of the relation of self to the natural world.

The peculiar genius of the saxophone is to have combined the amplifying brass horn with the fibrous reed, the public declamation or call with the solitary woodland or pastoral song, in effect personalizing the public voice in the way that sensitive broadcast microphones created the torch singer and the talk show host. Phalanxes of saxophones formed the front line of assault in the big swing bands; but in rhythm and blues it was primarily a solo instrument, compounded, one might speculate, in ways that gratified the African American imagination in the years of the great migrations. If the affinities of the jazz trumpet are with ballrooms, dancehalls, nightclubs, with the public personality and the stage "showman"—only Miles Davis seems to have succeeded in fully personalizing the trumpet for modern jazz—those of the saxophone are with the smoky jazz dive and lonely street corner, deep introspection, intense personal striving, intimate disclosure, emotional anguish and conflict. The saxophone's hoarse, grainy sound, moreover, pervasive in African and Afro-American vocality, in "Honky Tonk," somehow picks up the smoke and grit, the weird heavy overcast skies, the vast faint din of toil and noise, the rough, unyielding surfaces of the urban industrial zone. The entire tune is powered, plugged in, like a small machine shop isolated on the blackened ground of some great foundry: a current runs through the organ and into the low-fi monophonic guitar amplifiers, transforming the otherwise hollow resonances and reedy exhalations of acoustic instruments into a dense, fluid, tempered substance, a processed raw material or an electromagnetic wave shaped to carry its cryptic but eloquent message. In the little guitar bridge preceding the final chorus I can almost detect a visible scene: the blank windows, the little yards littered with rusty old machine parts with no names, the chain-link fences and inscrutable chemical storage monoliths . . . I'm trying to evoke the landscape of small factories, warehouses, freight depots and so on that in the 1940s and 1950s were the lifeblood of Chicago's South and West sides, and, as Nick Lemann has suggested, the economic underpinning, now withdrawn, of Chicago's migrant black community.

With its small combination of distinctive textures and tone—the drifting, bursting soap bubbles of the guitar notes, the viscous electric organ whose sounds seem to have been synthesized in a Dupont chemical laboratory, the shimmer of brushes and cymbals—one feels that "Honky Tonk" carries the blues away from Canal Street to say, Halstead or Polk Street, from a world of saloons and brothels, the St. James Infirmary and the local police precinct, to a world of pawn shops, cheap furniture stores, crooked currency exchanges, and savings-and-loan agencies; from a world of spats, derbies, cigars, and spittoons to one of zoot suits, watch chains, broad-brimmed fedoras, and cigarettes; from an age of railroads and trolleys to one of noxious buses and bulbous aerodynamic automobiles—one can almost see the grille of a 1949 Ford or Hudson parked in the sun by the curbstone and reflected in a plate-glass window. To take a literary analogy, it seems to register that wartime shift in the African American urban lifeworld from south to north, following a path that leads from Richard Wright and Ralph Ellison to James Baldwin and Chester Himes. While granting the stereotyped character of these associations, I nevertheless maintain that they form a kind of interpretative backdrop against which the particular statements of the music, as indeed of the literature, have their meaning.

"Honky Tonk" is for me both shaped by and shaping of these images, as surely as "Honky Tonk Train Boogie" is by and of a railroad train. For me, it was neither the music nor the environment by itself, but the convergence of "Honky Tonk" with the otherwise unrepresented and unnarrated landscape of my childhood that rescued that landscape from cultural nonbeing and installed it in my imaginative life with all the authority of a canonical novel, a socially prestigious orchestral concert, or an art gallery exhibit.

In Chicago in the late 1940s and 1950s, a new form of the blues, not entirely anticipated either in boogie or in rhythm and blues, but arising more directly from the Delta tradition carried into the region by migrants from Mississippi and Arkansas, was developing in the South- and West-side black ghettos with a raw, throaty, dusky, electric sound and a shrieking, over-amplified electric guitar pioneered by Muddy Waters. The Chicago blues volatilizes almost to incandescence the sound of the harmonica and guitar, and sets the bass line into the role of a collaborative second lead. Whereas the amplifier in the music of the first generation of migrants was an expedient of the street or the rent party, in the achieved Chicago blues it is a structural element—all sounds, of voice, guitars, harmonicas, meet on the quaking surface of an acoustic membrane stretched to the breaking point. It is the sound of an exposed nerve, and it seems to evoke a different kind of city—not the mighty industrial city, full of forbidding beauty and strange promise, but a more brutal one, full of frustration and despair.

Listen to Howlin' Wolf's monotonic shout, "Smokestack Lightnin'."[13] Chester Burnett was born in Tupelo but moved over to the Dockery plantation in 1926, where he began to learn guitar from Charlie Patton. Later he played on the streets with Robert Johnson, and settled in Chicago in 1952. I don't know what "Smokestack Lightnin'," in any programmatic or lyrical sense, is about; but for me it recalls the night scene across Lake Calumet from the Pittsburgh Paint factory, where the air smells of sulphur, and where at the top of the huge stacks of the mills at Whiting, East Chicago, and Gary strange gaseous bonfires illuminate the overcast sky with a lurid red glow.

It is interesting then to compare Doggett's rhythm and blues to the postwar Chicago blues in light of their closely adjacent historical settings. The unperturbed and fluid Hammond organ, an instrument associated, in the African American urban community, with respectable churches and social clubs (as opposed to storefront holiness churches and taverns), the easygoing guitar riff, the textured and insistent but technically complex uptown saxophone—the rhythm-and-blues ensemble as Doggett conceived it was an artifact of the urban industrial black working class in a period of wartime prosperity, and would seem to be comparatively at ease with itself in that moment; the much more raw Chicago blues, still making-do in the country way with slide guitars, a diatonic harmonica, and, in its song lyrics, the old rural belief system—got my mojo workin'—records a far more vexed and troubled encounter with urban life, relegation to a secondary class status within the black community itself, and ultimately with the deterioration of urban black culture altogether, as in the later postwar years its industrial supports gradually withered away.

The Chicago blues was at once an innovation, a folk tradition turned to the business of confronting and absorbing a new environment and a new way of life, but a return, too, to some of the speech-derived rhythmic and melodic principles of African and African American music. Whatever the evolution of the blues may mean in a strictly ethnomusicological sense, the music seems to confirm the instincts and impressions of thoughtful musicians and composers that the meaning of music is rooted deep in our cultural experience; and it ought to suggest to us, I think, that between music and culture, as of course between all art and all culture, there is a kind of dialectic through which culture both reproduces and originates itself, and that music can be read not only as a record of the cultural moment but as a discourse in which to renegotiate the terms of culture's contract with the real: the sense in which music is "ideological." A folk music revival can be explained, sociologically, as a kind of reaction; and in a society pervaded by ever more various broadcast and recorded sounds, the sounds of an Appalachian fiddle or a bottleneck guitar from the Mississippi Delta, sounding its timbres in wholly alien communities, have become a constant accompaniment to the conduct of life, reconstituting existence itself and building in consciousness a kind of secondary endowment that rechannels, reshapes, distorts, or resists the dominant cultural message. And yet we might hazard, paraphrasing Shelley, that music is the unacknowledged legislator of the world, with a predictive as well as a responsive power.

Every musical species seems both to sustain and to engender such subcultural or epicultural modes around it, modes that, with the exponential expansion, through digital technologies, of access to musical styles and kinds, approach the threshold of completing the decoupling of music from its cultural contexts that began with the advent of recorded sound. This decoupling will have approximately the same double effect that the steam-driven rotary press and the mass production of the printed word had in the early nineteenth century: a steady out-migration of lingering local and parochial forms into the global technological and commercial network, and the emergence of a new kind of artist capable of capturing, musically, the sense of life in an information-based global economy. Indeed, I suspect that this double effect may be, as it was in literature nearly two centuries ago, really one effect, as traditional musicians and singers from the Caucasus, the Middle East, South and East Asia, from Eastern Europe, and inevitably, from West Africa and South Africa, migrate to the studios of Paris, London, and Los Angeles to speak in music of the strange intimations, fresh and full of possibility, of a global world still struggling to be born out of the durable horrors of the past.

2 DARKLING I LISTEN

MAKING SENSE OF THE *FOLKWAYS ANTHOLOGY*

Harry Smith's *Anthology of American Folk Music* is pervaded by darkness: the darkness of recorded sound itself, which mechanically or digitally (and the difference is not immaterial) forges (as in "forgery") the vibrations of instruments and human voices at the same time as it imprisons them in grooves or codes, like Ariel in a cloven pine; the historical darkness of music whose origins, provenance, and meaning are obscure or lost; the social and political darkness from within which despised people speak in strange and forbidding, or ingratiating, irritable, or ecstatic voices; the intellectual darkness of caste and race under whose veil secret acts of love have engendered dispositions and powers now visibly abroad in the world. Finally the *Anthology* labors under a "dark conceit" of allegory, a cloud of obfuscating signs that a confluence of various forces in successive moments—war, economic expansion and collapse, exile, war again, and finally an acute recoiling from all that war represents, all that was required to promulgate it—have brought together into a system of signification that is perpetually renewing itself at the same time as it reincorporates its whole genealogy as a vital element of that renewal.

There is apparently no history as such in the *Folkways Anthology*, then, but a dense throng of stories, reports, complaints, confessions, outcries, choruses, dances, and the rest all driven by desire and terror, no one of them in the least intelligible relation to any other save in the few cases where they are sung or played by the same artist, and in no systematic relation to the history that, it must be supposed, over two or three generations produced not only the performances themselves but the conditions under which recording machines and performances came together to issue in an inchoate set of recorded performances: or rather the *sounds* of performances. From the body of the music, then, not a history but, perhaps, a kind of alluvial sediment, a sort of cultural bottom-land; or, more to the point, an aural iconography that like Renaissance magical iconographies—indeed like Theodore de Bry's *Celestial Monochord* that Harry reproduced on the first cover of the *Anthology*—salvages from various discarded inventories and lapsed epochs signs, symbols, icons, and images that in their collage-like adhesiveness vibrate with a kind of Masonic inscrutability.

Yet human sounds will not be altogether disconnected from their discursive matter. In this sense the *Anthology* resembles, but is far from typical of, other collections of folk songs, such as those of the Lomaxes, that necessarily embody the moments of their making and the predilections of their collectors. Among a multitude of other historically situated events on the *Anthology*, two presidents are assassinated, and two murderers executed by hanging. A riverboat dandy shoots his adversary over a poker game, and a betrayed woman shoots her man, *in flagrante*, through a solid oak door. Two trains crash, the *Titanic* goes down, and several farms fail. Story-songs reference historical and legendary figures such as William McKinley, John Henry, Casey Jones, and Cole Younger, as well as particular political issues, such as worker displacement and convict labor, that might tempt us to locate the world of the *Anthology* in or around the turn of the nineteenth century.

That is sensible, ethnomusicologically, as much of the body of folksong commercially recorded for ethnic and regional markets in the interval between the First World War and the Great Depression, what was then and is now called "old-time music," had been shaped by the experience, including the popular musical experience, of the late nineteenth century. Much, but not all. Sentimental parlor ballads are conspicuously absent from the *Anthology*, as are, a few stowaways notwithstanding, any songs obviously out of the minstrel show. Blues, however, are plentiful, especially blues about misspent lives, ungratified desire, drink, incarceration, overwork, poverty, hunger, infidelity, loneliness, exile, abandonment, and abuse—country blues, for the most part, largely predating the postwar northern migrations. And scattered across the *Anthology*, as over the mountain ballad repertoire generally, are materials that, if somewhat altered by their long exile in a far-off land, are quite ancient: medieval, actually, peopled not with steel drivers, hoboes, and bandits but kings, queens, knights, and ladies, given to stabbing themselves and others, or to drowning or strangling them, over affairs of the heart, or to departing from them upon splendidly long voyages on ships as, apparently, tests of fidelity. These songs, however, are historical too, I suppose, insofar as they register the imaginative life in relation to which stories of bandits and steel drivers, and perhaps the drowning of Omie Wise at Deep River, North Carolina, in 1808, or of the hanging of desperado John Hardy in Welch, West Virginia, in 1894, have their meaning.

History is not quite, like balladry, a world of "passion and fury," in Northrop Frye's phrase, and neither history nor romance are as intimate as are myth, fable, and fairy tale, or the *Folkways Anthology*, with an auxiliary population of animals such as the goose, ox, horse, possum, rabbit, bird, and a catfish, all of whom play pivotal roles in resolving or failing to resolve some human predicament, or to whom, more famously, whole songs are reverently devoted: that well-known couple the mouse and frog; Clarence Ashley's very British cuckoo bird; Bascom Lamar Lunsford's reclusive mole and lizard; Jim Jackson's ever-loyal blue-tick hound Old Blue. As the human characters in these songs are in regular conversation or some other entanglement with animals, it is perhaps warranted to take them in an anthropological sense, as residues of frontier economies, or folklorically, as deposits from African and Anglo-American song stocks rich in animal fable. Fair enough; but poetically speaking these creatures are radioactive; one or two of them actually talk, or at least exchange knowing looks with their human associates; like the flaming and voluble eagles, doves, bears, lions, and fish of folktale, they are signs of inevitabilities, of the fates that are both kinds of habit and a kind of consensus. Mole, lizard, dog, mouse, frog: a humble menagerie, not emblematic of the great faiths, but pressed into service nearer the bottom and closer to the edge of the social body, field, yard, and household spirits that mediate between the human and the natural worlds, vibrating as if bewitched on the boundary between the commonplace and the uncanny. Official religion the *Anthology* represents mostly in unofficial form, in a range of vernacular hymns that highlight what for the truly wretched is the central doctrine of faith, the promise of reward in a better world beyond Death. Its main theme is release, its setting is social, as Harry made clear, and its emotional tone is joy—all of which are as evident in secular dance tunes like "Sail Away Ladies" or Eck Robertson's "Brilliancy Medley" as they are in the ecstasies of the shape-note hymn "Rocky Road" or the sheer pandemonium of "Fifty Miles of Elbow Room."

But as we have said, the *Anthology* is really an order of sounds, more than of words, which is to say, a babble of voices. Oh those voices! They are, again, uniformly untutored, rustic, primitive. Among male voices on the *Anthology* there is occasionally warmth, sensuousness, relaxation—but more frequently the total absence of them. There are cozening and irascible voices, bellowing and officious ones; many are deadpan, dispirited, almost catatonic. Some of the blues and gospel songs sound as if they are being sculpted by chainsaws or being poured from hoppers, like cement, others crafted by dental drills or industrial forges. John Hurt, on the other hand, sings sweetly, youthfully, with a sense of humor, and Bascom Lamar Lunsford tenderly, avuncularly, with a suppressed laugh. Uncle Dave Macon sings grandiloquently, like a fifth-term mayor, and Buell Kazee with officious self-importance. Women warble, wail, crackle, and cry, or, especially in the shape-note hymns, seem nearly to giggle; there are no sweet-voiced, sultry or seductive voices, no pre-Raphaelite tresses, no evening gowns, no diamond tiaras.

As we enter this auditory universe, then, every performance becomes a kind of thicket in a synesthetic body of "verdurous glooms and winding mossy ways," in Keats's well-known phrase, in this case not only smeared with flickering apparitions like the walls of Altamira but layered with a kind of igneous compound of many musically and lyrically reimagined times and places. Such locales as the east Texas frontier, the Mississippi Delta, the north Georgia Hills, the Blue Ridge, the Big Bend Tunnel, Beale Street or Birmingham, are fields of repressed memory or unrealized possibility that because they constitute us cannot otherwise be known; in these locales lives a race of beings—rogues, gamblers and clowns, tramps and vagabonds, drifters, forsaken men, innocent girls, wounded women, a beloved uncle, and a goofy trail-crazed cowboy—whose sudden exposure in the immediacy of their own voices is, and must be, shocking, magical, frightening, and ultimately funny, because they are so precisely and fittingly recognizably unrecognizable.[1] I cannot but picture old Harry, shoulders hunched up, shaking with wheezy laughter—like the young Keats of "Ode to a Nightingale," sick and tired, but more worldly and more wise.

From darkness, light. Harry Smith's *Anthology* of "verdurous glooms and winding mossy ways" in fact forcibly recalls the "embalmed darkness" from within which the poet of Keats's "Ode to a Nightingale,"[2] listening to the warbling of a night-singing thrush, harbinger of the dawn, synesthetically guesses into existence, an invisible but palpable region where incense hangs like moss upon the boughs, moonlight touches the skin with the spring breeze, where space and color exfoliate out of natural music into a "melodious plot of beechen green and shadows numberless." Like Keats's *Ode,* Smith's *Anthology* both practices and inspires that visionary conjuring that refuses the intelligible world, with all of its habitual distinctions and received truths, to resurrect it from the borrowed materials of the tactile and auditory body, transforming it from a reflective surface to a vital organic motion, from a reactive to a generative act, its comprehension demanding a prolonged and profoundly inward meditation upon forms and meanings.

Like the *Anthology,* Keats's *Ode* is riddled with darkness, physical and moral. There is first the darkness of the poet's own mind—the heartache and a "drowsy numbness" that "perplex and retard" his brain, as if, he says, he had just taken opium or swallowed Hemlock—that would seem to have sprung from the darkness of despair. The world to him has become a charnel house, "where men sit and hear each other groan"; where "youth grows pale, and spectre thin, and dies," where "but to think is to be full of sorrow / And leaden-eyed despairs." Tuberculosis, which months earlier had killed Keats's brother and which as he wrote was killing him, and a passionate, reciprocated, but unconsummated love for a flighty eighteen year old, might account for the young poet's black frame of mind; but the "angelheaded hipsters" of another age, burning for the "ancient heavenly connection to the starry dynamo in the machinery of night," who as Allen Ginsberg wrote in "poverty and tatters and hollow-eyed and high sat up smoking in the supernatural darkness of cold-water flats floating across the tops of cities contemplating jazz,"[3] might recognize him as one of their own.

Poetry itself is in a sense always dark—its "viewless wings" can carry him, the poet, through the tactile and auditory flight of a nightingale's song, only into another kind of darkness, that of imagination when it turns self-consumingly away from loneliness and suffering towards its own resources in memory, knowledge, and feeling, to shape what inevitably becomes, the deeper is the heart's dedication to its own fabrications, to its own exile, the "faery lands forlorn" to which the poet arrives at the same instant as he awakens to the inescapable isolation of his "sole self." In this sense the act of listening is like an act of love—absorbed and all-absorbing, envelopingly sensory and ingeniously sensual, an object whose attainment is guaranteed to return us, with an even keener self-awareness and a deeper resignedness, to the very condition from which it offered to deliver us. Clarity and finality, one might think, would be the outcome of such an excursion; instead it is only a deeper and more perfect ambiguity, one that holds at one and the same time, like the music of which it is made, deception and the inevitability, hopelessness and necessity: "Was it a vision, or a waking dream?"

If there is light in *Ode to a Nightingale* it is only by an apparent paradox the light of musical sound and what can sometimes be, under its influence, that intoxicating excess of happiness—"not through envy of thy happy lot," says the poet, "but being too happy in thine happiness." Where that more glorious existence whose reality music persistently if deceivingly affirms—"Fancy cannot cheat so well as she is famed to do"—may be located is often sufficiently terrestrial that we can plausibly long to go there, sometimes perhaps with frequent-flyer miles, but far more often metonymically, through associations, and with the aid of wine, or music, or both, driven by a desire for warmth, for the gratification of appetite, for the light of another's eyes. "O for a beaker full of the warm South," cries the poet, oh for a "draught of vintage, tasting of the country green, of dance, Provencal song, and sunburnt mirth." Keats, like us, and he may be forgiven for it, might be said to be dreaming on the folk—of minstrels and troubadours, country weddings, and sun-baked grin-crinkled peasant faces with wine-hazed eyes, though he is perhaps endowed with an at once more discriminating and more sober sense of social actuality when he elects the viewless wings of poesy to get him there. Whatever else this place may be, he seems to know at the outset, it is never anything else but imaginary. "The warm South" is located in its own unlocatability, in the very process of sense-making that, while it may lead through images, codes, and representations to a verifiable world, can produce, by itself, only effigies of its own interiority. It is the process of listening itself that is meaningful, the transitive and immediate knowing of knowing, the dark energy that is as much the issue of the theory that predicts it as of the instrument that detects it, that ultimately validates what is known knowable as a human product. Let us then take stanzas 4 and 5 of Keats's *Ode to a Nightingale* as a prolegomena to the act of listening, and see if it does not reflect our own acts of listening when it comes to something as unexpected as Harry Smith's *Folkways Anthology*.

4
Away! Away! for I will fly to thee,
    Not charioted by Bacchus and his pards,
But on the viewless wings of Poesy,
    Though the dull brain perplexes and retards:
Already with thee! Tender is the night,
    And haply the Queen-Moon is on her throne,
        Cluster'd around by all her starry Fays;
            But here there is no light,
    Save what from heaven is with the breezes blown
        Through verdurous glooms and winding mossy ways.

5
I cannot see what flowers are at my feet.
    Nor what soft incense hangs upon the boughs,
But, in embalmed darkness, guess each sweet
    Wherewith the seasonable month endows

The grass, the thicket, and the fruit-tree wild;
  White hawthorn, and the pastoral eglantine;
    Fast fading violets cover'd up in leaves;
      And mid-May's eldest child,
  The coming musk-rose, full of dewy wine,
    The murmurous haunt of flies on summer eves.

"Away! away! for I will fly to thee." This threefold call to the act of listening banishes the poet's hideous vision of death and decay as well as the merely luxurious and stupefying seductions of wine in favor of the bold cavalier-like declaration that he will deliberately fly away on the conscientiously fabulous, if viewless, wings of Poesy. This is not merely an intellectual action, and in some sense not an act of mind at all, since "the dull brain perplexes and retards"—but more, it seems, a flight of the spirit out of the confines of thought and into the dark interior spaces, the "verdurous glooms and winding mossy ways," of the body itself. The poet has merely to close his eyes ("Already with thee!") and the night is turned to flesh, and we are in love with it; Keats has ushered us into what amounts to a love-bower, presided over by a matriarchal Moon-Queen and her fairy attendants.

As for the body into which the lover has gained entry, it is auto-erotically the poet's own—as it must be, of course, even, or especially, in an act of love—but one nevertheless enthralled by the song of a night bird whose mythical name is Philomela (an Athenian princess, her tongue cut out by the brother-in-law who has raped her, transformed into the songbird) and which in any case we already understand to be female, a "light-winged Dryad of the trees." Hence it is propitious that in this bower of love there should be no light, other than "what from heaven is with the breezes blown," and so on—a light, in other words, that registers its energy on the surface of the skin but whose origins are in heaven: not, in other words, a merely optical light, that nakedly exposes surfaces, structures, shapes, magnitudes, and proportions, that conceals in order to reveal, dazzles and deceives, but the celestial light of love that creates what it touches. This light opens access not to a world of surfaces but of textures, masses, densities, temperatures, tendencies and forces, of color, darkness and brightness, all indicative of living presence, as they are registered on a tactile spectrum that extends from the skin to that most delicate of tactile organs, the ear.

Though the image of "soft incense that hangs upon the boughs," very nearly assuming a botanical as well as a near-human anatomical mass, could hardly be more erotic, it is the poet's *musical* imagination that restores us and him in the space of a few lines to the world of memory and experience, where he summons into existence an exact, even a learned, inventory of hawthorn, eglantine, and violet, locating us near the grasses and thickets of Hempstead Heath in the "seasonable month" of mid-May, and even bending, it seems, to the smell of the musk-rose, that "murmurous haunt of flies on summer eves" which he audits so closely that we are almost peering into it. Keats knows his flowering plants. The "viewless wings of Poesy," then, have not recorded this world in any documentary sense, but figured it into existence, created in effect images, ideas, and objects out of a kind of tactile *aurora borealis* that reaches from the most delicate hairs of the cochlea outward to the skin, the hands, the fingertips, into what music perhaps most centrally arouses, the sensation of purposeful activity, and finally into things and the names of things. This process of creation, evident enough I suppose from the incidental images of the stanza, is clearly linked in the poet's mind to death—for he sees himself laid as if upon a bier with flowers at his feet, swathed in "embalmed darkness"; and yet the process of listening, far from a descent into unconsciousness ("to thy high requiem become a sod"), has been instead the unfolding of it, the active sustaining and arousing of consciousness in its fullness and integrity against the forces of dejection and illness that would drag it down.

Keats's hymn to Death, then, is a radical, if ambivalent, turn; his act of listening both restores the world and restores him to it, a poet no longer "half in love with easeful Death" and ready to consign his "mused rhymes" to Death to oblivion. If the act of listening has been a metaphorical kind of dying—or at least a descent into the viscera of perception, where the diffusion of self offers relief from pain by effacing the subject of it—the process itself, because it is imaginative, because it springs from memory, invention, and knowledge, unlike the mere amnesia of intoxication, recalls what for Coleridge was "the living power and prime agent of all human perception, and as a repetition in the finite mind of the eternal act of creation in the infinite I AM," that, as he famously wrote, "dissolves, diffuses dissipates, in order to recreate."[4] The poet may, then, at that consummate moment, suppose that it is "rich to die / To cease upon the midnight with no pain / while thou art pouring forth thy soul abroad / In such an ecstasy!"—but it is too late for that. The creative agent is restored, like it or not, to himself—and it is as a resignedly *mortal* being that he sings his paean to the immortal bird, not born for Death, whose voice "was heard / In ancient days by emperor and clown," and has opened "on the foam / Of perilous seas, in faery lands forlorn."

That is the phrase: "Faery lands forlorn"—the fatal but inevitable slip from what for Coleridge would have been from Imagination to Fancy, merely "a mode of memory emancipated from the order of time and space" receiving "all its materials ready made from the law of association;"[5] or as Foucault put it, from "imagination to voluntary memory, spontaneous attention into reflection, instinct into rational knowledge,"[6] or, finally, as we might say, from mimesis into agency, culture to ideology.

Is the *Folkways Anthology,* then, an "eternal act of creation" reiterated in each of our acts of listening, or simply a "mode of memory emancipated from the order of time and space?" It's up to us, I suppose—so let us attempt, not to calculate, study, reason, figure, or otherwise assemble but like Keats to *guess* the *Folkways Anthology* into existence, listen it to life.

Harry Smith, as we've seen, has taken many conscientious steps to lead us towards the former at the expense of the latter, by, for example, effacing all the racial, historical, occupational, and other distinctions supposed to be proper to the domain of folksong by which we locate and control it. The *Anthology* is instead, again, an order of human sounds, vocal and instrumental, that, considered apart from the body of scholarship and popular understandings that identified these sounds, that accumulated, collected, and recollected them, are diffuse and obscure in origin, parochial, momentary, in most cases idiosyncratic even within their own milieu and in the various remote settings into which sound recording has carried them, obdurately wondrous, grotesque, curious, queer, amusing, absurd, sometimes ridiculous, sometimes frightening, from time to time sublime. Keats awakens to the forlornness of a momentary vision that turns inevitably to what is "ready-made from the law of association"; we wake, I think, to the tooting of Henry Thomas's panpipes, in laughter.

Since our theme however is darkness, let's get into the dark matter of the *Anthology,* from which all its distinctive energy is invisibly emanating. Let us recall that as a visual artist Harry worked in a transitional zone between image and after-image, doodle and drawing, where a neurological *anima* aroused by its own activity meets itself in the process of creating an intelligible world out of the raw material of perception. He was not only a master of sensory transliteration—his mural of a Dizzy Gillespie solo at Jimbo's Bop City, preserved only in a photograph, seems as close to a picture of listening as any visual image could approach—but, as in his films, always worked directly in and upon, and not merely through, his medium.

Just what *are* Smith's anthologized voices, then, and what is the medium in which he is working? They are, first of all, the voices of the dead—dead because a world war and all the social and technical forces liberated by it threw a curse of obsolescence over them from which they were momentarily rescued by a reactionary fad, only to be buried less than a decade later by the same forces; dead because buried alive in a thick polymeric medium derived from crude oil, a kind of cultural fossil fuel, first to be retailed as a souvenir of time-travel and then, reverting to their material character, stockpiled as war *materiel* and charged with a new regimen of political, cultural, and technical energies; and not only dead but, in a sense, silent, because the recording process itself had stripped them like Philomela of their tongue.

All this is to say again that Harry the folksong anthologist like Harry the filmmaker has his hands directly in the medium, in this case the medium of recorded sound: not, ultimately, a *record* of anything but at best merely an impression or footprint, or a residue, never mind how accurate, faithful, or complete, but an impression nevertheless, of it, and as art meaningful as print or photography is meaningful in the particular way it transforms what it represents. As a reissue anthology, the *Folkways Anthology* is an accumulation of archaic commercial music originally directed at certain ethnic and regional markets long since dispersed. Hence it is first and foremost a gathering; as such it exposes what formerly could be experienced only in threads and patches as a total design, in a structure of fixed elements whose relationships are narratively as well as architecturally organized. What was many things, in a variety of moments and settings, becomes one thing, in its own moment and setting. The various signs of an old social ecology become signifiers in a catalogue of early commercial recordings, among other recordings of different types; they are appropriated again to become signifiers of "folk" culture, among other such collections, in an LP *Anthology* destined to become itself a sign, the sign of the folk—only to be appropriated yet again as a signifier, among other works of art, of the avant-garde and now, with the Smithsonian reissue, a sign of cultural preeminence. These many transformations are precisely the "verdurous glooms and winding mossy ways" of layered temporal and social contexts, each of which endows the selections with specific, but different, meanings. Each of the songs has its original life at some distant moment, and another in 1925, or 1952, or 1963, or 1997.

The *Anthology* further transforms technologically, by enunciating its own mediating power: the old *records,* not the old songs, are its subject, whose main interest therefore is that they are old and that they are records. Now all this is a good deal more complicated than it seems. That they are old means that the *Anthology* is among other things a salvage and recovery operation, a set of found objects, or more precisely, junk; and more than merely an accumulation, already partly accomplished by the War Department, they are a collection by virtue of which the whole acquires a value, simply as the outcome of human labor, greater than the sum of its parts. As an intelligent arrangement of elements, as a recombination, moreover, the *Anthology* becomes a kind of hypothesis, an archeological reconstruction, though which a total way of life might be imagined. Hence, at the most superficial level, there is the fascination of the antique, brought out of hiding in an unknown past, hence in a sense radically new and unprecedented, the more curious and quaint as the conditions of its former being are obscure, and the difficulty of comprehending it according to contemporary usages more daunting.

That they are *records* further complicates their intrigue, for what is really happening in the first instance on the *Anthology* is that it, or Harry Smith, is playing to us a collection of old records of a particular kind in a particular order. He is making designs upon us; but as our primary interest in the medium is the way in which it transforms what it represents, we'll first be conscious of the performances *as records,* and grasp them as performances only as they become transparent as records. But they don't become transparent, and they never will.

Here is one of the points at which Harry works his extraordinary magic. Speaking now of the vinyl, not the digital, release of the *Anthology,* certain mysteries present themselves: What are, or were, these records? What possible entrepreneurial, scholarly, or some other initiative, technical intervention, commercial field, or cultural moment can explain them? Like the 78–rpm stacks of fox-trots and light opera that used to gather dust in the Goodwill stores, they appear, misleadingly, to belong to a manifestly earlier stage in the evolution of sound recording, and that is part of what is interesting about them, the scratch, the hiss, and the hurry to the three-minute closing bell, through which, at some former time, people had to listen, more *for* their music than *to* it; on the other hand, unlike those fox-trots and operatic selections (typically marketed, as John Szwed points out, more by musical category rather than by individual artist, save in special cases like Caruso),[7] they do not carry much of any indication of their historical location.

On the contrary, it is all hopelessly muddled. Where are we, musically speaking? Not much help from the vocal styles. Some of the voices plausibly emanate from Memphis or Chattanooga, and some from the Kentucky mountains or the Carolina cotton mills. But, as Ralph Rinzler said of "Train on the Island," some might just as plausibly have come from medieval China,[8] or, we might add, from seventeenth-century Senegal or Mozambique. What is the connection between the material gathering on the one hand, a heap of forgotten phono discs, and an accumulation of musical performances? And what has the concentration of performances to do, if anything, with the collection of the "material" performed? The songs and accompanying instruments themselves can provide some orientation, since for the most part they belong to identified traditions—but, again, doubly removed, not only spun onto the surfaces of inaccessible old records (not to put too fine a point on it, it is the *sound* of the old records we have, not the records themselves, unless we happen to be in the Smith Collection itself)—but *already* culturally residual at the time they were recorded. Like all such collections of "folk" music, then, they are essentially thought experiments, cultural fictions: newer than new, as it were, and older than old. And they lead us, finally, to the *Anthology's* central mystery: How can *these* performances have found their way to *those* records? Or better, these records to those performances?—questions that would not arise at all were it not for the still deeper question with which Harry has confronted us: *What is a record?*

Harry has placed us roughly where the listeners to Edison's phonograph were, phenomenologically speaking, in the early weeks of its public unveiling, when, according to the editor of the *Scientific American,* "The machine inquired as to our health, asked how we liked the phonograph, informed us that *it* was very well, and bid us a cordial goodnight."[9] At succeeding demonstrations young women fainted; eminent scientific heads were convinced it was a trick of ventriloquism; a Yale professor pronounced it a flat-out hoax. What was this machine that could steal the human voice? That could make absent people present—or was it that it rendered present people absent? That immortalized the human voice, but at the same time abolished it? What can one say of a machine that brings the dead back to life, but in the same instant buries them again? "Was it a vision, or a waking dream? Do I sleep or wake?"

Now sound may be a summons, an alert, an emergency, a stimulus, an incentive, an inspiration, an urge—but in all these cases it is, as Keats's metaphor suggests, necessarily a brush with death, a descent into the "verdurous glooms and winding mossy ways" of synthetic neurological processes by which we bring coherence and intelligibility to the "booming buzzing confusion," in William James's phrase, to the message of the senses. The same could be said, perhaps, about any of the senses abstracted from the sensory body, since without the interplay of the senses there is no world, or no imagination to complete a world, only its disembodied force, or impress, or reflection; all acts of perception are interpretations, recognitions and misrecognitions, but in any case subjective creations. Recorded sound, by definition divorced from the spatiotemporal point of its production, in a sense reverses the calculus of recognition, unlike either touch or sight, going out of existence just at the point that it is coming into existence, in a sense creating itself just as it undoes itself wholly through our power of inference. As this sound is always revealed by the imagination to be that—a creaky floor, a distant thunderstorm, a Fender Telecaster—so recorded sound, and particularly *musical* sound, compels the process of listening that is somehow akin either to drowning or to saving oneself from drowning or both, essentially a decision about whether life is worth the effort it takes to live.

All this turns upon the processes of sense-making that the obscurity of recorded sound necessitates; like Harry himself, transmuting a Miles Davis or Dizzy Gillespie solo into a visual pattern of whorls, angles, globes, bubbles, and lights, we are confronted with the finally impossible task of making *The Folkways Anthology* real for us. It is a faery land summoned out of the play of memory and sensation whose aim, as in all of Harry Smith's work, is to "make sense" of the world as mystery, which is what we call those patterns, processes, and designs in art and in the world that open to perception—and invite, through signs, prolonged contemplation of—the unity of consciousness and its object. It is a process of knowing, an essentially scientific investigation, which as Bertrand Russell pointed out has historically been a process of elevating notions such as mass derived from tactility into an understanding of the nature of the energy that works upon the eye. But unlike the physics of which Russell was speaking, Harry Smith's science is of a Rosicrucian character, not dedicated to a description of reality in terms of orders and relations of magnitude but in registers and hierarchies of human value: not the science of hypothesis, which is never in touch with its object, but the science of revelation, which *is* its object.

My own dull brain "perplexes and retards"; but after forty years of listening, the soundscape of the *Folkways Anthology* has begun to fix itself in my imagination as something very close to the iconography of magic with which Harry was so fascinated. There are the animals, of course—a lizard, a mole, a dog, and a bird, all somehow endowed with the gift of speech. I fancy I can see there, too, with an inward eye, a heavenly choir and a blind beggar; a eunuch, perhaps, selling a remedy for impotence; and perhaps a leper, possessed by the voices of spirits and demons. There is a weeping woman, and a man in chains; I think a see a field hand, and a house servant, and, to borrow from Thackeray, "a vagabond with a corked face and a banjo [who] sings a little tune, strikes a wild note, and sets the heart thrilling with happy pity."[10]

But there is also a sturdy farmer with a hoe, and his wife; some hungry, hollow-eyed children; a schoolmaster and a schoolmarm; and a kind of citizen, a businessman, a Mason perhaps, with a round belly and a gold watch. And three young men with blueprints and micrometers: mechanical engineers, out to make a more efficient loom or a stronger bridge. I would say it was a world of this place or that, at some time or another, were it not for Ragtime Texas Thomas, the street singer, who carries quills in the pocket of his suit-jacket and whose two-dollar shoes, in the mud of the riverbank where he's gone a-fishing, leave cloven prints. He is perhaps the spirit who has presided over the central *musical* story of the *Folkways Anthology*, which is the story of two great traditions, African American and Anglo-American, coming together to become one in the crucible of southern vernacular life. A moment's thought will suggest the intense irony of this tale, so subtly told in the sounds of the *Anthology* that it scarcely seems to have been told at all, how its gay, even merry comedy, embodied in such voices as Uncle Dave Macon's, Bascom Lunsford's, as well as that of Ragtime Texas Thomas himself, strives bravely against a historical tide of almost incomprehensible suffering to which the music consistently alludes and whose emotional residues it consistently delivers up in fantasy, obsession, resentment, anger, and ecstasy. I do not mean the suffering of slavery and its legacies only, though these are appalling, but also to the ugly material and moral consequences of the slave and plantation systems for poor, despised, and disenfranchised whites whose misery and oppression is stridently registered in the *Anthology* in voices strained, stretched, and pinched to the point of comic absurdity.

The *Anthology*'s color-blindness, then, is only an aspect of a more comprehensive effacement that yields up an imagined people of no-race, no-time, no-place, a "folk" in the sense that in certain conditional passages of our "unofficial" or unstructured existence we are all "folk," people-as-such prepared by the disarming oddness of the sounds, and by Smith's discontinuous sequencing that tends to defer or subvert any intellectual closure, to project in a nearly Jungian sense our own repressed humanness, with its own debts to pay, onto their tunes, their stories, and their voices. "In that condition of life," as Wordsworth, speaking not ethnographically but poetically, said of the "humble and rustic life" that he chose for his *Lyrical Ballads,* "the essential passions of the heart find a better soil in which they can attain their maturity, are less under restraint, and speak a plainer and more emphatic language." But he might better have said, *appear* to be—for as he himself well knew, his real subject was ever and always his own spiritual life, and the manner in which, through the "spontaneous overflow of powerful feelings," and the "association of ideas in a state of excitement," poetry, wherein "ordinary things are presented in an unusual aspect" in a "language really used by men," might reveal "the primary laws of our nature."[11]

The world of *The Folkways Anthology,* like that of Keats's "Ode to a Nightingale," is one of heartache, forgetfulness, disease, decrepitude, injustice, loneliness, and despair, but also of sunshine, laughter, intoxication, joy, and fun. Like Keats's poet, we look longingly away from the charnel-house of mid-twentieth century America, as Smith did, or, as the case may be, from the twenty-first century's crumbling Temple of Mammon, to a dream of the "warm south," of song, dance, and "sunburnt mirth"—but find ourselves transported instead, under the dark spell of the music, into the depths of our own bodies, a region of life-in-death and death-in-life, where, guided by the secret knowledges it is the business of mystical contemplation to summon up, we seem to make a path through our very substance. But the spell, in and by the very act of its enunciation, must ultimately be broken, and our eyes opened; the voices of the *Anthology,* like the nightingale and its song, are after all only visitors from another place—"faery lands forlorn" from which, as for the poet, only the sound of a living voice, our own, can deliver us. Like the wild Heath that lay just up the road from the suburban garden in which Keats composed his poem and to which his harbinger bird ultimately returned, Smith's "old weird America," as Greil Marcus calls it,[12] though always near at hand, is directly knowable only through transient and irrecoverable experiences we usually associate not with beauty in any conventional sense but with that more jealous apprehension of it that as a kind of revelation glances back at us from what is rude, ugly, frightening, obscure, despised, or merely plain—from what, in a word, we have discovered for ourselves.

If we like Keats have been half in love with easeful Death, it is perhaps on account of spatiotemporal change so ruthlessly accelerated that we are as good as continually dying, no sooner consolidating selfhood than packing it up for storage, no longer living *to* music but living *on* it to the point of becoming it, until the very point of selfhood seems to have been lost. Listening to the *Folkways Anthology* we are, like Keats in his *Ode,* at once playing at death and playing with it, for the purpose—if the evolution of Keats's meaning can be called a purpose, since it is as much our own as his—of wondering whether we are asleep or awake, seeing or dreaming, and whether it is ever possible to know the difference, or whether it makes any difference that we can or can't.

3 THE MAGIC 8 BALL

FROM ANALOG TO DIGITAL

On my desk I keep a Magic 8 Ball, which I bought recently at a shopping mall; I had one as a kid. The Magic 8 Ball, you may remember, is really only a little bottle filled with an inky fluid in which an obscure shape, or shapes, inscribed with twenty some odd "messages"—"Ask again later," "Don't count on it," "Better not tell you now," "Cannot predict now," "Signs point to yes," and so on—drift up out of the darkness to a little round window upon which the 8 Ball rests. That shape is some sort of polyhedron, I guess, or several of them—but of course I haven't actually seen it; you can't, unless you tear the thing apart, as I finally did with my childhood toy, to see how the damned thing worked. It is more a kind of ideal form, a pure idea that we not only can't see but that can't really exist in the world. We can only construct it by inference, with repeated consultations.

Since I bought this one a few weeks ago I've been casually consulting it, experimentally, on a certain minor anxiety that's been nagging at me, and I'm happy to report that its answer—it came up three times in a row, too consistent to be merely accidental—is just the one I wanted. The trick was making up the right question. That way, you tell your own fortune.

The 8 Ball has all the answers; but it is we who must find the questions. The burden is on us. You have to concentrate—because if you don't, it'll put you off; it'll protect you if it thinks the time is not right ("Better not tell you now"); it is sometimes uncertain—"Very doubtful"—and can even be disabled: "Cannot predict now." It'll even betray the fact that it doesn't really know, itself, what to report; that it depends upon intermittent contact with something still more distant and obscure: "My sources say no," "Signs point to yes." Hence it doesn't, *by itself,* predict the future or explain the past, or fathom others' motives or intentions—like a computer, it has no mind of its own. But it is hard not to attribute mindfulness to it, because in spite of the fact that it is an obviously rational mechanism with a finite structure of possibilities, it speaks to us. Since its messages come up without evident reason or purpose, at random, it is easy to project reason and purpose into them. But they are our purposes, and our reasons.

I think the Magic 8 Ball makes a good metaphor for Harry Smith's *Folkways Anthology of American Folk Music*—its eighty-four facets, each one inscribed with a riddling, arcane, complex, and cryptic musical message, seem also to drift up out of an inky blackness, with no context but what they summon up collectively out of themselves, what George Trow, writing almost thirty years ago about what has become, fortuitously for him, the present, calls "the context of no context." The *Anthology* has all the answers, each one more hauntingly enigmatic than the last—answers to questions we haven't yet learned, or have forgotten how to ask; like the 8 Ball, it demands of us a special kind of mental effort, innocent and open-hearted on the one hand, even naïve, and crafty, even self-deceiving, on the other.

The *Anthology* has always seemed to be audibly in touch with something at once shockingly actual and fascinatingly obscure, the soul of a dead world, it seems, which can only communicate with the living world through a medium, in shadows, and indirectly, by means of an occult mechanism, like a great underwater creature that can only be glimpsed in parts, and that if we are not careful can swallow us up. The *Folkways Anthology* seems to have an imaginary form lurking inside it, a form that some of us think we may have glimpsed, just for a moment, as time and time again its many faces heaved up into view, a bristling, unwieldy, prodigious shape that seems to speak of another world—an "Invisible Republic," as Greil Marcus calls it, the "old weird America."[1]

That strangeness and elusiveness is partly a quality of recorded sound itself: as present and as imperative as any music or speech, as full of intimation, and also out of reach, inaccessible, even sometimes, implausible or impossible. That is what happens, the moment you steal sound away from what produced it. You thrust it back into silence and darkness, and, though you may be able to carry it away to "Pakistan or wherever you might be," as Harry Smith drolly observed,[2] you can't really know it. You can only listen, and listen, and listen to it again, and guess.

The essence of magic, by which I mean the yoking of real elements to ideal forms, usually by some symbolic means, is poetry—which is to say, art. But magic wants more than beauty; it wants influence. Not content with the power of metaphor, it wants the power of causes. We have recourse to magic at those crises of perception brought about by a sense of historical rupture, and all the available means of reality-making lie in a heap at our feet. This was the crisis of the Renaissance, when, the old scholastic story having lost its credibility, but still lying around in a heap of allegorized signs and symbols, magic began to challenge authority for an account of God, calling upon queer new manipulative processes like memory theaters to fathom His Creation and alchemical experiments to test it out: to absorb the human mind into God's own.

It is the crisis of our own period, I think, for whatever the analysis offered to explain our situation, whether it is the implosion of capitalism or the final triumph of it, the emergence of "flexible production" or of decentered worldwide electronic communications, few would quarrel with the notion that we have in some sense experienced the "end of metanarratives," or that, in Jameson's words, we have somehow lost any possibility of "positioning the cultural act outside the massive Being of Capital."[3]

Magic yielded to science—and all the great scientists, Galileo, Copernicus, Bacon, Descartes, even Newton, dabbled in magic and mysticism—when Leibniz and Descartes realized that magical symbols, which worked by resemblance, were not in actual touch with reality: the new reality, that is, of things, made like the terrestrial moon of actual *stuff,* that could be weighed and measured, carried away, or exchanged for money. Symbols were mere shadows, traces, leavings, films, footprints, contaminants from a fallen human nature still clinging to its projections. Numbers, on the other hand, as Pythagoras had taught, were the root of truth. They were *their own* reality, entirely clean and self-consistent, meaningful entirely in terms of one another. That was, after all, the secret of money. Like the economic system that engendered it, its knowledge was extractive, nonrenewable, continually sweeping away the old in order to make a place for the new. Relations among numbers could express relations among things; manipulations of those relations represented, potentially, manipulations of things. Whatever could be expressed in number could be brought into relation to everything else that could be expressed in number; hence the tendency was towards totality.

Science and magic are never far apart. Their ends are the same; only the means differ—and that with vanishing subtlety. Consider, for instance, Jackie Kennedy, who, in the instant after its disintegration, knowing that life and form are one in the same, tried to restore the integrity of her husband's body. She was only trying to achieve by magic what the surgeons a few minutes later tried, and failed, to achieve by science. Since then we have struggled, by a process at once thoroughly scientific, and yet wholly magical and symbolical, to restore the integrity of the event that preempted the history we otherwise might have enacted in our collective life, to put all of its elements into their proper relation. The "book depository building," "Dealy Plaza," "the grassy knoll"—these are but figures of the intellectual, imaginary, and political forces that make the historical moment in America: the dream of an enlightened democracy, the dream of a public sphere, the dream of national innocence; and the presiding characters, America's most famous ninety-eight-pound weakling Lee Harvey Oswald, Abraham Zapruder, the Sam Goldwyn of postmodernity, John Connally the pol, Jack Ruby the crook, and the rest—they were the *dramatis personae* in the final scene of a postwar Noh play in which the spirit of war, which had won dominion over every department of life, is finally defeated by the spirit of collusion, in which the Spartanization of the world gives way to the corporatization of it.

Harry Smith's moment was similarly fraught—a moment when history, like Coleridge's wide wide sea, was eerily becalmed, temporarily out of service, and the world suddenly taken over by the hurley-burley of daemons and spirits. It was the end of modernity, and not yet the beginning of whatever it is that we called postmodernity for lack of a better word and now call global capitalism. What could we do but summon our ancestors, consult our gods, fashion hexes and signs and fetishes? Modernity had brought us a new way of knowing—turning imagination, as Foucault put it, "into voluntary memory, spontaneous attention into reflection, instinct into rational knowledge;"[4] now, with modernity in collapse, it was time to reverse direction, to study the old books, to restore memory to its real seat, in the imagination. That is, to create the world again out of the wreck of the old.

All this should be suggestive for us, when we consider the Smithsonian's conversion of the *Folkways Anthology* from analog to digital form, from the echo of a sound to a measure of it. The original Smith *Anthology* yoked palpable earthy sounds, harrowing stories, aged symbols, and sprung human voices to intuitive sequences, intellectual patterns, and abstract forms. It was a cultural alchemy that transformed *materiel* (Harry had obtained the bulk of his collection in wartime when the old-time records were being stockpiled for shellac) into *material,* martial energy into imaginative force, and in so doing permanently altered the atomic structure of cultural memory. In an economy of abundance, exploitation, and waste, of which of course war is the supreme manifestation, Harry Smith, the hunter-gatherer, the likable moocher and sponger, discovered traces of a culture that like himself was a creature of salvage, providence, and scarcity. Out of the discarded old-time records he made a fantastic new object, like the tinfoil-and-bottle-cap castles and towers of the outsider artist; his was the art of the scavenger, the homeless man who rummages among the detritus that always lies in the wake of the capitalist juggernaut, retrieving what it does not know and is too drunk to care is the substance of its wealth and power. In a culture of the burn and the clearcut, he went into the rain forest to gather mushrooms; like Katherine Ann Porter's hired hand Helton, the escaped lunatic in *Noon Wine* who retrieves bent nails and picks up the corncobs that drop off the end of the wagon, culturally speaking Smith saved the farm.

The *Folkways Anthology* was not recorded music, strictly speaking, but recorded music recorded, a recording of recordings. It was lo-fi faithfully reproduced in hi-fi, square reclaimed as hip, vernacular culture inscribed upon the surface of the avant-garde; ephemeral emanations of disparate sources, locations, and moments became a single emanation from one source at one location in a single prolonged moment of strangeness and surreality. Like much of Harry's art, it tampered with the synesthetic machinery of perception, playing at the boundary between the spatial and temporal, visible and audible, static and dynamic, pattern and flux, enforcing the boundary at the same time as it smuggled the specters of perception across it, flushing sound out of image and image out of sound. Like montage or collage it was about obsolescence, technical, social, cultural, the fascination of it, the strange hallucinatory quality of objects out of their practical and temporal milieu and thus in effect about the transformative force of time itself, and hence ultimately about death, or more precisely the dead body, which is precisely the object out of its living medium, of the world.

And that's why, if I may quote Pete Reiniger, supervisor of the analog-to-digital transfer of the Smith *Anthology* to the Smithsonian-Folkways CD set, it became necessary, now that the winds of history are blowing again, albeit in a direction we can't fathom, to make it "sound real again."

Music predicts: as Benny Carter predicts the Buick 6, and Elvis Presley "the sixties." The Smith *Anthology* weirdly predicted the strange retreat of the whole world, as the sea level rises and a tide of geological time literally rolls over us, into the mystifying obsolescence into which all the songs on the *Anthology* had already retreated when they were originally recorded, a past made unnaturally present and urgent but, like any hallucination, insubstantial, ungraspable, out of reach. Fifteen years before the Beatles, Smith had discovered the deep structure of the LP, which is the structure of hallucination, exactly the quality of life where magic—of an incantation, a hallucinogen, of a technology—produces a rift between history and materiality. And he did it with music whose doubled obsolescence was our only way of experiencing it, disinterring the exquisite corpse of what Harry somewhat recklessly but provocatively called "American folk music." As achieved, the *Anthology* is suffused with asthmatic nicotine-stained Beat laughter, with crazy, compulsive, wounded joy; the mood is not nostalgic or romantic but gaily psychotic, the mood of the permanently traumatized man, at first a threnody of the absurd, but in the end, by the time we get to Dave Macon stomping on the floor and Henry Thomas tooting on panpipes, transcendently comic, the mood of the pilgrim soul, a divine ecstasy.

. . . .

I've listened to the new *Smithsonian-Folkways Anthology*, as I'm sure you have, and I wonder if you've noticed how subtly, how profoundly, it is all changed. The thick fluid medium is gone—clarified, brightened, sharp and astringent as ether, more gas than liquid; the tunes do not drift up out of some inky blackness but come on all at once, suddenly, luminous and quick as liquid crystal. A gate has opened, a top come off, a veil thrust aside; the music comes forward, right to the edge, no longer painfully weighted with its own pastness, or drowned in the displacements of the recording medium, but made anew, as fresh, indeed, and as incorruptible as the binary numbers of which it is newly made.

CDs, as everyone knows, are less "warm" than the old analog recordings—in much the way, I imagine, that Descartes' Analytic Geometry was less warm than Robert Fludd's cozy Memory Theatre—but also sparer and more elegant, less dreamlike and more acute. The new *Anthology* is not a recording about recordings. In a sense it is not a *recording* at all. Its *content* is Smith's mystical design—but its medium is number and light. It comes to us as it were by fiber-optic cable, like one of those long-distance phone calls that makes your niece four thousand miles away sound like she is in the next room; ears that touched Smith's music like hands feeling shapes in the dark now seem almost to *see* the music, shimmering like Princess Leia's hologram before us.

What has happened of course is that the Smithsonian engineers have simply exploited superior technologies—retrieving in some cases technically superior pressings of the original discs, or Asch's tape masters, correcting distortions of pitch and tempo arising from the older technologies, optimizing the ratio of music to noise, in at least one case actually patching in a missing note from another place. Then, like a tailor measuring for a suit, they ran the entire collection through a software program that digitalizes the sound and encodes it onto a laser disc. However subtle or sensitive, the analog recording could never have been anything but a trace, a footprint, like the old cabbalistic and alchemical symbols. But the digital recording strictly speaking records nothing; it offers to reproduce through number the sound in its actuality—the sound, in this case, of a recorded sound. It might be said that as an extension of the auditory apparatus digitalization shifts the function from vibrations and waves to the quantitative processing of those vibrations in the tactile seat of human calculation, in the inner ear—from a mechanical to an intellectual imitation of the act of hearing.

To have "sampled," which is to say, *sounded* the depths of Harry Smith's *Anthology of American Folk Music* makes it navigable again in immediate cultural terms, no longer surreal but hyperreal. The three precincts of Marcus's Smithville, story, sociality, and self, are all still there, the dialectics of isolation and celebration, bondage and freedom, pain and the release from pain, the oddity with which Harry marked it all is all still there; but now no more alien or surreal than what is being recorded in Madagascar or Indonesia or Senegal, a music that reveals "American folk music" to be global music in approximately the same sense that planet Earth is already in outer space. In other words, it makes plainly audible what Harry Smith, an ethnographer and anthropologist virtually from birth, already knew and was trying to get across. And its background research, its protocols of credits and permissions, its documentation and its technical medium, moreover, restore it to its own history and to the musical revivals it engendered, as well as to the new global medium of commerce and information; it has become, as they say, an "interactive" medium, which as Jeff Place writes in his supplemental notes, admits of continuous growth and change, "in a discourse of feedback and sharing."

"Sampling," I think, is the key word here. Like the sampling of census-takers, it is a result achieved through technics, theory, measurement, estimation and judgment, essentially a *prediction* based upon a probability, which in an odd way thrusts the music, not into the irretrievable past of analog recording, but into a kind of speculative future where a memory has become a hope, where what *was* has become what in all probability *is*.

And it is this *hypothetical* quality, I think, rather than any acoustic property—we cannot literally hear the "gaps" in the music that digitalization creates—that accounts for the hollowness or emptiness that we think we hear in digital recording, as well as for the sense of immediacy and presence. The digital recording is not, again, a trace or a deposit, like the analog recording; unlike Edison's cylinder or Berliner's disc it is no longer a form of "sound writing" or even of sound picturing but of sound measuring or figuring; hence however bright or immediate it cannot be anything but theoretical, *never* actually in touch, acoustically speaking, with the no-longer-present musical performance, and hence no longer "rather hurtfully out of reach,"[5] in the way that the original old-time and bluegrass recordings were, by the sheer fact of acoustical reproduction destined to sound their own pastness. Instead it is always already present, and far more than any form of acoustical recording, admits of manipulation and change *in* the present, its text-like fixity permanently dispelled. While the cylinder or the disc tended to decontextualize and objectify (or "commodify," if you will, and quite literally) the discrete performance, and the LP to enable collage-like constructions of deracinated sound-texts, the CD, by appropriating the musical effect for cyberspace, rescues music from its entanglement with history and transforms it into what amounts to a medium of exchange, which like money, as Marx remarked, "does not disclose what has been transformed into it."

Hence paradoxically the *absence* of the musical performance has been brought to a kind of consummation in its technical disappearance; once "measured" by the digital software it is at once infinitely reproducible and wholly irrelevant. Hence it is absence, not presence, that the signal processor buttons on a CD player—mine are labeled "Hall," "Church," "Jazz Club," "Stadium," and "Disco"—are designed to simulate. Perhaps the more sophisticated machines of the future will provide buttons to simulate performances in schoolhouses in the Kentucky coalfields, the kitchens of mountain cabins, or the recording studios of Memphis, circa 1954. For it is absence that indicates the embeddedness of the performance in history.

My point however is not really a technical one, though there is much to be said I think, musically speaking, for the analog recording; my point is that when music for whatever reason loses its power to transport us into putative realms whose very essence is absence it has ceased to be music. Cybermusic, which is still in an early phase of its technical evolution that structurally reproduces the exigencies of the medium that preceded it (which has become its content) will eventually find its own nature, materially and formally, and while I am no prognosticator, it is suggestive that what is everywhere and always available (as on the Internet) can have only a momentary and contingent value. In the way that the real *metier* of sound recording was orders of sounds, not of words as Edison had supposed, the real *metier* of digital reproduction is precisely orders of data, not of sounds. What this may mean culturally for music I can't imagine; but I am tempted to say that it will arouse a desire to rediscover the origins of musical value, and ultimately to recreate its historical and cultural foundations, its "context"—not, as in the revival, through the recovery of some imaginary spatial or temporal realm, but through an original invention of them, a kind of emancipated culturality, an ethnogenesis.

Contexts change. The Magic 8 Ball is out of date; I know this because I had to go all over hell to find one. It was discontinued at Toys-R-Us, Kay-Bee Toys, and Playhouse Toys; none of the independent toy stores had it either. I finally found one at one of those novelty shops that sells things like Nixon masks, lava lamps, risqué cocktail napkins, and telephones shaped like '57 Chevys. The Magic 8 Ball is a nostalgia item; its ideological engine, like so much of the pop culture of the postwar era, was the bourgeois myth, reinvigorated by adolescent culture, of personal destiny. What can be the interest of such a quaint little toy to the preadolescent imagination in the world of Beavis and Butthead, Smashing Pumpkins, and the Web, where the number of messages that can appear in the magic window is not twenty or eighty-four but an infinite number of messages, most of them in some way commercial?

It is difficult, in the twenty-first century, to become enchanted by the notion of a special destiny; virtually the whole phantasmagoria of identity is or will be out there, on the shelf, present and accessible to everyone—at least to everyone who can afford it—all at once. The context of no context *is* our context; on a planet where the web of information reaches to the ends of the earth, there can be no other. If the Magic 8 Ball was a kind of model of our own souls, that dark place to which we looked for whatever answers conscience or training or reason or imagination could provide, the current generation has seen it pried open, unscrewed, and spilled out, its substance somehow both catastrophically wasted or squandered and at the same time always everywhere. Once we were merely invisible; now we're globally dispersed, like carbon dioxide.

Thus our characteristic gesture must be precisely algorithmic, a cultural procedure for "sampling," selecting, filtering. It is the only way to learn, to get along; there is too much information, too many sounds and images, at too many times and places. One does not consume or accumulate information; one gets caught in it. One must *process* information, not only technically but socially, culturally, spiritually, find a path out of the background noise, from optimum point to optimum point, a shifting stratum on which life can actually be lived. Mark Edmundson says it is essentially the mood of the consumer, a cool self-protective detachment, and blames it on television; I think it is more the attitude of the tourist, who cannot find the opportunity to write the postcards she wants and needs to write. In any case, the algorithm is the new emblem of personal identity—and each of us needs to conceive our own.

We should not be surprised that an abundance of accessible information, like an abundance of accessible things, may have spawned contempt, or suspicion, or at the very least, boredom. That's natural; what is everywhere in supply cannot be much in demand. There doesn't seem to be much we can do; not only have we created a machinery that's taken over a vast proportion of our work, and does it better and faster and far more powerfully, but a machinery that in large part operates us. Naturally, then, we idolize it, just as we did writing and the book before it, and poets and priests, and for that matter, idols, before that. And like the idols of the past, this one, too, will eventually prove, and I think is already proving, to have clay feet. No doubt the Internet is a wonder; but to my mind it often resembles, more than a global village, a vast business office, where the whole world, isolated in its cubicles and literally sitting on its ass, is communicating with itself through inter-office memos, bulletin boards, and ring-binders. And what is called the Information Highway often looks to me more like a gigantic rumor mill than a library or an encyclopedia. You can't fool human nature.

Capitalism will not really have done its work in the world until like all magic it finally betrays us—until it reveals to us, again, just what it *is* we do that none of our devices, from the Magic 8 Ball to the parallel processor, can do without us, which is to ask the questions. It is well to have outdone ourselves with our machines; but to produce anything worth knowing, we must first know what it is we don't know. This is just the problem Descartes and the others faced—to rediscover the roots of knowledge, to summon knowledge out of ruin. In this, the current generation has much to learn from Harry Smith and his *Anthology of American Folk Music*. For Harry I think anticipated all this. I think it was what he was getting at when he spoke to John Cohen of "programming the mind"—it was *our own* information storage and retrieval system that so fascinated him. He wanted to influence it in a way that like the old memory theaters would somehow impart the mysteries, natural, celestial, and spiritual, to the understanding, and fix them in memory. "The major message that has to be brought across," he said to John Cohen, "is that everybody is thinking the same, although the stuff that is passed down or inherited determines the things that are thought about."[6]

Between thought and what is thought about—that is where he went a-hunting; neither visible nor audible, but intimated in the disembodied spirit that passes from sight to sound, sound to sight, now audible, now visible, like messages from the dead. That is what we see in Harry's uncanny visualizations of a Charlie Parker or Dizzy Gillespie solo,[7] what we hear in the vocalities and the rhythms of the *Folkways Anthology*, that run through it like an electric current: a blueprint, evanescent, of the human lifeworld. Now in postmodernity, where *everything* is refuse, so much so vastly and so comprehensively obsolete, including (it often seems) we ourselves, it is we who must in a sense unhouse ourselves, become like Harry the hunter-gatherers of cultural memory, to discover anew everything from which the ever more Hobbesian global marketplace has tempted us away: real intimacy, real personhood, real community, and real life.

4 THE INVISIBLE SCIENCE

THE SPIRIT OF CALCULATION

"See we not plainly," Hooker wrote in 1593, "that obedience of creatures unto the Law of Nature is the stay of the whole world?" Edmund thought so; Nature was his goddess—"to thy law my services are bound."

The new order, more natural than divine, that *King Lear* introduces into literature was of course already well abroad in the world. In the generation before Shakespeare's birth, Calvin and Copernicus had written; in Shakespeare's lifetime Drake had sailed up the West coast of North America, while England, already trading in the Baltic and the Mediterranean, had established a foothold at Jamestown. Three years after the publication of Lear, Galileo built his telescope, and Kepler articulated laws of planetary motion that demonstrated a mysterious compatibility between numerical calculations and natural processes. In the year that Shakespeare died, William Harvey, using calculations of volume, concluded against his better judgment that blood flowed towards, as well as away from the heart, displacing, with numbers, the teachings of Galen; Galileo, with algebra, inclined planes, and a pendulum, was presiding over the demise of an even greater philosopher, Aristotle.

Every student knows that the modern world, of science, technology, and literacy, of individualism, capitalism, and democracy, came decisively into existence in the seventeenth century. The seventeenth century brought Bacon, Descartes, and Newton, and an end to the authority of traditional wisdom on all subjects—an end, indeed, to authority of every kind save the authority of the independent original mind, what Descartes called "the simple and natural reasonings of a man of good sense, laboring under no prejudice concerning the things which he experiences."[1] The orderly medieval cosmos, which was in effect a vast allegorical poem, pervaded by the principles of resemblance, analogy, and metaphor, dissolved to reveal "the awful silence of those infinite spaces" of which Pascal was so terrified. The patristic universe, uttered in time as if God had spoken it, had fallen silent; in its place was its own representation, a kind of gigantic planetarium, fashioned by a celestial mechanic who, though his mathematics were impeccable, had not lingered to contemplate his work, nor had left much behind in the way of instructions.

Developments in science, moreover, began the long technological evolution that in the West today forms a kind of secondary natural environment. The steam engine, for example, which began life as a kitchen implement, became, with the application of Boyle's law, a pump that made it possible to dig ever deeper and more extensive coal mines; the cannon, its power enhanced by better metallurgy and its accuracy by Newton's calculus, enabled European governments to consolidate their power on an unprecedented scale, and to dominate not only their own but the rest of the world's people by force of arms. Thus it appears that the exploitation of natural resources, which is the fountainhead of technological development, and the centralization of political power, which characterizes both the modern state and the revolutions mounted against it, begin in effect with one idea: for, as Lewis Mumford observes, the steam engine is but a reciprocating cannon; the massive project of maintaining, clothing, and equipping such large standing armies and navies as the new technology produced, he adds, provided the pattern of mass production and consumption that would shortly mark the industrial age.[2]

One of the most characteristic motifs of modernity is its discontent with itself. A long lament to our squandered powers and exiled divinities, and a concomitant fascination with custom, tradition, belief, ritual, enchantment, and the supernatural, often associated with the primitive, the peasant, or the folk society where all these seemed still to prevail, began well before the dust of the scientific revolution had settled; neither Heisenberg's uncertainty principle or Kuhn's sociology of the scientific paradigm, meanwhile, has done much to discourage the exposure of nature's secrets to empirical observation. Mortally ill, we may turn to the ancient remedies—but that is only because we believe they may contain the germ of what science will someday recover as a finding. Though we long ago repudiated the triumphant positivism of the nineteenth century, we have yet to dislodge the prestige of scientific explanations, even while suspecting that a kind of magic somehow akin to Prospero's own must underwrite what can only be called, still, their unceasing and astonishing expansion.

Irrepressible recuperations of belief and ritual notwithstanding, it seems unlikely that modernity could ever really content itself with all that has fallen, since Galileo and Newton, and continues to fall, into the abyss of superstition and error. No genuine reenchantment of the world, probably, is on the horizon, the various worldwide religious revivals notwithstanding. But would it not at least be consoling to know in what way scientific knowledge, which can never know absolutely, nor ever transgress the boundaries of the natural, may be grounded in those same resolutely unempirical human processes that would otherwise populate the universe with spirits and fashion entire cultures around the propitiation of them? To know that the boundary that modernity has drawn between itself and all that is not itself is not an unbridgeable gulf between minds so differently constituted that no possibility of understanding exists between them, but nothing more than a kind of imaginary threshold across which knowledge and wonder find themselves captured by a kind of irresolvable mutual deference?

. . . .

The history of knowledge is continually vexed by the difficulty of assigning priority to any of the material causes that, precisely because they have been enlisted in the genesis and representation of knowledge, tacitly defining its domain and insinuating their own forms into it, are not themselves objects of it. Among such causes speech and writing, number and the assignment of number, considered as concrete social practices, are at once the most evident and the most contingent—but it is precisely in terms of these practices that such a history might be written.

Until some time near the end of the sixteenth century, to know, meant, practically speaking, to have been told, usually by an ancient writer, and most importantly to remember what had been said by ancient writers—for though books and manuscripts were of course a basic element in learning, they could not be said to "know" in and of themselves, for knowing consisted in the organic unity of the mind with its object that memory signified. Despite the centrality of books and manuscripts in the scholastic tradition, writing had not so decisively broken off from the spoken word as it would by the print-dominated nineteenth century, so that the process of learning, and beyond that, of investigation and inquiry, was chiefly carried out in the medium of the spoken language, to which writing was a kind of servomechanism, by communities of scholars related not primarily to the phenomenal world through observation and experiment but to each other through dialogue and debate. What was known was principally what was agreed to be known, with all the force of tradition, community, and authority behind it, and that could be represented, retained, and deployed again in speech, formulated in ways that facilitate communication and stimulate the memory—in the use of proverb and aphorism, for example, in redundancy, euphony, repetition, and figure. The fruit of study was eloquence, and the abuse of it, as in too mechanical reliance upon books, pedantry, and buffoonery: such is the comedy of Shakespeare's Polonius, who represents the obsolescence of the tradition in the face of a new "method."

As Walter Ong first observed in *Ramus, Method, and the Decay of Dialogue,* dialogue and all that attends it was the "scientific method" of the scholastic philosophers, whose body of learning was the science of the late Middle Ages.[3] Its basis was received truth, recovered from antiquity, embodied in forms of speech and retained in memory often in conjunction with a visual image, a legacy of ideas that could be brought to bear in systematic ways upon any question by means of debate. This method, called dialectic, was every bit as rigorous as the experimental method that displaced it: but it was, again, social, not individual. An individual and essentially visual method of investigation emerged early in the seventeenth century as book learning replaced dialogue in the universities. The new method was all the rage—anyone might become, after all, a philosopher by means of it: even a gravedigger. Hamlet was interested in it, of course, though it failed him; Bacon, Leibniz, and Descartes were too, though only Bacon hesitated to make the leap from verbal and iconographic methods, which bore traces of the dissolving medieval allegory, to mathematics. The Cambridge divines made it the engine of their theology, and actually believed that by means of it they might cleanse the intellect darkened by Original Sin. Ultimately it became the hobbyhorse of butchers, bakers, and candlestick makers.

However we must not suppose that because the schoolmen could not come up with the laws of thermodynamics or of relativity or even with an idea of motion free of occult forces that their science was inadequate to the questions that scholasticism mainly addressed, questions essentially metaphysical or theological. The arts of eloquence—for that is what scholasticism actually was, a sophisticated, formal, and dialogic oral tradition—produced a science that explained the world in terms of the world: for that is in the nature of language, where Being itself is irreducibly metaphorical.

The roots of the scientific revolution lay deep in scholasticism and in the scholastic imagination, where the very exigencies of dialogue, oral discourse, language, and learning demanded a science of memory by which the scholar-orator could retain his knowledge both for deployment in speech and for contemplation. All this has been engagingly set out by Frances Yates: Aquinas, drawing upon Aristotle and Quintilian, suggested that memory was best served by visual images, and instructed the scholar to link his ideas to certain visual images—the more grotesque, the more memorable—arranged in a particular sequence based upon some familiar place: a temple perhaps, or an amphitheater.[4] Sequence was the secret of this occult practice, as it is of course in oral performances of all kinds; and at the heart of sequence lies the principle of number.

Descartes understood that the mainspring of memory was order, or sequence, not image, however concrete or abstract, and that "the right order is that images should be formed in dependence upon one another." But he went further. The force that drove the orator's mind from one image to the next was the causal contiguity of the underlying structure in which he had placed his images. Five hundred years of reflection upon memory, and the increasing tendency to visualize and mechanize processes of thought through images, symbols, and schematic or diagrammatic arrangements of them, had brought philosophy to the point at which Descartes could at last identify memory with our mysterious capacity to attribute and apprehend causes, the principle betrayed, he thought, in the curious affinity of memory for order and sequence. "All vanished images," he wrote of the art of memory, "can easily be found again in the brain through the impression of the cause. This is the true art of memory."[5]

Science in the modern sense emerged when language, specifically learned Latin as written and spoken in the universities, lost its authority as a mode of representing reality rationally, having come to be seen, as Descartes expressed it, repudiating even the "sciences found in books" that had shaped his childhood world, "the accumulation of opinions of many different persons";[6] when visual images, first, and then visual symbols, and then mechanically manipulable systems of images and symbols, and finally and most decisively mathematics itself, became the systems of signs mediating between knower and known—the known becoming, magically, a thing inherent in the signs themselves and in their relationships. This was the change that liberated scientific inquiry from the nexus of authority and brought it into the purview of individual observation, reflection, experiment, and order.

Like writing, visible images and symbols did in fact "remember" what they represented, and so like the memory theaters performed part of the work of thinking for us; but whereas writing remained bound to language, and hence to authority, society, and self, visual symbols objectified the content of knowledge, and at the level of abstraction achieved by, say, Descartes' analytic geometry, could secure a truth in the form the system's own laws.

A geometrical account of celestial motions, or a numerical calculation of the volume of blood pumped in an hour—Harvey arrived at the idea of circulation before capillaries were known to exist—migrates out of consciousness to become an object of it among other objects and in relation to them. Such an account, whether it is a drawing by Leonardo of human anatomy or Harvey's numbers, might be adjusted and adjusted again to conform to local and momentary observation, building and retaining the particular pauses of the eye upon its object into a total structure of observation, in effect bestowing upon the eye, which can focus only upon one thing at a time, the power of the ear to attend to many things at once, as if the eye could compose itself and listen to the universe. It isn't of course that science confined itself to the exploration of visible phenomena, but that all phenomena, of space and motion, mass and volume, even time and energy, could be converted into the systems of signs visually conceived, represented, remembered, and contemplated. These systems, whose internal relationships were supposed to reflect those among phenomena so signified, might be internally developed and manipulated until hypotheses about the world might be shaped by means of the system, and experiments contrived to bear them out.

Was language, then, as a medium of intellectual investigation in a social milieu, entirely displaced by the mathematical sign? As Julia Kristeva observes with reference to signification, the idea of causality, so fundamental to modern scientific method, is itself grounded in Indo-European linear syntax, whose structural hinge, the subject-predicate connection, is a generative cause through which, by identification and determination, our sentences complete themselves and become utterances.[7] Hence, although through method the voices of schoolmen may have fallen silent in favor of the experiment and calculation, the ghost of language lives in the apprehension of linear causality derived from what is essentially a process of "reminding," in which the proximate element is covertly governed by a syntax that assigns it the authority of the cause; in other words, the cause, syntactically speaking, is doubly constituted by what it arises from and by what arises from it, as Abraham is constituted at once by he who begat him and by whom he begat. Hence all scientific accounts, as has now frequently been observed, are underwritten by tacit discourses or narratives, "paradigms" (a term appropriately derived from grammar), that are the authentic parties to any competition between theories, as that, say, between the germ and the stress theories of disease—two not-entirely-incompatible stories, one that figures the human organism as the site of natural invasion, the other that figures it as a defensive system against invasion.

"Bring out weight and measure in a year of dearth," writes Blake. If experiment and calculation are implicitly discursive, however, it is in a medium that like language itself is culturally situated. Thus we must look to the poets, not the philosophers, to discover where morally the spirit of calculation belongs in the human breast. In Goneril and Regan, in Edmund, "twelve or fourteen moonshines lag of a brother," in Edgar the pictorialist, and even in Lear, "every inch a king," we meet it, or Shakespeare's angry parodies of it.

The spirit of calculation has two sides, an intellectual and a moral; it is among other things that species of forethought that contrives through prediction to turn events in the direction of itself, as well as a methodical way of organizing empirical observation, particularly through the manipulation of numbers. Both senses, moral and scientific, imply manipulation, and both in effect supplant direct and immediate interpretation of the world with a sign or signs of our own making, social or scientific, verbal or mathematical—Edgar's dissembling is carried out in signs, too. Calculation divides occasion and act, sense and understanding, transforming, as Foucault writes, "imagination into voluntary memory, spontaneous attention into reflection, instinct into rational knowledge."[8] Thus transformed, from a story told by human voices to a toy of the conscious will, the social and phenomenal worlds suffer a loss of presence that baffles the processes that join human action to its sources in the moral being. Edmund of course is not the only villain spawned by this new sleight of hand; no sooner has she swallowed the apple than Milton's Eve learns selfhood, deception, guilt, and death at a blow. "But to Adam in what sort shall I appear?" she asks, the wedge already driven between appearance and reality, the manipulation of appearances, representations, for certain ends already predicted by moral hypothesis, in this case of Adam's choice.

Perhaps the spirit of calculation arose first, as Mumford suggests, in the canonical hours of the monastery, and the ringing of the monastery bells that marked them. The monastic life was a strictly disciplined one, the bell a regulating force, a rhythm, in the life of the community, coordinating its activities by extending to all within its hearing, enforcing the solidarity and coherence of community life; the rhythms of the bell tower still prevail, even where no bells ring, in many rural European communities, where the cycles of sleeping and waking, eating and drinking, marketing and householding, occur in concert, as if the community breathed with one breath. But in spite of the mechanical devices that regulated them, the bells remain a kind of voice, and hence a call, ringing, when they ring, in us; while perhaps mechanically regulated they have not made time mechanical, a thing that transpires without and in spite of us; they prompt, but do not prod us.

It is the clock, and its seedling the personal watch, that, like Gulliver, we worship. The domestic clock that emerged in bourgeois northern Europe in the late sixteenth century, and ultimately the watch (a word that should remind us of its communal origins), while it synchronizes vast areas of human enterprise, at the same time isolates the individual in his or her own sphere of activity, making of society a vast machine in which no one part can quite know the function of the part laboring beside it. Here is a true scientific instrument—a device whose "face" and "hands" control the dialectic of space and motion we call time, assimilating the power of tactile discrimination, which from infancy we learn in our mouth and hands, to much finer visual discrimination, by means of the sweep of a needle at a uniform rate around the circumference of a circle divided into an arbitrary number of arbitrary segments arbitrarily understood to be what materially they cannot be, perfectly equal, which is to say, identical. The digital "watch," empty of spatial relations, transforms time, and life, into pure metric, no longer sweeping across the face of the day but perpetually counting it up or down, accumulating or evacuating it.

The watch is the type of every scale, scope, meter, and rule that has converted force—the revolution of the earth, the weight of a stone, the amplitude of an electrical current—into its value in a uniform and comprehensive system of quantities by which it can be brought into relation to and integrated with every other quantity as well as into relations to relations of quantity. Its genius, of course, of the spirit of calculation, is that is has substituted, by analysis, one set of relations for another: the relation, say, of yesterday's hope to today's disappointment, or of a fertile valley to a rocky slope, to the relation between four and three, or four and five—displacing meaning onto the relation itself, the order or sequence, and creating out of the arbitrary unit of measurement a new appearance: the minute or the mile, and a new idea out of the marks that distinguish them, the instant or the boundary line, which we can represent but never conceive.

The world takes on the character of the instruments by which we know it. A mathematical universe, not surprisingly, must be a relative one, as mathematics are, as Ernst Cassirer observes, a system of relations; and nowhere will those relations be more apparent than in the irreducible particles that are essentially projections of the integers by which we represent them.

As time is a dialectic of space and motion it should not surprise us that the White Rabbit is in such a rush, for it is with reference to a watch that he is late for his very important date. It is a simple triangulation: as time can be constituted by the relation between space and motion so can motion be constituted by the relation between time and space, and space by the relation of time and motion. It is by isolating the idea of the instant that visual art learned the discipline that produced Edgar's speech to Gloucester at Dover Cliff—the instant that arrests the temporal activity of the visual field and permits its analysis into the lines and planes of linear perspective, a kind of space that, time having been seized and confined to the instant, can be abolished only by motion: of the eye that paces across the irrecoverable horizon, of the ship that tacks from point to point across the plates that Mercator's projection laid across the face of the waters. The new space of surfaces, the containing space of Euclid, analyzed like the clock face into a pattern of uniform sections, while developed in art, established itself into the social and political realm as well, where it shaped new notions of private property and of the body politic. One has merely to glance across the map of the United States to behold its emergence: a world organized around the course of rivers and mountains, of distances measured by the tread of ox or man, or by the drifting of a boat, of settlements clustered together into webs of human interdependency, gives way as the eighteenth century passes and the new civilization moves West to a patchwork that records the struggle of the surveyor's lines with natural features and finally to an orchestral swell of, in desert regions, pure geometry.

The spirit of calculation, then, made us masters of space and slaves of time, and set us in perpetual motion between them: but from whence the spirit of calculation itself? Certainly it has an important ancestor in the marketplace—it is perhaps this realization that made King Charles laugh when he heard that the Royal Society was undertaking to weigh air: as if they hoped to sell it to the French. Time is, after all, or was, money. It is gratifying, at least, that the human heart does not readily lose its hold on the world, either of time, or of space—the development of linear perspective was a discipline akin to the mortification of the flesh—or of wealth. We have waited until now, how many hundreds of years, for money to distill itself into pure number without palpable embodiment. As gold, it was something rare and beautiful, dug at great cost out of the gorge of the earth; in the form of coin it bore the image of an emperor, and was both a token of his power and a means of paying tribute to it. In the English banks today there are still in existence scales for weighing coin, and a love of crisp new bills, that betrays an ancient reluctance to disassociate signifier from signified, which only the true capitalist can accomplish and which is the germ of his power.

Time is money—and money, in a curiously literal way, talks. Perhaps no analytical incursion into the human frame has been deeper than that of alphabetic writing into language, and none more far-reaching than the gradual assimilation of the idea of language, and the ultimate dispersion of that idea into society and thought, to its embodiment in writing and print. Writing draws the word out of its psychic and social matrix and, like the clock face, makes of it a picture—a "speaking picture" in Sidney's oft-misunderstood phrase; print, as has now frequently been observed, carries the process still further, making of discourse, now embodied as text, into an item of manufacture and of trade so detached from the nexus of communication that the act of reading becomes not only an interpretative effort but a restorative and purely inventive one. Aural performances in the old communal cultures, even, as we have seen, in the Renaissance university, had shaped speech to meet the exigencies of aural perception: to establish itself in memory, to promote fluency through formulism, to clarify and secure its message through redundancy and repetition, in a general way to conserve through the arts of speech the social, moral, political, and sacred orders in a richly inflected, pervasively musical, and deeply imaginative medium—which, indeed, the Latin language, one of the ancient aural languages, was until the paradigms of grammarians purified it out of existence. In an aural culture, we seek knowledge through counsel and dialogue, which even books can supply where aural conceptions still prevail; because language is social, knowledge cultivated by means of it is of necessity communal and traditional, deeply saturated with the archetypes of human thought and feeling. In a prescientific age it might be said, then, that society itself is the scientific instrument.

If in an aural or residually aural culture language is the preserver, in a literate culture it is the thing preserved. In the visible language of print literacy, where the babble of communication is dissolved into a network of silent isolated writers and readers, where the transient formations of heard speech are displaced by the discrete material tokens of letters and words that seem to have analyzed the language into its irreducible constituent parts, language itself changes fundamentally. It writes itself onto the cellular maps of the visual memory, word-hoards from which one builds structures of meaning—not performances or dialogues but texts; it becomes a system of normative relationships between what are apparently permanently and ineluctably alienated signifiers and signifieds, in effect a scientific instrument like the clock, seeking through economy, precision, and originality an exact accommodation between itself and a referent posited on its behalf, banishing the magical generativity of traditional, eloquent, and inspired speech and with it the deeply polarized ideas and images of aural culture, favoring a realistic depiction of scenes and events, and an abstract, analytical, exhaustive, in short a scientific description of reality.

Even the syntax of English, perhaps more than any other European vernacular language, has taken on the relational character of number, having lost most of its inflections and assigned the parts of speech to particular positions in the sequence of the sentence. It is under just such conditions that literature as such comes into existence, as a thing distinct from drama, eloquence, and song, which we identify with departures from those normative relationships—in fictionality, say, or in metaphor, both of which offend the normative adjustment of words to the world and require that new or "imaginative" adjustments arise out of the imputed relation. Literature, it appears, talks in much the same way that money does. Where literature, with its apparent iron grip upon discourse, prevails, the arts of persuasion, which in aural cultures are essential for the governance of society, the transmission of its laws and traditions, become "mere" rhetoric, merely ornamental, something spurious and superficial.

The process of purifying language of its aural features was one of the favorite pastimes of seventeenth-century writers, and one of the pet projects of the Royal Society. Along with it went of course the elimination of idolatry, superstition, and error, indeed nearly the whole field of popular belief, and the concomitant identification of truth with documentation and of documentation with bureaucracy. In the courts the laws of evidence replaced traditional methods of determining guilt and innocence, while traditional rights, such as the right of a peasant to occupy manorial lands that his family had occupied for generations, might be denied simply for lack of a document to support them. It is difficult for us to imagine, in an age of electronic communications, the ubiquity of documentation that by the eighteenth century had absorbed nearly all the offices of public speech: nearly every formal human relation, of marriage, say, of indebtedness, any form of incorporation, was secured by written contract; indeed such contracts, which were produced by the thousands, in daily economic, political, and commercial transactions, are the basis of Locke's concept of the "social contract" and of constitutional forms of government. Traditional law had been on the tongues of the ruling classes, and hence was inseparable from traditional authority rooted in descent and in the very being of the men and women who embodied it; written laws drew their authority from assent, and hence were an inexorable democratizing force. Indeed, the whole of vernacular literature, in the forms of broadsheets, ballads, newspapers, journals, personal letters, and the like, had created, on the one hand, a traffic in popular opinion that was the basis of popular democracy and an important instrument of revolution, and, on the other, a popular imaginative literature closely akin to folklore, which indeed from an early period provided matter for the insatiable printing press.

Scholasticism, monasticism, mercantilism—historically the spirit of calculation can be found in many places, depending upon one's starting point; the broadest perspective suggests that the vast tide sweeping across northern Europe from roughly the tenth century onwards that brought all three to fruition in the seventeenth century was a vast achievement of the human imagination: namely the closure, through dynamic systems of signs—signs of symbols, signs of words, signs of numbers, and signs of signs—of the human sensory apparatus that without such systems could find closure only through its direct contact with a culturally constituted life-world, which it sought to shape to the imperatives of its own moral being. This short-circuit of the "precious square of sense" initiated modernity's pervasive dualities, the gulf between reason and imagination, perception and knowledge, flowing with those objective systems of signification that became the immediate environment of consciousness. All cultures, of course, create, and are, systems of signs—but outside of Western scientific and commercial culture there are few, if any, that so fully procure the release of signification from representation. And it is extraordinary that the reabsorption of the representation into the sign in fetishistic and iconographic forms should power the postmodern commercial and political marketplace.

Much has been made of the cultural, indeed the evolutionary and even the physiological priority of the eye in this process. Indeed, the eye seems to have been primary in all scientific enquiry, in the new conceptions of space especially, as reflected in the visual disciplines of Renaissance art, and in the rise of print literacy. But, as the example of the clock I think illustrates, the eye is only one element of a more complex psychosocial process. The eye, like the other sense organs, is no mere mechanism like the camera. Eyes are imaginative; they see angels as well as ethers, can see to touch and to hear, and are constantly engaged in drawing inferences from the other senses upon themselves. All our manifestations of the spirit of calculation bring the hand and the eye into an imaginative coordination, offering us visible tokens that imaginatively or actually we discriminate according to intellectual processes derived from touch—this coordination of hand and eye is, as is well known, developmentally fundamental and begins in the later stages of infancy, not surprisingly, in conjunction with locomotion, as the dialectic of the clock, wherein time crawls, or flies, or stands still, rather elegantly illustrates.

The projection of invisibilities by this means into the foreground of experience and into the realm of visual-tactile manipulation transforms the universe of perception into an excrescence of human cognitive processes, which like infants we manipulate and smear over and around us, accumulating, shaping, amassing it, saving and spending, sharing, stealing, wasting and losing it, ultimately, one must say, eating it, whether it is as elusive as time or as malleable as gold. Is it surprising that the precious metals should have been dug out of the bowels of the earth? We are, it seems, little better off, morally, than the barbarians who, having lost the arts of manufacture, could supply their wants only by conquest, hoarding and rapine, of which it seems industrialism, capitalism, and imperialism are but clever elaborations.

It is perhaps signification itself that fractures the original unity of the mind with its object; but it is the objectification, or more precisely, the materialization of the sign—never, in speech, complete or perfect, but always elusive, assimilating the sign to memory, dialogue, to the personal and social body—that produces Lacan's signifying chain, that endless process of deferral that perpetually forbids contact of the sign with its object. For the sign, as object, must itself be signified, must perpetually relinquish its status as sign, must perpetually defer to another signifier, in order to be in itself known. In this process, out of the original difference between signifier and signified, mind and world, language signifies itself in difference, producing meaning out of its own deterioration.

But the numerical sign arrests this endless deferral, captures the ever-receding mirage; it signifies itself in identity, produces identity, devours itself in identity. It is its own signifier, not deferred but absorbed, collapsing into itself, a semiological neutron star of infinite density and infinite interiority. If, as Lacan writes, the signifier, as index and as agent, represents the subject for another signifier, the numerical sign represents, indeed is the subject. It must be in the subject, then, *subjectively,* that some unbidden displacement actuates the massive paradigmatic shift such as that which marks the seventeenth century. Where in the "subject," resolving and dissolving in the human imagination, might one locate the principle of number? Where does the human sense of degree, of proportion, of quantity and congruency, and the "certain and evident reasons" in which Descartes anchored his method, lie?

We observed that at the heart of language, what might be called the structure of its structures, lay the principle of causality that Descartes seized upon as the key to method: method itself having evolved out of a system of dialogic practices driven by memory. Method in effect retrieved from language, through many intermediate stages, its primary intellectual form, which in many symbolized elaborations made abstract "narratives" that might be experimentally tested against physical phenomena incorporated through calculation into the new denatured "language." This retrieval entailed the thoroughgoing sublimation of all that can be regarded as linguistic, reducing syntax to structure, semantic to metric, reference to relation. The suggestion here is that in the transformation from a dialogic or residually oral to a scientific culture, language was not simply jettisoned but transformed, dialogue not simply silenced but displaced; that the aural and, more significantly, the social element of language, like its syntactic, semantic, and performative elements, was pursued introspectively to the most naked and irreducible of its determinations, its very corporality, and redeployed as a pure disembodied function, reconstituting the representation to an apparent equivalence virtually neurological in its priority.

Hence for the seat of calculation we must look first to a tactile organ so delicate that nature has sequestered it from the world of substantial objects and placed it where natural forces arise as a play of spiritual presences in a surrounding medium coextensive with consciousness itself; we must consider it as an abstract, symbolic, and mechanically ductile projection of the sensory modality in which all the preliterate peoples of the world encounter first, their gods, and after, themselves: the modality of the ear.

Thousands upon thousands of tiny filaments, each attuned to a particular frequency, lie in sequence along the expanding spiral of the inner ear. Making many fine and precise discriminations among these frequencies, measuring their relations, discovering their ratios and proportions, the auditory imagination, the great natural calculator, combines and recombines them, by inference from experience attributing to each audial impression its cause in the tactile and visual world, and, where experience has not supplied an image of the cause, by imagination refashioning from experience a new image or idea in which to posit a cause. By a swift and invisible calculus, the same that empowers us to appreciate and to be moved by music, the ear joins memory to understanding and awakens in the mind all its "vanished images."

"From harmony, from heavenly harmony, this universal frame began," wrote Dryden in 1687—the same year that Newton published his *Principia*.

If by the eighteenth century science seemed to have revealed a divine harmony in the universe it is because harmony is the manifestation of order in the auditory realm. The music of the spheres had been silenced, and its score, which in the eighteenth century was a musical one, had begun to be written. Science began by organizing visual space, the space of surfaces and the reflection of light from them, according to the principles of the auditory imagination, translating its fine discriminations into morphological distinctions whose psychological origin is in touch. This initiated a three-hundred year process that in physics at least ended of course with Einstein's formula, that elevated mass, notions of which we derive, as Russell pointed out, from tactility, into a mathematical relationship with the nature of the energy that works upon the eye.

The eye is analytic: that is the nature of its movement over the visual field. It moves restlessly about, attending phototropically to one thing at a time, associating discrete elements, each distinguished by means of what one researcher has called a cellular "alphabet" of "iconic figures,"[9] according to some conception supplied to the senses by culturally constituted forms of representation. There is no "totalizing gaze"—the eye is blind to everything around and behind it, and can only strive for totality through some system of accounting such as a number that can record and fix its observations in spatial relationships. Having invested the eye with the auditory function—for it is the ear that, at the center, attends to the entire universe around it and all the voices in it—we sense a loss of integrity, continuity, and contiguity that it becomes our obsession through the conquest of time and space to recover. That is why we cannot bear the space that divides us from our objects, the time from our purposes, and why we must have highways, jets, rockets, computers, guns, and bombs to overcome them.

In our period the eye has lost its primacy as the organ of science, at the same time as the mathematical universe, having finally taken on entirely the relational character of the system in which we describe it, has found means of measuring and of representing, as well as of manipulating itself, that do not depend upon visuality or mechanicality. Moreover, the analytical power of science has moved beyond the purely auditory to the deeper realms of the nervous system, which the scientists tell us is itself "preconsciously monitored" by systems of electrical frequencies and their relationships, listening, in effect, at sub- and supraauditory levels. Having thus bound the sensorium even more tightly to the wheel of its own physiology, at the subatomic and supergalactic levels where Newton's instruments play with a strange and beautiful dissonance, science again finds itself in a scholastic—read metaphysical and theological, agonistic and rhetorical—mode, confidently grounded in pure speculation.

It is perhaps only by restoring the auditory projection into the empirical field that we can cross the boundaries of speculation into new knowledge. Consider a recent experiment in cellular motion: it assigns the numerous dimensions of a computer-generated image of a moving amoeba to a series of orchestral instruments, which, through a synthesizer, play back the acoustic equivalents of those movements as a kind of symphony. Listening to it we learn what the visual image could never tell us—that she moves like a courtesan, with the gorgeous liquefaction of gathered silks across a ballroom floor where men in black part to let her pass.

part II

FEASTS OF UNNAMING

5 FEASTS OF UNNAMING

FOLK FESTIVALS AND THE REPRESENTATION OF FOLKLIFE

Folk festivals bring folk culture and official culture into a mutual embrace: the one to win honor from the attention of cultural institutions allied with education, science, commerce, or government, the other to disseminate the influences of folk culture into the popular imagination and, by way of advocating and sustaining it, into the commercial marketplace or public policy. A folk festival thus reframes folk culture as an element of a legitimate, polite, or elite culture, typically under the auspices of institutions representing these interests—a school, university, or museum, a municipality, a historical site, a public park—and with the sponsorship of various establishments, foundations, corporations, governments, agencies, and the like.

Yet a folk festival is typically not one event, really, but the scene of many events, formal and informal, public and private, prescribed and spontaneous, a social, political, and aesthetic phenomenon of sometimes incomprehensible complexity whose energy reaches, through its impact on individual people not only into local communities, but also into arts agencies, preservation societies, academic departments, state and local governments, commercial institutions, and folk communities themselves to disturb the surface and sometimes redirect the channels in which our cultural history flows. In the great public festivals such as the Smithsonian's Festival of American Folklife or the National Folk Festival, public audiences constituted both by particular local communities and visitors from distant parts can encounter folk artists, craftspeople, cooks, storytellers, and musicians, their appearances often mediated by professional folklorists and anthropologists, representing a startling variety of the world's ethnic, regional, tribal, occupational, and voluntary cultures normally present to them only as names or at best as musical recordings, photographic images, caricatures, or as the subjects of books—or never known to them at all.

In this laboratory of cultural negotiation, a negotiation that for many may occur only in imagination, artistic power can penetrate thick cultural barriers; private idealism can be restored; class antagonism can be quelled and the old incessant cravings put to rest; neglected parts of personality may assert themselves, and even erotic force, in one way or another, find expression. At the Festival of American Folklife, as Alan Lomax once exclaimed, America falls "in love with itself"—and even "tired old Washington sometimes is beautiful when the American people gather to sing and fall in love with one another again."[1]

At the same time, as an ethnographic study of the Festival of American Folklife suggested,[2] the reframing of folk culture by high cultural institutions can be deeply confusing and potentially painful, as well as encouraging, empowering or enlightening, for festival participants. Ethnographers at the Michigan section of the 1987 Festival of American Folklife discovered that festival participants in some instances did not understand what a folk festival was supposed to be or why they had been invited to one, and in contriving their various performances and demonstrations found "a lack of consensus and explicitness among the festival staff to guide them."[3] Some men and women who had some understanding of the concept of "folk" were uneasy to have been so regarded, not only because several of the participants had had professional training or held advanced degrees, but also because they perceived the designation as implicitly degrading. Some were embarrassed to be viewed as such by audiences whom they mostly perceived, and mostly correctly, to belong to the social classes above them. Some rejected membership in the cultural group with whom the festival had identified them, while others struggled with the question of their own role—were they guests, hirelings, or honorees?

In ways that in later years more experienced public folklife presenters have come to recognize,[4] most of the participants arrive with well-developed and fully articulated political and personal aims: to wield political influence in some area of importance, to expand a clientele, to accomplish a specific project of work, or simply, and perhaps most tellingly, to earn some money. Many found their personal needs, such as an opportunity to clean up for an evening reception after a day in the sun, neglected, and occasionally experienced the habits of other participants, from other cultural groups, as grossly discourteous or intrusive. Nearly everyone felt strongly the honor conferred by an invitation from the Smithsonian—but in one or two cases, only to meet, upon their return to their home communities, the resentment and jealousy of people who had not been so honored. On the whole, it seems, folk festivals have their origin in an intellectual tradition that cannot wholly credit the full personhood of the participant nor thoroughly conceive his or her fundamental cultural difference *as* a difference.

Historically speaking, the public folk festivals of the post–World War II period, which include various university concert festivals such as those at Chicago and Berkeley, the Newport, Philadelphia, and Monterey folk festivals, the new National Folk Festival, and, particularly for this discussion, the Smithsonian's annual Festival of American Folklife, can be understood as outgrowths of the 1960s "folk revival." "Folk revival" is the name we assign, somewhat misleadingly, to the sudden explosion in the commercial popularity of folk song and folk music in the years when John Kennedy presided over the nation's cultural and political reawakening. With their repertoire supplied by extant folk song anthologies, field recordings such as those deposited at the Library of Congress, and esoteric record albums, their musical backgrounds often squarely rooted in the original rock and roll of the 1950s, young men and women of college age or slightly older, now familiar names such as Bob Dylan; Joan Baez; the trio Peter, Paul, and Mary; and the Kingston Trio, whose best-selling recording of the Appalachian murder ballad "Tom Dooley" widely popularized the movement, won considerable fame both as interpreters of folksongs and as original songwriters, spreading their music, their social and political attitudes, and their often dashing personal styles throughout the expanding college-age population. A complex mix of class alienation, political disaffection, arty bohemianism, and messianic communalism, the folk revival was the reaction of postwar youth, newly conscious of itself as a group, against a cultural landscape regimented, Spartanized, and bureaucratized by the social and political fallout of a war they could not remember and would never fully understand. It was a kind of unofficial cultural recovery program, innocently seeking a return on the promise that aspiring postwar families, in glad conspiracy with the postwar commercial establishment, had made to their children that life in America was something colorful, fulfilling, and fair.

We call the "folk revival" what we do because in the popular imagination, and on the historical surface, it seems temporarily to have lifted the oppressive weight of history and civilization upon old traditional music. But in fact the gravitational force of folksong, folktale, folk crafts, and folk culture generally upon the minds of ordinary people, though it subsides and revives, has, historically speaking, always been there; it has been there for hundreds of years, well before there was even a word, in English, for "folklore." This has been particularly true in America, which was not only the native home of a complex and extensive aboriginal civilization, but also has been the adoptive home, from day one, of innumerable ethnic, religious, economic, regional, national, and minority groups from which have evolved, in the American setting, thousands of diverse folk communities, urban and rural, with many residual, syncretic, and emergent folk traditions. Among these is of course one of the world's most fertile and indomitable folk cultures, the African American, permanently locked, it seems, in a social, political, economic, and cultural symbiosis, often, sadly, a hostile one, with a racist official culture. There is, in America, scarcely a realm of human endeavor that has not enlisted the force of folklife, or representations of folklife, in its service.

Let us look briefly, then, by way of illustration, into the shallow prehistory of the folk revival. The Kingston Trio's "Tom Dooley" was not the first commercially popular folk song—not by a long shot. A folk song quartet, the Weavers, had made Woody Guthrie's "So Long It's Been Good to Know Ya" the best-selling song of the year in 1950 and sent several other folk songs to the hit parade; had show business blacklisting not scuttled their career they might have sustained their success until 1958 and recorded "Tom Dooley" themselves. And yet commercially popular folk music, strictly speaking, did not disappear from phonographs and radio stations between 1950 and 1958, for the rock and roll music that dominated the popular music of the period was, originally, a musically and commercially potent mix of African American jump, doo-wop, and other varieties generally called "rhythm and blues" by disc jockeys and record companies, and "rockabilly," a folk form of southern white dance music shaped out of the black influence upon commercial honky-tonk, bluegrass, and other kinds of "hillbilly" music, all of this a folk response to the sudden postwar urbanization of southern rural people, black and white.

Why had the Weavers been blacklisted? Because certain political opportunists, notably Senator Joseph McCarthy of Wisconsin, had found it expedient to exploit a national paranoia, whose origins were in the presidential campaign of 1948, that the worldwide communist conspiracy promised after the war by Joseph Stalin had contaminated certain quarters of American life, including not only the State Department but the labor movement, the intellectual community, and the entertainment and the art worlds. Considering that they were often allied with all of these enterprises at once, the tiny cadre of left-inspired folksingers such as Pete Seeger who had performed at labor union, Communist party, Spanish Civil War relief, and other progressive functions were a conspicuous target for political witch-hunters. Blacklisting drove professional folksingers into the relative obscurity of college campuses, schools, summer camps, local recreational programs, radio stations, and small independent recoding companies, where their influence upon young people would, ironically, almost guarantee a new folk revival, while many amateur enthusiasts, frightened by FBI investigations and wiretaps, packed up their guitars and banjos for good. At the same time, however, folksong was being introduced in the music curricula of elementary schools under the direction of the American Folklore Society, and folk stories and themes increasingly into popular entertainment: remember Disney's Mike Fink and Davy Crockett?

The suppression of folksong was a peculiar and unexpected development, and, to the folk revivalists themselves, certainly a kind of betrayal, considering the ground swell of feeling for American life and culture, a kind of cultural patriotism, in which folk music and folklife during the Roosevelt era had allied itself with political policy. In the economic and social emergency of the Great Depression, which to many seemed without benefit of hindsight a kind of economic apocalypse, the collapse of capitalism itself, the Soviet experiment did not seem conspiratorial to many young and thoughtful people; rather it appeared, from this distance at least, to embody the very ideals that to save itself American democracy urgently needed: an intelligently managed economy, a regulated industrialization, heroic measures in engineering and technology, and, above all, social justice; and these demanded that America learn something about itself, especially the ordinary people, above all the dispossessed and forgotten, who would be the designers and builders of a better democracy.

. . . .

The New Deal brought the most concerted multilateral documentation of American life and culture we have ever known. The Federal Writers' Project sent reporters into every state to record cultural life as it was actually lived, to collect not only what Ben Botkin, director of the project's folklore section, called "living lore," but also to take the testimony of living European immigrants and former slaves, as well as to depict, journalistically, the entire sense of life in given regions and urban districts. The Farm Security Administration sent writers and photographers into stricken agricultural areas to record the lives of men and women and children, and the circumstances in which they lived, in literary and photographic documents such as James Agee and Walker Evans's *Let Us Now Praise Famous Men,* which remain touchstones of America's image of itself as an agricultural, popular, and folk society. The Resettlement Administration engaged musicologist Charles Seeger to find ways, through the encouragement of indigenous musical resources, to foster the consolidation of communities around the project of economic and social self-help. Muralists glorified the working life in countless public buildings, and a vast pictorial record, in photographs and drawings, of American folk crafts, *The Index of American Design,* was initiated under government auspices. The Roosevelts themselves opened the White House in a series of nine concerts between 1934 and 1942, on one occasion with the king and queen of England in attendance, to traditional singers and musicians, including the North Carolina Spiritual Singers, organized by the Federal Music Project; a mountain string band called the Coon Creek Girls; an old sailor from Virginia, Dan Hunt, who sang sea chanties; and, because he and his father were the foremost collectors of them, Alan Lomax to sing cowboy songs.

With a cumbersome wire-recorder built into the back of their car, Alan and his father, John, had set out into the rural South in 1930, after a bank collapse had cost the latter his job, to search out what would become the mother lode of southern song, particularly of black song, in the holdings of the Library of Congress Archive of Folk Song. In the Angola State Prison they met a man called "Leadbelly," Huddie Ledbetter, who with his encyclopedic memory, siren voice, and engine-like twelve-string guitar became, after the Lomaxes had helped coordinate his release and brought him to New York, for the intelligentsia a living symbol of the black folk tradition, and as such was often misunderstood by well-intentioned but naive young radicals who had little acquaintance with the facts of black life in the rural South. Leadbelly and Woody Guthrie, whom leftist actor Will Geer had coaxed to the city in 1939, seemed to divide America's folk heritage between them, picturesque characters whose genius brought the cloudy idea of "the people," so fundamental to what was called "twentieth-century Americanism" during the days of the Popular Front, down to earth.

The folk revival began in the 1930s, then, under "the man who couldn't walk around," as his friend Josh White called the president in a blues song. Well, not really. The Roosevelt administration had simply reached out into what by the 1920s had already become a brisk trade in the representation, as well as the commercial, political, and social exploitation, of folk culture. Pioneer record-company advance men such as Ralph Peer and Art Satherly, beginning in 1923, had begun to tap the immense resources in nineteenth-century social and display music, folk and commercial, still flourishing in southern folklife: now-familiar figures such as the Carter Family, the

Stoneman Family, and Jimmie Rodgers won fame as performers and recording artists playing and singing traditional songs, of which they were both collectors and creators, to regional audiences. A parallel development was occurring on the vaudeville circuit, where singers such as Ma Rainey and Bessie Smith supplied the urban and rural African American marketplaces with a newly introspective blues and jazz music, opening the way for many black rural singers and guitarists such as Charlie Patton and Robert Johnson who left behind them on "race" records documents of prodigious musical and poetic power. Commercial broadcasting, with its institution the radio barn dance, initiated by Nashville newspaper humorist George Hay's "Grand Ole Opry," brought traditional dance fiddling, minstrelsy, and the Saturday night play party, in performers such as Uncle Jimmy Thompson, Uncle Dave Macon, and Dr. Humphrey Bate and the Possum Hunters, to parlors urban and rural throughout the South and Midwest, recalling, with gentle satire, the old times before the First World War. This was a "folk revival" too.

Not all the activity in folk music was commercial. The intense concentrations of European immigrants in urban ghettos, the squalor and desperation occasioned by it, documented by such works as Jacob Riis's *How the Other Half Lives* (1890), had stimulated an anxious nativist movement among people who believed—their fears aroused by the lurid and monstrous ethnic stereotypes promulgated by newspaper cartoonists, pulp novelists, and the vaudeville stage—that the Anglo-American root stock and its values were threatened with extinction. This outlook was often conjoined with the related idea that the agent of extinction was the spread of commercial entertainment, including the aforementioned radio barn dances, but especially jazz, which to the nativist imagination was a poisonous brew of primitive racial elements both Negro and Jewish: what Robert Winslow Gordon, founder of the Archive of Folk Song, called "Hebrew Broadway jazz."[5] Modernity generally, or more precisely, its threat to the cultural hegemony of the Anglo-American middle class, in fact, was the enemy, and folk culture, understood as a survivor from a more elegant and innocent, but above all more refined and respectable, past, might be a bulwark against it.

Class anxiety and ethnocentrism, then, occasioned by swift social and technological change, provided an atmosphere in which, in 1926, the regional office of the Ford Motor Company in Louisville sponsored a fiddlers' convention, bringing together the winners from local contests held at Ford dealerships in the middle South. Industrialist Henry Ford, an outspoken anti-Semite and isolationist, was, like John D. Rockefeller, inspired to memorialize the preindustrial artisan economy that his own enterprise had done much to abolish. While the Rockefellers were collecting folk art and underwriting its exhibit in New York and at Colonial Williamsburg, Ford was constructing his historical museum at Dearborn, Greenfield Village, which, like Colonial Williamsburg, would be a pseudo-environment constituted from the relics of a renovated and rewritten preindustrial past. "Folk art," in this context, was really the folk *objet d'art,* with the craftsman or craftswoman herself quite eclipsed by it—precisely the condition of its "folk" status.

A new regional folk festival, music teacher Annabel Morris Buchanan's at White Top, Virginia, drew national attention when Eleanor Roosevelt visited in 1933; but another visitor, Charles Seeger, who came in 1936, was troubled by the strange parochial attitudes of a coterie of managers who seemed motivated as much by their contempt for what Buchanan called "crude modern folk productions with cheap tunes based on ancient Broadway hits," and a hatred of urban culture generally, as by a love for "the highest type of native material." They saw no contradiction in excluding from the festival local people who could not pay the forty-cent admission fee. "Elizabethan frankness may be tolerated," Buchanan wrote of her festival, but "vulgarity is barred. The folk festival is not concerned with products of the streets, nor of the penitentiaries, nor of the gutter . . . high standards cannot walk hand in hand with simon-pure democracy."[6] Seeger called the affair "reactionary to the core," detecting in it a veneration for Anglo-Saxon culture, which, with its apparent indifference to actual mountain music and mountain people, was at bottom not musical at all, but social, the idol of a self-styled cultural aristocracy. "Not for the mountain people alone," Buchanan intoned, "not for one region alone not for one class alone: the White Top activities, if they are to endure, must be wrought slowly, carefully, measure by measure, for a race . . . for after all, the White Top festival belongs to the folk. And we are the folk."[7]

Seeger was much better pleased by the Mountain Dance and Folk Festival, established in 1931 by local lawyer, collector, balladeer, banjo picker, and square dancer, the "Minstrel of the Appalachians," Bascom Lamar Lunsford, whom the Asheville, North Carolina, Chamber of Commerce had enlisted to add a program of folk music and dance to its annual Rhododendron Festival. Asheville's development boom, founded in a feverish speculation in real estate, which in the previous decade had more than tripled the town's population, was on the wane, and waning with it was the hope that Asheville, "The Land of the Sky," might become the holiday, spa, and resort center of the East Coast.[8] Such was the occasion—but Lunsford's love of mountain people and culture was genuine, and his understanding both of the tradition and of the concert stage profound. Lunsford located and invited to his festival many of the most interesting mountain ballad singers and musicians to have emerged in the twentieth century, including banjoists Obray Ramsey, Samantha Bumgarner, and Walter Parham, and balladeers Cas Wallin and Pleaz Mobley, people whose vocal and instrumental styles, the mountain origins of which no one could doubt, had nevertheless enjoyed the pacifying influences of a prized first- and second-generation literacy and the late-nineteenth-century parlor.

Conservative in politics and manners, and a former schoolteacher himself, Lunsford saw in the domestic music and social dance of his region a reservoir of the old-fashioned rural gentility that a generation earlier had flowed from the country schoolhouse, the law office, and Baptist pulpit, so that virtually all of his participants represented in fact the culture of a particular socioeconomic class, a kind of mountain yeomanry, and Lunsford himself a kind of local squire. He would not brook a hell-raiser or a rogue, types not unknown either in folk music or in mountain society, and certainly not a convict or a tramp; normally he did not extend his hospitality to the occasional visitors from the urban folksong movement, whom he saw largely as frauds. Often sheer personal regard, as well as an interest in the upcoming generation, not musicianship alone, determined who would appear on his stage—an indication that in spite of the far-flung audience and reputation it won over the years, the Mountain Dance and Folk Festival was at bottom the effort of a specific historical community, formed by a specific conjunction of regional, economic, and social factors then in decline, to turn the local real estate collapse into its own cultural opportunity.

Tourism provided the incentive for other festivals as well, such as the American Folk Song Festival, begun in Ashland, Kentucky, in 1930 by former Kentucky court stenographer Jean Thomas, the "Traipsin' Woman," whose experience in New York and Hollywood had taught her the commercial potential in bringing regional stereotypes to life, not only in her own gingham-clad Dogpatch persona, but also in a commercial icon of her own making named J. W. Day, a man whom she presented to the world, on records and in a book, as a blind Kentucky fiddler called "Jilson Setters," the "Singin' Fiddler of Lost Hope Hollow." All hope was not, however, lost: Setters, his sight miraculously restored, ultimately performed in England for George the Fifth.

Boosterism does not of course entirely preclude cultural authenticity. The Kutztown, Pennsylvania, Folk Festival, conceived in 1933 by an Allentown newspaperman named William Troxell, or "Pumpernickel Bill," grew out of Pennsylvania Dutch community picnics and apple-butter boilings.[9] Unlike the concerts at Ashland and Asheville, however, Kutztown was participatory, inviting the visitor to handle tools and chat with straw stackers, harvesters, shingle makers, soap boilers, and other traditional craftspeople and agricultural workers. Dialect speeches and ethnic humor nevertheless indicated that, like other festivals of the period, Kutztown was undertaken in the awareness of, if not entirely on behalf of, the gaze of the outsider. By the late 1950s, though, self-satire was replaced by seminars and panels in such matters as witchcraft, "powwowing," and the conduct of funerals, and the term "folklife," which the Smithsonian was to adopt for its own festival, was introduced to describe, more accurately than "folklore," the festival's focus upon the agriculture, domestic economy, and cottage crafts of the pre-automobile era.

But let's not forget the Rhododendrons, or Jilson Setters, or Pumpernickel Bill. What appear to be merely the occasions or expedients of these folk festivals are far more significant as signs of the essential and fundamental involvement of folk with official culture, the involvement that, because official culture absorbs all authority, prestige, and power into itself, providing social and political standards and proofs, opens culturally unincorporated tracts in which folklife may build according to its own codes. "Official culture" is—or at least the phrase implies it is—the sum total of those august institutions with which we identify our historical moment and level of civilization: the state, its governing bodies, its educational and business establishments, its corporate structure, commercial interests, its systems of transport, communication, production, and exchange, and so on, institutions that are, indeed, "official" because they are configurations of the forces that in any society shape all of its human processes and determine the sources of authority itself in human needs and wants.

The folk festivals at White Top, Asheville, Ashland, and Kutztown are bound up in various ways with these institutions, not only as expedients and occasions, but, more importantly, as forces in relation to which both the old local parochial culture and an embracing cosmopolitan culture understand themselves and the other—a fact that, in turn, shapes what each of these cultures is: what it values and devalues, the ways it addresses itself to itself and to the other, the ways in which that address shapes its own development. That such affairs should be bound up with tourism, and hence with travel, money, and, say, advertising and communication, is interesting because it suggests the deeper and more extensive forces that bring tourists and folk cultures together. We may suspect, for instance, that hard-surface roads, balloon-tired automobiles, and broadcast radio are all implicated in the emergence of the folk festivals of the late 1920s and 1930s, just as interstate highway and jet air travel, and certainly long-distance telephone, and now the computer, form part of the understructure of the Festival of American Folklife and other public festivals of our epoch. Interesting, too, is the variety of ways in which festival organizers integrate folk culture with projects of a personal, political, or educational character, bringing intellectual, social, and economic resources and advantages to the husbanding and sometimes the engineering of folk cultural resources according to ideologies usually quite alien to ordinary people.

But the presentation of folk culture cannot arise in a vacuum. The tacit system of shared understandings that makes any presentation intelligible—in this case, a ductile system of stock characters, stereotyped locales, old stage dialects, typical occupations and pastimes, and, above all, a fixed social and moral hierarchy—demands a tradition of representation in which and through which folk festivals have their meaning. The representation of folk culture, moreover, whether literary, popular, or social scientific, constitutes and frames the category of folk culture itself, opening in official culture an imaginary space that reduplicates the cultural opportunity in which folklife has its existence. In that framework, folklife may be only a pure stereotype, a fantasy; but like any fictional frame, it can, with application, assiduous inquiry, and deep imagination, be penetrated; in fact, one can, like Alice into her mirror, disappear in it. As many folklorists have discovered, the careful field investigation of a folk community does, after time, gently do away with the conceptual frame that permitted the identification of the field to begin with, and gradually reveals particular people, with histories, personalities, and names, gifted and versatile people, with many kinds of social and cultural affiliations, not all of them, in the strict academic sense, "folk"—doing all kinds of interesting, real things.

Probably no society in the world is as fully represented to itself as ours. After the Civil War, and grounded in its technological, managerial, and productive requirements, began a sweeping and inexorable expansion, and a concomitant consolidation of forces of every kind that historian Alan Trachtenberg has called "the incorporation of America."[10] Trade between the Northeast and the Ohio frontier had been briefly consolidated in early decades of the twentieth century by a system of canals, a fact crucially important for the birth of our popular music, in what was originally a folk form, blackface minstrelsy. In the decades after the war, however, the extension of the railroads into lumbering and coal areas, and into newly opened western lands, violently contracted the continent, opening to consciousness its vastness and variety, and at the same time blighting the old provincial life with obsolescence.

The developing transport network, with its sense of access, became simultaneously the superstructure of the vast telegraphic system of information processing, which lent lightning mobility to written communications between remote parts and urban centers—communications in turn amplified to godlike resonance by the steam-driven rotary press, whose massive productive capacity was readily served by the scope of rail distribution. The concentration and movement of capital and goods, the expansion of markets and of access to raw materials, the concentration of industry in urban centers and the formation of corporate monopolies, and, above all, the virtually universal ascendancy of print communications, markedly facilitated by the invention of the typewriter, the linotype, and the telephone: all of this, by the First World War, was plain fact—but far from a universally comprehended, not to mention an accepted fact.

At the center of the popular mythology of this epoch was the encounter of country and city, with its emblematic popular types, the hayseed and the city slicker, reiterated in popular and even literary fiction in a zillion different incarnations; the mythic journey of the period was of course from country to city. Think of Sherwood Anderson's George Willard, the young newspaper reporter of *Winesburg, Ohio,* whose ritual departure on the train to Chicago, leaving behind him a handful of sadly isolated and grotesquely provincial people, is his passage into manhood. There is no irony in the fact that Anderson himself had made this journey, and had peopled the fictional community of Winesburg with figures he knew in a Chicago boarding house. *Winesburg, Ohio,* with its idyllic pastoral name, had become itself little more than a boarding house, for America had become a nation of transients, and the old local community, with its intimate and personal interactions, its close economic interdependency, its social and cultural self-reliance, if ever such a community existed, had been replaced by a conceptual community of separates, their interaction and interdependency mediated by steam engines, electric wires, and printing presses.

The "incorporation" of America suggests of course a new unity and integrity, a transcontinental nation-state tied together by rails and wires, ever hungry for news of itself, as any emergent nation must be. But in linking us to one another technologically, such systems, we sometimes need to be reminded, also break us apart, transforming the individual into a tiny island of invisibility and powerlessness who can ratify his or her personal existence only by coupling it to massive collective projects and movements, or by somehow magnifying the personal—as a voice, as an image, as an action—until it has the visibility of "news," which is our name for the information that establishes and defines our connectedness to others. It is voice, literally and figuratively, the ability to exteriorize consciousness and win the attention of others to it, that secures our reality as social beings, without which we are scarcely human at all. Society is, after all, a field of conscious awareness differentiated by cultural codes that provide for the articulations of individual personality. In the period after the Civil War, America was a Babylon of such voices, speaking voluminously in print to themselves and to each other, from, to, and within marginal communities and central ones, generating the panoply of ideas, images, narratives, and characters who became, imaginatively, the American civilization that apart from such representations could not be conceived at all.

Elite monthlies such as *Harper's* and the *Atlantic,* mass-circulation weeklies such as *Ladies' Home Journal* and *McClure's,* local and regional newspapers and story-papers, the funnies, serial and dime novels, western pulp romances, ethnic and foreign-language tabloids such as the *Jewish Daily Forward,* joke books and dialect books, lithography, sheet music and product packaging, photography, and eventually, photogravure and halftone reproduction brought the work of innumerable regionalists, local colorists, realists and naturalists, humorists, genre painters, book illustrators, and even song and tale collectors, some of America's first deliberate folklorists, into the popular imagination, furnishing it with a rich inventory of images of the American common life. All of it was reportage, a message sent along the newly constructed lines of communication, marketing, and transportation from one enclave, locale, or center to another, its kinds distinguished not so much by the nature of the message as by the direction in which it traveled. The great proportion of it, of course, was romantic or sentimental, much of it simply a record of the covert shaping force of ruling ideas and values upon images of little-known and little-understood people. The superiority of the Anglo-Saxon "race," or, collaterally, of the white male, the subordinate role and innate inferiority of women, and so on were ideas reiterated in pictures and stories of life among the Indians, on the plantation, in the ghetto, and out West in narratives whose subtext, in spite of exotic exteriors, was often simply an old story of masculine autonomy and female purity. The very term "stereotype" is borrowed, interestingly, from a printing process, for it is in the realm of print that the necessity of stereotype, as a means of organizing social information, becomes most urgent.

Some of it, though, we remember. Mark Twain's "The Celebrated Jumping Frog of Calaveras County" brought oral tradition into print. His Nigger Jim and Injun Joe and Pap owe a good deal to newspaper and minstrel-show stereotypes, but a moral complexity and penetration under the regionalist masks has given these characters continued life. The Atlanta newspaperman Joel Chandler Harris's Uncle Remus stories do considerable violence to schoolroom orthographical conventions in their effort to get across the Gullah dialect, but as a kind of proto-ethnography they do a creditable job and provide us with a fair record of a tale tradition whose roots are in West Africa. Frederick Douglass's harrowing narrative of his escape from slavery has the sloping, melodramatic contours of abolitionist oratory; but the report itself—of actual social conditions on the Maryland plantations, of actual cruelties exposed to keen psychological analysis, of work songs and field hollers as they actually struck the ear of one who remembered and felt them—rings appallingly true. *Forward* editor Abraham Cahan's story of Yekl the greenhorn's Americanization lies somewhere between literary naturalism and a Yiddish folktale, but the collapse of traditional values under pressure of assimilation, with its consequences for men, women, and families, and the taxing adjustment to new conditions, are set in a context of convincingly human personalities. Greek American Lafcadio Hearn's lurid descents into the nocturnal underworld of Cincinnati's riverfront Bucktown are probably the best disclosures of the interaction of black and white on the folk level in the 1870s we are likely to get. And, to cite one more example, George Caleb Bingham's *The Jolly Boatmen,* actually an entire family of related paintings, much reproduced, of trappers on the Missouri River, is a masterpiece of composition and color, but also a document in which folkways, or their signs, have been carefully observed and recorded.

This traffic in the popular representation of folklife after the Civil War produced a number of pioneering collections and studies as well as fictions and fantasies. A classical scholar named William Francis Allen, who visited South Carolina and Arkansas as a government agent after the Civil War, became interested in black language and song, and with two others who had collected Afro-American songs, Charles Pickard Ware and Lucy McKim Garrison, daughter-in-law of William Lloyd Garrison, published the first collection of Afro-American folksong in 1867, *Slave Songs of the United States.* Harriet Beecher Stowe, author of *Uncle Tom's Cabin,* itself a virtual sourcebook of regional and stage stereotypes, also published a collection of New England folktales called *Old Town Fireside Stories* in 1871. Another novelist, George Washington Cable, whose subject was the Creole culture of New Orleans and whose work had won the endorsement of the establishment periodical *The Century,* published two articles in that magazine in which he argued, first, that the banjo, commonly regarded as the signature instrument of the plantation slave, was actually little used in the South, and second that Negro songs had originated in Africa: issues over which folklorists still puzzle today. *The Century,* incidentally, had published both *The Adventures of Huckleberry Finn* and William Dean Howells's *The Rise of Silas Lapham* between 1884 and 1885.

The invention of America, or what Whitman called the "democratic nationality," did not of course commence with the invention of the steam-driven rotary press. Washington Irving had drawn upon Teutonic folktales for his "Rip Van Winkle" and "The Legend of Sleepy Hollow"; both have become, in a sense, allegories of the displacement of traditional ways of life by popular democracy. Revolutionary poets, educated in Cicero, Horace, and classical rhetoric, inspired by Milton but trained to Dryden and Pope, attempted prophetic blasts of heroic verse such as radical republican Joel Barlow's *Columbiad* of 1807, on the future of the new utopia. Longfellow attempted it too, in historical narratives such as "Evangeline" and "Paul Revere's Ride," but especially in "The Song of Hiawatha," which he modeled on a national epic pieced together by folklore scholars, the Finnish *Kalevala,* using Ojibwa tales from Henry Rowe Schoolcraft's *Algic Researches.* Travelers and diarists, too, like Fanny Trollope, A. B. Longstreet, Caroline Kirkland, and Charles Dickens left vivid and discerning accounts of life on the old frontier.

But in the early nineteenth century the real office of defining the national character fell to tradesmen, artisans, frontiersmen, and adventurers, not to mandarin poets and novelists. The much-maligned, little-studied, and little understood tradition of blackface minstrelsy, the single most popular and pervasive entertainment of the nineteenth century, was largely the property of this class. Layered with ironies comic and tragic, inscribed by suffering, an almost pathologically complex masking and unmasking ritual of dreamlike donning and doffing of imaginary identities, minstrelsy ought to be taken as a paradigm of the elaborate process of cultural negotiation at the folk level from which new manifestations of the American identity are continually being formed. T. D. Rice, banjoist Joel Walker Sweeney, and the other "Ethiopian delineators" who brought black songs, dances, fiddle and banjo tunes, street cries, costumes, language, and gestures into the circuses and theaters of the 1820s and 1830s, many of them professional entertainers, were nevertheless largely footloose young men, many of Irish descent, moving along the edges and close to the floor of society in a condition of unending social and economic ambiguity. Minstrelsy provided them with a socially and culturally negotiable role as deliberate messengers and agents of the fertile cultural syncretism that had been transpiring along frontier river and canal routes and on the plantation for several generations.

Dan Emmett, the founder in 1842 of the Virginia Minstrels, the first blackface minstrel ensemble, gave us "Turkey in the Straw," "Old Dan Tucker," and "I Wish I Was in Dixie's Land" (not a martial song originally but a plaintive "walk-around" or cakewalk derived from the African American ring-shout). He was a blacksmith's son from the Ohio frontier, a fiddler with a head full of traditional dance tunes and hymns, a rudimentary literacy that permitted him to compose original words to them, and an education in frontier banjo playing from an enigmatic circus character named Ferguson, who if he was not racially African American was certainly one culturally. Emmett's apparently fruitful interactions with a local band of black musicians, the Snowdens, has been richly and provocatively documented.[11] What the minstrels called "Ethiopian" in any case was really neither African nor European but a folk-cultural creolization of Irish, Scots Irish, German, French, and African styles in language, music, gesture, bearing, in personality itself, an emergent indigenous type in whom Whitman recognized the "indescribable freshness and candor" and the "picturesque looseness of carriage" of the new American.

Whitman himself was a carpenter's son and a carpenter, who later tried his hand at newspapering. His "barbaric yawp," flooded with the babble of newspapers and of hundreds of popular books of poetry, fiction, and science, was a response to the dizzying sense of the expansion of access to the continent that constant exposure to images seemed to make possible. He saw them everywhere: "in paintings or mouldings or carvings in mineral or wood," he wrote, "or in the illustrations of books or newspapers, or in any comic or tragic prints, or in the patterns of woven stuffs or any thing to beautify rooms or furniture or costumes, or put upon cornices or monuments or on the prows or sterns of ships, or to put anywhere before the human eye." When the vast miscellany of American life came together in one place, as it did—significantly for our discussion—at New York's Crystal Palace Exhibition of 1853, Whitman was enchanted, and adopted as an important stylistic influence a popular poetic description of the fair.[12] Whitman's supernaturally mobile imagination moved, with the enthusiasm of first-generation literacy, in a nation of representations, which, poetically transformed, became present to him, touched with a love and desire that took virtually everything and everyone for its object; and his voice, though we have not really heard it until now, he broadcast from what he knew was the "rooftop of the world," newly synthesized by organs of mass communication, whose culture he never learned to despise.

Its "incorporation," then, altered fundamentally the nature of community and identity in America. New affiliations, more virtual than actual, formed in new configurations of printed communications, and new identifications gathered around new lodestones of prestige and power. Freemasonry, voluntary associations, clubs, societies, organizations, parties, auxiliaries, and guilds accomplished social differentiation where commerce, mass production, and communication were introducing an unprecedented level of homogeneity on an unprecedented scale. "Ethnic" groups, as Werner Sollors observes,[13] formed from communities often not connected in Europe but consolidated here by their contrastive relation to the Anglo-American elite; the "regional" and the "local" emerged as categories in a civilization no longer a loose federation of such communities but a dense urban commercial and technological nexus that seemed to marginalize them, categories embracing essentially every folk community that by definition remained economically and culturally unincorporated. Among these regions, locales, and ethnic groups was, for example, a population of leisured and literary middle-class women, which in regional writers such as Willa Cather, Kate Chopin, and Sarah Orne Jewett expressed itself not only as a consciousness of sexual oppression but also as a sensitivity to the details of social, domestic, and psychosexual culture—read female culture—which male writers either satirized or tried to escape, or of which they were mostly ignorant. Print and its cheap reduplication in the post–Civil War decades helped to amplify the hitherto inaudible voice of the community of women, who as popular writers gradually rose to a position of cultural preeminence in the religious, social, and domestic life of the classes otherwise dominated by commercial men. The late nineteenth century was the age of the "New Woman," as political satirist Finley Peter Dunne dubbed her in 1898, asserting her sexual and economic independence and learning to translate it into social and political power and influence.[14]

The response to the newly commercialized and metropolitanized society, then, tended to divide along gender lines, and the uses of folklife that emerged around the turn of the century were to reflect that division. To many men and women comfortably accustomed in the material luxuries that industrial capitalism could produce, life had become, as Jackson Lears writes, something unreal, amorphous, and, in Nietzsche's word, "weightless," personal identity something shallow and vacillating, human drives dull and diffuse.[15] In some sense these changes represented, in Ann Douglas's now well-known phrase, a "feminization" of culture,[16] particularly in the parlor and the parish house, the enclaves into which culture, understood as a special area of activity insulated from the marketplace, seemed to have retired; hence a masculine and "muscular" reaction, symbolized by hunter, soldier, explorer, and physical culturist Teddy Roosevelt, that laid emphasis upon male independence, strength, autonomy, and virility, stressing the self-sufficient outdoor life of the scout, the cowboy, the wilderness guide. It was Teddy Roosevelt's endorsement of John Lomax's *Cowboy Songs and Other Frontier Ballads* that hastened its popularity and inspired similar collections in a similar spirit, such as Carl Sandburg's *American Songbag* and Robert Winslow Gordon's "Songs That Men Sing," a column he wrote for *Adventure Magazine*. This movement lingered in our culture until well after the Second World War in innumerable summer camps, scout troops, YMCAs, outing clubs, and the like, many of which became repositories of revived folk crafts and folksongs and were among the contributory streams to the postwar folk revival. The ballad "Tom Dooley," for instance, had first been collected from mountain singer Frank Proffitt by a recreation director for the YMCA, folksinger and summer camp counselor Frank Warner; and the Kingston Trio learned the words to the song from a collection of folk songs published by the collegiate International Outing Club.

A parallel tradition developed among reform-minded women who found among the many varieties of socialism emanating from England an opportunity for personal fulfillment outside the home, a more Spartan and rigorous existence than that of the kitchen, garden, or parlor, and a definite object toward which to direct their intellectual and spiritual energies. Socialism, represented by such writers as the Welsh industrialist-reformer Robert Owen, art and architecture historian John Ruskin, and the poet, designer, and printer William Morris, was and is a complex synthesis of utopian thought and romantic feeling occasioned by the profound bifurcation of the social order into antagonistic classes by industrialization. In general it sought to relieve the physical deprivation and psychic alienation of industrial labor and to raise the aesthetic standards of art and manufacture through various configurations of model communities and enlightened leadership. Morris, for example, took the medieval crafts-guild as his model, and with Ruskin and others shared the object of redefining, morally, the process of work itself as an agent of communal interdependency on the one hand and of artistic self-expression on the other.

Medievalism was a diversion, a masquerade and a romance as well, an idealized realm of passion and color in a world whose passion and color seemed to have drained away. But socialism advanced the timely and potent hypothesis that social forms, power relations, and the culture that reproduced them formed around modes of production: a hypothesis whose immediate implication was that shifts in modes of production might bring about shifts in the organization of communities, and, still more fundamentally, that society, understood as a structure erected upon the basis of economic relations, might be reconstructed from the ground up—not merely as a political order secured by contract, but as a whole way of life. Hence medievalism and socialism were at bottom one idea, the substance and the structure of one deeply paradoxical idea that culture is, can, and must be deliberately produced, and that once produced tends to reproduce itself: produced, that is, by a powerful class whose power it is the purpose of culture to maintain. If bourgeois life had come to seem artificial, it sought its salvation in an artifice even more complete, laying claim to an omnipotence once thought to belong only to history, to nature, or to God.

In Jane Addams's Hull-House, and throughout the settlement movement, these ideas, or ideas very similar to them, shaped and were shaped by the practical business of social service, but in an important new context: ethnicity. Ethnicity, again, was in America often a redefinition of otherwise highly diverse racial, cultural, social, and even linguistic groups according to nationality, mediating the relations between the European immigrant and the ruling Anglo-American order by means of a contrastive identity, which served them mutually, and a relational identity that distinguished national groups among themselves and differentiated them to Anglo-America. At Hull-House, ethnicity was reconstructed symbolically in cultural remembrances, reenactments, and retrievals, including instruction in native language, literature, and the fine arts, and, most significantly for us, "folk festivals"—one of the earliest uses of the term—in which immigrant groups performed native music and dance for themselves, for one another, and particularly for the younger generation in whom Addams hoped to inculcate a sense of historical continuity and cultural pride.

In such symbolic reenactments ethnic identity at Hull-House certainly lightened the heart and brightened the morale of dislocated and disoriented people urgently effacing their habits and customs in favor of the language and imagery of the fashion magazines, the newspapers, and the street. But a whole way of life could not of course be summoned up in a Hull-House library or gymnasium. Ethnicity had become something specular and ceremonial, a representation among other representations that in the end fostered successful assimilation into the industrial work force by attaching itself to the occupational communities forming within factories and shops. Nevertheless, it was a form of social identity that time has shown to be negotiable currency in our cultural economy, and a psychological mainstay against the vicissitudes of wage labor. It is likely, too, that ethnicity at Hull-House, particularly as spectacle, lent something of its own color to the lives of earnest feminist reformers: for among the new Balkan and Mediterranean immigrants of the settlement period, many from areas of Europe little touched by industrialism, capitalism, or democracy, were nonliterate peasants pure and simple, the primitive "folk" originally imagined by German romantics such as Johann Herder and the Grimms who saw such people as the wellspring of national culture.

Ethnicity at Hull-House, then, which in effect laminated national identity to folk culture symbolically reenacted, was an expression of that romantic idea. This was particularly true as the feminist reform movement extended from the liberal Northeast into Appalachia to create missionary and settlement schools, folk schools in the Scandinavian model, handicraft guilds and craft cooperatives in the tradition of William Morris: "psychic, educational, and cultural aid stations," writes David E. Whisnant in his admirable *All That Is Native and Fine,* "for the bruised and dislocated victims of advancing industrial capitalism."[17] Among those social workers was Olive Dame Campbell, founder of the John C. Campbell folk school, on whose heels came the English folksong collector Cecil Sharp. But, as we noted in the case of the White Top Mountain folk festival, and as Whisnant explains at length, the quasi-religious idealism of enlightened crusaders such as Olive Dame Campbell could be almost indetectably poisoned by cultural manipulators for whom a vision of historical-cultural purity was part of an implicit, perhaps even unconscious program of cultural totalitarianism. It is difficult not to admire, or to escape, the influence of men and women who believe strongly in what they believe and have a courage in their conviction that perhaps surpasses our own; but cultural evangelism, like its religious counterpart, is sometimes blind and deaf to what others actually believe, want, and need.

The first folk festival to conscientiously address, with clearly articulated social and political aims, the culture diversity of American civilization, and to adopt that diversity as a structural principal, was Sarah Gertrude Knott's National Folk Festival, introduced at St. Louis in 1934.[18] Knott, like Annabel Morris Buchanan, was concerned about the leveling effects of commercial records and radio, and, like most folklore scholars, regarded folk culture as an endangered species; but, far from an exclusive commitment to a particular vision or strain of culture, with all the social and political allegiances such commitments imply, her outlook was generously, even exhaustively democratic, not shrinking from the historical moment but sensitively integrating its liberal ideals, from decade to decade, in the folk festival enterprise. Whether the preservation of traditional cultures, or the promotion of international understanding and tolerance, or, after the Second World War, the improvement of new leisure time occasioned by automation, and finally, in the postwar folk revival, anticipating what would become a complex theoretical discussion in the social sciences, a renewed interest in distinguishing between what she called "survivals" and "revivals" in folk tradition, Knott was able to ground her work in the ideological moment.

For Sarah Gertrude Knott, representation in a festival was as important culturally as it was politically in legislative bodies. Representation, she understood, was the primary medium of negotiation between official and unofficial culture; in a festival, moreover, representation took on, potentially at least, the imperative character of actual human relations, with their charge of moral, ethical, and emotional energy. "The festival reflected the broadened attitude of our people," she wrote during the Second World War, "and symbolized the democracy we claim and were fighting to protect. . . . We were more convinced than ever that interchange of folk expressions in festivals breaks down barriers, helps to eradicate racial and nationalistic prejudices, and lays a foundation for better understanding and stronger national unity."[19] Knott was a native Kentuckian and as a student of the University of North Carolina had been a member of the Carolina Playmakers under director Fred Koch. The Playmakers were part of a regional theater movement, inspired by the Abbey Theater in Dublin, that sought to erode the dominance of Broadway by appealing to native or "folk" materials, which the young playwrights imported into their vignettes, skits, plays, and pageants, usually in picturesque stereotyped forms.[20] In 1929 she took a position as director of the Dramatic League in St. Louis, working with both blacks and European immigrant groups. Bascom Lamar Lunsford's Mountain Dance and Folk Festival, which she attended in 1933, inspired her to produce a festival in St. Louis—but her aim from the outset was diversity rather than uniformity. "Our national culture is being woven from the warp and woof of the variegated and colorful strains of many nations," she wrote. "No one would want to dull the richness of that pattern. How bleak indeed would be the cultural outlook for the future if we overlooked the distinctive, individual cultures in a universalized, standardized, regimented culture."[21]

Early National Folk Festivals included Native Americans, British, Spanish, Irish, Scottish, French, German, and black singers, musicians, and dancers, as well as the songs and music of occupational groups such as lumberjacks, miners, cowboys, canal men, and sailors. Eventually her festival widened to embrace the folk traditions of Hungarians, Yugoslavs, Lithuanians, Poles, Greeks, Norwegians, Italians, Jews, Bulgarians, Chinese, Finns, Romanians, Filipinos, Portuguese, Russians, Czechoslovakians, and Spaniards, in recognition of the fact that "these newer groups are keenly aware of the value of folk activity in binding themselves together, in maintaining *esprit de corps* and national identity and spirit."[22] A diversity of audiences was essential, too, so that she moved her festival from city to city—from St. Louis to Chattanooga to Dallas to Chicago to Washington to Philadelphia in the prewar years.

Knott's festival was the first to join the folk festival enterprise to folklore scholarship through teaching workshops, demonstrations, seminars, and lectures by noted collectors, folklorists, musicologists, and artists—indeed the entire folk arts community at one time or another seems to have rallied around her, including of course Bascom Lamar Lunsford, with whom she retained a lifelong association, and the "Traipsin' Woman," Jean Thomas, who brought "Jilson Setters" to perform. George Pullen Jackson, well known for his studies of southern shape-note singing, involved himself, as did Zora Neale Hurston, the black anthropologist and novelist who had studied under Franz Boas. J. Frank Dobie, the collector of Texas folklore; George Korson, a pioneer collector of coal-mining songs; Benjamin Botkin, the aforementioned federal folklorist and popular folklore anthologist; George Lyman Kittridge, Harvard editor of the Child ballads; John Lair, founder of the Renfro, Kentucky, Barn Dance; Arkansas folklore collector Vance Randolph; and Stith Thompson, compiler of the monumental *Motif-Index of Folk Literature*—all folklorists, academic or popular—became Knott's advisors. Even regionalist painter Grant Wood added his voice: an impressive, if diverse, group.

To appreciate the "colorful strains of many nations," of course, one's viewpoint must be beyond and above, rather than tangled in, the pattern in the cultural weave. This persistent blind spot in the panoptical ideology of cultural diversity remains its most vexing element. Knott's background was in theater, and her festivals, which like parallel festivals of the period, were essentially theatrical concerts with a visible emphasis upon picturesque promotional graphics heavily dependent upon ethnic and regional stereotypes, colorful pageantry and costume, and the sheer numbers of groups represented. In several days' time the National Festival program could saturate an audience's capacity for appreciation, requiring it to supply imaginatively the cultural contexts that had not been supplied in other ways and frustrating the passion for more thorough understanding and more intimate association that such performances often inspire. In the National Folk Festival, the cornucopic outpouring of cultural voices met the relatively narrow limits of concert presentation. In the radio age, the fantastic diversity of a civilization now virtually stunned by the aural intensity and immediacy of its communications with itself seemed to urge a mastery of the diversity that theatrical presentation symbolically accomplished. But mastery, actual or symbolic, was utterly inimical to the festival's social and moral aims.

The National Folk Festival, which continues today under new auspices, those of the National Council for the Traditional Arts, led by Tennessee-bred producer and folklore specialist Joe Wilson, elevated the festival enterprise out of its milieu of cultural and political reaction on the one hand and sheer commercialism on the other and laid the groundwork of a festival ideology that could inform the relation of the folk festival both to its public and to public policy. Its problems arose out of Knott's ambition, idealism, and daring, and the still often elusive solutions to them engage all of the vital social, political, and aesthetic issues surrounding folklife and cultural life generally.

Both the Festival of American Folklife and the current National Folk Festival, and the increasing number of state and local festivals modeled upon them, follow Knott's example in seeking the guidance and participation of academic disciplines such as folklore and anthropology, which bear upon folklife and festivity and help in defining them. And in addressing the National Folk Festival's overriding problem, the theatrical insulation between participants and audience, both the Festival of American Folklife and the new National Folk Festival have been years in developing such counterstrategies as the construction of small community settings, modestly scaled performance and demonstration venues, discussion workshops, multiple staging, and, most significantly, the development of an "inner audience," which, through the natural influences that work in small assemblies, particularly the infectious and knowing enthusiasm of the cultural familiars within it, can encourage a visitor's more thorough participation and richer understanding.

In recent years the National Folk Festival, which had been sited at Virginia's Wolf Trap Farm Park near Washington from 1972 to 1982, has returned to Knott's practice of moving from city to city, mounting its exhibition in the postindustrial, multiethnic cities of Lowell, Massachusetts, Johnstown, Pennsylvania, and Bangor, Maine, actually and symbolically joining, within the boundaries of an urban national park, the folk festival to kindred projects in historical preservation and local economic revitalization. Here the audience for various ethnic displays is formed from local ethnic communities, while local organizations such as the Lowell National Historic Park and the Laotian-American Organization of Lowell, or the Johnstown Area Heritage Association, assist in the planning and production of the event. In 1990, the National Council for the Traditional Arts, while moving its festival to Johnstown, continued in an advisory capacity to Lowell's local apparatus in hopes of converting the folk festival there to an annual community event.[23]

The deeper social, economic, and political character of the folklife festival, however, begins to suggest itself when we place it in the context of the broader history of cultural exhibition, particularly through the Festival of American Folklife and its parent institution, the Smithsonian. For analogues in the history of international fairs and festivals we might look back, with the assistance of Robert Rydell's excellent history, *All the World's a Fair,*[24] at the great industrial and cultural exhibitions of the nineteenth century such as the Centennial Exhibition at Philadelphia in 1856 and Chicago's World Columbian Exhibition of 1893, both of which drew significantly upon the ideas of Smithsonian natural scientists and anthropologists as well as the material resources of the institution. These were not of course "folk festivals," but celebrations of technological and scientific progress, industrial might, the exploitation of the world's natural resources, the expansion of capital markets, and, above all, of Anglo-Saxon racial superiority—in short, festivals of colonialism whose anthropological theme, which reflected the period's rough conjunction of scientific and popular thought and ran comprehensively through the organization of the exhibitions, was the progress of humankind from its dark and savage beginnings to its zenith in European industrial civilization.

That the first of the great international exhibitions, Victoria's Crystal Palace Exhibition of 1851, and its sister event in New York two years later, took place under what was in effect a giant greenhouse is significant: though its purpose was to exhibit England's primacy in steam engines, power looms, and other machinery, as well as the textile, iron, and other products manufactured by them, the glass canopy overhead, formerly an exclusive feature of the nobility's gardens, intimated that the exhibition's deeper purpose was, in some elemental sense, cultivation and nurture. That culture had become, by the 1870s, thoroughly machine driven, was a dismaying and colossal reality. At the Philadelphia Centennial Exhibition of 1876, an aging Walt Whitman, bound to a wheelchair by a stroke, lingered half an hour before the huge, insinuating, Corliss Engine that silently presided over a brood of mechanical innovations including sewing machines, refrigerators, telephones, and the Westinghouse air brake, promissory notes of epochs to come. "Type of the modern," Whitman wrote that year, "emblem of motion and power—pulse of the continent . . ."

Spencer Baird, assistant secretary of the Smithsonian under Joseph Henry, had sent John Wesley Powell and others on a pioneering expedition into the West to retrieve Indian pottery, weapons, tools, and the like for exhibit in the Smithsonian's section of the Government Building. Here Indian artifacts were mingled with a full-sized tepee and a sixty-five-foot Haida canoe alongside photographs and wax and papier-mâché figures of Indians that in their crass verisimilitude turned the romantic conception of the noble Red Man enjoyed by the novel-reading public into fear and revulsion. Living Indians had arrived from the West too, though not by invitation, and had made an encampment on the fairgrounds under the supervision of a Texas Scout and Indian fighter named George Anderson. African Americans were represented in a private concession operated by an Atlanta businessman, which presented "plantation darkies" singing and strumming the banjo and rattling the bones in a kind of outdoor minstrel show.

Ethnographic exhibition under the auspices of the Smithsonian, then, is nothing new. In a manner anticipating Secretary Dillon Ripley a century later, in fact, Joseph Henry sought to extend the institution's influence increasingly into public education and edification; in the twelve years after 1880, the Smithsonian erected industrial exhibits in Chicago, Philadelphia, New Orleans, Louisville, Cincinnati, Minneapolis, and Marietta, Ohio, as well as Berlin, London, Paris, and Madrid.

The structural parallels between the Festival of American Folklife, then, spreading itself out over the grassy Mall between the alabaster Capitol dome and the Washington Monument, and the Columbian Exhibition at Chicago in 1893, are all the more arresting. Overlooking Lake Michigan at the 1893 exhibition was a plaster-of-Paris White City of lakes and fountains, domes and columns, which shone with a vastness and glory reminiscent of the visionary cities of antiquity painted by Claude Lorraine or Thomas Cole. These utopian images, touched over the centuries by a sublime religiosity, and at least since Bunyan's City Beautiful an archetype of popular culture, left little doubt as to the nature of the hope and faith the official culture of the age had placed in the scientific and technological progress the White City was meant to consecrate.

Within the walls of the White City, several structures were either dedicated to or included exhibits of anthropological or ethnological import. The Anthropology Building itself was the work of Frederick Ward Putnam, of Harvard's Peabody Museum of American Archaeology and Ethnology, who had been placed in charge of the exhibition's anthropological exhibits. This was a thoroughgoing anthropological college, with a reference library, a laboratory, reference collections in religion and folklore, and exhibits of artifacts from around the world—Japanese and Indian toys and Mohammedan, Hindu, and Jewish ceremonial objects. In the Government Building, the Smithsonian's Bureau of American Ethnology, under anthropologist Thomas Wilson, assembled figurative groups—familiar to us now from our experience of natural history museums—of life-sized Indian families, framed on the nuclear model of the American middle class,[25] dressed in traditional costume and engaged in various labors in simulated natural environments. The government of Spain offered life-sized models of peasant women in costume in the Women's Building, where another Smithsonian scientist, Otis Mason, mounted an exhibit of the three "modern forms of savagery," American Indian, Negroid, and Malayo-Polynesian, in twelve groups of artifacts representing particular art forms.

The contributions of foreign governments were in several instances quite spectacular. Norway built a replica of a twelfth-century church, Spain a reproduction of the Valencian stock exchange, and Germany a kind of fifteenth-century city hall. The Sultan of Johore sent artifacts representing all of the ten or twelve distinct ethnic groups of his tiny state in British Indochina: models of the native dwellings of aboriginal Saki and Jacoons; a Malay audience hall, mosque, and palace, complete with kitchen and baths; the weapons and utensils of Malay and Chinese, a blacksmith's forge and tools, and costumes representing every social class from aboriginal hunter-gatherers to the robes worn by the sultan's company of Chinese actors.

Interestingly, primitive arts and crafts in these exhibits were taken as indicators not of the accommodation a particular community has made to the conditions of life, but of the early stages in the history of civilization, a history simultaneously projected upon the racial categories of humankind that physical anthropology had posited. Crafts, then, an index of technological development during a period in which Thomas Huxley was popularizing the ideas of Darwin in America, were taken as a measure of human biological evolution. A visitor to the Anthropology Building, indeed, could participate in the advance of anthropological knowledge by volunteering for an examination by a physical anthropologist, who would determine his racial type!

Such vortexes of official culture as the White City naturally engender colonies of unofficial culture around them. The Philadelphia exhibition had generated a flimsy but festive "Centennial City" of beer gardens, ice cream parlors, peanut stands, pie stalls, fruit and sausage vendors, strolling players, brass bands, dioramas, and freak shows, which extended in ludic counterpoint the official program of science and machinery. At Chicago, flowing westward from the White City along a wide avenue of turf nearly a mile long, which today separates the campus of the University of Chicago from the inner-city neighborhood across Sixty-third Street, was a mall called the Midway Plaisance.

Historian Hubert Howe Bancroft has given us a vivid recollection of it:

> Entering the avenue a little to the west of the Women's Building, a visitor would pass between the walls of medieval villages, between mosques and pagodas, past the dwellings of colonial days, past the cabins of South Sea Islanders, of Javanese, Egyptians, Bedouins, Indians, among them huts of bark and straw that tell of yet ruder environment. They would be met on their way by German and Hungarian bands, by the discord of . . . camel drivers and donkey-boys, dancing girls from Cairo and Algiers, from Samoa and Brazil, with men and women of all nationalities, some lounging in oriental indifference, some shrieking in unison or striving to out-shriek each other, in hope of transferring his superfluous change from the pocket of the unwary pilgrim. Then, as taste and length of purse determined, for fees were demanded from those who would penetrate the hidden mysteries of the plaisance, they might enter the Congress of Beauty with its plump and piquant damsels, might pass an hour in one of the theaters or villages, or partake of harmless beverages served by native waiters. Finally they would stake themselves to the Ferris Wheel, on which they were conveyed with smooth, gliding motion to a height of 260 feet, affording a transient and kaleidoscopic view of the park and all it contains.[26]

This officially unofficial folklife festival was an effort by Putnam and his associates to take advantage of what they knew was the attractive force of such commercial strips by introducing into it their own living ethnological exhibits. Some years earlier in Paris, at the International Congress of Prehistoric Anthropology and Archaeology, held in conjunction with the Paris Exhibition of 1889, a popular "colonial city" had presented upwards of two hundred Asians and Africans in simulated native villages. Within the White City, on the Shores of the South Lagoon, Native American representatives had built a Penobscot village; several Iroquois bark houses and a "long house," in which the visitor could meet Tuscarora and Seneca men and women from New York; a Navajo hogan that housed a native blacksmith and weaver; and an entire Pacific Coast village peopled by members of the Kwakiutl tribe. Totem poles stood before these structures, and canoes drifted by on the lagoon, while Franz Boas, one of the founders of modern anthropology, lurked about examining artifacts and conducting interviews with the participants, preparing to overturn the entire intellectual structure in which the exhibits had been reared.

But stretching beyond the White City along either side of the Midway Plaisance were the houses and shops of an astounding variety of exotic peoples. Here, as a contemporary observer described it, was a Turkish village, with a bazaar, mosque, and theater; and an Arab encampment, where a wedding, mock combats, and a traditional drama were in progress. A Damascus house, with its domestic customs, lay hard by a Cairo street, where two Sudanese families provided music, dancing, and soothsaying. An Algerian and Tunisian village included a café and a "torture dance" in which the dancer "ate live scorpions and broken glass, grasped red-hot irons, and drew needles through his flesh, while apparently under the influence of some drug."[27]

A South Sea village consisted of houses brought from Samoa, Fiji, and the Wallis Islands, while in a Javanese village over a hundred natives from a colonial plantation engaged in batik dyeing, target shooting with bows and blowguns, and kite flying. A wedding occurred here too, with attendant festivity, as well as an actual funeral for several of the participants who had succumbed to their violent physical and cultural dislocation, a fact that did not prevent one commentator from observing that among the Javanese "good nature and merriment constantly prevailed, and life seemed a perpetual holiday."[28]

Best remembered of the Plaisance villages, however, because pioneering work in African music was performed there by ethnomusicologist Henry

Edward Krehbiel, was a village of thirty thatch-and-plaster huts, entirely enclosed by a high stockade—the Dahomey Village, inhabited by sixty-nine men, women, and children from the French settlement of Benin on the west coast of Africa, who on an open square in the center performed native music and dances, ornamental painting and goldsmithing, and religious ceremonies, including the sacrifice of a bull. The Dahomey Village, alongside settlements of Dakota Sioux, Navajo, Winnebago, Apache, and Pueblo, arranged through Indian agents, occupied the far end of the Midway, while nearest the White City stood the German houses and two Irish villages—an arrangement that one observer called "a sliding scale of humanity," descending from the Teutonic and the Celtic, through the Middle Eastern and Asian, to the African and Native American.[29]

Lest we laugh too derisively at the overt racism of some late-nineteenth-century anthropological representations, let us recall that while ideologies come and go, the cultural traditions that gave rise to them, and the social experiences that continually drive them home, persist. The White City and the Midway Plaisance are merely momentary expressions of ideas, political and pastoral, that have been with us for centuries in thousands of varied embodiments, among which is the nation's capital itself; and, while most of us would like to think we have jettisoned the racist evolutionary assumptions of our grandparents, the social landscape around or before us, where difficulty, disadvantage, and outright oppression continually shape and reshape privilege and power along racial and cultural lines, sends our best convictions into an airy, abstract realm, which the passionate intensity of racial confrontation can blow away in an instant. They were not all racists, after all; an interesting young character from San Francisco called Sol Bloom, who installed the Midway Plaisance exhibits, found a "spiritual intensity" in Bedouin acrobats that exceeded the "emotional power of a Renaissance tapestry," and an Arabian sword swallower whose level of culture to him was higher than that of Swiss peasants making cheese and chocolate. Bloom's head was clear—and it seems fitting that in later life he should have been one of the drafters of the United Nations Charter.[30]

It is more than intriguing to place today's Festival of American Folklife in the context of these symbolic and ideological structures of the past. The nineteenth-century federal White City of Capitol and Monument now linger in remote and silent watchfulness on the margins of the National Mall, while the festival draws onto the sunlit grass growing at the middle of things, into the social scientific as well as the touristic gaze, its own federalized Midway Plaisance. In the rotunda of the old Arts and Industries Building, hard by the Smithsonian Castle and the symbolic heart of the National Museum, an evening reception for festival participants, staff, officers, federal and foreign service dignitaries, and invited guests takes place amidst exhibits from the Philadelphia Centennial Exhibition of 1876. Science, industry, and technology in their modern forms are all there too—half hidden in the months of phone calls, the stacks of computer disks, the paperwork, Xeroxing, and faxing, the air and highway travel, the electrical and communication systems, and all the rest that it takes to produce a folklife festival. Even the Smithsonian's nineteenth-century anthropological paradigms survive in the institution's current initiatives in African American, Native American, and Pacific cultures.

Roger Abrahams has given us a powerful metaphor for understanding what, culturally, these structural and historical reconfigurations mean, particularly in the original nineteenth-century context of manufacture and trade.[31] Trade, Abrahams observes, implies the crossing of frontiers and demands the creation of special zones outside the contexts of family and community in which people otherwise insulated from one another may come together for exchange. Typically the marketplace occurs "at the crossing points between two worlds," such as in the seventeenth-century suburban London "liberties" or unincorporated tracts outside the city gates, or on the borders between two precincts, or at international crossroads: a desert Palmyra or modern jetport with its unincorporated city beyond the last suburban tract.

The marketplace, Abrahams explains, is essentially cultural; though it may have evolved, anthropologically, from the festivals of tribal or communal societies, market society festivals, such as our national holidays, summer vacations, and long weekends, reflect the production calendars of complex market economies. At festival times, which are temporally as well as spatially unincorporated, situated between seasons, at moments when productive work is temporarily suspended, economic exchange retreats before the cultural exchange that is its social foundation, moving expressive activity dramatically into the center. The social hierarchy is inverted; an outpouring of symbols, effigies, and images bewilders perception; imitation, mimicry, and parody lift cultural identities out of their fixed positions in the social structure and bestow upon them the mobility and the appeal of commodities; sheer plentitude relaxes customary prohibitions, and a kind of erotic energy suffuses the festival space with the spirit of play and the promise of riches.

Though the Festival of American Folklife arises from a concentration of economic and political power, though for some participants its festive character is compromised by their hired status, though for others it represents an economic as well as a cultural and political opportunity, with its historical and institutional links to nineteenth-century anthropological exhibitions, and its place on the Mall outside the gates of the Capitol and on the summer holiday calendar, it is manifestly a festive event. But what is the nature of this festivity, and what is its meaning for us, particularly in its symbolic movement into the center and onto what has been called the "national front lawn," where in 1964, in one of his first actions as secretary, Dillon Ripley installed a carousel and turned the statue of Joseph Henry around to face the Mall? Why, indeed, the millennium now already almost a decade behind us, is the public folk festival, burdened as it is with discredited social and anthropological ideas, grounded in a thoroughly suspect concept, still invested with the dusky glow of old romance, aggravated by ideological conflict and class antagonism, a feature of the cultural landscape at all?

A folk festival, as I hope the foregoing discussion suggests, resituates, reconstrues, and recontextualizes, by means of public reenactment, displaced and decontextualized folk cultural performances. These are the variables—decontextualization, reenactment, and recontextualization—that determine the several kinds of folk festivals we have considered; and these variables, as we have seen, are themselves shaped by various motivating ideologies and interests; social, historical, technological, and other larger forces; and by the several modes of presentation available for folk-cultural display.

Let us consider then, each of these factors in turn. The regional festivals of the 1920s annexed themselves to and assimilated certain local forms of presentation such as the singing convention, the camp meeting, or fiddlers' contest, or, as in Lunsford's case, the annual Rhododendron Festival, mounted for tourists. At Kutztown, a seasonal celebration, the apple-butter boiling, provided the occasion and its structure. The present-day National Folk Festival has been linked to particular historical sites and national recreation areas and is exhibitory in character; other folk festivals have been more strictly theatrical, beginning with settlement house presentations and including of course Sarah Gertrude Knott's festival and most of the university-sponsored concert festivals of the postwar folk revival. The Festival of American Folklife provides perhaps the only real instance of a folk cultural exhibition whose models are the great exhibitions and world's fairs of mature industrial capitalism.

Each of these modes of presentation suggests particular processes of recontextualization and the audiences associated with them. All folk festivals are themselves contexts, of course, in which particular folk cultural performances are redefined and interpreted in relation to the other performances on the program, the total body of performances promulgating, though rarely articulating, a tacit theory of a particular folk culture or of folk culture generally. The regional folk festivals of the 1920s and 1930s strived for cultural definition or reinforcement, usually driven by certain ideological commitments arising from particular institutions such as a crafts cooperative, a settlement or folk school, or, as at Asheville, a business establishment. Where tourism or some other form of economic traffic—trade in local crafts, for example—is the object, recontextualizing, as in Jean Thomas's "Traipsin' Woman" festival, may involve a deliberate gratification of the cultural stereotypes that tourists bring with them. Or, as in the settlement house or folk school festival, recontextualization may consist, as we have suggested, in the "construction" or encouragement of ethnicity: to enhance what Knott called "*esprit de corps,*" to assist in the process of assimilation, and to acquaint the insulated middle class with the real culture of peasants and serfs. The new context here, of course, is life in the industrial working class.

In the case of theatrical and exhibitory presentations, recontextualization is more problematic. In Knott's festivals, and in the many concert presentations akin to hers, presenters seem to assume, probably accurately, that audiences are already furnished with whatever rudimentary cultural information may be required to make the performance intelligible. This may be some kind of formal or informal learning, a benign sentimental stereotype, or even something as simple as a belief in cross-cultural understanding or a love of the exotic. It is the aim of such festivals to validate and satisfy such beliefs and desires, which are all predicated upon secure social standing and a tacit conviction of cultural legitimacy or even of superiority. Various textual and oral mediators mounted in association with the performance, though, may promote and shape a recontextualization of the performance along educational or ideological lines.

"Cultural conservation," a policy initiative outlined in various federal documents and articles during the 1980s,[32] is one such ideology of recontextualization, in this case highly concrete and pragmatic, one that aims to shape existing social, economic, and political structures in ways that will nurture the folk-cultural performance, and with it the folk culture itself: by heightening awareness of itself in itself and in others, by strengthening cultural self-esteem, by opening potential markets for music and crafts, by preserving natural and cultural raw materials, by influencing favorable legislation, and so on. The synthesis "cultural conservation" represents, of the concepts of natural conservation, historical preservation, and economic revitalization, within the domain of federal authority, strikingly materialized at the National Folk Festival at Lowell, which attempted to summon various ethnic communities together around their own cultural performances in an architecturally preserved urban national park adjacent to the old cotton mills.

There is a close connection, of course, between a festival's mode of presentation, its interests, and the character of the folk performance itself. Performances mounted in conjunction with a regional celebration or local fair—a fiddlers' contest, for example, or a street fair—may be thoroughly traditional in themselves. But reframed as tourist attractions, they are assimilated to stereotypes; reframed as cultural recoveries, they are assimilated, say, to nativist, Anglo-Saxonist, socialist, populist, preservationist, or other ideological romances. What is "traditional," however, at a particular historical moment, may already have been constructed commercially, a generation or so earlier: by minstrel and tent shows and Wild West shows, by record-company advance men and concert promoters, by regional writers and local colorists, cartoonists, and photographers, even by folklorists like John Lomax. Postwar revivalist concert festivals in the university and the Smithsonian's Festival of American Folklife have enjoyed a background of commercial, political, and academic constructions of folklore extending into the nineteenth century, with certain periods, such as the populist 1930s, contributing mightily to the concept as well as to the various claims made on its behalf.

A folk festival structurally reduplicates the social arrangements that make the concept of folk culture possible to begin with and in a variety of ways seek to drive that concept home—and with it, its enabling social arrangements. We have already noted that a folk festival is itself a context; this fundamental recontextualization *must* occur—hence, always, a folk *festival*: because the idea of the folk cultural performance is implicitly decontextualizing. Whether romantic or reactionary, explicitly political or methodologically ethnographic, the concept of the folk cultural performance has already bracketed the many social, economic, technological, and especially the historical factors that join folk culture, and more importantly, the people who bear it, inextricably to official culture, established institutions, and reigning technologies. By identifying, soliciting, organizing, and presenting the reenacted cultural performance, the folk festival formalizes that decontextualization so that *re*contextualization can occur under its own auspices and in the service of its own interests.

Because social differentiation and historical change have already created the conditions of the folk festival, it may consequently be said to be a kind of symbolic response to such differentiation and change: typically to reconcile or to resist it. In celebratory events, the anxieties occasioned by an aggravated economic inequality, say, or by the emergence of a depersonalizing mass society, or the decline of social power at a particular social stratum, can be contemplated as joys; the grief attending the loss of tradition, community, or place can be temporarily assuaged. Nativist and Anglo-Saxonist festivals, for example, which may appear to have preserved traditional performances in contexts already in place, in fact occurred under pressure of an anticipated or perceived deracination arising from disconcerting, even traumatizing, technological and social change, not only European immigration, which in Appalachia was a distant reality at best, but the entire modern world, the deep cultural ambivalence modernity inspired, and especially its apparent collapse in the Great Depression, which certainly inspired the idea of return to customary ways in newly modernized communities. Knott's later festivals have as their historical context the vast social, economic, and human catastrophe of global war: it is almost as if in her teeming multiethnic gatherings she was endeavoring symbolically to put the broken world back together again.

Finally, we must consider social class itself and the cultural stereotypes that arise from and reinforce it as a psychosocial form of the process the folk festival recapitulates. In culturally heterogeneous societies the folk cultural performance, or its image, perceived across a social boundary and radically decontextualized in its passage, becomes the nucleus of a complex figure whose recontextualization, out of and on behalf of the perceiver's own cultural endowment, fixes and revalidates the distance that occasioned it.[33] That is the "stereotype"; and the process of its formation is precisely the process that the folk festival, by introducing itself at the moment of the transformation, seeks either to realize more perfectly or to radically disrupt.

The concept of folk culture finds itself embodied, and hence seeks a kind of fulfillment in cultures decontextualized by literal displacement—by immigration from abroad, say, or by country-to-city migration—communities in which cultural knowledge has been in a sense mentalized by its withdrawal from the practical field. Displacement need not be so literal, of course: the recent National Folk Festivals presented in Lowell, Massachusetts, and Johnstown, Pennsylvania, are addressed to groups whose ethnicity, long a coefficient of working-class social life, has been in a sense laid bare by the deterioration of the industrial base that originally grounded it. In these cases festival recontextualization mimics and in many cases seeks to influence the cultural process that any displaced community must undertake in new circumstances. Hence the concept of community has in most respects displaced the concept of folk culture as the mainspring of folk festival planning and production, since sociologically speaking at least community at once constitutes and recontextualizes the folk cultural performance.

The aim of the folk festival, then, should be to identify, summon up, and perhaps in the end to reintegrate itself with community. In the community-oriented or community-based folk festival, the fixed categories and unilinear narratives of the old ethnology and folklore are gone; gone, too, are the strict identifications of the kinds of human communities with their specific historical manifestations in, say, certain nations or races. Such equations are of course axiomatic in the cultural mathematics of evolutionary narrative, folklore types, keys to mythology, and other idols of nineteenth-century social science.

Let us look, then, by way of conclusion, at the role of community in the Festival of American Folklife and the National Folk Festival. Communities are always formations, like whirlpools, rather than forms, like squares and circles. Some may arise under the pressure of insulation or enclaving—regional and ethnic groups, for example, bounded by the economy and the polity of a particular region in Mississippi or Kentucky, the Smithsonian's "featured states" in 1973 and 1974; by the binding force of a language such as Cajun French, for many years with Cajun music a conspicuous presence on the Mall; or by economic and historical factors that drive particular groups into particular urban areas and industries. Some folk cultures arise out of their forced exclusion from official culture: African Americans, enslaved, economically and socially isolated, ghettoized; Native Americans, driven from native lands onto reservations—both compelled to forge syncretic cultures out of complicated and diverse legacies. Others are voluntary: labor unions, sister- and brotherhoods such as the community of the hearing impaired, or enthusiast groups such as citizen band and ham radio broadcasters or Hawaiian hula dancers. In 1986 the Festival of American Folklife controversially transgressed the bounds of public folklore practice by admitting a professional organization, the Association of American Trial Lawyers, also one of the festival's donors that year, to the festival as a "folk" community.

Some folk cultures, violently uprooted from one way of life without having yet accommodated, culturally, to the new circumstances, are in a state of becoming. These are ethnic protocultures—refugees, such as the Vietnamese and Laotians, mountain people such as the Hmong and Kmhmu, dislocated by war, or Latino national groups seeking temporary or permanent employment. In them we can observe a folk culture in transition, as, for example, Hmong embroiderers, settled in church-sponsored communities in small-town neighborhoods, adapt to the American crafts economy by creating designs in our patriotic colors, or narratives of the war that drove them from their homes. Finally there are kinds of folk community that arise within certain webs of relation, embracing many different kinds of occupations, ethnic groups, economies and ecologies, and the rest: the Chesapeake Bay fishery, for example, or the California winery. Some associations seem purely natural, such as families, or children, or the elderly, all of them represented at different times at the Festival of American Folklife, and others purely economic—occupational communities such as cowboys, loggers, railroad workers, taxi drivers, or telephone workers, all of which have been represented over the life of the festival from its beginnings in 1987.

A folk festival is "festive" because of the abundant multiplicity and simultaneity of performances: musicians playing, singers singing and dancers dancing, craftspeople crafting, sculptors sculpting, workers working, talkers talking, and children playing. In this theater the whole range of human ingenuity—crafts subsistent, domestic, preindustrial, and industrial—finds a specific form for presentation, ranging from potters' wheels and kneeling looms to temporary oil derricks and steel-girded buildings. Open tents shelter Bengali effigy makers or Italian American stone carvers preparing finals for the Washington Cathedral Chinese dragon dancers, Serbian string bands, Spanish bagpipers, Kentucky tobacco twisters, Lumbee Indian May Day players, a Finnish Laskiainen winter festival, Macedonian polkas, New Mexican adobe builders, Korean masked players, Philadelphia break dancers, bluegrass bands, blues singers, tamburitza and mariachi and corridos and Cajun and zydeco and samba and reggae and a hundred other musics, as well as Lebanese, Mexican, and Ukrainian and Chinese and Ghanaian cooks—no list can even so much as suggest the number and variety of participants in twenty-five years of the Festival of American Folkife. They practice their art before small, often intimate audiences in whom the public and democratic spirit of the Mall often takes on a warmly communal character.

And there, in the festival's own "communities," fleeting as they are, but often unforgettable, whether it is an audience under canvas, or the community of participants that in its two weeks together works out its own set of codes and forms its own alliances, or in the community of volunteers that gathers around the festival and returns to it year after year, or of the staff with its ideas, its projects, its responsibilities, and its inevitable office politics, or in the many combinations and permutations of all of these, that the purposes of the Festival of American Folklife are best achieved—when they are achieved—where the cultural recovery of the folk performance is, if temporary, more than didactic, theoretical, or imaginary.

It remains to be seen, however, whether the grand experiment on the National Mall, with its variegated public audience of tourists, suburbanites, students, civil servants, bureaucrats, legislators, executives, and professionals, as well as its tiny implanted "inner audiences" of Washington refugee, ethnic, and minority residents, will not eventually be displaced by localized events such as the National Folk Festival, the Cowboy Poetry Gathering at Elko, Nevada, the Conjunto Festival at San Antonio, Texas, and many other grassroots events inspired by public folklore work. At Lowell, musicians, singers, dancers, and craftspeople of British, Irish, Swedish, Italian, Armenian, Polish, Greek, African, Caribbean, Portuguese, Brazilian, Puerto Rican, African American, Native American, Laotian, Vietnamese, Cambodian, French Canadian, Lithuanian, and Filipino heritage, all of them residents of Lowell or of other small cities in New England, performed both to the festival's audience of folk culture enthusiasts and their own families, neighbors, and friends. Such a festival strives for, and in a sense constructs, its own indigeneity, building its cultural bowers in the ruins of the postindustrial age.

With each new contraction of history a new world comes closer to birth. Pilgrims from the obsolete but still prevailing age, its structures still standing and its business still transpiring all around them, colonize the unincorporated zones, bringing their old cultures with them, or fashioning new ones, their existence scarcely detectable until their new order has by ineluctable degrees displaced the old. The Dutch trading companies of the seventeenth century, for example, with their corporate organization, contractual ties, and written charters, a phenomenon of the merchant towns without legitimate place in the official discourse of the period, became, early in the seventeenth century, a metaphor for human society, and protoforms of constitutional governments that would be secured by revolution against traditional power. Standing armies founded on protective armor and the rolling cannon, and the provision of them, prefigured the factory system, the bureaucracy, and mass society, whose consummation was the radio age, and whose apocalypse the atom bomb.

Our own folk festivals are footholds on a cultural future that we in a global society, still defining ourselves in relation to the lost modernity, can but dimly discern. We seemed to have entered a new age of diffuse and shifting Empire, where web-like social structures and effectively instantaneous communications fully global in extent throw an entirely new light over the entire issue of cultural difference, indeed seem to compel a new notion of culture itself, one far more transient and adaptable than the old. When he was an employee of Pan American Airways, in the early days of the jet age, the late Festival of American Folklife founder Ralph Rinzler was discovering what he called, using an airline metaphor, "hubs" of alienated cultures flourishing around their imported expressive forms in taverns, clubs, theaters, and other spots, and at weddings, dinners, and other celebrations in New York, London, Paris, Istanbul, and other cities to which the airline took him. He was catching the scent, perhaps, of a new cultural synthesis of which his own early exposure to Library of Congress field recordings, and to the pioneer reformer-revivalist Pete Seeger, had been full of forebodings. A localizing of culture was following paradoxically from a new expansion of the global order. For this phenomenon geographers have since coined a new word: "glocalism." The new order, it seems, is not yet another "shrinking" or implosion of the planet, facilitating travel and communication, bringing distant places and people closer, a "global village" or world culture. On the contrary, it is an evaporation and precipitation, a kind of inundating cultural rain, an "information explosion" so vast that culturally it denatures information and levels the semiotic field. Culturally speaking, it is tantamount to no information whatever. It overcomes the power of human imagination to orient itself on its own terms and in its own scale and demands that we rediscover the basis of culture in immediate human interaction, conducted under the auspices of our God-given sensory and intellectual equipment, even while as cultures—and only as cultures—we are able to participate in the political and economic consolidation of a global civilization. It is a curious situation, that at the end of history, or of a certain phase of it in any case, we seem to have arrived at the beginning.

Though many may yearn for it, many struggling to create or to recreate it, the homogenous cultural community is precisely what most of us do not experience, and we would feel culturally imprisoned if we did. In the information age, community no sooner forms than it deteriorates—and its deterioration is perpetual. In the evanescent, momentary reality between these impermanences culture springs forth out of acts of making and relating essentially imaginative and improvisatory. The idea of the homogeneous cultural community, which in spite of recent theoretical refinements is still tinged with the old socialist romance, must ultimately give way to a concept of culture grounded not in specific social formations but in the agencies of psychic differentiation in which those formations are themselves grounded. That, I think, is what is indicated by the empty proliferation of the many names—endless lists of regional, national, ethnic, occupational, and other groups, musical varieties, material kinds, crafts types, and so on—without which neither the Festival of American Folklife nor the National Folk Festival can refer to itself or its history. These names speak of course to the perspicacity of fieldworkers, the wonderful diversity of people and their arts, the dizzying abundance of folk festival displays, and the bewildering process of planning and producing what is finally a mysterious and spontaneous social and cultural phenomenon well beyond the reach of mortal understanding. But they are, after all, only names, and, impressive as they are, do not say what the Festival of American Folklife or the National Folk Festival actually is or does.

A folk festival is not in the business of naming things, really, but of unnaming them—of reaching into the little structures of figurative comparisons and self-serving judgments by which we at once admit and dismiss one another in our thoughts to pluck out the vague effigies, made from the scraps of our own culture's representations, that hold such structures together. Bring them to the festival we will and must—they are simply images of unknowns, like the "x" in the equation, through which we assimilate the image of another and work out its value in our own known quantities.

But at the festival this cultural algebra becomes wholly inadequate to account for the chemistry of personal encounter. The sheer reality of the person, the rich exactitude of her presence, the keen imperatives of his art, empty our hopeless conceptions and bestow a gift of permanent love. If the festival has done its work—and it cannot always, of course—we can never think of him or her, or of human nature itself, in the same way again. At the very least we will have felt the nagging unease that comes of being, at this time and place, who and what we are, and for one naked moment perhaps watch as outsiders as the gift of complete humanness falls into hands other than our own. For there will never again be any Corliss Engine nor any merry Javanese to place us at the summit of history, seated on the throne of the human race.

The folklife festival is a practical investigation of the genesis of social experience in a world where the boundaries between cultures are no longer geographical or political but personal, in which the person is in himself or herself culturally not one but many, capable of moving within and among many communities, in which "culture" itself has emerged as the force that secures the connection between reality and the individual soul. In this world folklife is not the culture of the rude peasant or the rustic mountaineer but a very model of the ways in which we are at this moment learning to reinvent our humanity.

6

WHITE CITY ELEGY

MODERN AND POSTMODERN AT THE WORLD'S FAIR

Look on my works, ye mighty, and despair.—Shelley

There was much engineering, but little "architecture," at the White City of 1893—not, at least, unless structures made to dissolve, to be dismantled, sold, and carried away in pieces can be counted as architecture. "Buildings in their proper sense they do not pretend to be," wrote the official historian of the World's Columbian Exposition, Hubert Howe Bancroft. Instead "we have what may be termed so many architectural screens . . ."[1]

Any architect must make concession to, and to reconcile, the transitory nature of earthly materials; but few frankly capitulate to it for the sake of greater imaginative license. It was such a capitulation that erected and defined the White City of 1893, what British traveler James Fullarton Muirhead called its "pathetic transitoriness"—one that still sighs elegiacally in the deteriorating surfaces of our own civic infrastructure, especially where, as in the few traces of Burnham's City Beautiful that survive on Chicago's lakefront, the grandiose imperiality of the fin de siècle commercial city succumbs to the prolonged melancholy expiration of the millennial dreams that gave rise to it.[2]

That melancholic strain French journalist Paul Bourget marked on his own departure from the White City. "All white they had been that morning, the morning of my farewell," he wrote of the buildings, "white as a marble town outlines against a sky untarnished as themselves. How they stood out, still white, in the dense enshrouding fog; but it was the whiteness of a phantom village, whose contours were merged in mist, whose domes, colonnades and towers lost all solidarity—a dreaming vision of architecture, vague scenery about a phantom crowd. . . . In the last glance I gave that fading, shifting panorama, it seemed to me . . . I had experienced in a few short hours the extremes of that city's fascination: first, its dazzling brilliancy, then its fading gloom. . . . I had realized the melancholy touch with which every human masterpiece requires to make it truly beautiful—effacement in the past."[3]

Manufacturers and Liberal Arts Building, with Rostal Column and fountain in foreground. Courtesy of the Chicago History Museum (ICHi-02254).

The meaning of the White City is bound up with this odd contradictory fusion of monumentality and ephemerality, of grandiosity and sham, which the design and execution of the Exposition buildings conscientiously revealed in scales apparently enlarged beyond the limits of physical possibility, in styles capriciously detached from place and time, and, primarily for this discussion, in a fiber-and-plaster sheathing material called "staff."

"Great is 'staff!'" exclaimed architectural critic Clarence Clough Bird. "Without staff this free-hand sketch of what the world might have as solid architecture, if it were rich enough, would not have been possible. . . .

A workman may walk to his job with a square yard of the side of a marble palace under each arm and a Corinthian capital in each hand. While it is a little green it may be easily sawed and chiseled, and nails are used as in pine. . . . Great is staff!"

Staff introduced into White City architecture a dramatically accelerated transitory element apart from which no other aspect of the buildings could really be understood or experienced. The coordinated spatial inflation, stylistic riot, and temporal acceleration of the White City confounded customary spatial-temporal assumptions, disordered the relation of the visitor's body to the built environment, eroded the distinction between exterior and interior, public and private, civic and commercial space, and offered to reverse the flow of historical time.

Architect Daniel Burnham, the Exposition's Chief of Works, conceived of the White City buildings as "great architectural sketches, carried out with sufficient elaboration and finish to give an effect of solidity and magnificence."[4] The key word here is "effect." Architectural critic of the period Montgomery Schuyler captured the moral basis of this emphasis; he attributed the success of what he called "cloud-capped towers and the gorgeous palaces" to "unity, magnitude, and illusion." Classical forms, having "lost touch with their origins, become simply forms . . . used without a suggestion of any real structure or any particular material." Their essence, he noted, was insubstantiality; "inordinate dimensions" distracted from the empty gesture. The buildings "have realized in plaster," he said, "the illusion of monumental masonry, a painter's dream of Roman architecture."[5]

The White City raises a number of issues that bear upon the complex interrelations among modernity and postmodernity, modernism and postmodernism, particularly with reference to the fact that apart from the design contributions of any particular architect to it, and apart from the considerable feats of ironwork, steel manufacturing, engineering, and bureaucracy required to carry it out, the White City was only a mock-up, perplexingly suspended between reality and representation, summoning to perception a scene, which, though constituted in its particular elements by what had been seen before in the world, can never have nor could ever exist in it, in many respects a simulacrum formally indistinguishable from its postmodern counterparts in theme parks, shopping malls, and redeveloped urban centers.

Bancroft saw in the White City "the forums, basilicas, and baths of the Roman empire, the villas and gardens of the princes of the Italian renaissance, the royal court-yards of the palaces of France and Spain";[6] art historian

W. Lewis Fraser "a union of Rome, Palmyra, Athens, Venice, Constantinople," but what in reality was "only a collection . . . of plaster shells."[7] Here was material sufficient, added painter Hopkinton Smith, "for all the painters of the earth, with almost every variety of subject." Zeim and Rico and Whistler "could float in Venetian gondolas along the edges of white palaces that are as real in color, form, and water reflections, as their beloved Bride of the Adriatic. Tadema could find porticos, loggias, and courts—backgrounds for his figures—infinitely more perfect and useful in his studio than could be discovered in a year's travel along the Mediterranean."[8]

This confusion of representation and referent, signifier and signified, throws the White City squarely into the problematics of periodization associated with the idea of the postmodern. Insofar as it conjoined "transient, fleeting and contingent" materials with architectural ideas supposed to be "eternal and immutable," the White City belongs, as art, to modernism, at least as Baudelaire thus formulated it; insofar as it called upon advanced techniques of steel-frame engineering, quasi-military management, and top-down corporate administration to do so, it was outspokenly modern; insofar as it presented a systematic heterogeneity of stylistic allusion, quotation, and metaphor, much of it imitative and all of it simulated, it was curiously postmodernist. With a convergence of races, tribes, states, and nations, moreover, the Exposition looked forward to the social condition of postmodernity, with its general collapse of boundaries and its pervasively touristic social surface.

Monumentality and ephemerality both have their meaning, not only as possible ways of manipulating space or matter, but as temporal projections embodied in those manipulations. Monumentality of course implies permanence, invested in structures and materials; but ephemerality in architecture belongs mainly to modeling, sketching, or representing, as we find it in the grottoes, ruins, cottages and temples of a landscape garden or on the stage. Were such representation simply a matter of appearances, however, as in art formally so marked, its nature would be comparatively unproblematic; but at the White City, as in the landscape garden, perception and apprehension are squarely at odds, for we have in effect stepped into the frame, and become art ourselves. "The aesthetic sense," wrote Muirhead, is "as fully and unreservedly satisfied as in looking at a masterpiece of painting or sculpture, and at the same time soothed and elevated by a sense of amplitude and grandeur such as no single work of art could produce."[9] What appears to be for all time or utterly out of time is demonstrably of the moment, as transient as sugar-candy; what is manifestly artificial is nevertheless obdurately real; out of a cosmetic expedient arises a transcendent beauty.

"There was an air of unreality about this congregation of edifices," Bancroft averred, "so strange in dimensions and design."[10] H. C. Bunner echoed his sentiment:

> Perhaps the first thing that would strike a stranger entering the World's Fair grounds in the summer of 1892 would be the silence of the place, the next the almost theatrical unreality of the impression by the sight of an assemblage of buildings so startlingly out of the common in size and form. . . . It is not only the grouping of the huge white and pale-yellow buildings that gives this impression, although it is hard enough to believe in that at first sight: for it cannot but suggest the extravagant fancy that a dozen or so palaces from distinct lands—some unmistakably out of the Arabian Nights—have taken a sudden fancy to herd together. . . . You watch two or three workmen moving apparently aimlessly upon the face of what seems a stupendous wall of marble. Suddenly a pillar as tall as a house rises in the air, dangling at the end of a thin rope of wire. The three little figures seize this monstrous showy shaft and set it in place as though it were a fence-post. Then a man with a hand-saw saws a yard or two off it, and you see that it is only a thin shell of stucco.[11]

The substantiality of the scene had already been compromised by the imaginary historical narrative implicit in it. Within mid-to-late nineteenth-century outlooks normally thought of as romantic, and reflecting the impact of the social changes broadly associated with industrialism upon the sense of historical time, monumentality, particularly that of the classical world, was already conceived in terms of decline, decay, disappearance—as in, for example, Thomas Cole's "Course of Empire" of 1843, throughout the century one of the most popular and widely reproduced visual statements of the theme. Cole's painting "The Consummation," third in the series after "The Pastoral State," might have inspired the White City itself, miraculously raised in a year in the Jackson Park swamps:

> The rude village has become a magnificent city. . . . From the water on each hand piles of architecture ascend—temples colonnades, and domes. . . . The harbor is alive with numerous vessels—war galleys and barks with silver sails. . . . The statue of Minerva with a Victory in her hand, stands above the building of the Caryatids on a columned pedestal, near which is a band with trumpets, cymbals, etc.

> In this scene is depicted the summit of human glory. The architecture, the ornamental embellishments, &c, show that wealth, power, knowledge and taste have worked together, and accomplished the highest meed of human achievement and empire . . . man has conquered man,—nations have been subjugated.

Yet neither Cole's narrative nor the White City ends or can end here. "Luxury," Cole observes of the next painting in the cycle, "Destruction," "has weakened and debased. A savage enemy has entered the city. . . . Description of this picture is perhaps needless—carnage and destruction are its elements." At last, in "Desolation," "Daylight fades away, and the shades of evening steal over the shattered and ivy-grown ruins of that once proud city . . . the empire is extinct."[12]

The cyclic theme, and the elegiac tone, reconciles monumentality and ephemerality, turning them to an allegory of the futility of human efforts against time and mutability figured as social breakdown. Thus within its founding paradigm the White City is already implicitly marked for decay, deterioration, and, ultimately, ruin—a process vividly dramatized in the use of staff that, however practical for its purpose, began to decompose almost as soon as it was applied, its projected life of six years quickly compromised by Chicago's extremes of climate, and showed increasing signs of erosion throughout the summer of 1893; moreover the collective "story" of the Fair, as realized in journalistic and fictional narratives about it, almost invariably incorporate, with significant parallels to the Great Fire of 1871, the two fires, in November 1893 and July 1894, that brought thousands of spectators to the site and carried the great edifices away, leaving a vast plain of twisted rubble—and almost compulsively linking its destruction to a new "savage enemy," the legions of tramps encamped in the abandoned buildings.

That the White City was many things to many people goes without saying. But its grades of temporality, shaped by inference and interpretation of its various aspects—design, exterior covering, interior and exterior scale, interior structure, the contents of the exhibits themselves—point revealingly both to its role in the development of a popular urban culture and to the subtle social stratifications comprehended by its enormous public space. The by now facile symmetry, in the historical account, of a popular Midway and an elite White City, the idyll of the white Protestant imagination, a symbol of moral, racial, and sexual purity and respectable middle-class standing, with the increasingly bipolar industrial caste system, while broadly applicable, obscures the sense in which the White City was a site

Erosion of "staff" on the face of the Transportation Building. Courtesy of the Chicago History Museum (G1984:480, box 3; photographer Laban Deardorff).

Manufactures in ruins after the fires of summer 1894. Courtesy of the Chicago History Museum (ICHi-25231).

at which many sensibilities, of many origins and purviews, converged in the process of sense-making.

Such apparently different perspectives as the effete detachment of the well-traveled and self-involved *flaneur,* or the more naive delights of the amateur landscape painter or photographer, for example, each work to mitigate the fleeting grandeur of the buildings with more permanent visual images of them achieved psychologically, artistically, or technologically; a high-cultural elegiac vision of empire such as Cole's lingers to inform local contemporary narratives in which the Fair was embedded and which it actually played out; the assimilation of a popular, and provincial, Protestant eschatology with a popularized Spencerian notion of social and technical progress proved propitious for the eventual absorption of the century's strong millennial thrust into the commercial spectacle. These several viewpoints, taken together, seem to radiate, in spite of their apparently divergent end-points, from a common source, which is the general effort to reconcile the double consciousness of the White City's image and imagery with its acknowledged and visible impermanence and imitation, on the one hand, and on the other with its message of progress and power.

Hence the two prevailing views of the Fair, what broadly may be called the elite and vernacular, can be contrasted in terms of the temporal position to which each has assigned the White City. For the provincial visitor the Fair was a vision of an essentially utopian future, steeped in Protestant eschatology at once subverted by and displaced upon the wonders of technology and commerce. The elite response, however, that of the *flaneur* or grand traveler, belongs to a decadent romantic sensibility—a mere "passage," as Pater expressed it, "of impressions, images, sensations . . . the strange perpetual weaving and unweaving of ourselves"—luxuriously feeding on its own decay.[13] For the *flaneur* the White City, while palpably and materially present, was nevertheless dreamlike, elusive, shimmering in a border realm between object and subject, a contemplated perception almost purely subjective, a sensory text more durational than spatial—not a monument, but the ghost of one, to and of the past.

. . . .

The World's Columbian Exhibition, like its earlier counterparts in London, Paris, New York, and later in several American cities around the turn of the century, in general promoted economic development and mass consumption, and displayed economic and industrial strength in ideologically coherent spaces in which, from the perspective of the Anglo-

American ruling elite who were the principal investors, differences of race, class, and nationality were enlisted as elements in a grand narrative of social and industrial progress. Carrying the logic of its predecessor exhibitions to its ultimate paradoxical conclusion, the White City at Chicago at once epitomized and sabotaged the idea of progress by enfolding an emergent idea of time in a residual one, or to put this another way, by enclosing the embryonic body of the real future in the crumbling shell of an imaginary one. The past was subsumed by means of icons and relics already enshrined in the national mythology, such as the sword belonging to Judge John Hathorne of the Salem witch trials, a lock of Jefferson's red hair, or Miles Standish's pipe. Even the iconic Liberty Bell, guarded by police and decorated with flowers, rode on a truck spangled with soap ads.[14] Palpable artifacts of an ascendant species of power, on the other hand, many of them utterly unprecedented, shockingly novel, outsized, or magical—the first electric chair used at Sing Sing, the century's most extensive electrical network, towers of electric light, prodigious abundance of industrial or agricultural bounty, the forbidding Krupp cannon—opened to ordinary view backstage production and technical processes and massive wholesale accumulations from within what was both an engineering marvel and a simulacrum of old Europe.

In this respect the White City anticipates postmodern theme parks such as Disneyland, concentrating its touristic discourse of second-order signs in a dense environment of simulation, a kind of tour of the touristic, rallying its meanings on its own behalf. In *Scribner's, The Century Magazine,* and other highbrow periodicals that spread news of the Exhibition, including many of the pieces that form the research base of this essay, reports and pictures appeared directly alongside strictly touristic accounts of European journeys, lithographs of the White City placed on a continuum with images of Venice and Rome. Figured and represented in this fashion, the White City appears to magazine readers as an imploded domestic Grand Tour, with all of the social affiliations and cultural opportunities implied, animated by the activity of memory upon it.

Tourism, argues Dean MacCannell, is allied to postmodernity as "a kind of collective striving for a transcendence of the modern totality, a way of overcoming the discontinuity of modernity, of incorporating its fragments into unified experience."[15] It is, again, a Barthesian "second order" semiotic system, in which signs made meaningful in various social, historical, and cultural contexts, the tourist "sight" or site such as the Eiffel Tower or Ellis Island, are appropriated as signifiers in the special discourse of tourism, which is constituted by the totality of its literature, its art and photography, its commercial packages, and so on; the tourist seeks the sensation of recognition that arises when these displaced signs-as-signifiers find their referents in the tourist discourse—a moment sometimes reiterated to the point of transcendence when the actual sight/site, when we encounter it, at once summons its own representation and invalidates it, producing what Jameson calls a hallucinatory "breakdown in the signifying chain." Still further this moment of recognition, breaking through the tourist discourse itself, dips psychodynamically into the tourist's own reservoir of memory, imparting to the site, often in imperfect or ambiguous ways, its deepest significance, in which lies the quality of authenticity itself.[16]

These formulations would seem to describe both a range of responses to the White City as well as to its own idea of itself. Most telling, of course, is the fact that the production and circulation of images of the White City were strictly controlled, since it was the image of the site, quite literally the "sight," that was ultimately for sale. "Millions could not attend the Fair during the short season of its duration," reported George Herbert Markley, "yet it will be an insignificant minority in all countries who will not, at one time or another, have seen it photographically."[17]

The process was not left to chance. The Exhibition had contracted its own official photographers such as C. D. Arnold and Laban Deardorff, whose work has provided us with most of our images of the Fair, while two large commercial firms rented cameras at the gate. Personal cameras, without payment of a fee, were confiscated.[18] Surveillance was not limited to cameras. The easel painter F. Hopkinson Smith describes being stopped at the gate for attempting to carry in his artist's kit. The Guard's "orders were to seize everything that . . . might possibly reproduce any of the beauty and the glory of the white city within." Once having gained entry, moreover, Smith was again detained by an official who told him he could not paint without a permit.[19]

The authoritarian and inquisitorial character of the control exercised over images did not go unremarked by Teresa Dean, who saw it of a piece with a series of locked gates, barred doors, and "No Admittance" signs, but even more pertinently with the all-season passes issued to sixty thousand some odd people officially photographed for identification: "to be known," she wrote, "to the numerous Lord High Chancellors—collectively high, and individually very much higher—of the World's Fair, by number."[20]

In this officially managed production and reproduction of images we observe a tourist discourse, alongside a covalent system of surveillance, in the process of its formation, as well as the ultimate inadequacy of the image, once recognition of the site has been achieved semiotically, to represent the sight/site in the irreproducible intensity of its own being. "There's the unexpectedness of it!" exclaimed Walter Besant. "Never was anyplace so unexpected. The special correspondents and the illustrated papers have done their best to bring the place home to us: but, you see, description never describes . . . oh! you may point at once, on arrival, to the Woman's Building, or to the Manufactures Building; you recognize them because you saw the pictures in the Illustrated London News. Quite faithful pictures they were, yet—yet—did you expect, at all, what you see before you?"[21]

For many of its visitors, then, particularly for travel and nature writers, the site of the Exposition emerged as a storied, picturesque, or exotic region from which the writer might report, even if it would ultimately be visited by almost thirty million people. Cosmopolitan travel writers found no difficulty in treating the White City as an inventory of memories of European monuments, the psychological counterparts of the amateur photographer's collection of souvenir images. "Venice, Naples, Rome, Florence, Edinburgh, Athens, Constantinople," wrote Muirhead, "each in its way is lovely indeed; but in each view of each of these there is some jarring feature, something that we have to ignore in order to thoroughly lose ourselves in the beauty of the scene. The Count of Honor was practically blameless."[22]

"There are certain mastering impressions in one's life," recalled Will Low, searching for an analogy to the White City, "certain scenes which stamp the memory, like the priceless kakemono which the reverent Japanese withdraws from hiding when in the mood to enjoy it, rise obedient to one's thought in aftertime. Such a memory is that of a first sunny morning in Paris: a ride from the Madeline across the Place de la Concorde, along the Tuileries Gardens and the Louvre, across the Seine with the island and Notre Dame in the distance, and through older Paris to the gardens of the Luxembourg. Or, again, a certain moonlit evening in Florence, with the Duomo looming at the end of the street."[23]

This withdrawal into the stubborn, even petulant subjectivity of the elite decadent or exquisite traveler, heir of Baudelaire, Huysmans, and Wilde, rejects on aesthetic grounds the vulgarity of commercial appeals, the unseemly boast of industrial display, happily embracing, according to a doctrine that makes of all perception a kind of hallucination, artifice as such. "But your true *flaneur,*" insists M.G. Van Rensselaer, "feels a genuine interest in one thing—his own capacity for the reception of such new ideas and emotions as may be received with exertion of any kind. He does not care for facts or objects as such, or for what they teach, but he does care for their momentary effect upon his eyes and nerves. He does not crave knowledge, but he delights in thought of Chicago, because it suggests hard work at sight-seeing, and his idea is the easy work of holding himself passive yet perceptive."

If you go "in perfect freedom," Van Rensselaer wrote, "you will find such an idler's paradise as was never dreamed of in America before, and is not equaled anywhere in Europe today." He continues: "If, as I say, you go wholly consciousless,—not like a painstaking draftsman, but like a human Kodak, caring only for as many pleasing impressions as possible, not for the analyzing of their worth,—you will be delighted in the first place by the sight of such crowds of busy human bees, and the comfortable thought that, thank heaven! you are not as they. And what a setting for these crowds! What a panorama of beauty to drink in and dream over, and to carry home, in general views, and bits of detail, for the perceptive adornment of your mental picture-gallery!"[24]

Or as Besant put it, pointing superciliously to the bourgeois status of the entire enterprise, with its lurid paean to Progress, its naked hucksterism, and its cheap deceptions, "What I have desired all my life is an Exhibition without exhibits. . . . For the uncommercial drummer, the bagman without his bags, for one who is not in the least interested in machinery, processes, and the way in which things are made, there need be no exhibits at all and one can meditate undisturbed by the intrusion of exhibits, as long as he pleases, about and around and among the buildings, and the waters and the walks of the Fairy palaces beside the lake."[25]

Nevertheless, the comparatively accessible White City represented, particularly for its rural and small-town midwestern visitors, a radical democratization of the system of tourism, opening in simulated form opportunities for experiences—but experiences reduced, it must be added, to the purely visual—traditionally reserved for the privileged classes. "Oh, this dear old Fair!" cries a woman in Teresa Dean's report, tears streaming down her cheeks,

> What will I do without it?
>
> Only five days have I missed since the opening. They have been the happiest months of my life . . . we have taken chairs and have been rolled almost everywhere, it did not make much difference where, and have taken the electric launches, and the gondolas, and drifted up and down and around the lagoon. We have watched the sun set over the white domes and have waited for the illuminations to take away the gray,

weird mist of night. We have listened to the music, and to the trickling of the water from the fountains . . .

It has been the romance of our lives—journeying around the world. It was too grand to last. I came to-day for one more glimpse. The good-by is as sad as any I have known in all the years that I have lived.[26]

Naturally the opening of cultural privilege, as everywhere in tourism, implies the claim of social prestige. In Mary Catharine Crowley's didactic juvenile novel *The City of Wonders,* apparently constructed largely out of the Fair's official documentation, a middle-class family visits, among other locations, the Italian exhibit in the Liberal Arts Building, a collection of mosaic-framed mirrors, crystal vases, Venetian glass, marble statuary, bronzes, laces, and the like. "My dears," tutors Uncle Jack,

"such are the beautiful objects you would see in almost very shop window of St. Mark's Square in Venice, or through the streets of Florence."

"How foreign everything seems!" commented Ellen.

"Now we come to the English pavillion," said Uncle Jack. "The front is a reproduction of Hatfield House . . ."

"How delightful!" cried Ellen. "Can you not fancy, Nora, that we are traveling with the Colvilles?" . . .

"Yes, we shall be able to talk quite as if we had been abroad," declared Nora."[27]

At a deeper level, however, the White City initiated a psychological process where the various discourses of tourism intersect with the cultural systems in which their signs originally acquired meaning, stirring the compelling but often unconsummated process of recognition that lent to the White City its true mystery and grandeur, satisfying what John Ingalls called the "unspoken aspirations of the soul for unattainable beauty."[28] "Most of us, when we were young," wrote one visitor, "dreamed dreams and had glorious visions which in soberer years we dismissed as foolish and incapable of realization. It is only in this way I can account for the fact that the Fair impressed me with a strange familiarity. I felt sure I had seen it before, though I could not tell when or where. That splendid Court of Honor . . . all bore to me some incomprehensible affinity to something I had seen or read or dreamed in the present or a previous existence."[29]

This psychological neuralgia, defeating barriers to the willing suspension of disbelief that might have been erected against the Exhibition's explicit commercialism or the cheapness and ephemerality of its construction, paved the way for the transcendent experience most reported, not by international tourists, but by more naive midwestern visitors unprepared by tourist discourses for the encounter, and hence most vulnerable to it—"plain and unassuming people," as Dean wrote, whose "hearts . . . were always alive to the sentiment. Theirs were not the coldly critical eyes that saw 'staff' and effect. They lived contentedly in the magnificence while, perhaps, like everyone else, they could not always understand."[30]

"The class most largely represented in proportion to its numbers," wrote Robert Grant, "was the rank and file of the American people."[31] Walter Besant observed, "The great mass of people are Americans, and as might be expected, people of what in Europe they call the lower class . . . in a word, the Average People. It is for them that this Fair has been designed." He continues: "Let us remember that many of these people belong to that vast country west and south and northwest of Chicago which is newly settled, newly populated, and without noble or venerable buildings . . . here they see, for the first time, such buildings as they have never before imagined. These lines of columns; these many statues standing against the deep, blue sky; these domes; these carvings and towers are marvels reflected in the waters of the Lagoon . . . can they . . . ever forget the scene? Never. It will remain in their minds as the Vision of St. John—an actual sight of the New Jerusalem. . . . A new sense has been awakened in them."[32]

The White City evoked such quasi-religious or religious responses from sophisticated and unsophisticated visitors alike. Owen Wister was "dazzled to a standstill"; William James, in a letter to Henry, noted with bidirectional irony that in The White City people seem to "cast away all sin and baseness, burst into tears and grow religious under its influence."[33] Hamlin Garland, whose parents were pioneers in Iowa and South Dakota, described his mother's reaction to the White City: "Stunned by the majesty of the vision, my mother sat in her chair, visioning it all yet comprehending little of its meaning. Her life had been spent among homely small things, and these gorgeous scenes dazzled her, overwhelmed her, letting in upon her in one mighty flood a thousand stupefying suggestions of the art and history and poetry of the world. . . . At last utterly overcome she leaned her head against my arm, closed her eyes and said, 'Take me home, I can't stand any more of it.'"[34]

Clara Louise Burnham's Jack Van Tassel, mourning the death of his father while wandering amidst the White City palaces, catches a mysterious intimation. "Since such a miracle of beauty as now lay about him was possible in this lower world, might it not be indeed true . . ?" Gazing about him "with reverence and a species of awe," he finds that "The Court of Honor had given him his first approach to a realization of the possibilities of the Celestial City."[35]

Even as sophisticated an observer as Hubert Howe Bancroft could, with a stuffy circumlocution, make the religious inference: "As seen from the waters of the lake and especially at eventide, when their long array of columns and porticos, their lofty towers and stately domes, mirrored in the waters, stand forth against a glowing sky, they are in truth a revelation surpassed only by the inspired vision of him by whom was beheld the city not made with hands."[36]

That the World's Columbian Exposition was widely associated at the vernacular level with the sacred or secular end of history is suggested as well by some of the various proposals received by the directors in the planning process. A self-styled seer claimed the Fair had been foreordained from the beginning of time, while a self-appointed messiah offered to exhibit himself there. An inventor would bring the long-sought perpetual motion machine; a mathematician would square the circle; a cosmetician would transform a "wrinkled hag" into a beautiful young woman. At this level, millennial interpretations sink to the level of humbug—a fact to which L. Frank Baum, as a pioneer department store window-dresser and publisher of a popular magazine on the subject, might have been particularly sensitive. His City of Oz was an obvious allusion to The White City, which in the *Wizard of Oz* (1900) turns out to be only a mechanical fantasy, the cultural equivalent of the old traveling medicine show with its mendacious and pompous "doctor" and his ineffectual nostrums and elixirs—and perhaps connected in the same way to the wholesale distributor with his phalanx of commercial travelers. There's of course "no place like home" on the Kansas Farm, as the Exposition's most popular painting, Hovenden's "Breaking Home Ties" might suggest—but in Baum's many sequels Dorothy returns irresistibly to the glamorous Oz, for, humbug or not, no return is possible to the old preindustrial way of life, either for Dorothy or for Dreiser's Carrie.[37]

A condescending irony informs the work of two contemporary novelists who expose the provincialism of the business sensibility that erected the Exposition and that figures necessarily in the rhetoric surrounding it. "This is the American businessman's fair! The businessman—he did this!" boasts Will Payne's Mr. Arlington, a bank clerk who has risen to the eminent height of an officer in a coal company, making an "oratorical gesture" with his "short, fat arm," and adding, vaguely, "It shows what the Chicago businessman can do when he gives his attention to things of this kind—art, architecture, and so on!" Just what the White City may be to him, however, is not altogether clear: "All bore the air of something ancient, august, haunting the mind with an idea of power."[38]

Robert Herrick, in a conversation between his ex-governor Walton and the industrialist Colonel Stively in the novel *Waste,* who are recalling to one another the days when Chicago was only a frontier town set up on stilts in a swamp, outlines, with a kind of sad disparagement, the myth of cultural flowering out of capital growth, a book-club history of civilization that had justified the White City to its investors: "There was much talk about the significance of this great effort in Chicago, of the 'educational' and 'cultural' influence it must have on the nation; of the international aspect of these conglomerate gatherings of exhibits and peoples. . . . Growth, bigness, multiplicity, these they had witnessed, been a part of, struggled to achieve, and now came this soaring prodigal city of plaster, which to them seemed the acme of fine art, of beauty—the one accomplishment that hitherto had been lacking in their country."[39]

But even Herrick cannot entirely banish a certain ambivalence concerning the White City. He can chasten the elder generation (*Waste* appeared in 1924) only through two members of the younger, whose developing romance hinges on the innocent receptivity of the one as against the gritty (and *au courant*) realism of the other. "Oh Auntie—it's such a glo'rious day!" exclaims Walton's daughter Cynthia, leaning out of her hotel window on the morning after her arrival in the city. "I can see the Lake, miles and miles of it, all bluey gray and shiny. . . . And over there in the Park is a big white building. Immense'—some'thing like a Greek temple. . . . Oh, it's won'derful."

But young Jarvis Thornton, an architect, is skeptical. "You like this?" he asks her scornfully as they explore the Court of Honor, where "the somewhat grandiose scene of white buildings, gilded statues, dashing water, and human throngs thrilled her." The real Chicago, Thornton insists, "is back yards and tumbled down grimy houses and dingy brick blocks and dirty streets"—and offers to show her the Midway, which, he says, is "alot more like Chicago than all this white plaster stuff!" Yet when Cynthia opines that there must be more to Chicago than dirt and grime, Thornton concedes, revealing his own dedication to Burnham's vision, "Yes, there are the Parks—and the Future. In Chicago one lives mostly on the Future."[40]

"Vastness of all kinds oppresses the soul with sadness," Besant reflected.[41] What was dreamlike and transcendent, or, depending upon one's reading of its exterior materials, meretricious and false, could not but stagger the imagination nevertheless in the "stupendous" scale of the White City. Consider, by way of illustration, the enormous Manufactures and Liberal Arts Building. As the early visitor Clarence Bird testifies, it was "the unparalleled leviathan of the structural world"—the largest structure in history to that point.[42] To lay the floor required three million board-feet of lumber and five carloads of nails; the hinged iron trusses of the central hall, the largest in the world, weighed twelve million pounds. The central hall could seat three hundred thousand and the entire Russian army mobilized on its floor—that is, half a million soldiers.[43] The roof of the building was what Bird called "a noble nave" a third of a mile long, capable of "swallowing three coliseums," and comprehended a floor space of over forty-four acres.

The Manufactures and Liberal Arts Building challenged its documentors to record its magnitude in a variety of quantitative measures and scalar metaphors that called the nature of the building almost metaphysically into question, and, more than any of the other buildings on the Court of Honor, dislodged the appreciation of it from conventional markers of design and decoration towards a kind of modernist formalism whose root was the heroic engineering feat itself. Bird takes us to the giant footings upon which the building, like its lofty counterparts downtown, rested: "Each rounded base is hinged by a massive eyelet and a great tie-pin to the foundation-plate. Thus each truss arch (consisting of two parts like the span formed by the arms of a man raised over his head, with fingers touching), is pivoted at the bases; and when the halves meet in the peak they are again linked with a pin, the upper ends of the semi-arches, as well as the bases, being so rounded that with the changes in temperature their great masses may bridge or recede without cross-strain. The weight of each truss is 300,000 pounds; they were brought from afar, in pieces, and put together without an error in boring or bolt."[44]

While nearly every commentator remarks on the eclecticism of the building's ornamental exterior, for most its genuine beauty, as Bird's cathedral metaphor suggests, lies in its dramatic reconciliation of form to function. As Millet testifies, "The ugly forms of ordinary bridge builders' construction, which have hitherto been endured as necessary for rigidity and strength, have been largely eliminated, and graceful curves, well-balanced proportions, and harmonious lines unite to make the iron-work beautiful in itself"—promulgating the "great truth" that "the useful may be beautiful even in engineering."[45]

We can perhaps more immediately grasp the nature of these many and varied responses by comparing the White City to its contemporary counterparts. We have already invoked, as theme park, Disneyland; let us briefly consider it, then, in both material and scalar terms, with reference to the midwestern "Main Street" just inside the entrance gate. From Anaheim—a vast, diffuse, dim and featureless postmetropolitan automotive waste, we arrive by car at the postmodern equivalent of Jackson Park's featureless plain, the frontier of the even more arid and diffuse asphalt tundra of the Disneyland parking lot, whose margins dissolve and disappear into the smog that effaces the horizon on all sides. A shuttle bus, like a pilot boat though a fogbound harbor, ferries us to the gate; at this point we are almost literally nowhere.

But once we are through the gate, we are instantly commuted, as if supernaturally, onto a small-town midwestern Main Street of the 1880s or 1890s, realized in virtually indestructible polymer building materials, as spiffy as a brand-new tract house development, free of the merest trace of disrepair, decay, or dereliction, and thus frozen in time, continually policed of all refuse, and reduced, imperceptibly for most visitors, to five-eighths scale: a technique originally designed by Hollywood studios for the movie camera.

The sensation is one of physical seizure, as if by ten thousand invisible hands, and an accompanying sense of almost beatific relief, as if some constant physical pain or discomfort, so accustomed as to be almost forgotten, were to be suddenly removed, and a resulting exhilaration touches the scene with a kind of hallucinatory shimmer. From within the vast, dull, nameless oppression that is the postmodern urban landscape we have been suddenly released into a familiar world of which we are the undisputed masters; we seem to grow and expand physically; from a condition of temporal and spatial disorientation we are suddenly geographically, historically, and culturally, decisively situated, and endowed with a sense of personal power, social inclusion, and freedom from anxiety.

It is all, of course, an illusion. The visitor to the Columbian Exposition, whether farmer or *flaneur*, his sense of life perceptibly more confused and his social world at once contracting and expanding with increasing industrialization, metropolitanization, with the extension of railroad transport and telegraphic communications, his sense of personal significance concomitantly diminished historically and practically, moved typically on a train through increasingly complex, strange, forbidding, and unfamiliar rings of urban and industrial development until at the southern rim of the city at Jackson Park, on the lakefront, the accustomed scales, textures, functions, and forms of provincial existence were suddenly and violently eradicated and, as if by a kind of explosion, replaced by a visionary city of dreamlike proportions: but in visible, tangible, and familiar forms already imaginatively linked, either to upper-class European travel, or, through the imagery and iconography of evangelical Protestantism, to the consummation of history in the Celestial City.

If entrance to Disney's Main Street is a kind of rebirth, the moment of entry to the White City, then, was a kind of symbolic and virtual death: the sudden reduction of the visitor's body to a mere social particle in the face of an overwhelming creative power; its violent transport from congenial home circumstances to an exotic "Europe" more densely and essentially European than any actual capital could be; the absolute abolition of the sense of personal mastery, and, in its place, a sensation of ecstatic subjugation, as to a religious vision; a radical isolation, sense of powerlessness and insignificance, perhaps a kind of delirious happiness associated with what Lacan calls "the signifier in isolation." If on Disney's Main Street we are seized, situated, and enlarged, in the White City we are uprooted, dislocated, reduced, and dissolved.

In Disney's Main Street and the White City, then, a socially promulgated but interior vision has been in the manner of postmodern spectacle exteriorized and dramatized in ways—the reduction of scale on the one hand, the expansion of it on the other—that at once preserve the visionary quality and drive home its radically subjective character. If Main Street in modernist fashion encloses and concentrates subjectivity, the White City in postmodernist fashion must be said to have dispelled it.

If Main Street and the White City each in their different way invoke, arrest, accelerate, and project historical time, the interior spaces and the massive human and material aggregation they support concomitantly redistribute subjective experience into the sphere of public or official "history" and the rituals whose regular reiterations reinforce and sustain it. Only consider the situation of the White City visitor on Opening Day, overwhelmed by the vision of a Celestial City bafflingly realized in structures palpably unreal, who then passes into the Arts and Manufactures Building carrying the message of cosmic finality elaborated outside into the strangely familiar interior, part bridgework, part railroad terminal, part urban streetscape, where tens of thousands of souls have massed together in song, "a vast, whispering, rustling audience which could not hear."[46] Within the huge assembly hall, Daniel Gilman reported,

> perhaps one hundred thousand people—some say one hundred and fifty thousand—were gathered. . . . The military bands played while the cannon roared. An orchestra and chorus, said to number five thousand musicians, performed a new composition; but the notes of it were only faintly heard on the speakers' stand half-way across the building. A Methodist bishop and a Catholic cardinal, not unused to vast assemblies, offered up prayers, which we may hope were heard in heaven, but were not heard by most of the audience. The penetrating voice of a lady accustomed to public reading carried a musical note to a distance, but it was only a note and not a word. The Vice-President of the United States read an address, but his hearers might have been deaf for all the pleasure they received. Two orators of distinction spoke in succession,—men who are wont to appear upon the hustings,—but in the gallery directly opposite the platform their eloquence was that of the dumb appealing by gesture and attitude.[47]

It spite of Sullivan's remark that it had "set architecture back fifty years," the White City in fact structurally reduplicates the architecture of the Chicago School. It drew upon the basic innovation of the downtown skyscraper, the steel-truss frame, sheathed in staff as against terra cotta, and projected it horizontally in proportions that could never have been realized in stone. And, like the downtown skyscrapers, the buildings were for the most part literally floating on "spread" foundations, rather than set on pilings sunk to bedrock; the exceptions were the south half of the Liberal Arts Building and the northeast portion of Agriculture, which rested in a "crescent-shaped swale of muck."[48]

The Beaux-Arts style of Second Empire Paris that influenced the design has been misleadingly called "neoclassical," with emphasis laid on the late-nineteenth-century revival of classical forms. Its models however are, again, less Greek and Roman originals, or those of Italian Renaissance city-states, but, as Schulyer's painterly metaphor suggests, and steel-frame construction enables, merely their visual forms deployed in romantic dream-visions of ancient cities: massed piles of imperial power on a vast superhuman scale set against the background of a pastoral arcadia. Thomas Cole's work again supplies a clue to this aesthetic: Cole's "The Architect's Dream," painted in spring 1840 for New Haven architect Ithiel Town, presents an allegorical tableau of the history of the architecture of Mediterranean civilizations. It was, however, strongly influenced technically by scene and panorama painting, especially backlighting for theatrical effect, and by Louis Jacque

Mande Daguerre's diorama theaters in London and Paris, which used three-dimensional papier-mâché columns, pilasters, and other structures outside the proscenium to create a sense of "spatial progression."[49]

This Claudist integration of the idea of classical antiquity with an idealized pastoral landscape, with its increased emphasis on Roman models, the vast increase in scale, luminosity, mass, and antiquity, all in a sense "romanticized" and ultimately transfigured the neoclassical vision. Neoclassicism is a civic ideal, the architectural expression of the idea of polity; but the architecture of the Second Empire, as its name implies, was an emblem of imperial power, distant, impersonal majesty, and sublime grandeur. Projected imaginatively into a pastoral landscape, it drifts out of time in a limitless intellectual and finally subjective space, a dehistoricizing and depoliticizing form perfectly suited to emergent consumer capitalism with its faceless, ubiquitous, remote, and unaccountable authority on the one hand, and the passive, solitary observer, the consumer, on the other. "The Architect's Dream" places in the foreground, almost sitting on the frame, a solitary figure seen from behind, overawed by the architectural dreamworld rising before him.

The White City, then, as architecture, was made more of mental than of material stuff. And what of the exhibits within? The Liberal Arts Building, with its hardwood display cases, plate glass, velvet curtains, its decorative kiosks in the forms (to scale) of European churches, temples, guild halls, and so on, might have been a kind of cathedral of international trade; the Transportation Building, with its locomotives and ship models, might have been a kind of technological museum; Machinery Hall, with its power-driven lathes, woodcutting machines, power generators, engines, looms, presses, typesetters, canning machines, and so on, might have resembled a gigantic factory. In the "noise and confusion of Machinery Hall, writes Catharine Crowley, following her characters on a kind of factory tour, "It was interesting here to watch the processes of the arts of peace,—the manufacture of carpets, the looms with their mysterious patterns; and the weaving of ribbon, in which little boat-shaped shuttles, like toy skiffs, rode with a curtseying motion to and fro upon the waves of a many-tinted silken sea."[50]

The White City interiors, then, have been assimilated to factories, shops, stores, and even streets, at the same time as they have been transformed, by virtue of scale, into public, that is, into a kind of virtual "outdoor" space. In this respect they have been exteriorized, not unlike the "retail drama" of our own shopping malls—becoming in effect public thoroughfares, capable of housing entire structures such as tombs, churches, halls, and other architectural relics and the civic space of European culture, now consumed and supplanted by commercial space.

When the visitor enters Liberal Arts, wrote Ben Truman, "his impression will be that he is . . . visiting a city of palaces, temples, castles, arches, monuments, and hanging gardens. But his eye will necessarily be drawn toward a beautiful structure in the center of the building. The great central landmark, looking like a spire of a cathedral in alabaster, is the clock tower, 135 feet high." Its ringing chimes "sound like the music of heaven reverberating through the immense spaces of the building."[51]

As Bancroft notes, the interior aisles of Liberal Arts were named like city streets and lined with pavilions in which one might visit "the new German Reichstag, on the corners of which are towers surmounted by a dome, its apex in the form of an imperial crown, finished in burnished copper and overlaid with gold," or "the Bavarian pavilion, fronting on Columbia Avenue, and forming an integral portion of the German display. It is a temple-like structure, with arches, central portico, and roof, cornice, and frieze richly adorned with statuary and bas-relief." The Russian pavilion, following the thematic pattern, was built in "the ecclesiastic style of Russian seventeenth century architecture, with the principal entrance at the corner, in the form of a lofty arch surmounted by a tower."[52]

Not surprisingly this roofed city demanded reckoning with reference to the unroofed world. Of Liberal Arts, Bancroft wrote that "no better idea can be taken than to state that on its site could be erected about 500 residences, each with a lot of 25 by 100 feet, capable of accommodating in all at least 5,000 persons, and that with far less crowding than is felt in the more crowded portions of Chicago"—in effect transforming the floor of the building into an imaginary real estate development.[53]

Mary Crowley's characters recur to the same measures. When young Ellen observes that Liberal Arts is "a city in itself," her Uncle Jack replies fancifully that if it were possible to put the Rookery, one of the largest of Sullivan's great buildings, upon a mammoth wheelbarrow, and wheel it through the arch, it would not touch the sides or the top by several feet. "One thousand cottages" he adds, "could find room within these walls." Craning her neck to see the vast glass roof, Nora completes the idea by saying, "It is as if the building had a sky of its own."[54]

At the White City, then, inside is outside and outside is inside; private is public and public, private; commercial is civic and civic commercial. It is the ultimate festive inversion, turning the whole of industrial civilization into the content of a shallow and ephemeral cultural spectacle aligned to

Interior of the Manufacturers and Liberal Arts Building. Courtesy of the Chicago History Museum (ICHi-17532).

the purposes of commerce. Its second nature physically assimilated to first nature, capitalism had created its own firmament, and, in the darkened corridors of the Fisheries Building, its own inner sanctum, an exotic and mysterious Nature at the very heart of the industrial artifice:

> They advanced to a great curved corridor, behind whose crystal walls was a sea of green water, in which many kinds of fish were swimming about. In the middle of the Rotunda was an immense pool, from which rose a mass of rocks covered with mosses and lichens; and from between the crevices of the stones gushed forth bright streams, that fell sparkling amid the tangle of reeds and river plants below . . .

> . . . and arrived, finally, in the mysterious and exotic Egyptian building, at the "anemone grotto," where it was as if "they had been transported to an ocean cave."[55]

Kevin Lynch's *The Image of the City,* according to Fredric Jameson, argues "that the alienated city is above all a space in which people are unable to map (in their minds) either their own positions or the urban totality in which they find themselves: grids such as those of Jersey City, in which none of the traditional markers (monuments, nodes, natural boundaries, built perspectives) obtain. . . . Disalienation in the traditional city, then, involves the practical reconquest of a sense of place, and the construction or reconstruction of an articulated ensemble which can be retained in memory and which the individual subject can map and remap."[56]

From this perspective, Disney's Main Street is a kind of hypospace in which we remap our position, accommodating to its reduced scale, by moving nostalgically in history. In effect we have returned to the days of our collective but personalized childhood, finding that everything "seems smaller." John Portman's Bonaventure Hotel, as Jameson has explained, by contrast "aspires to being a total space, a complete world, a kind of miniature city" that corresponds to a "new collective practice, a new mode in which individuals move and congregate." Portman's buildings, according to Jameson, transcend "the capacities of the individual human body to locate itself," a symbol and analogue of "the great global multinational and decentered communicational network in which we find ourselves caught."[57]

Yet the White City, too, would seem to have aspired to become such a total space, a city unto itself, one that "reconquers" the surrounding urban grid with a utopian projection of it. If Disneyland shrinks the movie-studio Main Street for cinematic representation, the White City shrinks us, drawing us into a gigantic outdoor pageant-set that palpably and compellingly, but temporarily, even fleetingly, for the merest moment, realizes in steel and iron cloaked in staff the visionary seaport capitals of landscape painters such as Claude and Cole, ancient imaginary empires that are but compensatory historical fantasies designed to accommodate psychologically already achieved social transformation. Inside, however, a concomitant reduction in scale would have restored a sense of mastery over the historical legacy of Europe-as-tourist oyster, colonized in effect by the colonized.

The cognitive disorientation, moreover, that Jameson associates with the postmodern hyperstructure seems to have been equally characteristic for visitors to the White City. "In estimating the scope of the design," wrote Bancroft of Liberal Arts, "an observer would find himself at a loss for standards of measurement, for here the scale was so vast that there was nothing upon which to base a comparison. . . . To compare it with other buildings, either in Europe or America was impossible, for there were none in existence; and to compare it with those on the grounds would be equally impossible, for adjacent structures, covering several acres of floor space, were dwarfed and dominated by this mammoth edifice."[58]

Teresa Dean relates the stories of many people exhausted and lost, especially elderly people, including the story of a woman who thinks she's lost her children because she can't distinguish one corner of the Liberal Arts building from another. The wonders of technology, moreover, in Dean's account, touch most movingly upon older sensibilities anchored in the very structures those technologies would ultimately erode. She tells of a "gray-haired" old man who, hearing nearby the strains of "Annie Laurie," but unable to locate the source of them, approaches one of the Columbian guards: "'Them words sound sweet to me. It is a long time since I heard that'ere song. Ken you tell me who it is? I would like—I would like—of course I don't 'spose I could—but I would like ter thank some one for singing it. It goes right hum. You see, my darter—."

When the sympathetic guard attempts to instruct him on the wonders of the telephone, which can transmit a voice from New York, the old man first thinks it a joke. "When I passed on," Dean writes, "he was still asking questions. I heard him ask if he could hear his son talk in New York if he should come up to the telephone. The guard said 'yes.' His face lighted up, and I knew he had not heard the son's voice in a good many years."[59]

Foucault offers us, I think, some insight into the historical role of such an imperial spectacle as the White City. In his account of the Napoleonic moment in European history he writes:

> The importance, in historical mythology, of the Napoleonic character probably derives from the fact that it is at the point of conjunction of the monarchial, ritual exercise of sovereignty and the hierarchical, permanent exercise of indefinite discipline. He [the monarch] is the individual who looms over everything with a single gaze which no detail, however minute, can escape. . . . At the moment of its full blossoming, the disciplinary society still assumes with the Emperor the old aspect of the power of spectacle. As the monarch who is one and the same time a usurper of the ancient throne and the organizer of the new state, he combined into a single symbolic, ultimate figure the whole of the long process by

which the pomp of sovereignty, the necessarily spectacular manifestations of power, were extinguished one by one in the daily exercise of surveillance, in a panopticon in which the vigilance of intersecting gazes was soon to render useless both the eagle and the sun.[60]

It does not require too much interpolation to understand the pertinence of this formulation to the situation at the end of the nineteenth century in America, where the residual but pervasive presence of the imagery of the Protestant imagination, as well as more fully secular and class-inflected cultural ideas represented by old Europe and the Grand Tour, could be deployed by corporate and governmental power, "at the moment of its full blossoming," to posit a quasi-religious totalitarian vision, its surveillance and reproduction fully administered and controlled, of the end of history in a capitalist utopia.

This cultural statement—corporate capitalism as imperial power as consummation of history—through the sad relics of the City Beautiful movement, is still evident on Chicago's public face. The city's lakefront facade of boulevards, parks, and monumental buildings such as Shedd Aquarium, Soldiers' Field, the Field Museum, and of course the Museum of Science and Industry (the Exposition's Palace of Fine Arts), its public works, which continue the Beaux-Arts theme and even project onto the skyscrapers of the twenties, such as the Wrigley Building and Tribune Tower, are the cultural insignia of the city's corporate and technological might articulated as a Mediterranean imperial civilization mediated as a dream-vision, at once nostalgic and futuristic, an effort to reconcile the disorienting and inexorable thrust of technological and industrial development with a psychological attachment to the only imaginative resources available, before the decisive emergence of modernism in art, to realize such change as cultural.

The White City was not unprecedented; its original might have been found in the tropical capitals (Chicago's summer climate was regarded as such by Europeans) of France and Spain—architectural spectacles addressed to subject populations—in which staff had served the imperial design: Burnham himself was later to have a hand in the design of the capitol at Manila. "Staff is an expedient borrowed from the Latin countries, and is much cultivated in South America," Bird instructed his readers. Chicago was itself a kind of internal colony, its patterns of settlement and finance emanating from New York, New England, and London, driving its post-fire growth and shaping the attitudes of the men and women who planned the Exhibition.[61] In this sense the White City, especially given the central role of photography in promulgating, controlling, and distributing its image, may be regarded as a vast advertisement, enlisting cultural nostalgia, class aspiration, religious piety, and even haute bourgeois *ennui* on behalf of expanded markets, increased commerce, improved industry, and, ultimately, the greater concentration of money and power fostered by industrial capitalism.

And yet, as we have argued, this realized image of the consummation of history was not only manifestly ephemeral, but bound up with an elegiac narrative in which its own eventual ruin was already guaranteed. Like the landscape garden, a realized picture, the White City translated the formally insulated imaginative participation of art into a practical encounter secured by fictionality: which is to say, the visitor knows, and must know, that the buildings aren't real—for if they were they would become a display of technical, social, and political power nightmarish and horrifying in extent. In this respect the form, as against the function, of staff, becomes more evident: the buildings must be seen, instantly and on the visible surface, to be temporary, and, in a word, fake.

Like Cole's *The Course of Empire* or "The Architect's Dream," the White City was by implication an allegory; but it was also a sort of cathexsis, like the Portman hotel, of what was to become the "cognitive orientation" to the colossal crypto-natural economic/political/technological environment of corporate capitalism. Unlike Cole's paintings, however, it did not enjoy the formal condition of fictionality; thus at the same moment that the White City announced the new capitalist hegemony, it pronounced it humbug and predicted its ultimate demise.

To summarize, the White City projected a vernacular Protestant dream-vision that it at once exploited for eschatological meaning and exposed as a fantasy; it inverted private and public spaces, reducing the old European *civis* to the content of a commercial spectacle understood, and intended to be, hallucinatory. Like much of the high art of the late nineteenth century, it called upon the available resources of the cultural imagination, in the moment just preceding the advent of modernism, to figure Western society's most violent discontinuity as the telos of a received historical narrative that begins in Greece and ends, like the railroad, at Chicago.

What distinguishes the White City, however, is that it betrays the futility of that effort, the inadequacy of the received account to incorporate the historical rupture; the White City in effect bids farewell to the vision that summoned it, looks forward to its own ruin, and prepares the level plain of the Jackson Park muck upon which to erect a new but unknown world—a ghastly revelation of the expiration of what the cultural imagination had required ten centuries to create.

But it also promised metamorphosis. The meaning of the White City lies in the imaginary and actual epiphany that its whole existence implied, which was the moment when its plaster skin would ultimately slough off to reveal a new world, the modern, and modernist, world, of naked steel girders making bizarre designs against a furnace-reddened industrial sky. In this respect its architectural message, like that of the skyscrapers to the north, is also an ecological one. Certain architectural themes such as the Roman arch or classical column remained consistent as building fronts changed from stone or brick—which signify monumentality, stability, and power—to iron; but the conspicuous use of iron and steel in achieving these forms announced the ascendancy of the new sources of that power in mining, energy, heat, combustion, and fossil fuels—a fundamental shift in the material basis of society. If Richardson's Romanesque banks, houses, and stores were redolent of fortresses erected against immigrants and restive workers, and of traditional craft masonry, the iron fronts of the steel-frame skyscrapers belong to a new industrial world of foundries, boilers, coal-burning furnaces, machine-fabrication, mass production, and alienated labor.

If, however, as Debord argues, the image is the "final form of commodity production," then the "staff" of the White City facades is on a continuum with commercial advertising, housing and clothing and life "styles," and finally with the near total videoization of contemporary social and political life. As Edward Bellamy observed, "the underlying motive of the whole exhibition, under a sheer pretense of patriotism," was "business, advertising with a view to individual money-making." The Exposition inaugurated on an unprecedented scale the effort of a business elite to enforce what Henry Adams called the "capitalistic, centralizing, mechanical" forces abroad in society. But it went a step farther. If it is the case that the White City was designed to end in a photograph, the civilization it inaugurated has literally ended in an image, a society that consumes its own institutions on television and computer screens. In a sense, then, the White City already prophesied, at the apex of its aesthetic effect, the city of Chicago a century later, where in Grant Park a homeless man lies clutching himself on the seat of an elegant Beaux-Arts bench where wafer-thin plates of disintegrating concrete expose the rusted iron skeleton beneath, as if to suggest that the whole city, and capitalism itself, were sheathed, ideologically speaking, in "staff."

Traces of the hegemonic spirit of the Exposition were with us at least until the 1950s, the constituent elements of a national hagiography and iconography of social and technological progress, patriotism, and technological and commercial supremacy. By the time of America's defeat in Vietnam and the Arab oil embargo, when, in David Harvey's analysis, Fordist production gave way to a new capitalist regime of "flexible accumulation," this spirit had run its course, only to be revived on the political right in the form of a business agenda that, like the White City itself, is advanced under cover of religious and political shibboleths.

"And the buildings themselves have gone into mourning," wrote Teresa Dean near the end of the summer of 1893, "for 'the days that have been, and shall be no more.' They are grey and grimy. . . . Perhaps the leafless trees and the absence of contrasting colors have something to do with the apparent accumulation of Chicago coal dust, which seems to have appropriated what a little while ago was so brilliant and pure; but surely, now, the White City needs a bath of soap and water."[62]

But the White City's apocalypse was to come by fire, not water. On October 28, 1893, the next-to-last day of the Exposition, Mayor Carter Harrison was shot dead by a lonely, crazed civil servant, almost a modernist figure in himself—later to be defended by Clarence Darrow on the then novel claim of insanity—who imagined that the mayor had passed him over for a city appointment. On the last day of the Fair, on the Midway, one writer recalls, "brawling and lewd crowds, waving whiskey bottles and signs, rioted until the small hours," while at City Hall "weeping processions . . . viewed the Mayor's bier . . . he was buried, and at the same time the dream-city on the lake's edge ceased to be."[63]

The sad unraveling of the World's Columbian Exposition, far more than the event itself, exposes some of the understructure of life in Chicago as it was actually being lived. With the closing of the Fair and the descent of a particularly cold winter (as, to Carrie Meeber's distress, only in Chicago can winters be), the streets were clogged with the unemployed and homeless—beggars, peddlers, and tramps, many of whom took shelter in White City buildings that the city could not afford to maintain. "The most spectacular proof," wrote Hull-House culture worker Julia Lathrop, "of the poverty entailed upon Chicago by the general business depression of 1893, and locally by the human debris left by the World's Fair, could be daily seen during all the severer months of the winter of 1893 and 1894. It was a solid, pressing crowd of hundreds of shabby men and shawled or hooded women, coming from all parts of a great city . . . standing hour after hour with market baskets high above their heads, held in check by policemen, polyglot, but having the common language of their persistency, their weariness, their chill and hunger."[64]

Nothing perhaps more starkly exposes the grip of Cole's elegiac narrative upon the imagination of the urban elite than its tendency to associate and even conflate impending social and economic apocalypse with the literal fires that destroyed the White City. "About dusk on the night of January 8th," Bancroft writes, "a fire broke out in the casino and thence swept across the peristyle to the music hall . . . by a sudden shifting of the wind the flames were carried towards the Manufactures Building, and through its glass roof and the clear-story beneath, a shower of firebrands fell among cases packed with exhibits."

> On the evening of the 5th of July some lads at play near the terminal station observed a gleam of fire within; and entering the depot tried for several minutes to stamp it out; but these few minutes were fatal. . . . It was a hot summer day; the buildings were dry as tinder; water was scarce; the fire engines far away, and a fierce gale was blowing from the southwest. . . . By the time the engines were fairly at work the terminal station was one flaming mass, and leaping across the plaza the fire had seized on the Administration Building, the dome of which fell with an appalling crash, covering with burning cinders and brands the Mining and Electricity buildings, both of which were quickly ablaze. To these were added, a few minutes later, the halls of Manufactures and Transportation. . . . Meanwhile from the railroad terminus the conflagration had spread to the Machinery and Agricultural buildings, the one being utterly destroyed and the other damaged almost beyond recognition.

It was in the loss of the Manufactures Building, however, that Bancroft found both his "historical mythology" and its political theme:

> Almost as soon as the fire laid hold of it the vast semi-circular roof fell in. . . . Then it was seen that the whole interior was aflame, while from hundreds of windows tongues and jets of flame cast far on the dim waters of lake and lagoon their red and fearsome glare. Presently the frame began to totter; one after another the huge facades fell inward with a deafening roar, and of this mammoth temple of the Exposition there was nothing left, save for the lurid skeleton of a wall. It was now the time of the railroad strike, and as the conflagration reflected in the sky was seen by neighboring cities inland and on the shores of Michigan, mes-

> sages of inquiry came pouring in by the hundreds. Fresh in the minds of many was the great fire of 1871, and with anarchy and lawlessness still unchained, it was feared that the rabble was inflicting on Chicago a repetition of that dread disaster. As to the origin of the conflagration nothing definite was ascertained, though both were believed to be the work of incendiaries, probably of the vagrant horde which infested the streets by day and slept at night wherever darkness overtook them.[65]

It was "a fit apotheosis," wrote Robert Herrick, the "dream of beauty made of plaster" reduced "to ashes and twisted steel. . . . Those spectres of threatening disaster, unemployment and panic, that had haunted the imagination of its leaders during the summer of 1893 had arrived to take possession. Thousands of idle, starving people prowled the ice-cold streets and slept in the filthy alleys. Violence broke forth. Once more Chicago became the frontier village, unkempt and unsafe."[66]

Reflecting once more on the White City, the Beaux Arts tradition generally, and especially upon its broader impact upon the City Beautiful Movement and even, in decorative form, upon the steel-frame building, I am struck by the fact that the assertion of imperiality that all of these forms make, with its inevitable historical gesture towards an idealized but fallen Rome, Venice, or Constantinople, is the very thing that lends to the Chicago cityscape, then and until very recently, the strange and in many ways sublime forlornness that is the real subject of this essay and, I believe, the essential aspect of the elegiac White City.

Its hollow stylistic gesture, unrooted in the practical challenges of architectural science, while attempting to annex a history, both exposes its own want of history and saturates the field of temporality, in effect arresting or killing it; at the same moment that it animates a narrative whose implicit end is its own ruin it forecloses the possibility of all successive narratives, which can only be "inscribed" upon the surface of an appearance.

That is what is so profoundly melancholy about the city that Burnham proposed, one that only went out of existence, culturally speaking, within our own lifetimes. The urban landscape has since mostly succumbed to redevelopment catastrophes, while the new, emergent city, with its corporate trophy buildings and commuter archipelagoes is like the rest of urban America one of the outposts—and there are now *only* "outposts"—of global finance capitalism, pitched amidst the ruins, human and otherwise, of America's gloriously failed urban empire.

7 THE ANNUAL DANCE

FESTIVITY AND CULTURE IN "THE DEAD"

"Here we are," says Gabriel Conroy, standing at the head of the festive table, to the upturned faces of the guests at the Misses Morkan's annual dance, "gathered together for a brief moment from the bustle and rush of our everyday routine."[1] The transient moment, the interruption of ordinary routines and suspension of ordinary cares, the gathering together—these are the elements of festivity; and with them come the exaltations of abundance, the intoxications of plentitude, the stimulus of sociality, and, with music, story, song and dance, and other instruments of celebration and commemoration, the stirrings of desire, the remembrance of loss, and as Gabriel will find in the hours before dawn, the dissolution of identity and the premonition of death.

"Everybody who knew it came to it, members of the family, old friends of the family . . . and never once had it fallen flat. For years and years it had gone off in splendid style, as long as anyone could remember . . ." The Misses Morkan's annual dance, the subject of Joyce's story "The Dead," is, for its guests, as regular and perpetual as the holiday with which it is associated—which is the Feast of the Epiphany, a celebration of the revelation of Christ's divinity that comes at the end of the Christmas holiday season on January sixth.[2] And fixed at its center, in one of the story's most scrupulously attentive descriptive passages, in a prose dense with appetite and glimmering with the festive mood, is the treasury of all festivity, its own hoard or plenum, a great feast:

> A fat brown goose lay at one end of the table and at the other end, on a bed of greased paper strewn with sprigs of parsley, lay a great ham, stripped of its outer skin and peppered over with crust crumbs, a neat paper frill round its shin and beside this was a round of spiced beef. Between these rival ends ran parallel lines of side-dishes: two little ministers of jelly, red and yellow; a shallow dish full of blocks of blancmange and red jam, a large green leaf-shaped dish with a stalk-shaped handle,

> on which lay bunches of purple raisins and peeled almonds, a companion dish on which lay a solid rectangle of Smyrna figs, a dish of custard topped with grated nutmeg, a small bowl full of chocolates and sweets wrapped in gold and silver papers and a glass vase in which stood some tall celery stalks. In the centre of the table there stood, as sentries to a fruit-stand which upheld a pyramid of oranges and American apples, two squat old-fashioned decanters of cut glass, one containing port and the other dark sherry. On the closed square piano a pudding in a huge yellow dish lay in waiting and behind it were three squads of bottles of stout and ale and minerals, drawn up according to the colours of their uniforms, the first two black, with brown and red labels, the third and smallest squad white, with transverse green sashes.

In a narrative otherwise concerned with the sounds of speech, of dresses that sweep across the floor and heels that clack upon it, with a recurrent juxtaposition of the interior brightness and warmth of the Morkans' hospitable upstairs flat and the cold, darkness, and snow outside, and with the mercurial turns of Gabriel Conroy's nervous temper, this passage brings the tempo of the narrative to a virtual halt, arresting its momentum with a system of visual symmetries and the imagery of a secular, even an official celebration. As the narrator's gaze moves from end to end of the table, and to the top of the piano, the delicious banquet of meat and drink, fruit and nuts, spices, condiments, and sweets, the feast itself takes on a transparency through which, in a veil of metaphor, we seem to be on a kind of sunny parade-ground, on a municipal or national holiday, where the "parallel lines" of what could be football teams, marching bands, or uniformed soldiers oppose one another at their "rival ends," attended by "little ministers" of petty officials; the "squat old-fashioned decanters" suggest the distinguished mayoralty or councilmen, while squads of bottles, in uniforms of different colors, the whites traversed with green sashes, virtually march across the piano-top like police or firemen in ceremonial costume, displaying with a kind of military dignity patriotic colors across their chests. Indeed the dinner itself becomes a kind of parade, as the guests sing a "jolly gay fellows" to their hostesses, with "Freddy Malins acting as officer with his fork on high."

This heavily laden board is at once a harvest of the natural produce of the British Isles and its colonial dependencies and appendages, extending as far east as Turkey and as far west as New England, a concentration of the otherwise modest purchasing power of the three generous spinster ladies who sustain a precarious living with music lessons and niece Mary Jane's "organ in Haddington Road," and, through the aunts, Gabriel's deceased mother's sisters, a cornucopia of filial devotion and care. At the same time it is the traditional Christmas spread, with the voluptuous roast goose on its throne, and yet a kind of official pageantry, gaily regimented with martial metaphors, in celebration of civil and political order, of authority renewed, hierarchy displayed, of prosperity secured and of stability long guaranteed by superior force: in every sense a cosmopolitan and imperial, not local and parochial, board. The feast, then, is at once, and paradoxically, the heart of a festive celebration rooted in Irish traditional culture and a martial display of the British Imperium that has conquered and still reigns over it.

Thus Gabriel, we learn, "likes nothing better than to find himself at the head of a well-laden table," and plunges his fork firmly into the fowl, distributing first, under the auditory scrutiny of a narrator who seems to record every utterance no matter how apparently trivial, a "slice of the breast" to Miss Furlong, who conspicuously repeats his phrase. Gabriel is in his element, and with gallantry and charm undertakes his festive duty in a language that, in the ever-unfolding subtext laid like mosaic in the hard surface of the narrative, at once puffs him up with little pretensions and intimates the ultimate dissolution of them. "If anyone wants a little more of what vulgar people call stuffing," he announces, "let him or her speak," but upon the urging of the others turns to his own supper saying "kindly forget my existence, ladies and gentlemen, for a few minutes."

The festive mood is of course infectious, and in the first moments of their repast a theme of hilarity, of which the narrative itself somewhat breathlessly partakes, prevails:

> There was a great deal of confusion and laughter and noise, the noise of orders and counter-orders, of knives and forks, of corks and glass-stoppers. Gabriel began to carve second helpings as soon as he had finished the first round without serving himself. Everyone protested loudly so that he compromised by taking a long draught of stout for he found the carving hot work. Mary Jane settled down quietly to her supper but Aunt Kate and Aunt Julia were still toddling round the table, walking on each other's heels, getting in each other's way and giving each other unheeded orders. Mr. Browne begged of them to sit down and eat their suppers and so did Gabriel but they said there was time enough, so that, at last, Freddy Malins stood up and, capturing Aunt Kate, plumped her down on her chair amidst general laughter.

But in all human celebrations, all fleeting, all undertaken in anticipation of their end, there is a kind of arc that leads from the gladness and relief of the opening moment, when care is put behind us, to the apogee at which, with the morrow lingering below the horizon, that happiness seeks with a kind of recklessness to escape its own demise with feats of intoxication and heedless small adventures, to the inevitable letdown, when we grieve again over expended sorrows and allow sleep and dreams to carry us over the awful isthmus back to the waking workaday world. For festive holiday occurs on an axis that turns every week or every year upon the same bearing in time and place as it turned the last, swaddling itself in the consciousness of time and mutability at the same moment as it seeks relief from them.

It is not entirely clear what Gabriel is thinking of—perhaps of his dead mother—when in the midst of his speech he alludes momentarily to "sadder thoughts," "thoughts of the past, of youth, of changes, of absent faces that we miss here tonight," though we may read into these lines, retrospectively, the eruptions from the past life of his wife Gretta that shape the end of the story. But along with him the entire party, just at the height of its conviviality, has been overtaken by a spirit of reminiscence. Bartell D'Arcy, the tenor turned by his very name into a kind of a fop, defends, against the combined sentiments of the elder hosts and guests, the reputations of contemporary opera singers, naming Caruso among them, and explains away the lackluster character of Dublin opera by locating the centers of high culture on the Continent: in London, Paris, Milan. Kate and Julia meanwhile, and the incorrigible old Mr. Browne, are stuck on the great old days of the Dublin music scene, when boys would dismiss the horses and pull the prima donnas behind them in their carriages. Aunt Kate unearths the forgotten name of one "Parkinson," an English tenor whom she has over the years nursed a hitherto unrevealed affection, for "the purest tenor voice that was ever put into a man's throat."

By a kind of shadow thrown over it by recollection of the past, the conversation, even as the sumptuous pudding is set before them, grows, as the narrator notes, "lugubrious." Mrs. Malins has made reference to her son Freddy's impending retreat—for the cure, we assume—to the monastery at Mount Melleray, where the monks, we learn, never speak, and sleep in their coffins. Mr. Browne, the Protestant, is hard put to understand this, and expresses a cantankerous, somewhat petulant, and not altogether honest disbelief, wondering that a spring bed wouldn't do them as well as a coffin. Kate's unamplified insistence that it is simply the "rule of the order" does little to clarify the problem for him, and Freddy's brief awkward discourse on the concept of the remission of sin is ineffectual; the subject is finally "buried in a silence of the table" as Mary Jane piously reminds the group, in a phrase that becomes the eschatological core of Joyce's magisterially orchestrated conclusion to the story, that the coffin "is to remind them of their last end."

Indeed, as its very title indicates, "The Dead" takes the pulse of festivity at its most vital and sensitive spot, where each surge of life it sends forth intimates the deep sources of our existence and expires in a momentary pause that contains the whole expanse of our mortality. There is a quality in the narrative—its auditory surface, perhaps (from which the brightly visualized feast is a significant departure), buzzing with voices, the tinkling of the silverware, the "distant music" of the piano in a farther room, the sweeping of skirts across the floor—and its tendency to linger upon moments framed by joviality, or mirth, or by anxiety, such as Freddy's arrival, Gabriel's exchange with Miss Ivors, or his horseplay in the downstairs hall at their departure, or the hilarious confusion with the cab driver, which lend to the entire story the quality of memory and touch it throughout with a tint of expiration and obsolescence, right up to the moment just before dawn that Gabriel imagines himself with his hat in his lap at Aunt Julia's wake.

In fact, as Richard Ellmann suggests, Joyce in "The Dead" is remembering not his own, but his parents' generation, and the annual parties at the house of his great aunts Mrs. Callahan and Mrs. Lyons, and Mrs. Callahan's daughter Mary Ellen. "There every year," Ellmann writes, "the Joyces who were old enough would go, and John Joyce carved the goose and made the speech. Stanislaus Joyce says that the speech of Gabriel Conroy in 'The Dead' is a good imitation of his father's oratorical style."[3] Joyce was born in 1882; John Kelleher, with clues from *Ulysses,* places the party in the early 1890s.[4]

Perhaps in the fashioning of "The Dead" Joyce's imagination has been immersed in the memory of family and childhood, in the compelling mystery of his own origins, mysterious because it is a narrative generated out of nonbeing, out of the unknown and the unintelligible, before a coherent social identity has formed to dress the still immature and naked personality. That Joyce has perhaps projected certain aspects of his own time and circumstances, particularly his marriage to the uneducated Galway country girl Nora Barnacle, and the epoch of the Irish Revival, into his parents lives, is perhaps prescient for a story about festivity, for festivity is a crisis of identity. It is in the social nexus, with its welter of functions, roles, relationships, and affiliations, and the several registers of education, class, culture, and other systems that articulate them, that we have our social identity, and precisely the suspension of these structures that marks the festive occasion. In festivity, identity is consistently at issue, at once dissolving and coalescing, shifted into a contested realm where make-believe and play, that is, fictional masks and "parts," and symbolic social rituals such as pageantry and dance take the place of the ordinary roles and functions from which genuine social life is constituted. In festivity the sutures of social identity, destabilized by the continual flexion of inversion, parody, fantasy, and sheer plenitude, separate to expose the interior of the deeper human drama of which society as we have it is but one transient manifestation.

Festivity is a psychosocial vortex around and into which the primordial energy of culture flows as glowing matter into a collapsing star. As a literary theme it provides, in "The Dead," an occasion in which the naked personality can confront itself in a cultural as well as in a psychological dimension, in which culture is deposited at levels of the psyche far deeper than individual identity or even ordinary consciousness can penetrate, where identity and society, psyche and culture, are in effect one, the substance and the medium of an unconscious at once historical, political, and personal. If we habitually associate festivity with ethnomimetic or "folk" culture, indeed look to festivity for enactments and representations of folk culture and tend to identify festivity with folk culture, it is because festive occasions recapitulate structurally, but temporarily, the relationships between official and unofficial, disciplinary and adisciplinary cultures that for folk cultures are mandated by the actual structures of class and power. The crisis of identity characteristic of festivity is in folk society a persistent condition normalized by a cultural life whose very authority, as we have suggested, consists in its excorporation. The festival feast, moreover, a harvest of natural plenty, assimilates itself symbolically to the cultural plenum that play and make-believe, song and dance, open to view—a connection that we implicitly acknowledge in our "treasuries" of folk song and "harvests" of folktale and, indeed, in our folk festivals, as if culture were at once a natural resource and a treasure, like diamonds or truffles: festivity is a revisiting and renewal of the ethnomimetic ground of culture.

"There are two ways of conceiving" the term "folk," writes folk art specialist Zo Za-Yong: "One is the general concept of 'common folk' in terms of social structure; and the other is the image of what may be called the naked man, man as a humble being on earth. It is not just country farmers who feel childlike happiness on New Year's Day or at Christmas. There are times when everyone wants to escape from his social position, high or low, and go back to being just a plain naked creature."[5]

This assimilation of the "naked man" to "country farmer," and the association of both to the happiness of children on feast-days, may perhaps be odious to social science, which rejects the ethno- and sociocentric tendency of ordinary bourgeois people to call folk cultures "childlike" and to identify them persistently with peasantry. Nevertheless, this metaphorical triad—festivity, peasantry, and childhood—points suggestively to a particular psychosocial territory, whether framed by an annual ritual, by social hierarchy and privilege, or by the life-cycle itself, in which ethnomimetic processes, in their dialectic with social institutions, carry the soul on the one hand towards the artifices of social construction and on the other on a blind tack towards the erotic sources of being; and it is a relationship that points to the system of metaphors through which Joyce in "The Dead" has traced this dialectic in Gabriel Conroy.

In "The Dead" folk culture and personality contend both on the bright, buzzing social surface and in the shade-ridden underworld of Gabriel's soul, "that region where dwell the vast hosts of the dead," in which he finds himself when frustration, disappointment, and fatigue have undermined his capacity to keep his social mask and self-definition intact. It is precisely Gabriel's dilemma, and that of Irish society itself, that in laboring under the twin yokes of English colonialism and the Catholic Church that it remains politically and culturally in a condition of historical becoming—at once mired in and vivified by the old enchanted communal world from which it both needs desperately to free itself and is profoundly reluctant to surrender—or, where it has surrendered it, registers its bereavement in the form of a politically "progressive" Gaelic revival movement. It is not in any case Shelley's veiled Demogorgon, Freud's faceless Id, or Eliot's featureless wasteland that Gabriel encounters when in the course of the evening his pretensions to the status of the modern European bourgeois give way to his profound ambivalence, but the anchoring miracles of his own being, reflected in the half-familiar faces of a beloved young woman and passionate young man whose identities are only a little displaced—and as such the more uncanny and powerful—from their divine originals.

Insecure and uncertain of himself, Gabriel Conroy's sudden immersion in a family festival is, as we shall see, deeply threatening to his still-fledging adoptive social identity, both because the occasion is far removed, socially and culturally, from the field in which he has constructed that identity, and because the old family culture inherently gives the lie to that identity, repudiating its claims with a kind of uncouth familiarity, exposing its dissimulations and threatening to draw the self back into the darkness and confusion of its own beginnings, a threat made all the more potent because the obliteration of the self in the unconsciousness of the womb, or of the mother's embrace, while a kind of suffocation or death, is also a union with the sources of life and the root of that desire whose myriad differentiations, displacements and elaborations diffuse the erotic drive into every corner of human striving and shed its charm onto every object we are capable of desiring, even onto death itself.

Festivity, then, as a theme, goes to the heart of the human mystery, which, as a symbol, greets us in the very first word of the story, the name of the housemaid Lily. Death and resurrection, sexuality and hierarchy, demarcating the social and cultural field in which Joyce's narrative will play itself out, converge in her, who is a maid, that is, a servant-girl, a virgin, and a daughter whose name is at once the death and resurrection flower, symbolically linked through the Annunciation both with the angel Gabriel and with the Blessed Virgin.[6] The phrase that situates her socially, "the caretaker's daughter," even before the story's first sentence is complete, also situates, and in a sense isolates us with Gabriel in the class above her, though the narrator catches the atmosphere of excitement and anticipation by reporting, and in a sense implicitly recalling, that she is "literally run off her feet" in attending in the pantry to the gentlemen's overcoats as the "wheezy hall-door bell" summons her again and again.

The language of the opening paragraphs—"It was well for her she had not to attend to the ladies also"; "It was always a great affair, the Misses Morkan's annual dance"; "Never once had it fallen flat"—moves like a barometer through the idioms of gender and class, absorbing what might be the vocality of the sisters in their recollection of the evening, even years beyond it, and at the same time addresses itself, through Lily's consciousness, socially upwards, deferentially, to "Miss Kate and Miss Julia," who had thought of everything, and, a moment later, confidentially to a member of her own class: "They were fussy, that was all. But the only thing they would not stand is back answers," words that could easily have been exchanged in the pantry. Simultaneously, the narrator takes the "great affair" from the perspective, perhaps, of its guests, who share the aunt's social milieu, the respectable petite bourgeoisie, and with the redoubtable pride of that class reviews the history of the family, from their removal to the "dark gaunt house on Usher's Island. . . .thirty years ago if it was a day," to the present, acknowledging that niece Mary Jane, who has the organ in Haddington

Road, is "now the main prop" of the household. The aunts, then, are in a position of a disquieting, if unadmitted, social insecurity, the specter of destitution below them while above them, among Mary Jane's piano students, hover the daughters of the "better class families on the Kingston and Dalkey line."

The narrator's social mobility is more than simple "omniscience."[7] His, or her, movement—for at the outset and at many points beyond it the narrative seems to be filtered through a feminine consciousness apparently an aspect of Gabriel's own—through the registers of gender and class sounds a variable modality of social discourses, including of course Gabriel's own polished, cosmopolitanized, if affected language, which, with the entire tissue of social and sensory details that make up the surface of the narrative contribute to a pervasive sense of superficiality and with it, a kind of dramatic and rhetorical tension that begs for the exposure of the cultural and emotional forces that undergird the story and for a language, forged unawares in Gabriel's mind out of the sensory and linguistic detritus of the evening, capable of embodying them. On the narrative surface itself is a painstaking record of various greetings, introductions, pleasantries, niceties, farewells, and so on—at the end of the story we get eleven "good nights" in succession—which polishes that surface so that it in effect shines, returning its own reflection; even Gabriel is dazzled by the waxed floor, while he himself is hidden, even to himself, behind the polished lenses of his glasses. This reflective sensory surface, moreover, extends its influence over the event itself, lending to its delicate social equipoise a quality of mendacity or falsity, "reflected," for example, in the enthusiastic applause of three young gentlemen who in fact have not listened to Mary Jane's histrionic performance of an academy piano piece.

And among the most apparently superficial of the guests, of course, is Gabriel Conroy himself. What Ellmann calls Gabriel's "private tremors, his sense of inadequacy, his uncomfortable insistence on small pretensions"[8] break upon the buzz and gossip of the opening paragraphs like a smoke alarm as soon as he opens his mouth. Miss Kate and Miss Julia, says Lily, had feared he and Gretta would never come; "I'll engage they did," Gabriel affirms with a stuffy phrase out of some university common-room, and adds, with an effete construction out of casual blueblood hyperbole at Gretta's expense, "but they forget that my wife here takes three mortal hours to dress herself." Gabriel, it is clear at once, is an amiable poseur, advancing to his harmless aunts and a servant girl a fashioned personhood that in this setting, already socially charted by the modulations of the class-conscious narrator, is wildly out of place. He is, as he later acknowledges himself with a kind of literalized metaphor, catching a glimpse of his "well-filled shirt front" in a mirror, literally something of a stuffed shirt, destined from the beginning for the chastening of his pretensions.

For Gabriel, the social and sexual worlds are vertically arranged, and in parallel; it is important for him, particularly among his relatives and family friends, in whom are lodged both the culture he has striven to rise above and the nurture that shaped his ambition to rise above it, that he be seen to occupy its higher reaches, for it is only in his inherited position at the head of the family, otherwise unoccupied, that he is entirely at ease. Even Aunt Kate, who acknowledges to Gretta that she is always more at ease in her mind when Gabriel's around, what with the possibility that Freddy Malins may turn up "screwed," is cognizant of the role that Gabriel has assumed in a family that seems to lack a legitimate patriarch, whose presence, therefore, may perhaps ultimately be supplied in a less literal way.

But where relations with women are concerned, an area in which his insecurities seem most treacherous and he himself most imbalanced, the world's comfortable vertical arrangements are persistently in danger of inversion. Gabriel smiles condescendingly at the three syllables that Lily gives his surname, a fact that as Torchiana suggests[9] links her to Gaelic Ireland, and in the next instant, the relation framed at that moment by a tentative verticality of sex and class, he glances at her, "a slim growing girl," in a consciousness of her sexuality. For Gabriel this sexual stirring, potentially disruptive and confusing, always puts him on his guard and causes him to draw around himself the protective cover of social and cultural superiority; here, though, the class difference operates as a kind of sanction, permitting him to strike, first, a manly pose, in part paternal, but also in part a sexual display, which scripts his incursion, in the guise of pleasantry, into her intimate life.

Is it snowing she asks—and he answerers gravely, like a preoccupied father, "Yes, Lily," and adds that he thinks "we're in for a night of it," as if they were in for a night of artillery shelling. Perhaps the British control the weather. Savoring the sense of dominance he enjoys with her, Gabriel looks up at the pantry ceiling that is shuddering with the dancing on the floor above, feels for a moment his isolation with her and perhaps the sexual suggestion of the couples moving overhead, and glances at Lily, who in a gesture suggestive of a kind of domestic affection is carefully folding his overcoat at the end of a shelf. There is the faintest suggestion here of romantic feeling; later we discover that as she serves the dinner guests Lily reserves three potatoes especially for him. Under its impetus Gabriel, after discovering the girl is out of school, forefends that "we'll be going to your wedding one of these fine days with your young man, eh?"

Having failed to reduce her to the status of a schoolgirl, he attempts to incorporate her with a complacent bourgeois story of love and marriage and the social-sexual role prescribed for her. But his recourse to these conventional narratives as a way of asserting his social superiority is suddenly demolished by Lily's retort: "The men that is now is only all palaver and what they can get out of you." With this, which is in part a sign of some bitter disappointment and in part a reaction to his unwarranted intrusion into her private life, she refuses to elevate him to the pantheon of gallantry he wishes to occupy but consigns him to the sorry class of "the men that is now," mere sexual opportunists and charlatans, and in a sense suggests that in sexual matters she is more experienced than he. And there is the slight suggestion, too, that her unprettified encounter with predatory sexuality is a function of her vulnerable social standing, which both her class and her sex have conspired to create; that Gabriel himself, a man of books, romance, and monogamy, has to this point been insulated from the ungovernable trespasses and harrowing shocks of sexual rivalry, betrayal, and passion from which the authentic human story is mostly written. That, at least, is how a man such as Gabriel, or a man in Gabriel's state of mind, could conceivably take such a remark; not implausibly, however, the girl's retort may also carry both a complaint and an appeal—to Gabriel's age and breeding, his sympathy and his social stature, in a sense a moment in which she has paid him the compliment of taking him into her confidence.

As a last resort, coloring from this unexpected parry, Gabriel attempts to regain his dominance by offering the girl a coin as a Christmas present: if class and gender won't work to sustain his power, the sacred calendar, defiled by a coin, will. And yet what Gabriel sees as his failure with "the girl in the pantry" does not sully the narrator's view of him; indeed just at the moment of Lily's retort, as Gabriel attempts to recover himself by flicking at his shoes with his muffler, and as if in response to it, Gabriel's embarrassment provokes a closely descriptive portrait of him that proceeds both from his own heightened self-consciousness and from an awareness not altogether his own that is more taken with him than he is with himself. For though he is painfully self-conscious, he is not narcissistic. His hairless face and polished gilt-rimmed lenses give him the aspect of a sexually nascent young scholar, a sort of seminary lad; but the tender movement of the narrator's gaze, from his cheeks to his forehead, to his "delicate and restless eyes," to the "long curve" of his hair to where it "curls beneath the groove left by his hat," is a fond one, and certainly womanly, the precise density and tempo of attention that one would expect from a wife or lover, with its touches of admiration, sexual feeling, love, and care. Gabriel's self-consciousness at this point, as elsewhere in the story, is framed on the one hand by a feminine awareness somehow incorporated with Gabriel's own self-awareness—a psychological legacy, perhaps, of his own mother's abdicated love—and on the other by his nagging sense of sexual inadequacy.

Significantly, though, it keeps alive, entirely unbeknownst to him, even below the polished lenses and "well-stuffed shirt front," an affirmative sexual viability that forestalls our ever accepting Gabriel's dejected self-estimate, and on the contrary prompts us to form an idea of him that overflows the boundaries of his constructed identity into the young hero Michael Furey, who at the end of the story emerges out of the past to rival him for his wife's affection, but who in part is a projection of Gabriel himself.

His discomposure further stirred by the sound of skirts sweeping against the floor of the drawing-room upstairs, Gabriel's sensitivity to sexual indications suggests his own smoldering sexuality, that of a still youngish man—Joyce was twenty-six when he wrote the story, though he seems to conceive his character about a decade older—some years along in marriage and the father of two young children. Lily's remark makes him gloomy, not only because it has embarrassed and demeaned him but because it has brought him briefly but violently into contact with an unsentimental eroticism against whose rough surfaces the protocols of romance offer little protection.

This lower grade of unsentimentalized, predatory sexuality is in fact pervasively present in the story through its principal proponent Mr. Browne, who loves a double entendre.[10] "I'm the man for the ladies," he announces at once, offering three young women a ladies' punch he calls "hot, strong, and sweet." A jest about whiskey causes the girls to laugh uncomfortably, "swaying their bodies to and fro, with nervous jerks of their shoulders," while his "hot face" leans towards them "a little too confidentially" with an ambiguous quotation, in a "very low Dublin accent," from "the famous Mrs. Cassidy"—"if I don't take it, make me take it, for I feel I want it"—which the ladies, "with one instinct," receive in silence. Browne's social habits suggest an exclusively masculine milieu, where sexual innuendo can be relied upon to communicate its meaning, even where no such meaning is intended. Late in the evening, as Gabriel and Browne come back indoors from hailing a cab, Browne remarks that he'd like nothing better than "a fast drive with a good spanking goer between the shafts." In the scrupulously polite social atmosphere of the story Browne keeps us mindful of a sexual force below the level of polite social convention and of Gabriel's own romantic sexuality that, like the story's other's deep currents, will ultimately erupt into his otherwise well-defended physical and emotional life.

Not surprisingly, Gabriel attempts to dispel the gloom induced by his encounter with Lily by arranging his cuffs and tie, and by reviewing the notes he has made for his after-dinner speech, almost literally refurbishing his disheveled persona. But the interview has so blighted his self-esteem that even his notes look wrong, and only exacerbate his ambivalence about himself. He finds, of course, an occasion in them for renewing his sense of social superiority, the ego being ever vigilant after its own aggrandizement, in his bookish quotation from Robert Browning, only to revile himself because he anticipates seeming to his audience only to be "airing his superior education." With the self-indulgence characteristic of wounded vanity he predicts that he will fail with them just as he failed "with the girl in the pantry," and immoderately condemns his speech as "a mistake from first to last, an utter failure," even while the "indelicate" clacking and shuffling of the men's shoes on the drawing-room floor remind him, reassuringly, that "their grade of culture differed from his." Nevertheless he remains preoccupied with Lily, particularly when he hears below him her voice laughing with another, that of the newly arrived Freddy Malins, which only aggravates his sense of failure and exclusion.

Gabriel's internal struggle, already fully engaged in the first few moments after his arrival at the party, points to the utter inadequacy of his adoptive social identity to insulate him against a deeper conviction of ineffectuality, sexual and otherwise, which seems to be rooted in a mistrust of that identity itself and an ill-formed, inarticulate suspicion that the others, even his old aunties, in spite of their lower social station and inferior education have something that he does not: what may perhaps be what we would call today their ethnicity or their "culture," their very Irishness, and the community formed on the basis of it. At several points the narrator calls attention, not only to Gabriel's cultural affectations, through which he attempts to "rise above" his Irish origins, but to what is almost a luxuriousness in him: his stoutness, his plumpness, his waistcoat tightly girt around his body, the fact that he "likes nothing better than to find himself at the head of a well-laden table." How can a man in early middle age, getting a bit wide in the girth, a bit stuffy in speech and formal in his manner, such a fellow might wonder, compare to a pale young consumptive named

Michael Furey, many years in his grave, who like some hero of the border ballads catches his death in the rain for love? At the level at which Joyce approaches the erotic, Gabriel's anxieties run deep into the wellheads of culture, where love, death, and redemption are the antipodes of a human identity that cannot be mapped on the longitudes of social life but must be sought archeologically, in the depths of imagination.

Who is Gabriel Conroy? What can we infer about him apart from the interiority to which the narrator gives us access? That he is capable of inspiring a woman's affection we have already been subtly reassured by touches of description; but where does he fit into the social and cultural community of his family and their circle? Gabriel is the son of Kate and Julia's dead elder sister Ellen, who had married T. J. Conroy of the Port and Docks—the son, that is, of a mid-level public servant. As Professor Kelleher notes,[11] the Port and Docks Board was an Anglo-Irish preserve, and the Monkstown address a good one for a middle-class Catholic; Kelleher adds that Ushers Island, once a highly fashionable Protestant enclave, represents, socially, the family's rise in social standing since the generation of mill-owner grandfather Patrick Morkan, whom Gabriel gently ridicules later in the story.[12] Gabriel's aunts, however, though they have procured for the dinner "the best of everything," are, at best, impecunious, a "plain roast goose without any apple sauce" having "always been good enough" for Aunt Kate "and she hoped she might never eat worse." Socially at least theirs is far from an influential family, though a penchant for music, as well as the undying bourgeois struggle for distinction, may suggest that the impulse towards social betterment is still quite alive in them.

In the aunts, then, we are seeing, specter-like, variations upon social themes of which Gabriel's own mother was also of course a variation: insofar as she is present, she is present in them. Aunt Julia is gray and infirm, "stupefied," as Ellmann puts it, by her own advanced age—and yet Joyce curiously places in her throat, as part of the evening's entertainment, a youthful soprano voice that Gabriel compares to the "excitement of swift and secure flight," albeit in an old song, "Arrayed for the Bridal," which looks simultaneously towards virgin purity on the one hand and on the other towards the dark, sinister groom that robs us of purity, youth, and life; the song seems to depart her almost as a pure soul from the vestment of the mortal body. Aunt Kate, on the other hand, named like a milkmaid, with an apple-doll face, a nut-brown complexion, and old-fashioned braided hair, is closer to the earthy, robust Connacht peasant, and unlike Julia endowed with a lively intelligence and opinions of her own, even where the Pope is concerned—on driving women out of choirs to "put little whipper-snappers of boys over their heads."

In Julia there is something abject, refined, and, like the suggestion in Gabriel's own name, angelic and ethereal; but that ethereality is unhappily lodged in age, dullness, and decline. Kate is resilient, true-hearted, and proud, and in spite of her disclaimer—"Oh, I don't question the Pope's being right. I'm only a stupid old woman . . ."—she has not fallen entirely under the sway of the Church. This is in contrast to niece Mary Jane, who of the three hostesses perhaps most closely approaches the stereotype of her gender, class, and unmarried status. With her ambitious piano display piece, which Gabriel doubts anyone present is capable of appreciating (including himself), her penchant for smoothing out the potentially disruptive ripples on the social surface, her piety concerning the choirs—"Well, isn't it for the honour of God, Aunt Kate?"—and the monks of Melleray, the "talented, cheerful, hard-working" Mary Jane, as Gabriel draws her in his speech, is a dismally virtuous young woman just past thirty who has been sadly thrown back upon the arid middle-class repertoire of female "accomplishments" and the unimpeachable routines of religious devotion. Moreover, she has been driven into the second-class citizenship of spinsterhood by a romantic Catholic culture that constructs the feminine almost exclusively as virgin and mother and the masculine, in its relation to woman, as gallant and as master. As Mary Jane's cousin, of her own age and generation, Gabriel is in a sense her contrasexual counterpart, and doubtless sees in her all the marks of the social oppression he wishes to escape; but particularly in his sexual attitudes and feelings he is as much marked by it as she is, and like her frustrated by the incompatibility of gender ideals with gender relations, and sexual identity, as they actually are.

And what, indeed, of motherhood and maternity in "The Dead?" We see, briefly, Lily as a child, nursing her rag-doll at the foot of the stairs, and Mary Jane as "a little girl in short clothes." Aunt Kate asks Gretta if she is not anxious about her own children, who have been left with a sitter. But in a story of absences, which include old Patrick Morkan and his horse, the tenor Parkinson, and of course Michael Furey, as well as the absences foretold of Aunt Julia, who will "soon be a shade with the shade of old Patrick Morkan and his horse," and of Gabriel himself, a most significant absence is that of Gabriel's own mother. Contemplating Aunt Julia's crewelwork on the wall and speculating on the sisters' schooling, Gabriel recalls, in fond and homely detail, down to its little foxes' heads and mulberry buttons, a waistcoat that his mother had made for him as a birthday present.

He gazes on a photograph of her, the "serious and matronly" sister who in the photo is reading to Gabriel's brother Constantine, and we learn that, being "sensible of the dignity of family life," she had chosen both of the boys' grandiose storybook names. With his university degree and his literary aspirations, it seems that Gabriel is playing out a destiny designed for him at least in part in his mother's own aspiring imagination.

The central conflict of the story emerges, then, in connection with Gabriel's remembrance of his mother, whose opposition to his marriage "still rankled in his memory." In his own mind he is still defending Gretta to her, denying that she is only "country cute," as his mother had suggested, and, as if his mother were still alive to hear his thought, countering somewhat irrelevantly that Gretta had nursed her through her last illness. Gabriel splits hairs even to Miss Ivors by acknowledging that Gretta's "people," but not, by implication, Gretta herself, originate in Connacht. Indeed, Gretta moves into the foreground of the story precisely at the point at which the aunts' "dead sister Ellen" is introduced—the object of Gabriel's "admiring and happy eyes," of his uxoriousness, his solicitude, "a standing joke with them," his amusing overprotectiveness of her and the children. To the vivacious Gretta, "galoshes" is simply a word that reminds her of a minstrel show—perhaps of the names of one of Christy's goofy end-men, like "Alyoshus"—and in this she somewhat exposes her class affiliations, since minstrelsy was chiefly a "vulgar" entertainment. But to Gabriel galoshes are, along with green eyeshades, dumb-bells, and the stir-about, little stratagems set to foil Death's nesting in the petty negligences and insufficiencies of life.

How is Joyce, who in *Dubliners* refuses to dissolve his characters' moral natures in abstract psychological analysis, but in the exposition of their inner life deploys a symbology derived from their own immediate experience, to expound what even on a superficial view is Gabriel's unresolved dependency upon his mother's apparently conditional love? This dependency he continually reenacts in all his relations with women, who if they do not utterly worship him will it seems throw him into fits of self-abnegation that only expose to him the fraudulence of the improvised postures and pretenses with which he has tried to shore up his wildly unbalanced and contingent self-estimate. From her, all reassurances of existence flow; but she is dead and gone, her power lingering now in the perilous magnetism of women and particularly in Gabriel's attachment to Gretta and through Gretta into the mother culture that his own mother's ambition for him has compelled him to repudiate.

Mother and mother culture are conjoined in Freddy Malins, too: "a young man of about forty, of Gabriel's size and build,"—a phrase that only readers over forty could take at face value—"a grosser edition" of Gabriel, writes Torchiana,[13] to whom Gabriel is consistently contrasted and compared, but in any case regularly linked. In Freddy, Joyce has created a kind of X-ray image of Gabriel's emotional nature, unfortified by education, travel, and books, still mired in essentially infantile dependencies. Freddy, who actually arrives with his mother, is in essence a great lumpy child, "rubbing the knuckles of his left fist backwards and forwards into his left eye," whose sleepy, heavy-lidded eyes and disordered hair make him look like a toddler at bedtime; at the same time he is a kind of grotesque, strongly reminiscent of newspaper and stage caricatures of the Irish, not to mention minstrelsy's stage-Negro, with "coarse features, a blunt nose, a convex and receding brow, tumid and protruded lips." Freddy seems to embody a kind of Irish curse, a pathology at once social and psychological emblemized in his alcoholism, in which are united both his infantilism and his ethnicity, the problem of individuation in a context of maternal dependency being in fact the site at which in a traditional culture under the stresses of Western domination a personal sorrow becomes social and endemic, a point at which cultural endowment and cultural opportunity come squarely into conflict.

And yet, at the deepest emotional level, Freddy is a kind of touchstone of candor, sincerity, of unprepossessing innocence. "It takes Teddy to find out the really good things," avers Browne, with ambivalent irony; but it is Freddy who fully and openly acknowledges, without embarrassment, his inhibition perhaps relaxed by drink, what the narrator has already certified to us, the success of Julia's "Arrayed for the Bridal." "Upon my word and honour that's the truth," says Freddy, positively beside himself. "I never heard your voice sound so fresh and so . . . so clear and fresh, never."

With Joyce's characteristic impulse to exteriorize all the resources of his narrative, it is difficult sometimes to anchor our own characterological judgments in some reassuring narrative irony; Joyce's narrative in "The Dead," which cleaves so closely to the processes of Gabriel's own mind, itself responsive to the feelings, the speech, and the social place of others, to some extent partakes of the violent unbalance of his self-estimate, so that we may be temporarily persuaded that he is, after all, only a "well-meaning sentimentalist," the "pitiable fatuous fellow" he catches a glimpse of in a mirror, and fail to detect how such an immoderate self-condemnation measures against a portrait that is, in the main, affectionate and sympathetic, as if Gabriel had incorporated into some part of himself an admiration that emanates, as we've suggested, from hidden and mysterious feminine presences. I do not say that Gabriel's dead mother is the "narrator"; but in a sense she is literally and figuratively the "mother" of the narrative. Thus Joyce can level a barb against Gabriel with the confidence that it will not penetrate to the marrow, and direct ironies against him already paled with ambivalence.

Gabriel's story of Patrick Morkan and his horse, for example, which he tells in the hall at the conclusion of the evening, is quite amusing, and Gabriel tells it amusingly, with a high rhetorical tone that ridicules the old fellow's social pretensions, those of a "glue-boiler" who, wishing to "drive out with the quality to a military review in the park"—we might recall the feast here, which on the figurative level is itself a kind of military review—goes out "in grand style from his ancestral mansion somewhere in Back Lane, I think," on an old workhorse who mortifies the old man by plodding round and round a statue of "King Billy," as if he were back at the starch mill. The story is hilarious, and Gabriel, as he paces around and around the hall in his galoshes in imitation of the horse, utterly charming. And yet the story, like the feast, is a kind of pantomime as well, one that has Gabriel vainly circling around and around a symbol of British power. "King Billy" is of course none other than William of Orange, William III, Ireland's seventeenth-century conqueror, whose triumph at the Boyne, Kelleher writes, turned the Irish into "hewers of wood and drawers of water to the conquerors, so thoroughly beaten that they seemed almost in love with defeat,"[14] a people whom Joyce elsewhere calls "the gratefully oppressed." Gabriel's circle around the monument to King Billy, moreover, duplicates the Orange commemorations of the battle of the Boyne,[15] while Back Lane, Kelleher reminds us, locus of the family's "ancestral mansion," was the site of the Back Lane Parliament that in 1793 demanded and won the Relief Act that abolished the remaining clauses of the Penal Code, admitting Catholics to the franchise and to university degrees[16]—an act of which Gabriel has been a direct beneficiary. The statue of King Billy in any case was repeatedly vandalized by Irish nationalists, until in 1929 it was finally taken down.[17] Hence Gabriel's amusing story is a political allegory in small.

These themes—Gabriel's pomposity and awkwardness, his still rankled and defensive reminiscence of his mother, his uxoriousness, the implicit connection of personality with a larger cultural and historical context that Freddy, Mary Jane, and Gabriel all embody, and, finally, British power itself—Joyce dramatizes, in their interconnectedness, and most appropriately for a festive occasion, on the dance floor, where chance encounters bring unexpected intimacies that in turn shake the foundations of our customary world. In his failure to grasp the nature of the interest being paid to him by the Irish Revivalist, freckle-faced Molly Ivors, with the high collar and the brooch with the Irish motto, Gabriel is a kind of comic knucklehead, failing utterly to see beneath the surface of her "enthusiasm" to the more personal and perhaps even slightly dangerous sentiments that inform it.

Joyce, as Ellmann reports, distrusted all enthusiasms—and Molly Ivors is an "enthusiast."[18] Of the Irish Revival he was disdainful, but cautiously so, portraying it in another *Dubliners* story about a mother's social ambitions for her daughter as little more than a fashion in Gaelic lessons for the kids and a lively trade in picture postcards. But as Ellmann observes of Gabriel, the question of Irish nationalism, and the wellspring of its folk culture to which Yeats and many others had turned for inspiration, was "far from settled for him."[19] The assertive and independent Molly wishes to "pick a crow" with Gabriel over the political implications of his affiliation with a pro-British newspaper, and calls him a "West Briton"—that is, an Anglicized Irish Catholic, or as the character "Molly Ivors" explains in John Huston's film version of "The Dead," "one who looks to England for our salvation." Joyce's attention to the etymological nuances of words may, however, be of passing interest here: "Briton" means an Englishman, and a "West" Briton is one who lives to the west, that is, in Ireland; the derivation, however, is from the name of a pre–Anglo-Saxon Celtic tribe, and in the "west" lie the territories into which the Celts were driven by Germanic invaders, an ancestral homeland: Gabriel's deep confusion etymologically encapsulated.

Gabriel is nevertheless so uncertain of himself that Miss Ivors's playful and affectionate rebuke, which is actually a kind of invitation, is for him an ordeal. It is perhaps exceeding the mark to say that Miss Ivors is flirting; but it seems plain that between "friends of many years standing," whose "careers had been parallel, first at the University and then as teachers," that is, between Gabriel and a female contemporary with whom he has more in common culturally than he does with his own wife, there is a good deal more than a fine ideological point. Is Miss Ivors merely an ideological irritant? Hardly: we learn at once of her freckles and her prominent brown eyes, which Gabriel in his pique resentfully transforms to "rabbit eyes," and with a negative descriptive gesture—"she did not wear a low-cut bodice"—infer all at once what she is wearing, a high collar, that the other ladies are not wearing high collars, and finally that Gabriel is not indifferent to these details, sexually, politically, or socially.

In her "aren't you ashamed of yourself?" there is a touch of the maternal, a sensitive point with him, and in her unmasking of him, especially as she couples it with her frank admiration of his book review, of the coquette—also a sensitive point, and for the same reasons. She grasps his hand warmly, and when, at a later point in the dance, realizes she has offended him, furrows her brow to make him smile, as if he were a pouting child, and to Gabriel's surprise presses his hand firmly. These gestures, and even her whispering "West Briton!" in his ear, are, however subtle and slight, stolen intimacies, and against their backdrop her invitation to join her and her friends on a western tour issued in the first moment to him alone as if they were still school chums and him not yet a married man—she includes Gretta, somewhat patronizingly ("It would be splendid for Gretta, too . . ."), as an afterthought—has a sense in it, though admittedly subtle, both illicit and poignant: as if these two, romantically speaking, have somehow missed one another. She's only teasing: but her premature departure from the party remains enigmatic, the more so for the cheerful face she puts on, the Irish blessing, and, perhaps, the self-concealing laugh that only leaves Gabriel more perplexed: "Gabriel asked himself was he the cause of her abrupt departure. But she did not seem to be in an ill humour: she had gone away laughing."

It is intriguing that Joyce places this incident hard on the heels of Gabriel's reflections upon his mother, the waistcoat, and her opposition to his marriage. Miss Ivors confronts Gabriel at a moment when he has been temporarily thrust back into obsolete relations and made vulnerable again to now illegitimate claims. But in the intimacy of the dance, briefly isolated with Gabriel outside the circle of social proprieties, Molly Ivors's frank admiration, her physical warmth, and her friendly but well-targeted admonishments all suggest that in this opportunity, precisely the psychosocial domain of festivity, she is seeking to make momentarily real a connection that in regulated social life has been overlooked or passed by. Because Gabriel "can't risk a grandiose phrase with her"—that is, cannot define his relationship to her in the vertical way his uneasy sexuality demands, he remains blind to, unable to participate in, and bereft of the transient but reinvigorating joy to be had in the covert mimesis with which festivity keeps alive, and brings to conscious awareness, the secret allegiances and unacknowledged possibilities that thrive in the interstices and under the surfaces of the festive ritual—and that may, through festivity, provoke their eruption into social reality.

If we take Molly Ivors as Gabriel inclines to, defensively, as a propagandist merely, then perhaps she departs the party early out of indignation, indifference, or even contempt; or perhaps she is on her way out to a political meeting, as John Huston rationalizes her departure. Perhaps she is hurt that Gabriel can have been so obtuse; perhaps she is a little in love with him; or perhaps she has only wished to affirm, after the passage of years and his withdrawal into family life, the old friendship between them. Or perhaps, like Gabriel, she has also sought, but in a different direction, transcendence of the old bourgeois culture that has hobbled Freddy and suffocated Mary Jane, and sustains, with fine dramatic sense, the claim of her achieved self by leaving a kind of triumph behind her and avoiding the further exposure of her cause at the dinner table. Her "propagandism," like Gabriel's grandiose "Continental" manner, is a way of escaping a stultifying social atmosphere.

Molly Ivors's judgment of him, however, sticks in Gabriel's craw. After what to him has been a blistering dressing-down he retreats into the idle chatter of the feeble and empty-headed Mrs. Malins, whose hackneyed report on the beautiful scenery of Scotland is the shallow touristic counterpoint to the authentic claim of a native place of which Miss Ivors has just spoken. Gabriel in the meantime occupies himself with defensive and ineffectual attempts to dismiss Molly Ivors on the grounds of rudeness—"there was a time for all things," and besides, she had tried to make him look ridiculous. But at the same time he is somewhat remorseful about his own intemperate response: "I'm sick of my own country, sick of it!"—which of course has only confirmed, again, that there are for him, perhaps, a number of issues that are "far from settled": not only his position on the "Irish question," but indeed the entire groundwork of an existence constituted by marriage, fatherhood, education, reading, European travel, a small-scale literary vocation, a few choice phrases, and a pair of shirt cuffs. Even while going over the headings of his speech in another effort to reconstruct his adoptive identity, lingering self-consolingly upon a precious Yeatsian phrase, "thought-tormented age," he finds himself preoccupied with Molly, unnerved to imagine her looking up at him from the dinner table with her "critical quizzing eyes," and forges for his speech a new passage directed against her as a member of "a serious and hypereducated generation" that lacks the qualities "of hospitality, of humour, of humanity" of the "generation which is now on the wane among us." Ironically, she has forced him back towards the very position he had repudiated, and leveled against her a criticism that just as credibly might have been leveled against himself. Of Gabriel's insecurity and inadequacy we are by this time well-acquainted; but Miss Ivors has closed off his accustomed avenue of escape from the claims upon him of his own culture: she has made him feel unworthy in what he has become.

It is perhaps worth mentioning here parenthentically that as Ellmann reports Joyce had not, to his surprise, found much hospitality of the Irish kind in the more industrialized and bureaucratic Europe, where in exile he began to recall what to him was Ireland's greater natural beauty, and to remark the "ingenuous insularity" that to him was a sign of a deeper civilization: in his exile, in other words, it seems that Joyce had begun to reinvent Ireland as his origin and as his home, and in terms strongly suggestive of the literary and antiquarian traditions in which folk cultures typically since Herder have been conceived.[20] Hospitality is of course an ancient traditional virtue associated with the heroic age; and incidentally it is a violation of the laws of hospitality that leads, in the story told in "The Lass of Aughrim," to a tragic loss. When in his speech, moreover, Gabriel complains that "we are living in a less spacious age," we may perhaps hazard the guess that Joyce had begun to sense the differences between clock and machine-driven modern bureaucratic society and a traditional culture calibrated to the more "spacious" sacred, seasonal, and family cycles and calendars.

Gabriel is saved from Molly's critical gaze by her early departure, and the instant she is out the door feels relieved and "ready to carve a flock of geese, if necessary." Once enthroned at the head of the table he is "quite at ease." But the political and cultural issues that Molly Ivors has raised with Gabriel are nevertheless far from impertinent, especially as they are tied up in the course of the dance with Gabriel's crisis of identity and still more deeply with the anxieties that bring the forces of culture, maternity, and sexuality into a psychic alignment whose immense gravitational pull upon social identity threatens to weaken and ultimately destroy it. The intersection, through Miss Ivors, of the Irish Revival with the Misses Morkan's annual dance situates the story historically; but it also provides its author the opportunity to explore the question of Irish identity at a level deeper even than politics, where culture is tangled obscurely with questions of what, at the end of the nineteenth century, was a volatile compound of history, nativity, language, and belief roughly comprehended by the concept of race, which was Joyce's term for the Irish people as a historical culture.

Indeed, Joyce touches twice in the story on the issue of race as such and joins it explicitly on the one hand to cultural representation and on the other to cultural power. Gretta finds the curious French-derived word "galoshes" amusing because it reminds her of the Christy Minstrels: and I wonder, just for the record, whether the wordman par excellence, who never chose a word arbitrarily, nor without a consciousness of its sounds, its cognates, and its derivation, might not for symbolic purposes have seen the possibilities of the long vowel in the name of the old minstrel-man. It is a "Negro chieftain," too, in the Gaiety pantomime, like minstrelsy a more "vulgar" production, that Freddy Malins, who has already been assigned the features of a Negro stage caricature, sensing Bartell D'Arcy's prejudice, defends at the dinner table: "And why couldn't he have a good voice too? Is it because he's only a black?"—thus in a sense defending himself.

That ordinary Irishmen should have seen something of themselves in minstrelsy, with its comic negotiations between oppressor and oppressed, is probable. In Emmett's, Christy's, and other mid-nineteenth-century minstrel troupes, frontier or famine Irishmen typically played, in blackface of course, the roles of rustic plantation blacks, often in counterpoint to interlocutors of Scots-Irish or English extraction. In the early period of minstrelsy such men in any case shared with manumitted slaves and free blacks a social niche on the margins and near the bottom of American society. The minstrel show, moreover, was immensely popular in Dublin and London, from T. D. Rice onwards. "The Dead" is about such divisions, divisions that in Joyce's time were, again, largely comprehended by race, a concept that captured the mysterious coherence of peoples and the persistence of traditions and traits we now sacralize as "culture," which in an increasingly rationalized, atomized, and secular society had begun to reveal itself *as* itself.

Through "The Dead," then, runs a deep and forbidding fault line across personality, society, and culture and riven deep in what Joyce's Stephen Dedalus would call in a famous phrase "the uncreated conscience of my race": that is, the domination of Celtic Catholic Ireland by British Protestant power. Molly Ivors's "enthusiasm" is on the one hand perhaps only a matter of a brooch, a motto, and a summer holiday, little more than a touristic diversion; but these are all tokens of resistance to British domination, as is, of course, her demonstrated independence of conduct and of thought, which in the name of cultural revival invert the received valuations of ethnic, political, and gender identity, all of which perpetuate the structures of social power. That Molly picks her crow with Gabriel in the passages of a dance, with playful and affectionate gestures, suggest that her challenge to Gabriel's social mask, her subtle disruption of society's comfortable, even complacent accommodations to sexuality, both as gender and as force, and her revivalism itself are all meant to be taken in a festive spirit. But like all festive inversions, her covert and overt demonstrations stir in the very bedrock of psychic integrity and social order a deeply disquieting instability.

The fault line as we've seen runs through the hearts of the characters as well as between them; but it runs deeply into the narrative itself, too, sounding litanies of picturesque Irish names against the ornamental "Gabriel," the foreign "D'Arcy" and the dull British "Browne," setting the dazzling social surface against the cold and dark of the night and laying under it powerful erotic undercurrents, all the while keeping these bifurcations in strict alignment, ultimately to summon out of them resounding cadences that radically invert the story's social, psychological, and cultural formations.

The erotic and cultural drama of "The Dead" is, of course, to be played out in the relationship between Gabriel and Gretta. The "row" with Molly Ivors has already come between them in a sense when Gabriel disingenuously divides Gretta from her Connacht "people;" it does again when he remarks coolly to Gretta that she may go if she likes to the Aran Isles; he will take his usual bicycle tour to France and Belgium, "to keep in touch with the languages." Against such a backdrop—Yeats, the story goes, had sent John Synge to the Aran Isles to find his destiny—Gabriel's highbrow tourism looks facile and effete. And, if Gabriel has been obtuse with Miss Ivors, he is here selfish and almost brutal with Gretta, who at the notion of a western holiday "clasped her hands excitedly and gave a little jump," her lighthearted and genuine innocence: "Oh Gabriel, I'd love to see Galway again"—guaranteed to win male readers at least to her against her sullen husband and to prompt in her, not implausibly, a readiness to journey back, emotionally, to the period of her girlish innocence before her marriage. For if Gabriel has been made to feel unworthy, he has made his wife feel abandoned.

It is at this point that Gabriel's consciousness, through which the narrative has been largely mediated, begins to reflect, through warring claims upon his attention, the impact upon the actual structure of perception of what to this point has been mainly a thematic strain. The feast, as we have seen, is a scene of happy festivity continually subverted by the weight of the past, by an underlying tension, with suggestions of class and ethnic rivalries, between the older folks who favor the old Dublin opera and D'Arcy, who favors the contemporary continental singers, and by the oppressive weight of the discussion of the monks who sleep in their coffins. Gabriel rises to give his speech at the moment at which Mrs. Malins's comment on the piety of the monks is met in the narrative with a delicious savoring of exotic Middle Eastern desserts: raisins, almonds, figs, apples, oranges, chocolates, and sweets—a keen juxtaposition of renunciation and pleasure, guilt and innocence, death and life, and the first faint intimation in the story of a darkly sensuous imaginary world into which Gabriel's language and thought will wander.

Gabriel's own mind sustains this division; facing the attentive guests, hearing again the waltz and the skirts sweeping against the floor, and raising his dazzled eyes to the chandelier, his imagination strays to the pure air outside the window, to the park where the air is pure, the trees are "weighted with snow," and "the Wellington Monument wore a gleaming cap of snow that flashed westward over the white field of Fifteen Acres." Indeed, the associations attached to these places seem to have permeated even the feast itself, for as Torchiana points out, many a British military review had been conducted on the "Fifteen Acres."[21] A moment earlier, as he reviewed the headings of his speech, we had seen Gabriel's "warm trembling fingers" tapping the cold pane of the window, as he imagined "how pleasant it would be to walk out alone. . . . The snow would be lying on the branches of the trees and forming a bright cap on the top of the Wellington Monument." That "cap of snow" would seem almost to be an officer's cap.

Gabriel wastes the dedicatory eloquence intended for the absent Miss Ivors in order to showcase his protomodernist phrase "thought-tormented age" and to display a grade of culture that smacks not only of tourism but of imperialism, praising Irish hospitality as "a tradition that is unique as far as my experience goes (and I have visited not a few places abroad) among the modern nations." But his pomposity at this point rings especially hollow, as the real impetus of the speech, liberated as Gabriel is now from Miss Ivors's scrutiny, is to repair the damage to his pride. To this end he delivers his tribute to "the Three Graces of the Dublin musical world," his aunts and his cousin. It is an elegant literary allusion—to the graces, brilliance, joy, and youth, whose purpose in classical mythology is to make nature, society, love, and truth attractive to the human soul.[22] That they are attendants upon Eros, Aphrodite, and Dionysus assures their presence at festive occasions; but Gabriel conflates, as is traditional, the Three Graces with another story, the Judgment of Paris, in which the young Trojan shepherd boy refuses the wisdom and power Athena and Hera have offered him in favor of Aphrodite, who has promised him the fairest woman on earth.

It is only an allusion, of course, and only a story; but the evidence is superabundant in Joyce's work that the discourses of classical literature and of Catholic doctrine intersect pervasively with it and provide a matrix within which an exhaustive inventory of historically contingent details, apparently arbitrary incidents in apparently accidental sequence, highly particularized characters precisely situated socially and culturally, and so on becomes a structure that assimilates and is assimilated to the Western world's primary narratives. With his allusion Gabriel charmingly adorns his hostesses with a garland of his learning; but for Joyce the allusion opens into the story a new territory, far beyond and much vaster than the walls of the house on Usher's Island, one in which the soul is the scene of a congress of divinities who carry out human beings' own unconscious designs, whose history is the history of their intervention in human affairs, and whose topography is the topography of the cosmos in which they move.

By increments it becomes apparent, from many subtle indications, that "The Dead" must be read, and reread, on this cosmic plane, where the feeble posturings of the human ego pale before the immense forces of youth and renewal, nurture and love, sickness and death, and particularly of the supernatural gift of grace given out of mercy to unworthy beings for their spiritual regeneration. The beautiful boy who chooses love is, simply, a boy who loves and is beloved. But he is also an Adonis, slain like Michael Furey in the bloom of youth and preserved for his continual return, in an endless cycle of death and rebirth, from his sojourn in the underworld. Let us recall that mythographically the "authentic form of the treasure hoard," our emblem of culture, and the ethnonoetic plenum that is its social and organic seat, is the "release of life-giving powers that come with spring and the rain": natural powers that every human being and every human society has in some way attempted to turn towards its own renewal.[23]

What is important is that Gabriel's own consciousness is furnished with the discourses from which he will forge the story's "uncreated conscience" and that in the course of the story by a kind of unconscious scavengery he gathers from the sensory surfaces of the narrative a language of emblem and symbol that will embody it. Hugh Kenner has described this technique as one in which the narrator appropriates his character's own modes of expression to sustain the narrative;[24] a bit more accurate to say, I think, that since the narrative is mediated to a certain point through Gabriel's consciousness, Gabriel himself assimilates new experiences by means of the sensory and linguistic resources of the old, and that the narrator, with a distance that is occasionally tense with irony, reports this process, at once holding the character at bay and tracing his experience as it unfolds out of itself.

Thus "The Dead" is in a sense replete with "foreshadowings"—though not in the dramatic sense, as they do not look forward, nor inspire any anticipation; they are a kind of sensory and linguistic trail of crumbs that lead into the terrifying psychic vacuum created by the final collapse of Gabriel's putative ego and form there the indistinct shape of an authentic cultural identity that can hardly be said to be individuated or in any sense subjective at all, but is a kind of immanence of pure power, morally charged, with a human face, a local habitation, and a name.

Let us reflect for a moment on Joyce's suggestive use of names: and, for the moment, let them rest as suggestions. We have already paused at "Lily," the caretaker's daughter. "Gabriel" is of course the Annunciator, declaring (Luke 1), appropriately for this story, the coming of the Messiah. Molly "Ivors" suggests of course ivy, symbol of Irish nationalism and Parnell's anniversary. Gretta is a diminutive of Margaret, or "Pearl": she is perhaps the pearl of great price for which the merchant in Jesus's parable (Matthew 13:44–45) gives all he has.

But by far the most resonant and powerful name in "The Dead," however, is that of Michael Furey. Both the surname and the given name are common Irish names, even characteristically so, particularly in Galway,[25] and hence at once powerfully Christian and powerfully native, naming the messenger of God, called the "prince of snow" in both Christian and Jewish traditions and associated with silver,[26] at the same time as it names the Irish nationality as "fury." "Furey" means of course vengeance, violence, rage—and, if we accept the interpenetration of classical allusion into "The Dead," it hearkens to the Furies, souls of the slain and agents of retribution against trespass upon the laws of natural piety, from which arise such naturally human sentiments as love of country and the laws of hospitality. Now here is a most curious turn: the Greek word for the Latin Furiae is Erinys, with its rare English derivative "erinnic" (OED)—no relation etymologically to the Old Irish Erin, "Ireland"—but nevertheless contained, homonymically, in it.

Gabriel's triumph at the dinner table at once fortifies him and puts him at his ease, preparing the way both for his entertaining performance as Patrick Morkan's horse, in which he freely partakes of the mirthful spirit of the general departure, and the fantasy in which he indulges at the foot of the stairs, modeling himself as a sort of pre-Raphaelite painter who will render "a woman," whose face he cannot see but whom he identifies by the terra cotta and salmon-pink panels of her skirt as his wife, standing in the shadows near the top of the first flight, listening to a man's singing from one of the upper rooms. "He asked himself what is a woman standing on the stairs in the shadow, listening to distant music, a symbol of."

What, indeed? The coloration, which includes the blue felt of Gretta's hat, suggests, as Tilly Eggers points out, conventional chapel images of the Blessed Virgin.[27] But as the reduction of these colors to black and white seems to indicate, Gabriel has forgotten this meaning, and senses that he has forgotten it; unapprehended and unnamed it strives to restore itself to consciousness through all the associations, figures, and displacements that subconsciously recall but do not identify it, filling the field of awareness with a significance that consequently must be sought again. "If he were a painter he would paint her in that attitude. . . . Distant Music he would call the picture if he were a painter."

The repeated phrase secures the irony directed against Gabriel's private self-indulgence that like his many other gestures in the story seems to offer him relief from an ill-formed contempt for himself that he cannot confront directly. But while arranging his shirt cuffs and affecting British upper-class speech will perhaps mislead others, here Gabriel is himself misled, particularly in the fact that by this stratagem he depersonalizes his wife, and deflects the perception that in her "mystery and grace of attitude" lies a subjectivity in her inaccessible to him—she is at this instant simply "a woman," the woman with whom he will within the hour come to feel that he has never lived as man and wife, and hence the last in a series of female objects whose conquest, in some form, seems essential to the maintenance of his self-esteem. And yet she is his wife: the past companion of his romantic life and the woman in whom he enjoys the complete social legitimacy of sexual consummation. In the course of the evening Gabriel has been repeatedly rebuked and rebuffed in his efforts at gallantry; but here is an object, and an occasion—they shall be spending what remains of the night in a hotel room, away from the children—in which he can make a final effort to reclaim his manhood.

"The Lass of Aughrim," which Bartell D'Arcy is singing and to which Gretta has paused to listen is a ballad in the "old Irish tonality," and "made plaintive by distance and by the singer's hoarseness," tells the story of a young woman's seduction by the great Lord Gregory, who in the song's final verses refuses entry to the girl and her baby, condemning her and the infant to death in the rain, or, in many versions, the snow, on the steps of his mansion. Aughrim is at once the name of a village near Gretta's native Galway[28] and of another city south of Dublin that was the scene of one of William's important victories. D'Arcy breaks off his song abruptly and once downstairs barks rudely to his hostesses: "Can't you see I'm as hoarse as a crow?"—embarrassed, perhaps, that an old half-remembered Irish song can have frustrated his effort to identify himself or to be identified with the great singers on the continent; or perhaps that the charms of Miss O'Callaghan can have persuaded him, against his better judgment, to try to sing over his cold. Perhaps "Bartell D'Arcy" is not his name at all, but an adopted one. Maybe it is really something like Patrick O'Casey or Kenneth Kilkenny. Indeed, if Freddy Malins is in some sense an unaccommodated Gabriel Conroy, Bartell D'Arcy is all accommodation, a fabrication imperfectly sealed against disruption by baser impulses and invading infections.

He blames his cold: and Mary Jane quotes the newspapers that "snow is general all over Ireland." Snow has of course been a presence in the story from the first moment that Gabriel is introduced: no sooner has he spoken his first words in the hall than we see him scraping the snow from his galoshes, entering the house it seems almost as a kind of effigy, snow lying on the shoulders of his overcoat and cold "escaping from the crevices and folds" as he removes it—a frozen life that the warmth of the party will restore. We have seen, moreover, Gabriel's attention persistently diverted by the outdoors, and his positive longing to be freshened and purified by the cold.

It is an important turning point when, after a chorus of good-byes that our narrator almost mechanically records, Gabriel and Gretta, alongside Bartell D'Arcy, step out into the wee hours of the morning. Here is a fundamental change in the texture of the narrative, its obverse side, in which a physical world still under the spell of darkness summons out of the methodical descriptive empiricism with which Joyce elaborates the social surface a system of metaphors through which the rational universe is gradually displaced by a dreamworld synthesized out of various romantic, Catholic, and classical elements, with folkloric overtones of the Celtic otherworld.[29] "A dull, yellow light brooded over the houses and the river; and the sky seemed to be descending." "It was slushy underfoot; and only streaks and patches of snow lay on the roofs, on the parapets of the quay and on the area railings. The lamps were still burning redly in the murky air and, across the river, the palace of the Four Courts stood out menacingly against the heavy sky." Joyce projects Gabriel's subjectivity, with its sense of weight and of menace, onto a landscape whose features—a palace, parapets, lamps "burning redly in the murky air," a dark river—are thereby transformed from fixtures of a modern municipality into the magical signs of a kind of underworld or Hades: like Yeats's Byzantium a city poetically transfigured that exteriorizes and concretizes the mind's consciousness of itself. This anomalous condition, an uncanny world, familiar if not entirely commonplace, in folk cultures, has in our society been marginalized and delegitimized as pathological, primitive, or criminal; there is nevertheless one area in bourgeois society where its cultural sanction, until our own time at least, has remained strong, and that is in the social, economic, and sexual adventure, touched with the hue of the illicit, of romantic love.

In the moments before their exit, as "the rich bronze of her hair" picks up the gaslight, as he recalls the image of her drying her hair by the fire, and notes on her face the emotional signs of a cause still unknown to him, the high color of her cheeks and her shining eyes, we have seen Gabriel fall in love with his wife. "A sudden tide of joy went leaping out of his heart." With the transformation of the story's physical setting and emotional atmosphere comes also a transformation of its rhetorical texture. A newly romanticized and exotic language emerges, in which we can detect, as with accumulating phrases he seems to read and to incorporate into his own thought the very narrative from which his existence is spun out, Gabriel's rehabilitation of himself as romantic hero, the blood "bounding along his veins," thoughts "rioting through his brain, proud, joyful, tender, valorous." A kind of Middle Eastern enchantment overtakes him, reminiscent of the spell that sends the young hero of "Araby" on a vain crusade to a commercial fair in the service of an idealized fifteen-year-old Madonna. With adolescent insouciance, Gabriel wishes "to run after her noiselessly, catch her by the shoulders and say something foolish and affectionate into her ear," to "defend her against something and then be alone with her."

This is a romance whose object is not ultimately the beloved, of course, but the male hero idealizing himself to himself, as he does here literally as we read. Among the tender memories of "their secret life together" that "burst like stars upon his memory" is the image of a man they had seen together making bottles in a roaring furnace, whose recollection inspires "a wave of yet more tender joy" and "like the tender fire of stars moments of their life together . . . broke upon and illumined his memory"—as if Gabriel himself has seized the narrative, wresting out images to deploy as phrases and phrases to suggest further images, writing himself headlong towards his own undoing.

Like the young hero of "Araby," surely a kind of juvenile version of Gabriel and no doubt projected like him out of Joyce himself, Gabriel is calling upon the language of popular romance, with its valor, virginity, and blood, whose cultural origins it is important to remember are in the aristocratic literary and cultural codes of the Middle Ages, which modeled sexual and religious devotion together around the image of the Virgin and shaped the courtly hero to the romantic quest on the one hand and the knightly crusade for the liberation of Jerusalem on the other: hence the "eastern enchantment," the lurking figure of the Saracen, and an atmosphere of sexuality sublimated by religious feeling. "For the years, he felt, had not quenched his soul or hers," one could almost say, Gabriel *writes*; "Their children, his writing, her household cares had not quenched all their souls' tender fire." Indeed, Gabriel's own words—"Why is it that words like these seem to me so dull and cold? Is it because there is no word tender enough to be your name?"—words that Joyce had actually used in a letter to Nora, inscribe themselves upon the narrative and "like distant music" are "borne towards him from the past."

The language of enchantment, the well-known Orientalism fashioned by a popular press out of an eclectic mix of medievalism, illustrated storybook, fairy tale, and *The Arabian Nights,* is an aristocratic secular mythology that by repressing or displacing a divine figure or sacred event throws the emotional tone of that figure or event, and its sense of deep meaning or importance, over the entire extent of what would otherwise be sheer fantasy, persistently implying or intimating it but, unlike orthodox enactments or remembrances, never permitting its closure in a thorough conceptualization. Yet without its institutional anchor, the sacred readily transforms itself into, and reveals its affinities with, the profane. Gabriel's inventive sublimations, proceeding not only from the humiliations of the evening but from the small exhilarations of his eloquence and his wit, arouse him with an energy that at the touch of his wife's body, "musical and strange and perfumed," as if she were a Turkish princess, sends through him "a keen pang of lust."

Though Gabriel has been, and continues to be, foolish and self-centered, and cannot escape the chastening of the gentle irony Joyce, by the activity of context, has directed against him, it is hard to find fault with a man who at the end of a festive evening wants to make love to his wife. One could say confidentially that such would seem to be the very end and purpose of festivity, to drive men and women in that direction. Though couched, perhaps, in the self-indulgent discourse of romance, his memories of their past life together, in their concreteness and particularity—her letter in the heliotrope envelope, the railroad ticket in her glove, the birds twittering in the ivy on their first morning together—surely betoken the emotion our culture has construed as romantic love, particularly as they erupt through Gabriel's consciousness of their "dull existence together" and bring a sense of festive renewal, as if "they had escaped their lives and duties . . . and run away together with wild and radiant hearts to a new adventure." Insofar as we can identify Gretta with Nora Barnacle, who like Gretta lost a young lover from Galway to consumption (and I think we can identify them very closely indeed), we cannot, I think, doubt Gabriel's love for her, the woman who, as Joyce wrote to Nora, "from whose love and whose company I have still to learn the secrets of life," nor doubt that she is connected in his mind, as Nora was in Joyce's, with his native country. Nor, finally, can we overlook the fundamental contradictions inherent in a love projected perhaps out of a repressed contrasexual aspect, an anima always either idealized or degraded: "One moment I see you like a virgin or madonna," Joyce wrote to Nora, "the next moment I see you shameless, insolent, half naked and obscene!"[30]

And yet, in a narrative newly tinted, though subtly, with a Catholic conscience, the very word "lust," which is after all one of the Seven Deadlies, brings something craven and urgent into the story, and as Gretta ascends the stairs with Gabriel behind her, her "head bowed in ascent, her frail shoulders curved as with a burden, her skirt tightly girt about her," Joyce communicates with an almost pornographic intensity the palpable sexual need, a "fever of rage and desire" in which the mood of enchantment suddenly dissolves. In the wee hours the hotel, with its porter dozing in his hooded chair, the thick carpeted stairs, and the guttering candle, is moreover strongly reminiscent of an empty church, and though Gabriel sends the candle away and locks the door in anticipation of love, the room in which the couple finds itself is less a honeymoon suite than a kind of crypt, where "a ghastly light from the street lamp lay in a long shaft from one window to the door." Romance and ghost story are not far apart; within sexuality itself lies the dread of violation and obliteration, while beyond adventure and consummation lie gloom, desolation, grief, and loss.

Something sinister, evil perhaps, has entered the story, sown by Gabriel's own self-absorption, his rebuff to Gretta, the failure of his imagination to reach out to her as anything more than a figure in a story of his own making, and further, a woman whose own independent subjectivity he has denied. As Gretta unhooks her waist we feel Gabriel's almost uncontrollable urgency, and the horrible gulf that has opened between his "riot of emotion" and the banality of their conversation. What had been pretentious in Gabriel now becomes false, and struggling with "diffidence" he delivers an awkward, fatuous, and arrogant speech about the "poor fellow" Freddy Malins so remote from his thought that it seems more to speak him, as if he were diabolically possessed. As Vincent Pecora notes, Gabriel ironically makes a convincing show of generosity to Gretta precisely at the moment he is, to us, at his worst—but would we prefer that Gabriel entirely ignore his wife's mood and, in effect, rape her?[31] Gretta, though "abstracted," and who seems scarcely to be listening, rewards him with a spontaneous kiss in tribute to his generosity—he has lent Malins a sovereign—drawing Gabriel into a moment of tenderness that he misperceives as a sign of sexual compliance. As he draws her to him, and in an almost paternal way attempts to coax her out of herself—"Tell me what it is, Gretta. I think I know what is the matter. Do I know?"—Gretta offers her confession, breaking away from him and hiding her face on the bed rail, that she is thinking of "The Lass of Aughrim." Gretta's substitution, at precisely that moment when, in Gabriel's scripting of the moment, she would have signaled her compliance, or actually commenced it, works like a razor to separate Gabriel's consciousness of himself from himself, and as he approaches her he catches a sight of himself, a kind of stranger, in the mirror, "his broad well-filled shirt front, the face whose expression always puzzled him when he saw it in a mirror, and his glimmering gilt-rimmed eyeglasses."

Perhaps on some level Gretta's decision to disclose the memory she had "locked in her heart for so many years" arises from anger against her husband for his treatment of her: an anger, perhaps, whose history long antedates this evening's unkindness. Torchiana makes the affecting suggestion that in fact, as Michael Furey had died at the same time of year, he has been on Gretta's mind all evening;[32] hence the "three mortal hours" it takes her to dress herself. And yet as its dialogic position indicates, Gretta's confession *is* also kind of compliance, a giving of an exceedingly intimate part of herself, more precious certainly at this stage than the mere gift of her body. Certainly Gretta's heart, too, has been melted by the festivity, opening her to an emotion that in other circumstances a married woman with children might dismiss, albeit sentimentally, as an infatuation, or in any case immature. But the story she tells is of a country girl, who walks with her lover along the lanes "the way they do in the country," and where courtship and love in any case cleave closer to the trajectory of adolescent sexual development than in an industrial society. No doubt both Gretta and Gabriel will feel better in the morning—but for now, her grief is real: and if Joyce has intended to wreak vengeance upon Gabriel Conroy for his failure of imagination and his violations of natural piety, then Gabriel has more than met his match in Michael Furey.

Michael Furey! What mortal could exceed, for sheer beauty, force, and innocence, this delicate boy in the gasworks, rescued by death "in the full glory" of his passion from the ignominy of the human condition, which as Gabriel sees it can only be to "fade and wither dismally with age," like old Browne and poor Aunt Julia? The very name thrusts him into the story like a vengeful god out of Old Irish legend wielding a flaming sword, felling with mighty strokes the ugly human overgrowth of artifice, self-deception, and pride and freshening the world with the sacrifice of his youth.

Thus confronted, and so unexpectedly, Gabriel does not do well: for a moment he suspects Gretta of deceiving him concerning the trip to Galway, and there is a suggestion, a short time later, as he glances at Gretta's discarded clothes, that he contemplates the possibility of an undisclosed sexual intimacy between Gretta and Michael. With jealousy's self-confirming obsession he badgers Gretta to confess that she was in love with Michael; she will concede only that she "was great with him at that time"—as if, taking the phrase in another sense, she was about to give birth, a virgin birth in this case, to him—and perhaps for the first time thus acknowledges to herself, or finally accepts, that, as Gabriel will put it, "such a feeling must be love." With failed irony he attempts, of all things, to relegate the boy to some social category beneath him, as his tone of voice indicates. But Gretta sees nothing amusing, as perhaps a reader might, to find that a young lover who might have sprung out of folklore or balladry was a "boy in the gasworks"—for Joyce does not permit us to fall, with Gabriel, entirely under the romantic spell with which Gretta has surrounded her ballad of Michael Furey.

Even such a thing as pedestrian as the gas, however, cannot escape, by this stage in the story, at least the suspicion of symbolicity. We have perhaps as early as the story's opening scene seen Lily's pale complexion grow still paler in the gaslight of the pantry, though the gas paradoxically is the source of the light and warmth that permeates the aunts' house and that dazzles Gabriel's eyes. And as the guests depart we hear Aunt Kate say in confidence of Mr. Browne that he has been "laid on here like the gas," that is, "everywhere," recalling the Dublin proverb that "Death is busy everywhere"[33]—a funereal theme perhaps elaborated in the enigmatic cabman and his dark, rattling equipage. In the wheezy hall door that greets us at the outset, in Gabriel's fears for Gretta's health, in Freddy Malins's bronchitic laughter, in D'Arcy's cold, and finally in Michael's consumption, Death, as Torchiana suggests, seems to be attempting to enter the world, like gas, through the respiratory tract.[34]

Disconcerted by Lily and embarrassed by Miss Ivors, but in both instances still capable of rescuing the social identity he wishes to project with gestures, speeches, merry-making, and fantasy, Gabriel now takes a humiliating blow that strikes at the very root of his manhood and at last exposes him, striking off his adoptive self like a discarded mask: "A shameful consciousness of his own person assailed him. He saw himself as a ludicrous figure, acting as a pennyboy for his aunts, a nervous, well-meaning sentimentalist, orating to vulgarians and idealizing his own clownish lusts, the pitiable fatuous fellow he had caught a glimpse of in the mirror."

Here as earlier in the story Gabriel is too hard on himself; but the same capacity for literary invention that has facilitated to this point his cultural posturing and his romantic fantasy now serves to dispel them. There is little occasion or opportunity for pretense for a man alone with his wife, preparing to retire, in a darkened hotel room, as his failed boast about the sovereign has shown. Instead he experiences for the first time in the story a kind of psychological nakedness, and turns his back to the light so that Gretta will not detect "the shame that burned upon his forehead."

A "kinder note than he had intended" has entered Gabriel's voice, and his effort to continue his "tone of cold interrogation" founders in a kind of weariness. Yet Gabriel's mortification is not yet complete. Furey died of consumption, and Gabriel with his question suspects as much. But her answer resounds with a force before which the ordinary ego is powerless to withstand and which shakes to the foundations a nature grounded in self-love:

"I think he died for me."

In the double perspective through which Joyce narrates this scene we can detect in Gretta's pronouncement not only the influence of the folkloric landscape of "The Lass of Aughrim" into which she has written herself, where lovers languish and die for their disdainful ladies and are sung about in ballads, but also perhaps a mortally precise blow to her husband's masculine pride—indeed, to his confidence in his very existence. As Vincent Pecora points out, the boy, in Gretta's version, enacts the role played out in the ballad by an abandoned girl.[35] Beyond even the romantic turn of her phrase, "he died for me," there is an intimation that seems to shift the linguistic ground of the narrative, subtly displacing the narrative voice from its genesis in the point at which the narrator parasitizes Gabriel's consciousness and recentering it in the narrator's own commanding but impersonal intelligence, where the movements of Gabriel's mind are rendered in the narrative but not constituted by it, where a language that, only a few passages earlier, we could take as Gabriel's elated mimesis of particular romantic discourse now takes on original and literal force and authority. In short, the story seems to shift generically, sliding off the foundations of realistic fiction, with its naturalistic depiction, its real-world social intercourse, its philosophical impetus, and above all its personal voice, towards the realm of romance, ghost story, legend, and myth.

"A vague terror seized Gabriel at this answer, as if, at that hour when he had hoped to triumph, some impalpable and vindictive being was coming against him, gathering forces against him in its vague world." For this moment the story's real-world setting is done away with, leaving Gabriel alone on a kind of shadowy plain, almost as a kind of warrior hero, or in a kind of hollow darkness where beyond the horizon of his awareness lies a supernatural force, perhaps massive in extent, like an army, preparing for him some unimaginable retribution ordained by gods or by God. Gabriel's anxiety about his level of culture, his sense of sexual inadequacy, now gives way to a terrible surmise, of his innate irredeemability, a sense of moral unworthiness so profound that the universe itself can turn and expel him. It is an infantile terror, inarticulable, formless, a remembrance of a fear that with the loss of the mother's body will come darkness and annihilation—the dark underside of festivity, a transitional moment in which the ego is plunged into oblivion with no promise of return.

But he shakes it off, for the moment; and Gretta tells her sad story to Gabriel's now chastened, even indifferent ears, recalling the moment when Michael Furey throws gravel up against her window to bring her out into the garden, where, standing under a tree and shivering in the cold he tells her he does not wish to live. At the recollection of the news of his death Gretta breaks into sobs, and, as Gabriel leaves her to her grief, shortly falls asleep.

That a consumptive boy should have died like the Sweet William of the ballads for love of a girl is a sad and a touching story, though in the clear light of day it would perhaps be more entirely accurate to say unsentimentally that Michael Furey has died as much of consumption as of love. But we are not in the clear light of day; and in any case the import of Gretta's tale is as much in the sheer fact of it as in its substance for it is, again, ultimately a gift of love, whose power from this point forward will shape Gabriel's spiritual awakening. Never mind that a consumptive boy in the gasworks died years ago in the throes of a youthful passion. As far as Gabriel is concerned, a man has died for Gretta's sake, and against this measure of what is after all the ultimate sacrifice, as Gabriel is compelled now to interpret it, he can only think "how poor a part he, her husband, had played in her life"—a conclusion with which, again, in the clear light of day, we might wish to take at least partial exception: they have had, after all, that "romance in their lives," as Gabriel's own memories attest, and through marriage and children have shared what Michael and Gretta could not, the transience of the mortal life that compels us to love what we cannot have forever.

Thus that it is better "to pass boldly into that other world, than to fade and wither dismally with age," is a proposition that like the other self-estimates Gabriel offers in these closing passages Joyce cannot wholly endorse, but rather one that reflects his immediate recoil from a new perception of existence and the contraction of its limits. The chill of the first intimations of death seem to take on concrete form as Gabriel stretches cautiously, so as not to wake Gretta, under the sheets, his shoulders chilled by the cold air of the room. Joyce it seems has made us privy to the first moment in Gabriel's life when a consciousness of mortality, working its gradual purposes in the human career, as, looking upon Gretta's sleeping face he realizes that she is no longer the girlish beauty for whom Michael Furey had braved death, awakens a capacity for love not dedicated to the preservation of the self but like a parent's love dedicated, selflessly, to the beloved. That is what Michael Furey's sacrifice means to Gabriel, his eyes filling with tears, as he reflects upon it: "He had never felt like that himself towards any woman, but he knew that such a feeling must be love." And yet it is love—not a self-aggrandizing kind contingent upon mastery and control, but of the self-sacrificing kind that because it is divine can spread itself throughout creation, infinitely—that touches him when, as he gazes upon his sleeping wife, "a strange, friendly pity for her" enters his soul.

In the remarkable closing passages of "The Dead" Gabriel's identity dissolves, "fading out into a grey impalpable world," while the "solid world itself" is "dissolving and dwindling." In the moments before sleep, and it might be said that the closing lines of story are a representation of Gabriel's loss of consciousness and a descent into the half-life between thought and dream, Gabriel becomes a wandering soul, his social being in a sense sloughed off like the mortal body. The tears that well up in his eyes betray that dissolution of identity, for though they may be said to spring from grief for the loss of himself, they also betoken a deep empathetic absorption into Gretta and her bereavement, as he shares with her, in a sense becoming her, the image of Michael Furey's eyes and wonders at a constancy so great that she can have held it in her heart so many years, at the same time as he feels, empathetically, that same devotion.

When in the partial darkness he imagines he sees "the form of a young man standing under a dripping tree" he is still, in a sense, absorbed in Gretta, remembering Michael Furey; and yet "form" is abstract and empty, at once merely a form, a kind of half-perceived presence or shadow, and an idea, the form of a young man as it is ideally, and in which Gabriel's own existence has a part, especially since he cannot actually remember but must imagine the dead boy, and imagine him in relation to Gretta—and hence in some sense extend his own identity into the young man's, at the same time as he takes something of the young man into himself. Nor is the garden, without any particularizing elements beyond its dripping tree, simply the garden of Gretta's memory at Nun's Island, but an apparition, at once vividly sensory and shimmeringly hallucinatory, a visible darkness interior to consciousness but at the same time an object of consciousness and hence in a sense a kind of unbodied locale where imagination lends animation and presence to the stirrings of undirected or withdrawn perception, which on the one hand are the impressions of its own organic activity and on the other the phantom manifestations of unremembered images. Hence I shall forbear mentioning the Garden of Gethsemane, which seems hardly necessary to mention, and yet in a sense far too singular to mention.

Marvels and miracles, literarily and mythologically speaking, occur in such gardens. "Other forms were near . . . he was conscious of, but could not apprehend, their wayward and flickering existence." In their plurality, these "forms" acquire integrity and limit, no longer mere shadows nor "shades," though the earlier use of the term has brought us into a kind of Odyssean underworld, where Odysseus incidentally encountered among other ghosts his own mother—but imbued, if not with substance, with a kind of spiritual reality, like Plato's transcendent forms. "His soul had approached that region where dwell the vast hosts of the dead."

Gabriel is nearing the end of one journey and poised to begin another. He is a solitary soul, but nearing that "vague world" or "that other world" whose remote existence he first surmised in his fleeting moment of terror, an illimitable multiplicity—not, of course, some ghastly holocaust of heaped corpses, but of unexpired lives somehow consummated in their passage out of earthly existence. Death's harvest is appalling; but as he approaches the bourn of it his terror is gone, and instead he comes to feel with the dead, as he considers the solid world that they "had at one time reared and lived in," a kind of compassion or confraternity, one that points, certainly, to a sense of his own mortality, and to the solid world in which he can now perceive himself, with the dead, as an absence. What a moment before had been horrid now comes to seem a kind of natural wonder, and, like the falling snow, a beauty. The harvest of the dead is, paradoxically, also the multitudinous womb of life, the cosmos itself conceived, and conceiving, as an interior female darkness to which we at once continually return and out of which we are continually being born.

Is Gabriel then, when he turns again to the window, in the "solid world" of which we have been reading? It is, indeed, the very same panoply of commonplace forms—a hotel room, a bed, a street light outside the window—in which only a moment before he had lain down beside his wife. But we are, as it were, through the dissolution of Gabriel's identity, and the transmutation of a perception that has approached "that region where dwell the vast hosts of the dead," in a different kind of story, or rather, in a story in which one kind of language has gradually imposed itself upon and in effect replaced another, so that a narrative set in the objective rational world of fictive realism, precisely at the moment it returns us to that world with an empirical detail, a few light taps on the window, has become a kind of dream shaped by psychic and mythic, not physical or historical, forces.

"A few lights taps upon the pane made him turn to the window." It is the snow: attracting his attention again, as it has at several earlier points. But the taps on the windowpane commute us, too, retroactively, to the moment at which Michael Furey throws pebbles up against Gretta's windowpane; thus like a ghost Michael Furey is outside again, somehow embodied as the snow, perhaps "wayward and flickering" like the snow, beckoning to a soul so thoroughly absorbed in the identities both of Gretta and of her beloved that he can scarcely be called "Gabriel" at all—except that Gabriel, too, had tapped his fingers on the wet windowpane some hours earlier, his own gesture now reproduced in the presence outside the window, and, to repeat, in the narrative whose genesis is consistently out of the already deployed, but transformed, linguistic and sensory resources of Gabriel's experience. Psychologically, it is a moment forged in Gabriel's imagination out of love, memory, and approaching sleep; but the genesis of the narrative can no longer be said to rest with Gabriel or through him in any narrow psychological sense.

The deterioration of rational categories that comes with sleep and dreams, but particularly with the transitional state in which we find Gabriel in these culminating moments extends the narrative into a linguistic and psychic territory beyond the narrow pieties, domestic, religious, social, and political, in which the characters of *Dubliners* have their moral existence.

There is scarcely a story in the collection that does not show us a figure whose efforts to compensate lack, frustration, or inadequacy only snare him or her more fatally in the very deficiencies of character or judgment in which the predicament originates. It is not difficult to imagine a similar fate for Gabriel Conroy: a story in which, perhaps, he succeeds, after an evening of failure, in "overmastering" his wife, "crushing her body" against his own, or attempts and fails to overmaster her—thus joining the other louts, brutes, cads, and weaklings that populate the streets of Joyce's Dublin, a world that offers to the imagination no field in which to realize its own ends, or, as in "Araby," punishes the character who permits himself to be temporarily inspired by fantasies and wishes. Indeed, I suppose that even "The Dead" could be read in such a way. *Dubliners* speaks to a cultural impoverishment whose consequence for the personal life is moral entrapment; each character whom Joyce exposes, typically at an intimate or even purely interior moment, for his or her weakness, veniality, or brutality is also himself or herself constituted by institutional structures—marriage, the family, the household, the pub, the marketplace, the bureaucracy, the municipality, the church—that morally he can move within and among but not beyond.

We have had enough of these social formations, the church particularly; but we have had little of what the church represents. In the concluding passages of "The Dead," which also of course terminate the collection of stories, a pathway towards transcendence opens in the metaphorical landscape of the story, moving not away from Ireland towards "the continent," as Gabriel has done, but towards and into it, not merely as place or scene, nor, in the ethnographic sense, as a culture, but as a sacred order and the object of a spiritual quest. Were Gabriel a character in another story Joyce might simply have fixed him in his pretensions, mired him in his little failures, or perhaps condemned him to some sottish gesture, and worse, a consciousness of its sottishness, towards his wife. But we have already detected in the narrative a fondness for Gabriel, and the presence of a sensibility from which that fondness proceeds; and observed in him, not only genuine courtliness and charm, however misbegotten, but imagination and generosity, and even in the end, towards Gretta, friendship, tenderness, compassion, and love. In what, then, for Gabriel, can his redemption consist? It is perhaps a wayward intellect that absorbs, in the final passages, identities, memories, and sensory impressions into one another: but the ghost that beckons here with a few light taps upon the pane is a lover's ghost—and Gabriel, though he is not strictly speaking the socially masked Gabriel Conroy, but an unmasked soul, divested of self, having himself learned to love, is now himself beloved.

Something is calling to him, as Michael had called to Gretta—and not a thing that can be strictly identified with any palpable or impalpable manifestation: not the ghost of Michael Furey, though a momentary summoning of his ghost was essential to the quality of that moment, nor certainly the snow itself, which is nevertheless its indication, the flakes "silver and dark" recalling the archangel that brings the souls of men to judgment;[36] better to say, perhaps, that its mystery lies concealed in the curious verbal expedient of an impersonal pronoun, the "it" that snows and rains that is neither God nor nature but a kind of nonce made to perform the purely syntactic function of supplying the agent of a natural action. The snow, in any case, is a sign to Gabriel that "the time had come for him to set out on his journey westward."

It is a strange sentence: but we can learn much about it simply by its placement. Gabriel has been given a sign; and some imperative or duty until now postponed, but foreordained, and, it seems, a central and singular event in a lifetime—indeed in the broadest sense it is Gabriel's consciousness of mortality, his own and others', that prompts this recognition—now presents itself to him as timely, immediate, imperative. The west has already been associated in the story with the west of Ireland, the Aran Isles, and in turn with the folklife in which Ireland's authentic culture may be presumed to exist and where it may be searched out. On the shallowest dramatic level, Gabriel has merely resolved, in his half-sleep, to take a holiday with Gretta after all, as if it were something he can not only no longer avoid but in which he has found an act of self-abdication that relieves the burden of resistance he has carried throughout the story and that opens him to acceptance of that part of himself embodied in his love for Gretta. That he views the holiday in a larger sense, as an element in his own soul's progress, is indicated by the allegorical turn he puts on the idea with the phrase "journey westward": it is the turn we put on our life's significant pilgrimages, most particularly our returns, after long absence, to the home that in our adolescent pride and hope we have rejected: that, in any case, is the mythos to which, on this level at least, Gabriel's insight conforms, as he recognizes the universality of this juncture in his own life.

Yet, as we've said, we are in this concluding passage in a world noetically reduplicated and semiotically charged, a world at once natural and supernatural. On this level, Gabriel's journey westward takes place literally before our eyes, with a winged, aerial mobility fit for an archangel. His imagination follows the snow falling on "every part of the dark central plain, on the treeless hills, falling softly upon the Bog of Allen and, farther westward, softly falling into the dark mutinous Shannon waves." In rehearsing these place names and calling up the images associated with them Gabriel rehearses, as one who wishes to recover, his familiarity with the country and restores it in its integrity to consciousness. But this is not the quaint, kelly green Ireland of tourism, postal cards, and language lessons. It is a wilderness: a dark plain, treeless hills, a treacherous bog, and dark mutinous waves that like the eyes of famished sailors threaten the overthrow of all worldly authority, hardly a geographical locale at all, but a symbolic one, the godforsaken waste through which the soul on its journey, as those perhaps likened, in the old allegories, to a knight on his quest, must pass in its solitude and nakedness along his predestined route. Gabriel Conroy, gallant, courteous, eloquent, or at least attempting to be so, his head swimming in the language of literary chivalry as he styles himself a youth escaping with his beloved "with wild and radiant hearts to a new adventure," here ventures beyond the merely courtly code of knightly virtue, and the merely rhetorical flourishes of a cheap sentimental language, towards the heart of the deep historical culture that has made him, towards the remembrance of, and the encounter with, its definitive event.

At the end of this transition Gabriel finds himself in the "lonely churchyard where Michael Furey lay buried." Here the snow "lay thickly drifted on the crooked crosses and the headstones, on the spears of the little gate, on the barren thorns." We are at a graveyard in Oughterard; but the crosses, the upthrust spears, the thorns belong to the moment of Christ's passion and sacrifice. It is, to be exact, the imagery, and yet not quite the image of Calvary—for the fully formulated image, its name in effect enunciated, would only arrest its meaning in a culturally constructed, reified, institutionalized, and official imagery and mythology,[37] just as the mystery of Gretta's figure on the stairs would have been dispelled had Gabriel succeeded in making the association between her image and the conventional chapel image of Mary. Instead the graveyard in which Michael Furey lies buried, set out with the signs of the mythic event that it displaces but does not disclose, reiterates but does not replace, takes on the huge significance of that event without dispelling it in the customary and habitual embodiments, enactments, and expressions nor coupling it to the sources of social power. Like some strange anomalous emblem of folklore it renews the mystery of what it conceals by stirring to life, but neither recalling, identifying, nor naming, the basic cultural forms whose truth, like the truth of a repressed memory, remains quiescent even when the memory itself is staring us in the face: or perhaps because it is staring us in the face.

As Ellmann observes, Gabriel by "giving up what he has most valued in himself" has like Furey in some sense sacrificed himself for love: but, again, it is important not to draw the lines of identity, including the identity of signs and symbols, too sharply at this juncture in the story.[38] By calling upon the imagery of Calvary, Joyce is more than comparing Furey's sacrifice to the divine sacrifice, and more than placing the collapse of Gabriel's social being between the image of a romantic hero on the one hand and of a dying god on the other. No. They are all the same: the young man at once driven by love and in the grip of death, suffering, the love of a woman that Gabriel himself has felt keenly both as the urgency of desire and as the reminiscence of death, the gift of redemption through a god who died for love. In the conjunction of these images and these forces, consummating Gabriel's unsatisfied desire at the most sublime level, Joyce momentarily seizes for our contemplation the unbodied erotic force that is the creation, the life, and the reality of the world.

To forge this essential unity Joyce has called upon romantic, classical, and Christian discourses, and perhaps an Old Irish saga, synthesizing them in a depersonalization and diffusion of consciousness that absorbs Furey, Gabriel, and Gretta into one another and in the last sentence, with conscientiously fashioned assonant phrases and an inversion that call attention to the inscription as such, includes narrator with them and, in the last phrase echoes the Nicene Creed: "His soul swooned slowly as he heard the snow falling faintly through the universe and faintly falling, like the descent of their last end, upon all the living and the dead."[39] Gabriel is falling, or has fallen asleep in the last sentence, as its assonance, its heavily tolling triple accents, seem to convey, by slowing the momentum of the syntax, turning it momentarily back upon itself, as the narrative approaches its terminus; but his swoon is implicitly assimilated to Christ's on the cross, imparted by the previous sentence, and like Christ's swoon occurs in the cosmic setting that the imagery, the eschatological language, and especially the all-inclusive word "universe" all generate.

As Warren Beck observes, Gabriel's swoon "is neither inanimate repose nor collapse, but trancelike arrestment by an absorbing vision, in which the immediate and personal are diffused into the universal."[40] We find the same visionary swoon, and some of the same accompanying language, in *A Portrait of the Artist as a Young Man,* as Stephen Dedalus pauses to gaze upon a wading girl "touched with the wonder of mortal beauty": "The first faint noise of gently moving water broke the silence, low and faint and whispering, faint as the bells of sleep; hither and thither: and a faint flame trembled on her cheek."[41]

"Heavenly God!" cries Stephen's soul, "in an outburst of profane joy"—and he sets out across the strand, full of the ecstasy of his vision of a "wild angel, an angel of mortal youth and beauty," until he finds, as the day draws to a close, a sandy nook in which to rest:

> He felt above him the vast indifferent dome and the calm processes of the heavenly bodies; and the earth beneath him, the earth that had borne him, had taken him to her breast. He closed his eyes in the languor of sleep. His eyelids trembled as if they felt the strange light of some new world. His soul was swooning into some new world, fantastic, dim, uncertain as under sea, traversed by cloudy shapes and beings. A world, a glimmer, or a flower? Glimmering and trembling, trembling and unfolding, a breaking light, an opening flower, it spread in endless succession to itself, breaking in full crimson and unfolding and fading to palest rose, leaf by leaf and wave of light by wave of light, flooding all the heavens with its soft flushes, every flush deeper than the other.

It is a vision of warmth, sunset and light, rather than of darkness, cold and snow; but the pattern, of a revelation, a consciousness of the vast but tender presences of Creation, of a silence broken only by faint, scarcely audible or even inaudible sounds, of impending sleep, the withdrawal of the senses while sensation still plays upon them, and the outflowing of consciousness into the transformed world that seems to partake of the conscious interior and is indistinguishable from it, above all the sexual context, is Joyce's means of representing the expiration of personal, social, and even the cultural identity and the absorption of the soul into the female body of the world, where God, or the artist, creates, or recreates, "life out of life."

The literary mimesis by which language projected out of itself returns to constitute and shape the self is a technical displacement of the ethnomimetic process and both Joyce's technique and part of his subject in "The Dead"; but Joyce's representation, where Michael Furey and Gabriel Conroy are assimilated to and enact the passion of Christian culture's god incarnate, carries us with Gabriel to the heart of ethnomimesis itself, the "authentic form of the treasure hoard," where the ethnonoetic plenum yields up for human imitation its most holy form, the very form that festivity, with its death and rebirth of the self, enacts and reenacts.

Snow is metereological; but what can we say of a snow that falls, not only out of the early morning sky—let us recall that the end of the story, and of the collection, occurs at dawn—but that Gabriel hears falling, like words, throughout the universe?

The snow, it seems, is more than a simple rhetorical figure, and, if it is a sign, it is one whose signification modulates and modulates again so that it can be said, and has been said, more or less convincingly, to signify, among other ideas, purity, God and apocalypse, and even, perhaps, as we have just suggested, uttered words, that transform all forms into its own form, at once art and death. One thinks here of the "snowy landscape" in Hawthorne's *Blithedale Romance*, "a lifeless copy of the world in marble."[42] At one point the snow would seem to suggest pervasive oppression, perhaps at bottom political; at another it would seem to suggest precisely the transcendence of oppression. Among his many other intriguing suggestions is Torchiana's that in Irish folk tradition snow at Christmastime is a harbinger of early spring, reminding us that the party is in a house owned by a corn-factor.[43]

Snow is a negotiating term in "The Dead," one that through the transfiguring power of Gabriel's imagination organizes a certain inventory of ideas at several levels of metaphoricity, from the flatly literal to the ineffably abstract or mystical, absorbs them into itself and, in the story's conclusion, metaphorically saturated, precipitates them through Gabriel's consciousness, over all of Ireland, throughout the universe, and into the closing lines of the story itself.

These levels, to survey them briefly, are, first, the literal snow, falling onto the quay, in the light of the street lamp, and over Ireland; next, the snow as Gabriel perceives it, from which a number of related explicit comparisons arise; the snow as a narrative figure, where it both represents the shift in consciousness that we observe at the conclusion as he falls asleep, where indeed the snow is a kind of sightless picture of the closing down or obscuring of rational awareness with the coming of sleep, and at the same time an element in the formation of his thoughts as they move from perception into language and from language into an orchestration of imagery; as a coefficient in the story's oft-noted system of contrasts between light and dark, heat and cold, life and death; and finally as an immanence, all-embracing, that if we cannot actually identify as the body of God is something close, certainly, to what Stephen Dedalus in *Portrait* describes as the esthetic mystery and that can serve, I think, as a poetic account of the working of "The Dead":

> The simplest epical form is seen emerging out of lyrical literature when the artist prolongs and broods upon himself as the centre of an epical event and this form progresses till the centre of emotional gravity is

equidistant from the artist himself and from others. The narrative is no longer personal. The personality of the artist passes into the narration itself, flowing round and round the persons in the action like a vital sea. This progress you will see easily in that old English ballad Turpin Hero which begins in the first person and ends in the third person. The dramatic form is reached when the vitality which has flowed and eddied round each person fills every person with such vital force that he or she assumes a proper and intangible esthetic life. The personality of the artist, at first a cry or a cadence or a mood and then a fluent and lambent narrative, finally refines itself out of existence, impersonalizes itself, so to speak. The esthetic image in the dramatic form is life purified in and reprojected from the human imagination. The mystery of esthetic like that of material creation is accomplished. The artist, like the God of the creation, remains within or behind or beyond or above his handiwork, invisible, refined out of existence, indifferent, paring his fingernails.[44]

. . . and, we might add, impertinently, to this famous passage, the mystery of esthetic creation, in "The Dead," not only like, but implicitly likened to, material creation through the falling snow. This transformation from lyrical to epical, to use Stephen's terms, from personal to impersonal, occurs, again, in "The Dead" through the transformative power of Gabriel's imagination, whose lyrical turns upon the perception of the snow by steps exteriorize and sublimate themselves until they become, as his personality gives way, the world in which his spirit moves and over which presides an omnipresent awareness—no longer, at least not obviously, a distinctive rhetorical "voice"—projected into the narrative, not as a presence, but as a power, in the consecrating snow that falls through the universe.

We can trace this development. As Gabriel arrives at the Misses Morkan's house the narrator highlights the snow that he brings in with him from the outdoors with similes suggestive of the same festive spirit we detected in the metaphors of the feast: the snow lies like a cape on his shoulders, and like toecaps on his shoes, as if he were a gentleman in some sort of formal costume, undertaker or bridegroom or both; the snow, moreover, lies atop the Wellington monument like a cap, one that gleams and flashes like a badge or shield on a sunlit parade ground. These are all, of course, purely lyrical touches that like the feast itself connect the festive atmosphere to the imagery of social and political power. In them, however, begins, too, the system of contrasts that elaborates the cosmic topography through which Gabriel's soul moves. His coat is a "snow stiffed frieze" from which cold air escapes as if from an opened tomb; his "hot, trembling fingers" tap on the cold windowpane, as he contrasts the freshness and purity of the world outside to the stuffiness and confinement of the human warmth within. As he and Gretta stroll through the slush towards their hotel "moments of their secret life together burst like stars upon his memory" and the intense heat of a glassblower's fire that is among these remembered moments soon metaphorizes itself as the fires of lust that glow in his veins—all this in contrast to the darkness of the hotel room, the cold dismal rain in which Michael Furey had stood and caught his death, and finally the larger cavernous darkness of that "region where dwell the vast hosts of the dead." In these contrasts Joyce builds the universe in which his story will be played out.

We can observe Joyce commandeering these various strains, which begin with Lily and her pale, gas-lit face, and include the tapping of Gabriel's fingers on the windowpane, the ghastly light from the streetlamp, and so on, gathering to form the story's poetic finale. But we can best catch I think the function of the snow as a negotiating term by asking how it is that the penultimate paragraph, where Gabriel's soul approaches that region "where dwell the vast hosts of the dead," where he feels such compassion for and sympathy with them, a paragraph that carries us beyond the boundaries of ordinary realism without somehow disrupting our fundamental trust in it, can seem at once so uncanny and yet, in a sense, appropriate, even somehow familiar, the remembrance of the unremembered memory whose strange return we experience together with the narrator and the character. It is because we, with Gabriel, have already experienced it in a linguistic and sensory protoform that his language and imagination, in the conditions of dark and impending sleep, will transfigure: "Meeting a row of upturned faces he raised his eyes to the chandelier. The piano was playing a waltz tune and he could hear the skirts sweeping against the drawing-room door. People, perhaps, were standing in the snow on the quay outside, gazing up at the lighted windows and listening to the waltz music. The air was pure there. In the distance lay the park where the trees were weighted with snow. The Wellington Monument wore a gleaming cap of snow that flashed westward over the white field of Fifteen Acres."

Here, in the moment he begins his speech, is the seed of that formation that becomes the penultimate paragraph; here, in the people he imagines standing on the quay looking in upon the lighted windows, are the figures he transforms into the dead souls who look in upon the solid world they had once reared and lived in; here is the imagery of weighted snow that will fall over the churchyard and the compass or light pointing to the west into which Gabriel will take his long-deferred spiritual journey.

In Gabriel's lyric similes, with their festive quality, there is an essential recognition that the snow, as it touches us, and it touches all of us, and all equally, touches us with a kind of love and glory, almost, perhaps, a "strange, friendly pity," that is just the quality of the fringe of a cape over the shoulders or of a gleaming cap that in festivity celebrates what is, at bottom, what culture itself imitates, the bounty of God. The extraordinary snowfall, indeed, is itself festive; it seems to award itself to us, to honor, to *love* us. That is the recognition that Gabriel seems to have when he repeats to himself Mary Jane's words, themselves a quotation from the newspapers, that "Yes, the newspapers were right: snow was general all over Ireland." By taking up the headline Gabriel includes himself with all its readership, that is, the Irish people, a fact he had tacitly acknowledged when to Lily he averred that "we're in for a night of it," the greatest snow in thirty years being a cosmic event that involves, and in a festive spirit draws the entire people together in a collective and cosmic departure from the ordinary run of events.

But he also seems to have discovered in the words a metaphorical sense that he then affirms by repeating the expression. Yes, he seems to say, this snow that touches us all is general all over Ireland—indeed it pervades the universe. It softens the forms of all rationally constituted things and absorbs them into its own all-pervasive form; its vast hosts, in their infinite multiplicity, wayward, flickering, and numerous as human souls, fall softly, almost like a human touch, upon all the living and the dead, but faintly, too, for the assimilation of the literal snow to the pure universal snow of divine love is occurring, dramatically, in the middle zone of Gabriel's awareness where the snow figures in his dissolution of identity, the darkening of his conscious awareness, and the traces of withdrawn perception. If the story is as we've suggested a series of transformations, this series perhaps completes itself in these final phrases drawn from the pious lips of Mary Jane, whose piety, transmitted from the social to the sacred context, seems not merely the palaver of some frail mortal but an obdurate mystery, and a truth, that only a faith can penetrate. In the final self-canceling redundancy Gabriel borrows from Mary Jane, the snow falls "like the descent of their last end," an end to endings and hence a promise of eternal life.

Should Misses Morkan's annual *dance* recur next year, it will likely fall to Mary Jane to continue the tradition. Likely, too, however, that Gabriel will awake in the morning to the ordinary universe of petty inconveniences and quotidian concerns, particularly when the children have the sniffles, and there are a few feet of snow in the city streets; into the forestage of consciousness will return, again, his book reviews, his trips to the continent, the contents and discontents of a middle-class marriage on the threshold of middle age. New ghosts will succeed that of Michael Furey, who will not appear again in his own form, except as a boy in the gasworks, the lover of Gretta's girlhood, much diminished from his apotheosis on the evening of the Misses Morkan's annual dance. The mere conduct of life demands we conscientiously forget, even while sustaining them, the obdurate commitments in the absence of which there would be no life; how fitting, therefore, that the temporary abandonment of care should bring that festive epiphany, at once mortifying and glorifying, of what both constitutes and transcends us, the God whom we acknowledge precisely because we neither recognize nor remember him. This is a sublime, perhaps the most sublime cultural achievement, to discover—or is it to create?—in the empty universe an unconditional love that draws its protection around us, even against death, and around which we in turn form our human communities, our cultures. We cannot go farther than to say, following Mary Jane, that festivity is for the "honour of God," and that it is the register of such a faith.

part III

THE PARALLAX EFFECT

8

FANFARE FOR THE LITTLE GUY

THE SCOTS AND THE PICTS

Think, every time you pass the greasy alien on the street, that he was born thousands of years before the oldest native American; and he may have something to communicate to you, when you two shall have learned a common language. Remember that his very physiognomy is a cipher the key to which it behooves you to search for most diligently.
—Mary Antin, The Promised Land *(1912)*

The army must have been running out not only of men but of uniforms by March 1945, when it drafted Woody Guthrie for the third time, his two stints in the Merchant Marines not apparently having satisfied its thirst for his patriotism, because it couldn't find a uniform small enough to fit him. Many of us who have admired Woody Guthrie have seen the photograph of the new inductees at Fort Dix in May 1945, where a wiry long-necked fellow with a bushy head of black hair, at thirty-two visibly older than most of the rest of the men, looks as if he has got his suit on backwards. Like some impish impostor, he must be trying to fill the shoes and trousers of some real long-legged, barrel-chested soldier who has been swindled out of his clothes and who is shivering in his underwear in the barracks behind the group.

Measured against the fifty-odd other fresh-faced, scowling, or over-earnest young fellows extending across the frame, most of them filling their fatigues quite handsomely, nothing could be clearer than that Woody Guthrie didn't really belong. He seems almost to have sneaked into the picture, like the barber or the cook, or to be a kind of trick of it, like those wiseacres in group photographs who used to dart behind the old panoramic camera ahead of its arc so as to appear, in the final image, at both edges of the picture at the same time. You could almost say, so mobile is he, so impish, so droll, that Woody belonged to another race.

Woody's cultural proportions are large, even great, as great certainly as those physically more imposing men such as the athletic Paul Robeson or the lanky Pete Seeger, whose personal presence, in the many situations where the embodied man must for better or worse contend with the public

Woody Guthrie (far left) and others in front of army barracks, 1945.
Nora Guthrie Collection, courtesy of the Woody Guthrie Foundation and Archives.

persona, generally affirmed, or even enlarged, the authority and power already granted to them. Robeson was big, like his voice, very big; and Seeger stood, and stands, tall, as one who has made a career of principled opposition and indomitable, if at times insufferable, protest, must do. All politics is local, said the bearish and overbearing Tip O'Neill—as local, perhaps, as the few square feet of ground we require to stage a single interpersonal encounter. A mere handshake, a nod, a name enunciated—each is a subtle but seminal social moment that might first establish, and then endlessly reproduce, a routine of power that will ultimately manifest itself in movements, parties, elections, and regimes. No one knows this better than the professional politician.

If the personal is political, then at this irreducibly local level it is ineluctably true that the political is personal. At this level the personal is not merely a sluice through which subjectivity flows along its accidental meandering and ahistorical way, but a site at which the various streams of historical affiliation and collective experience, the social tributaries of the personal, converge with a kind of half-intelligible political meaning to which precisely because we cannot know it we must unconsciously submit. Struggle as we might in whatever way to extricate ourselves from the structures of power as we find them in whatever department of life, we remain mired in the personal, which is itself obdurately grounded, like it or not, in history.

Hence a relief map of social power, advantage, and preeminence, could it be laid upon the map of personal beauty, stature, and presence, if not quite congruent with it, would conform to it with startling regularity. Precisely at the point at which personal forces convert history into fate, and social forces gather fate up again into history, lies race—that most arbitrary of arbitrary signifiers that like all signs awash in culture and embedded in the thickness of history most unarbitrarily refuses to be dislodged from its significance. Race, as the nineteenth century knew, is located not in this place or that place, but everywhere, like culture; for "culture," in the anthropological sense, was what was then meant by the term; in the days before virtually instantaneous communications and global transport, race and culture appeared to grow up together, in the same human medium. That's why race, evolutionary theory, and social class could be combined to produce the weird science of phrenology, essentially a biological reinscription of the social hierarchy, implicitly inflected by race. Race was never what we thought it was, a class or a category, but rather a kaleidoscopically shifting human manifestation that marks the pauses and the densities of the social process as culture and history have shaped it. Race, it seems, is a marker of power, and distributions of power a kind of color-spectrum of race, so that while perpetually vanishing socially it is continually being recreated politically, asserting itself politically while concomitantly retreating socially. Where social differentiation produces the subtle or elusive distinction, we enlist "race," the more subtly and elusively, to enforce a practical division, while racial division fosters social distinction where no distinctively *social* factor would necessarily warrant it.

So various, elusive, and dynamic is race, as much so as today's configuration of clouds, that we sometimes yield to the temptation to distribute its properties as if they were fixed and permanent to people and cohesions of people for whom race, in the eye of time, is only a shadow that passes over, a rumor that passes through and is gone—as if race had an essence, an origin and an end, when in fact it has only formations, and endless transformations. Race, like music, is nowhere and nothing; and yet, like music, it always belongs to someone, someplace, and, migrate about as it will, finds itself burdened with meaning everywhere.

If race is so perfectly meaningless in itself that we overburden it with meaning, somehow finding in its myriad accidental associations and metaphorical resonances patterns of effects whose actual causes are long decayed and in any case buried in the past, it is because race, in a sense *is* history, an unconscious, yet visible, history. From it springs the dream imagery whose neurotic agitation haunts all our personal associations with unease and misgiving, stirs us with inexplicable attractions and repulsions, obscurely signifying where there is nothing significant. Hence it is full of signification, a kind of empty syntax ready to absorb to itself all the meanings of conquest, caste, and class, of peoples and their migrations, of specific historical enslavements, exploitations, and segregations, concentrations, and disperals that it both records and perpetuates. Despite our attempts to isolate it, to hold it up for scrutiny, as a biological, social, or political fiction, as an instrument for making, symbolically or actually, a better democracy or a poorer one, it remains tangled together with place and position, with allegiance, alliance, and belief, and hence with class, nation, and state, as a factor in human identity. That is because all of these forms of human social cohesion, insofar as they have histories, bring with them, however subtly or elusively, the racial markers that both indicate and have helped to produce and secure them.

The binaries of the racial semiotic inevitably accumulate at the sites of long-standing oppositions: Gentile and Jew, Western European and Eastern, Occidental and Oriental, White and Black, Anglo and "Other," and it is out of such binaries that we form the idea of race. But literary and pictorial traditions, with our happy complicity, have evolved a subtler racial language, where complexions fair and dark, features coarse and fine, statures tall and slender, short and squat, noses long and sharp or round and bulbous, lips thick or thin, eyes wide and narrow, brows low and high, voices shrill or deep have communicated as much social and moral information as would otherwise require whole treatises to elucidate. While in some respects a system of conventions peculiar to narrative or to drama, race is also a vernacular language in which meanings derived from one context may be recombined in new contexts to produce new and original meanings.

A French Canadian nose, for example, an Irish brow, and an Italian name (I am thinking of a character in a late-nineteenth-century novel called

The Cliff Dwellers by a smug Anglo-American named Henry Fuller) may summon in a few phrases an incorrigible and dangerous villain, while an African mouth, a patrician Anglo-Norman nose, and thick black Latin hair might produce an exotic sexual paragon (I am thinking of a fashion model). The traditional European systems of class, ethnic, regional, and national relations that were the milieu in which this racial language formed have in America been disrupted and scattered; from the minstrels and popular phrenologists of the nineteenth century to our own novelists, filmmakers, illustrators, photographers, and especially advertisers, we have been seeking as a culture to bring into alignment our European-derived racial language with our shifting power arrangements, to make intelligible on the landscape of American raciality the topography of dominance and submission, resistance and accommodation, center and margin, that have made and are making it.

None of us really escapes racial marking; it is only that we are more evidently "racial" as race the more transparently implies a social location. In this context "race" and "ethnicity" are of course simply alibis for social-political exclusion. By a kind of social trigonometry, these ideas reduce the complex fields of social distributions, of cultural, material, and actual capital into chronic alignments both conceptual and actual whose essence is violence. Here white and nonwhite, advantage and disadvantage, power and powerlessness all mean the same thing, so that "race"—as in "race records" or "the race"—becomes, not merely an evasion, but a kind of tautology: that is, you only have it if you are it, you are it if you have it.

Hence it is the racial anomaly, and its challenge to our system of racial understanding, that most fascinates us, especially, it seems, in the age of the reproducible image in which it is nearly impossible to dissociate the public figure from his or her image, where, indeed, in some realms at least, the celebrity or politician or even the author or musician may be said to be pure image, or *only* an image. Whatever our estimate of Elvis Presley as an artist, for example, surely the Mediterranean softness and sensuousness of his face, arrestingly and improbably yoked with the gestures and expressions of the working-class rural South, clowning, mocking, unprepossessingly "racy," wrought a mystery and magnetism utterly resistant to any easy racial description. Somehow in him, the youthful, innocent, even the feminine, was also urbane, exotic, and masculine; Neapolitan nobility mixed, as in a foundling's tale, with Scots-Irish peasantry; the smooth matinee idol was also the Podunk movie usher, the millionaire playboy the crunchy sharecropper's son, the baseball pitcher and the supper-club crooner, the maître d' and the busboy, congregated in one body. In the language of American raciality, Elvis was, and is, an utterly original expression, a living testament to the awesome significatory power of race.

We celebrate Woody Guthrie for his political conviction and his poetic genius. But others have evinced the same who have not been enlarged, as he has, to the scale of myth. Let us consider, then, that his myth has in it a racial aspect more difficult to fathom, and at the same time more durable and more fascinating for the deep unsolved symbolic riddle it poses, than the antic energy of his prose and the simple eloquence of his songs. If "Mr. Guthrie defines an essential character in the American dream," as a *Times* reviewer once claimed, then that essentiality, and that character, must at least partially inhere not only in his intellectual but in his corporal nature, not only in his life and work, but in *him*.

Woody was a skinny little splinter-boned guy with a head of springy black hair, a high sloping intelligent brow, sharp hooded, sometimes heavy-lidded scrutinizing eyes, a nose and mouth coldly faceted as if by a smith's hammer and yet, in the pronounced bow of his upper lip, touched with sensuality. He was, in a sense, homely, and in another, beautiful. His hands, moreover, his lifelong guitar picking notwithstanding, were plump like a woman's, languidly relaxed, possibly lovely. He had light, quick, animated movements, like Charlie Chaplin's, as if he had been cut from paper, with a quality of subtle self-caricature that accelerated the expressive tempo and sharpened the edges of his presence. His wide rectangular forehead and wiry hair gave him an elfin, childlike aspect, as if his entire body were made of intelligence. In sum, he was a sort of featherweight Robert Mitchum, transforming the sluggish irony buried in Mitchum's massive composure into a sparkling satirical effervescence.

On first glance you might have figured him, from his sometimes starved and arid features, a child of rural poverty, bred out of the red clay at the end of some overgrown lane; and yet these same features, with a shift no more pronounced than a shift in the direction of a breeze or the intensity of a shadow, might be utterly transfigured, imparting to him a sensitive, generous, vulnerable quality, as if tears had started to his eyes. His was a face and form that, like an actor's, might play many parts. Not only could he absorb the moral atmosphere around him, but he could model its expression to others; Guthrie was a metaphor maker in that syntax of human identity that articulates us all as individuals, as types, as classes and races, which locks us into histories we have not lived and locales we have never lived in, as well as to the ones we have. It was this same quality that allowed

Woody Guthrie in army work clothes, 1945.
Courtesy of the Woody Guthrie Foundation and Archives.

such young men as Jack Elliott, especially Bob Dylan, and even Bruce Springsteen—no, not to transform themselves into Woody Guthrie—but to transform Woody into themselves.

I speak, of course, not of the real, but of the mythopoetic Woody Guthrie, who belongs to a social imaginary usually more associated with literature and the arts than with ordinary social intercourse, but one that nevertheless is always ready to push through the social surface of things to lend its mystery, charm, and danger to real men and real women. These are the charismatic people who often find themselves gravitating as if by some irresistible interpersonal urging onto the stage, or before the movie camera, or into public life, precisely because their presence and their person work in marvelous and irresistible ways upon others, arousing some obscure attraction or fascination, preoccupation, infatuation, or love. They are not always beautiful; but they are always striking, full of obscure and impregnable import. Many become the victims of their own interest and beauty, of which there are too many well-known examples to name; some learn very early in life their own power of manipulation and make careers of it; and some, like Woody, growing gradually into a full sense of their own social influence, use it as we would use any talent or skill—not opportunistically, but tactically, as an instrument of adaptation and survival.

In the mundane, as against the mythopoetic world, Woody Guthrie was extraordinary not so much in his origins as in the events that thrust him out of them. There is no need here to recount the sad litany of misfortunes that unraveled the weave of his early years and turned him into an orphan, a refugee, even an outcast—but let us at least note that he was born of respectable and aspiring, if not exactly prosperous parents, and that if he could not ultimately enjoy the blessings of the middle-class standing he was born to, he had at least been decently educated, was a curious and eager reader, brilliant with words, and as a young man could reasonably imagine himself becoming, as he sings in "Ramblin' Round," a "man of some renown." In his work he aligned himself with working men and women of every stamp; but as Gordon Freisen reminded him, he had never harvested a grape in his life. Woody was essentially a poet and intellectual at a time when a nationalist embrace of grassroots imagery and expression, mixed up with an urban romantic conception of a heroic American People in whom one might detect the unquiet ghost of a revolutionary proletariat, had prepared a place for him, as Steinbeck observed, in a sense to *be* that People.

Guthrie was a westerner, out of the old Indian Territories, with Scots-Irish—read "hillbilly"—roots, and like his hillbilly-musician brethren, he had a knack for the African American way of diddling a tune, especially on that down-home, make-do, hip-pocket instrument, the harmonica. Once commuted to New York, however, the "clever little man," the "bantam rooster" as his friend Jimmy Longhi called him, the "real dustbowl refugee" and "the great American frontier ballad writer" could never again be seen in his mundane aspect, or even as a man with any history of his own; instead he would inevitably be woven into an essentially mythic web of a socialist heroic, replete with images and ideas of a glorified working people, of labor union triumphalism, Wobbly millennialism and, especially out of this last, the still unsung frontier epic we seem to glimpse in Woody's songs. In this story, cowboys and hoboes, wheatfield gleaners, peach pickers and grape harvesters, loggers and fishers and builders of giant dams are all toiling under the vast bright Western sky on behalf of a stolen dream. It is *your* hops we gather, he sings in "Pastures of Plenty," *your* beets we pull from the ground, *your* vines from which we pick the grapes, addressing the song rebukingly to the privileged classes; out of California, Arizona, Oregon, he conjures a nation of workers laboring "to set on your table" in some faraway city "your bright sparkling wine." A strange concatenation of abundance and privation, pride and resentment, alienation and fascination, Guthrie maps it like degrees of rainfall onto the great expanse of the continent.

It is the paradox evident in all of Guthrie's work—an imagery that loves, reveres, and glorifies, a language that points, exposes, rebukes—and one that time, where history is always transformed into romance, has largely resolved, sifting out of the ideologically inflected times in which he wrote and sang the essential ore of his idealism. Whether this is a reading or a misreading of the Guthrie legacy is not I think so much at issue as the fact that it has happened at all. Whether he liked or disliked "middle-class bourgeois people," in Moe Asch's phrase, and despite the rancor, resentment, and righteous indignation that, if not *everywhere* in his songs, is often the nub of their meaning—"some'll rob you with a six-gun, some with a fountain pen"—the fact is that Guthrie's *own* meaning lies neither in the singer nor the song but in the tension between them. Transfigurations of memory working upon his image and his images have finally yielded up a new Woody Guthrie for a new political moment. In the truth-vacuum that corporate capitalism has made of political discourse, a Guthrie renaissance has shaped itself out of strange mix of nostalgia and revisionism, where the very collapse of a progressive politics seems to have created an opportunity for its renewal, and where the exhaustion of a musical strain seems again to demand a return to, which is always a creation of, the roots.

No one I think captured Guthrie as imaginatively, with a precision that is as outrageous as it is uncanny, as his most vigorous champion and promoter the late Alan Lomax, who called him a "pureblood Neolithic Pict." This riveting and ineradicable bit of nonsense, more poetic than anthropological, and smacking of nineteenth-century racial fantasy, by its very defiance of possibility, its utter immunity from interrogation, its cheeky assault on the very notion of the historical, its covert appeal to the nationalist romance of originality, itself undergirded by ideas of savagery, the tribe, their ancient migrations and conquests, forms a sort of rough allegory, a structure of symbolic suggestion, a racial-political etymology that however true or false—and I am not so sure that there is not, in fact, a living race of Picts among us, or that I have not met one or two of them myself, especially once in a pub in the north of England—that points irresistibly to what we mean when we say "Woody Guthrie."

First, *Pict*. What, is, *Pict*? The Picts, as all the dictionaries say, and the Roman language tells us, were "painted people"—*warriors* with paint on their faces, with spears and arrows and coverings of animal skins, dark little tangle-headed savages from the north of Scotland whom early explorers to America could not help but to compare to the little swarthy naked painted people they found here, drawing them into their sketches of the American Indian to help the European imagination to get itself around what was not yet, but was in the process of becoming, the idea of a noble savage.[1]

Who were they? They are the people "about whom little is known," and much is conjectured, but above all a "race," a mixture of an invading Aryan "stock" and an unknown aboriginal people who at some immemorial time occupied all of Britain—that is, they are the original, no, the more than original, the indigenous, the autochthonous people—ultimately to be displaced by the Britons, whose Celtic language overmastered their own unknown non-Indo-European tongue, but who, being warlike, carried on sporadic border skirmishes with the Romans, joined with Irish raiding parties to assist the Saxons in conquering their own conquerors, were converted to Christianity by St. Columba in the fifth century AD, and by the seventh century AD had established their own Pictish kingdom in the north. By the ninth century they had come under the dominion of Kenneth I, a Scot, himself an invader from Ireland, and were absorbed into what would become the Kingdom of Scotland. The Roman historian Eumenius mentions them in AD 297 as invaders of Roman Britain; Tacitus, too, alludes to a dark-skinned people small of stature, of western Wales but possibly of Pictish origin, whom he distinguishes both from the Gaelic Scots and the Gallic Britons, tall and fair-haired and speaking Celtic language.

Thus far the dictionaries and encyclopedias. But folklore has elevated the darting, elusive, thrice-conquered Pict to a peculiar niche in the ecology of imagination, where in the glens, the thickets, the woods and watercourses the "little people," with their tiny voices and their elaborate courtly nocturnal convocations from time to time make their presence in human affairs known with enchantments, gifts, and the occasional wayfarer's tale, sometimes leaving behind a birthmark or a lazy-eye, or recovering a long-lost finger ring, to say they've been there. There is a vaguely Druidical cast about them, a ghostly presence that forms where history, memory, and dread meet in twilit forests and morning mists.

Whatever else may be said about this imaginary figure, the pureblood Neolithic Pict, it is certain that he is not well represented, the admitted exceptions notwithstanding, in, say, political office, among chief executive officers or elected officials, appointees to the directorships of federal agencies, nor among the military brass, or partners in Wall Street or K Street law firms, not much revered in Hollywood unless it is as the occasional character actor, or even, for that matter, much found among crew foremen or factory-floor managers or union officers or in less official positions of working-class leadership. Very occasionally you might find him in the U.S. House of Representatives—but almost never in the Senate.

The Pict is, by definition, the "little guy." He resides in the hinterlands, literally and/or figuratively, because ages ago someone pushed him back there. He knows his own smallness, his obscurity, and speaks of himself as such, the "little guy." Only a generation ago he might, though white, have been called a "boy," especially if he carried water for a road crew or a sports team, and like his cast-iron blackfaced counterpart, the livery boy, might be vaguely associated with the stable, horse racing being the one sport in which, as a jockey, he has excelled.

He might be in the trades, or even the professions, he might keep a store, but his strength, he knows, and his survival, must lie in cleverness, shrewdness, skill with words, for however physically powerful he may be, however intense his personal presence, it is useless to attempt to impress himself upon others in these ways. His Pictish nature, he knows, has for better or worse always been a factor in the history that brought him to the beleaguered position in which he finds himself. Deserved or not, he has a reputation for pugnacity. From his point of view, life has been a never-ending negotiation with a superior race, or at least a race that likes to think of itself as such. To them, to whom he is at once real and imaginary, he *is* elusive, and in a sense magical, having sprung it seems out of those long-lost miniature ages when the sleeping berths of sailing ships were the size of dresser drawers and the tombs of great armored knights could be mistaken for footstools.

I myself have encountered him once or twice, always under somebody else's eye or thumb, in his ill-fitting clothes: once on a highway construction crew, leaning on a shovel, where he called me "Bawb" and again and again asked me whether I thought I was going to "get to like it"—meaning the work (but the phrase had come from his wartime service in the Pacific)—and, most memorably, as I say, in a pub in the north of England, near the Scottish border. I had asked the barman where I might get a bite to eat nearby, his own kitchen having shut for the night, when a little fellow next to me with a head of curly black hair and pair of Buddy Holly glasses, who looked astonishingly like Woody Guthrie, recommended a place around the corner called Cheney's.

What was that? I asked. He peered up at me, his head no higher than my shoulder—and, reader, I am no lanky fair-haired Anglo-Norman, but a man of very medium build and medium height with a conspicuous ethnic marker in the middle of my face I am not altogether pleased to call my nose—and repeated, "Cheney's, richt arooned tha' coorner."

"Cheney's?" I repeated, finding a scrap of paper on which to spell it out, "Cee, aitch, heee, enn."

"Nair," he corrected me, 'Chey-neeze, chey-*neeze*!"

I had had a pint or two and was thicker than usual; but at last I got it. "Oh," I cried, balancing my eyeballs on the edge of their sockets as if I were trying to prevent them from falling out and rolling across the floor, "you mean Chi*nese*."

"Aye," he nodded—and apologized profusely for his Scottish "broooghe," came it seemed within an inch of curtseying and pulling on his forelock, though he didn't really have a forelock, and together we laughed at the miscommunication over another pint of bitter. It was New Year's Eve—and later, full of egg noodles and Mu Shu chicken, I spotted him and his two equally elfin mates lurching along the street, singing merrily and gallantly accosting the occasional pretty girl with admiring phrases and a few stolen pinches and squeezes through their winter overcoats.

A pureblood Neolithic Pict if ever there was one.

Lomax's grossly unscientific assertion, then, once untangled, exposes the web of symbolic relations in which the respectable small-town Oklahoma boy orphaned in the midst of the Great Depression who became a hillbilly singer, radio personality, political columnist, railroad tramp, and sign-painter betimes, and finally a "great frontier ballad writer" still has meaning for us. For that web is, after all, cultural, and still trembles when the bright ephemeral creatures of the social world blunder into it, their own substance drawn into the social imaginary to be spun again into fibers of weightless but absorbing illusion. Lomax's phrase inoculates one world with another, evokes and shatters the categories of which it is itself made, metaphorically infusing the present with the past and, like all metaphors whose fascination consists in the eerie intimation of their rational basis, demands we entertain, even if we cannot ultimately grant, its literal sense.

Guthrie's story is one of class and class slippage, of class as it is bound up with regional, ethnic, and ideological difference, of class as it is obscurely bound up with race, and finally of race as a conceptual stand-in for the cultural temporalities to which all of this ultimately adds up; the Pict's story is one of nativity, tribe, and nation, of conquest and reconquest, subjection, marginalization, oppression, and resistance. Guthrie's is a story of the industrial age in post-agrarian capitalist America, where social stratification, theoretically, follows the moraines of market flows through history's shifting social mass; the Pict's is of a feudal kingdom forming out of imbalances and equilibriums of martial force in the competition for protected spaces and fruitful lands, where social differentiation is made visible both on the earth's and in the human face. Guthrie's is of workers and bosses, the Pict's of warriors and kings.

In the most superficial sense, Lomax's complex metaphor simply figures Guthrie as an exotic, a kind of exile or refugee from the past, like Ishmael or Ishi the last man of a lost world; he asks us to imagine, not that Guthrie is *like* a Pict, but that he *is* one. Thus Guthrie cannot be in the social sense "white"—that is, he is neither entitled to nor capable of the range of material, social, and cultural privileges that constitute "whiteness" in Western culture, and consequently in a certain sense he must be, if not exactly "black" (though some have speculated as much), certainly somehow "other," ethnic origins notwithstanding, where that otherness is precisely the register of disadvantage for which it is the figure, the more pronounced as it challenges its own status with special gifts, a certain political agenda, or simply by his failure to observe the protocols of otherness. Set at large in society he is, like the minstrel or *jongleur* of the Middle Ages, a landless, lordless, unaffiliated man, both and neither peasant nor noble, as at home in the court as on the highway, at once master and mendicant, a near archetypal figure whose descent reaches on the one hand to the blind court singers of antiquity to Shakespeare's Tom O'Bedlam to the hired hermit of the eighteenth-century landscape garden with his hourglass, his beard, and his Bible, figures in whom the negation of social identity at once confers the privilege of emancipation from it and compels contemplation of the "poor, bare fork'd animal" we know ourselves to be in the absence of it.

But this is only so much fairy dust, the mere touch of a wand, until we attempt to make the Pictish metaphor intelligible in relation to the historical Woody Guthrie, of Okemah, Oklahoma, especially in the image-charged urban setting in which he at once achieved and was granted his mythopoetic status. Guthrie enlarged inestimably the power of his social critique by placing it in a context of bright hopes and unconquerable faith, an idealism just that much more violated and tarnished by failure and betrayal. Keepers of Guthrie's flame are quick to remind those who would like to turn "This Land Is Your Land" into the National Anthem that the song was born in anger as an answer to Berlin's pious "God Bless America," and in addition to the now familiar celebratory verses included this one:

Was a big high wall that tried to stop me
A sign was painted said: Private Property.
But on the back side, it didn't say nothing—
God Blessed America for me.

. . . and this one:

One bright sunny morning in the shadow of the steeple
By the relief office I saw my people—
As they stood there hungry,
I stood there wondering if
God Blessed America for me.[2]

But what is original in the song, and what song tradition has favored, is its ribbon of highway, its endless skyway, its golden valleys and waving fields of wheat. It is very nearly picture-scrapbook snipped from one of the commercial picture-magazines of the period, where domed parlor cars, rubber tires, and farm machinery are tying corporate enterprise to a populist-patriotic paean to the continent. The prick of cruelty, and the ironic cut, are sharp—but have proved transient. Embodied as it is now, in Guthrie's total story, as it has accumulated in various writings, representations, recognitions, and imitations, including Guthrie's own autobiographical prose, this tension between a promise and its disappointment, a kind of wounded love, takes on a troubling new dimension. Woody Guthrie embodies, not an eventual triumph over injustice and inequality, but the awful depth and tenacity of them in the human scheme; even as we thrill to his moral idealism and the luminosity of his vision we feel, as a kind of instinct, with the example and the person of Guthrie before us, the impossibility of any realization of them, or at the very least, the specter of that impossibility, in a world that seems daily more inhospitable to his social and political vision. Conduct border raids as we might, harry the rulers with infinite tiny vandalisms, even ally ourselves temporarily with invading barbarians—we sense that nothing much, finally, is going to change.

We are the Picts, they are the Scots.

Our fascination, love, and admiration of Woody Guthrie as with all such minstrels and balladeers must inevitably be entangled with the contradictions inherent in the interplay of identity and identification, the one a fact of our social location and the other an imaginative tendency arising from it, the one a structure of ideas, conditions, affiliations, and associations whose fixity and integrity we struggle to maintain against odds, the other a capricious and restless testing of the self against the whole register of social possibility in which it finds, loses, and finds again its own place. Without the power of identification, there would be no identity, no way to convert the intersections of subject and social place into the material of a lived experience; without identity there would be no identification, that is, no social place from which to experience and assess the otherwise unreflected social aspects of the self.

Our Woody Guthrie—the Woody Guthrie of the Left in New York, of the folk song movement and the folk revival, even the scruffy bohemian, and finally the stricken Guthrie of Washington Square, as against the western Guthrie of Oklahoma and California, the hillbilly radical—like his forebears in literature, on the stage, and in the landscape garden, morally strengthens and enlarges us with a message severely toxic to the status quo but whose very delivery of that message confers, homeopathically, a certain immunity to its effects. The inspiration, even the mighty inspiration, we take from Woody's moral courage and independence has its basis in the refuge we enjoy, and know we enjoy, from the implications of them; we are moved by his orphanhood, stirred by his days on the highway, the railroad, in the labor camps, but, as Lomax tacitly conceded, mostly in relation to our own relative comfort, security, and safety. We are high-minded; we want to feel and think the immense promise of democracy as Woody sings of it, and rouse ourselves to indignation at the insults to it that he catalogues. But the figure of the little Pict in whom we take this essentially aesthetic pleasure offers unspoken reassurances; though the hayricks may be set on fire, the granaries breached, and the sheepfolds thrown open, nothing is likely to overthrow the edifice of power and advantage whose foundations are not in justice and right, but in history and even more fundamentally, it is almost possible to believe, in race.

We are the Scots, they are the Picts.

That might be the end of the metaphor, were it not for the fact that the class consciousness fundamental to the political tradition in which Woody Guthrie somewhat cryptically included himself arises, as Marshall Berman brilliantly argues,[3] first in the wide new public spaces of the mid-nineteenth-century city, out of the glancing social encounters of an emergent class of respectable little men, the vanguard of the urban bourgeoisie, with officers and aristocrats on the one hand, the poor and the indigent on the other, in a new social theater where for the first time in history identity becomes conscious of itself not only as a social locus but as a public and hence ultimately a political performance open to the gaze of the socially, economically, and politically other. These characters, actuaries and clerks and scriveners, in patent leather shoes and morning coats, white collars "mounting firmly to the chin" and neckties "asserted by a simple pin," as yet without social identity or political visibility, essentially anonymous and faceless, becoming aware of themselves as individuals and as a class in the promenades, arcades, cafes, and parks of Paris and London, in St. Petersburg's Nevsky Prospect, felt the stirring of a sense of self actuated to the dynamics of power relations and to the flux of historical change in which it might itself play a part.

It was out of these multitudinous episodes of self-conscious social encounter that the idea of class struggle, wherein history endlessly produces and reproduces Picts and Scots in endlessly novel incarnations, finally emerged. Melville's Bartleby, Dostoyevsky's Underground Man, Eliot's Prufrock, even Joyce's Bloom are their literary reflections; cinema culture expressed the type in Charlie Chaplin—who, it is said, enacted some of his funniest scenes backwards in order to achieve the inimitable movements that appear when the film was run forwards—a pure artifact, that is, of the cinematic process. Hence the "Little Tramp," haplessly caught up in the machinery of social protocol, of constabularies, bureaucracies, factories, municipalities, indeed of machinery itself, like Guthrie not only performs but also embodies his own comic predicament, at the same time as he unwittingly engineers his own comic evasions of it—escaping the machinery of the modern by delivering himself over to it.

It does not need to be reiterated that the central stream of bourgeois sympathy flowed and still flows towards the glistening surfaces of ruling-class life and social, political, and moral reaction. But to those for whom that project seemed shallow or empty, or to whom it was essentially closed off, or both—most notably, intellectuals, Jews, and, preeminently, Jewish intellectuals—identity sought its reflected self, and its role in history, at the other end of society. In America, at a time when political and cultural elites were looking socially outward and downward for the vernacular energy that could resuscitate the collapsed economic and social system, they turned to the worker: figured, as all the heroic imagery of the period shows, as an impersonal regimental mass, a worker army, or as a godlike paragon of physical strength, wrestling with vats of molten steel or wielding nineteen-pound hammers, or as a sturdy farmer toiling behind a horse-drawn plough, or exercising his right of free speech on the courthouse steps, or facelessly presiding over the family table where all heads are bent in prayers of thanks.

But where in this epic synthesis was the urban little man with his frayed white collar, the immigrant shopkeeper, tailor, or machine operator, or his son or daughter, upon whom the Depression had fallen with a wretchedly personal and private weight, who felt most keenly the betrayal of the promise he'd hoped to realize for himself or his children or his children's children, to find his own revolutionary image? Was it in the "folk?"—the rural poor who unlike himself were not creatures of capitalism but whom capitalism nevertheless had ruined, as near to indigence as himself, in whose exhausted face he saw his own terror of penury and dispossession? Who were not, like him, mere human refuse used up and thrown away in another financial-industrial storm-cycle but lean and hungry native stock, rooted in the soil, in the rights and freedoms the Founders had assigned to it and ready by temperament and tradition to declare those rights and freedoms?

Yes: but the "folk" could not strictly be identified either with the socialist worker-hero or with the images of stark submission and defeat with which much of the documentary photography of the period had marked the rural poor; rather it was the Pictish zeal and pluck, springing out of wild hoedown fiddles and wicked comic songs, in outspoken blues ballads and cryptic work chants smoldering with anger, that one caught the revolutionary tone. In this setting no one better than a "real dustbowl refugee," his social conscience awakened by visible injustice, his verbal gift unsheathed by moral outrage and sharpened with satiric wit, his music rooted in a poor white rural tradition of Scots-Irish and African American origin, a man whose own physical nature and personal endowment placed him among the ever-dominated, never-defeated outlander race, could have been ushered into the place, and taken on the role, of America's "great frontier ballad writer."

"Our class struggle," Marx wrote to Engels, "you know very well where we found it: we found it in the story of the war of races."[4] In Woody Guthrie the comic majesty of hope plays continually in and against the tragedy of history. Like Chaplin, he was one with his medium, in effect *made* of it. His blood, mythopoetically speaking, is a mingling of the blood of all those conquered and exploited generations in whom the conqueror has searched out the sources of his own life. His *embodied* politics go deeper than the ground of things, the social and technical installations of production, to the living substance of flesh and blood, where injustice, inequality, and oppression are infused, and in which history has left a visible record of their expression. Hence the paradox of his songs is the paradox of him, and its very irresolution is what carries both his idealism and his realism, his rhapsody and his irony, beyond ideology and even poetry to what in postmodernity can perhaps no longer be called myth but that, like myth, can lend density and solidity to our specular and unreal world—not so much to enunciate belief as to lay a foundation for its possibility.

On a trip to Washington recently I happened in an idle moment to pick up from somebody's coffee table a newsletter published by one of those property-rights think tanks on Seventeenth Street. I can't explain the context—I didn't really read it—but my eye fell on this sentence, or something to this effect: "We don't want a 'This land is your land, this land is my land' sort of society."

If I am not mistaken, this egregious misreading of Woody's sentiment quite coldly exposes the fortress mentality—essentially the cowardice of conquerors—that has arisen again in one of capitalism's intermittent periods of retrenchment. There isn't enough to go around, apparently. If the little fellow in the crumpled outfit has come back to us out of America's racial unconscious, it is perhaps because under the new global capitalism, an oppression so vast, swift, invisible, and unreachable that we scarcely know what it is or what to call it, or what it is evolving into, we are all little guys again—as if the invisible legions of a master race, somehow more than human, fabulously rich and powerful, with an unheard of ability to communicate, to mobilize resources, to invest, divest, and administer on a global scale, were emerging to dominate the old human races of peoples and nations, and to efface once and for all with glamorous new lies the memory of the spacious and fruitful land that was our birthright. Maybe Woody has come to refresh that memory, and to arouse our Pictish indignation at its dishonoring.

9

A HARVEST OF ILLTH

BLUES, BLACKFACE, FOSSIL FUEL

Negroness is now being rubbed off by close contact with white culture.—Zora Neale Hurston to Franz Boas (1927)

*Formed like coal from the transmutation of living matter to release its energy in another world.—*Bluegrass Breakdown *(1984)*

. . . else, as mere accidental stays and impediments, acting not as wealth, but (for we ought to have a correspondent term) as "illth," causing devastation and trouble all around them in all directions. —John Ruskin, "Ad Valorem," from Unto This Last *(1860)*

. . . the profit system generates a loss which, in the multiple forms of wretchedness and poverty outside the system and of waste inside it, constantly turns production into 'expenditure.'
—Michel de Certeau, The Practice of Everyday Life *(1984)*

The abject hollows around Portsmouth, Ohio, are so charged with coal that the Welsh miners who emigrated in the mid-nineteenth century only had to plunge their spades into the hillsides behind their barns to profit in it. The region flourished industrially as a supplier of coal to a network of local iron furnaces until late in the century, when the discovery of iron ore in the Mesabi Range of northern Minnesota brought steel and iron making from the Ohio Valley to the southern shores of Lake Michigan. Today in New Straitsville, Ohio, a dour collection of wheezy dwellings on seven black hillsides, where the United Mine Workers had its first meetings in an abandoned mine shaft, the mine fires set by a militant faction of the nascent union are still burning, further depressing the chronically depressed economy and raising the local cancer rate. Now most of the old slope and pit mines are gone, and the desultory efforts of the Peabody Corporation to reclaim the naked hillsides have done little to conceal, even after more than forty years, the massive exposure by strip mining of the pale ground once bearded with forests of chestnut and oak.

In his *Jane Reed and Dora Hunt* (1941), Clarence Carter, who grew up around Portsmouth and whose early work documents the emaciation of the region by depression in the 1930s, two women wrapped in washed-

Clarence Carter, Jane Reed and Dora Hunt. *1941.*
Oil on Canvas, 36 in. x 45 in. © Museum of Modern Art. Used with permission.

out cotton shifts, their faces hidden under bonnets, their bodies lean with labor and with age, scavenge for coal along what must be the double tracks of the Baltimore and Ohio, somewhere upriver, perhaps, on the way to Parkersburg and Marietta. It seems to be early morning: a crescent moon tips backwards in the brightening sky, and a morning mist has settled in the cleft between two hills. One senses the river not far away. There's a chill in the air—the nearest figure, maybe Dora, with the coal-filled egg basket over her arm, is wearing her sweater. That could be her house on the nearest hillside, a one-story clapboard affair on a brick foundation, with a path through the bushes to a privy hard by the tracks.

We're following Dora close behind, almost crowding her—but from a viewpoint no higher, if it is as high as, the woman's waist; we could be watching her through the eyes of a child. Over all there's a quality of haste, of urgency, captured most graphically in the women's feet—Jane's wide apart as she bends down in what in a moment will be essentially a lunge towards the lump of coal lying in the middle of a crosstie, and Dora's, the sole of her left shoe exposed, tripping hurriedly ahead in a near run with the same end in mind. Technically, they're trespassing; they're on the railroad right-of-way. And the coal, dropped from the long trains of hopper cars headed up from West Virginia towards Pittsburgh and points east, belongs, strictly speaking, to the coal company. But coal is expensive and hard to get: at least for Jane and Dora. One cabbage-sized lump will cook the bacon, boil three pots of water for laundry, and heat the kitchen until noon. Maybe the women will put part of their morning's gleanings up for sale from their front porches, a nickel a lump, along with some kindling sticks from the woodlot.

It isn't only in rural southern Ohio, during these years, that the poor are scavenging coal from railroad tracks. It's everywhere supplies are short, the weather's cold, and the coal trains run. Like Mayhew's costermongers, or Dickens's dust-gatherers, or better, like Katherine Anne Porter's Mr. Helton, the solitary hired man of *Noon Wine,* who by saving every bent nail, every grain of chicken feed scattered on the ground, literally saves the farm, Jane Reed and Dora Hunt are salvaging the scat of the great lumbering bear of the industrial machine that by the sheer fact of its retrieval, and the labor required to accumulate it, becomes life-giving again. Hard-up mountain women coping with hard times, called "white trash" by those better off, the mean and dishonest slur oxymoronically "blackening" them socially, they're salvaging pieces of themselves, collecting the otherwise wasted fuel of a world, a life, and a dignity denied whose combustion defends them, however tentatively and temporarily, against utter destitution. For they are themselves, coal miners, ballad singers, and banjo pickers, like their black counterparts to whom the racial epithet eternally weds them, a kind of cultural fossil fuel, whom centuries beneath the immense weight of oppression in all of its forms have transformed into prodigies of invention, capable of making do with almost anything and of living on next to nothing.

"All that is solid melts into the air." After the gross national product, the national debt, the consumer price index, the federal deficit, the median family income, and the rest have all been figured, capitalism itself remains essentially ephemeral until, in flea markets, pawnshops, for-sale pages, thrift stores, recycling bins, and on the porches where Jane and Dora sell their coal, acts of unmediated exchange, like the minute transactions between cells that are the essence of life, its *capillaries,* expose the wellsprings of value. In the islands, the interstices, and on the frontiers of the global commodity system, market "forces," and vast technical infrastructures, capitalism is busily extending its vernacular dominion. Jane and Dora are the unwitting custodians of its shameful inefficiencies, recovering what was lost on its way to market, or, in another sphere, saving for use what the market never touched, or what the market has abandoned, or what, in time, may find a new market opening in its way, and thereby bringing capitalism to a condition of near perfect efficiency. Capitalism creates nothing, transforms everything; and in transforming, destroys, discards, pollutes, and wastes prodigiously, people and things: "produces," in other words, a colossal midden heap that, with its value set at zero, mocks us, in its stronghold of irrecoverable plenty, like wealth itself—the more so *because* it is wasted or despised, and wears its status like a badge of honor.[1]

Marybeth Hamilton's provocative and compelling work on James McCune, who collected 78–rpm discs of Delta blues recordings and stored them under his bed at the Y, ignite all at once, like a flame upon a lump of coal, what is discursively stored in McCune's collection, the metaphors of the residual that have dominated our thinking about blackness from minstrelsy's "Coal Black Rose" to John Coltrane and E. L. Doctorow's *Coal*house Walker. Race itself, as race theory explains, is a residue; it is always the other upon whom it has "rubbed off" or who "has" it—the racial substance with which the other is somehow endowed, imbued, touched, or otherwise "colored"; or to put this another way, race is, for those of us who happen not to have race, that is, to be white, a want or lack, and a signifier of it. Hence, one of the prerogatives of privilege is to appropriate the moral aura of enslavement, suffering, and victimization symbolically, salvaging its virtue, for good or ill, without the pain, the disgrace, or the social predicament that attaches to it. If moreover we are white and have, or are, nothing, then even race, which the other has and we have not, may inflame our resentment, even make us furious—because it is infuriating to hate what you want, and to want what you hate. Sheer necessity, perhaps, brings surrender, sends Jane Reed and Dora Hunt out to the tracks at dawn to gather coal, opening the flow of sympathy, even love, towards the other, where it finds not the ever-irreducible difference, but the shared sense of place that the racial residue at once marks and embodies.

What are the residues of blackness, which in this discourse, are *all* residue? The ash of mortification, that the mourner smears over his brow at the death of his lover or his God; the shine of respectability, scraped from a back-alley coal chute, with which the impoverished Jewish immigrant, someday to become a Hollywood magnate, blacks his shoes before appearing at the door of the famous silent film director; the burnt cork around the mouth of the famine Irishman, Jumping Jim Crow at the Bowery. On the brow of the smith, in the dust on the miner's face and in his lungs, the grease on the fingers of the bootblack, the soot on the cheeks of the chimney sweep; in the smoke of boilers, steam engines, and locomotives that blackens the sky over Pittsburgh and Chicago and deposits itself as black grime on the window sills—these are the original substance of the social blackening that culture appropriates as its marker. Black as ink, black as night, black as coal, black as the ace of spades—its residues burn where printing presses press, where the face of the rubber tire gnaws the road, where carbon brushes scour the armatures of electric motors. In short, they are everywhere. The discursive residues of race—not melatonin, but "blackness," "blackening," and "blacking up"—extend over the whole landscape of the cultural memory of modernity and *its* residues.

The genealogy of the collier, the smith, the sweep, the "mechanick," the engineer, the steelworker, and ultimately of the chemist and his/her laboratory, as well as of minstrels and bluesmen, begins with the discovery of coal on medieval estates, and with the unlanded, unhoused beggars, dwarves, and misfits sent down into the ground to recover it. The broader family of economic, social, and industrial relations thus summoned into existence leads, along one branch, to conversions and refinements of potential energy, natural, social, cultural, whether of carboniferous fossil deposits of coal and oil or of the social and political energy that develops under pressure of those relations, arising from the geological or the social depths to release itself in a kind of natural or symbolic combustion. Along the other branch it leads to the symbolic critique of modernity those conversions have historically underwritten, beginning, as Dale Cockrell has shown us, with the blackened faces of belsnickel rioters, Christmas mummers, blackface minstrels, and evolving, perhaps, to the titanic electrical currents flowing from coal-fired power plants into the cradling arms of rock guitarists.[2] Whether as spot, stain, smudge, badge, mark, or mask, the black residue signifies inversion, actual or symbolic, an energy mined out of dark ages and hearts of darkness. In minstrelsy, that inversion takes the form of class satire under guise of racial parody, descended from the social chastening that was the ritual function of mummers, belsnickels, and John Canoes; but even these energies will be harnessed, as street gangs and scandal sheets become fire departments, constabularies, and newspapers, as mobbers and "Indian" clubs become political claques, machines, and parties. Even rock-and-roll, it is evident, may be thematized, corporatized, and museumized.

Out of this gap, the gap between rule and misrule, law and lawlessness, social chastening and social control, the blues disc, dug like coal out of its social and historical milieu and swept up in an industrial and commercial process, but also marked like coal with the labor—or, as has been said and sung, with the blood and tears—of the black and blackened men who mined it, ultimately springs. In the blues disc, all the discursive residues of blackness come together.

The audience to Edison's first exhibition of his phonograph, who thought they had been defrauded, saw it as a kind of ventriloquist's dummy, "catching" the performer's voice. Somebody, they understood, had caught, or stolen, somebody else's voice. A phonograph record is on the one hand the indefinitely repeatable mechanical iteration of a unique, irreproducible and irrecoverable musical performance, or more precisely, the *sound* of a performance; on the other it is a unit of mass production, essentially identical to all other units and theoretically of uniformly equal value at its point of entry into the marketplace. As a disc, artifact of an industrial, historical and cultural moment, it can never be anything but residual, like lima beans in a tin can; as a recorded sound it is a human trace, in this instance of a singular musical performance that can never be anything but an echo of itself, what neither the most sophisticated technology nor the most exact "fidelity" can ever restore. Stealing sound, then, as a photo steals the image, the disc renders the performance silent, as the photo renders its subject invisible, each not merely representing, but replacing the other; hence the phonograph record produces music itself *as a residue of sound*. A commerce in sound, then, produces musical waste or pollution, "canned" music, a fact that live performers understood when they worried that a record might "use up" their repertoire. Today musicians mostly *are* their recordings, mere instruments for reproducing their own sounds in public, or they are *nothing but* recordings, or, as in live concerts or on MTV they are displays of what in music is occasioned by but is not identical to its sound. The history of recorded music therefore is perforce a history of recovery.

The peculiar enchantment of the disc is that it imprisons, like Ariel in his cloven pine, the sound of a musical performance that only Edison's magic can release. Thus liberated, it changes form; it fills the atmosphere with sounds that, like Ariel's siren sounds, are everywhere and nowhere, overflowing from scattered wellheads of mechanical recovery out of sources forever hidden and irrecoverable. The disc is unique in this respect—like a dinner plate or "platter" it is implicitly one instance of an issue or series and hence urges its own repetition: a disc, to complete itself, must either be played to death, in which case it in effect disappears, or indefinitely accumulated, until it need not be played at all. Disc collections, and the trade among collectors inspired by them, constitute a secondary system of exchange as well as a community of traders who engage in it. Within this community arises a musical culture within which the *material* priority of the industrial product facilitates the genesis of a body of imaginative processes attached to a set of particular musical forms, techniques, and practices, and carry a definite affective burden of a particular character: in other words a collective practice or "tradition," one whose wholeness, integrity, and shape belong primarily to the collection, and only secondarily to blues musicians and their social-historical milieu. Hence Marybeth Hamilton can confidently propose that the Delta blues begins under James McKune's bed in a Williamsburg YMCA. Unlike a scholarly enterprise such as Child's *Ballads,* that offers to consummate, and also to mark the demise, of a tradition, a traffic in discs creates both the tradition and the community to which it belongs. Like Child's texts, the discs are a reification; but collections and collectors represent an investment of labor, of hands and of hearts, in the making of a world reanimated by music.

The blues disc, then, is at once token, sign, text, and performance—as well as, I suspect, a kind of miniature or windup toy: anyone who has attended the explosive, almost frightening living performances of a Howling Wolf or Son House will know what I mean: at the same time as the disc may inspire a holy inference, a wild surmise, it does so under the conditions of its own fictionality, reducing, like Milton's *Pandemonium,* all the Powers and Dominions of the blues to what amounts to a tiny human effigy spinning merrily atop a piece of parlor furniture, "incorporeal Spirits to smallest forms / Reduc'd their Shapes immense." One thinks of Tiger Woods's golf stroke, recently captured as a computer file by outfitting him with a sensor-embedded electronic bodysuit from which the stroke can be digitally read, not "preserved for posterity" but embodied as the end and original of all possible golf strokes, at once consuming the game and resurrecting it as text.

It is not, then, the materiality of the disc alone that accounts for the transforming power of the blues disc—all that we have argued to this point could as plausibly be said about a collection of Souza marches played by the U.S. Army Band—but that it is a *blues* disc. The modernist search for the primitive, underwritten by Freud and the post-1918 triumphs of urban bourgeois life, with other influences had sponsored elite jazz collections, jazz club slumming, and the cult of Negritude; but by the 1940s, jazz, including the improvisatory hot jazz of New Orleans, had not only been revealed to be immensely sophisticated musically, but had become the mise-en-scène of a rarified and intensely cranial avant garde. The search for the primitive, then, understood at least since Hammond's *Spirituals to Swing* concerts in 1936 as a search for black origins, demanded a new African American music demonstrably grounded in the backwaters of the rural South, where racial mythology had located the beginnings of jazz music.

If taste as Bourdieu suggests is a "technology of dominance," blues connoisseurship is, or was, like minstrelsy, a technology of mischief. Delta blues, as has variously been observed, inverts the musical system in which it has its musicality. Notes are not played or sounded but sought out and won—trapped, bent, pierced, choked, attacked, throttled, stalked, snapped, ground down or out, extinguished and even "bombed." Musical movement is not among loci in a fixed harmonic space, nor a synchronization of accentual and metrical quantities, but a destabilization of the entire system of rhythm. Like a bus driver caught in a skid, Delta blues thrusts the musician into a swiftly proliferating emergency that tests not only his competence as a musician but his grasp of the whole nature of his body and his instrument in the midst of the wider context of natural laws of which he and it are parts. The blues musician wrestles or spars or fences with musical forces arising from within himself, and labors to direct or subdue them. Not merely a formal routine of "syncopation," "percussiveness," "microtonality"—the terms in which African American music is typically described—blues is a complete musical topsy-turvy: meter eluded, circumvented, delayed or prolonged, penetrated, arrested, even punished, tonality elasticized or liquefied; with the slide, particularly, the notes, or "frets," transferred from the instrument to the musician, become mobile and unstable, loosed from their moorings, like dogs out of their collars. In effect the player creates the harmonic system as he goes, recovering it at the same moment as he threatens to dispel it, not selecting from a field of preexisting notes but hounding, chasing, trapping, snaring, and finally, beating, which is to say, suffocating or killing them: as such terms as "frailing," "hammering," "choking" or actual pulling, snapping, or stretching all suggest.

These sounds are registers or readings of bodily force, its quality, intensity, and intention, like the sound of a bat hitting a ball, a point at which a specific form of human energy registers itself in the ductility, resistance, plasticity, and so on of material objects. As actions within a structure of music, like the play of intelligent activity in a boxing ring or on a basketball court, they dramatize the unfolding of thought, feeling, and idea in a field of contending human forces. All music, of course, can be understood this way, as the imprint of the performer, a series of symbolic actions in a differentiated symbolic space—but here the emphasis is upon the qualities of the actor as such, so thoroughly is the musical and poetic material conventionalized and formulaic. Melodies in blues conform so closely to speech contours that in blues language can be said to precede melody; so thoroughly conventionalized is the blues harmonic system—blues, after all, *is* that system—that a blues verse emerges as a kind of musical syllogism, essentially intellectual in form: harmonic shifts—two departures from home, the one tentative, the one conclusive—signal shifts of perspective upon a single idea, a process that issues in the birth of a concluding affirmation whose logic lies in the linkage between two ideas tied together by harmonic resolution.

Hence the Delta blues registers the bluesman's physical, intellectual, and moral nature, his strength, perception, precision, and power; it is a music erotic in an adaptive as well as a mimetic sense. What recording wastes, it intimates; what is residual in recorded sound, it recovers as meaning, through sound stealing back what sound recording has stolen. For sound recording depends upon the physical force of the sound wave and registers it *as* a force—not, as in the case of musical notation, as a text or an architecture, a script or procedure. In this respect the Delta bluesman, having turned, as a political matter, the musical system into a kind of seismometer for registering his own expressive force, both absorbs and is absorbed in, is at one with, the recorded medium. Of more sophisticated musics whose genius lies in the elaboration of the musical system itself, this cannot necessarily be said. Like blacks in minstrelsy who out-minstreled their white minstrel parodists, Delta blues *uses* sound to sound what recording silences.

Blues music, then, particularly the intensely fraught rural blues of the Mississippi Delta, musically enacts, and as disc materializes, the rituals of inversion, natural and social, written into the discursive residues of blackness. It comes up from underground. The performer and the recording, the music and its execution, are bound together in troubled marriages that at once bind them together and set them at odds with one another in a musical contest or struggle, forces that lie at the origin of life contending against those that would negate it. Like the miner with his pick, the black, blackened, and blacked-up musician must fight his medium in order to quarry it, living both for it and against it, releasing its stored energy in a combustion of affect that is the hallmark of the style—a drama that of course in a broader sense captures the condition of blackness itself, constituted by its own oppression and destined to carry out its acts of resistance in the forms of that oppression.

How fitting, then—and by this I mean the aesthetic fitness or unity of all of its constitutive elements—since we are concerned with the powerful convergence in the blues disc of an ensemble of social, imaginative, and natural forces, that the disc itself, whether made of bakelite, acetate, shellac, vinyl, or polymer plastic, should owe its material existence to carbon-derived fossil resources. Like other arts that fix their illusions to the hard materiality of the medium, like Henry James's sentences or Van Gogh's stars, the blues disc is phenomenal: in it the silenced bluesman comes to life again in the carboniferous body of the disc that has felt his authenticating touch as surely as a literary autograph. How fitting then that in the disc collection the culturally residual matter of the blues should be chemically and mechanically bound to the natural residues of the Carboniferous Age—and that the blues collection, finally, *as* a collection, a gathering of social-economic and cultural residues scattered in Goodwill stores, flea markets, and pawnshops, mere waste, junk, trash, should find their energies converted into a musical revival that has flowed from the cardboard boxes under James McCune's bed all the way to the tape programs of Starbucks Coffee and The Gap.

. . . .

A disc collection like any collection occurs in three economies, of the market, of society, and of the self. Collections of ephemera are not themselves ephemeral: accumulation eddies the flow of time and postpones oblivion. All collections—say of books, of opera or classical music, or for that matter of works of art—are effigies of treasuries, perhaps spurious, of accumulated cultural capital, a density of acquired habit, practice, and knowledge, implicitly social, transfigured as property and, in the mysterious way of property, capable of possession. They are a form of wealth that, according to Ruskin, "avails toward life, leads to it with its whole strength." But "in proportion as it does not lead to life, or as its strength is broken," says Ruskin, it is less valuable; in proportion as it leads away from life, it is unvaluable or malignant."[3] It is not wealth, but "illth."

It might be asked whether, in the end, accumulations of books, music, or of art, though they may be theoretically transformed into money, constitute wealth in themselves, except insofar as reading, listening, and beholding may restore them to our collective life. But it is certain that the blues is a harvest of illth, of servitude, exploitation, and degradation transformed by a kind of musical self-consumption into an affirmation of personhood. So, too, was the Delta blues collection, at the period McKune created his, a harvest of illth, essentially an accumulation of cultural, commercial, and industrial waste—but imaginatively transformed, like Nepalese shrines tendered on cow dung, into an "opportunity for devotion." In the three economies in which it occurs, a disc collection such as James McKune's or Harry Smith's transforms what is dispersed, discarded, ruined, and despised to what is recovered, concentrated, and renewed, rendering it at once rare and precious, scandalous and subversive. In the social archeology of consciousness, it is a repressive memory, whose appearance makes one's own despised or ruined condition available for contemplation and turns it, by virtue of our irrepressible sociality, into a source of cultural regeneration. In the economy of self, it is "a sign made to become a signifier" in the system of selfhood, by a sheer act of recognition setting fire to rejection, exile, and shame to drive the human engine with their power.

Here, perhaps, is the spark of sympathy that led James McCune, and others like him, to the Delta blues. His desire sprang *ex nihilo* from its own negation—a moral effect, ultimately, because we value what others value, as possession is a social effect, because we wish to possess what another possesses. His was an original cultural act, an act of awakening to the law of desire that inheres in sufficiency, for every sufficiency creates its own want, precisely what further sufficiency can never answer. In desiring what had been despised, he set himself against the prevailing moral order, already set against him; in possessing it, he adopted it as a token of personhood, and so located himself at the heart of a social formation of one, but ultimately of many, members; in collecting it, he not only defined a career of purposeful endeavor but, in the inverted economy that is the sacralization of waste, came into a fortune. Like the solitary driftwood collector in the ruined world of James McBride's early (1971) nuclear apocalypse film, *Glen and Randa,* who wanders the Pacific beach, accumulating the tangled pieces that wash up with the tide, collecting, sorting, accumulating into heaps, he saw that there was no order, no worthiness, no dignity, no belonging, no purpose, no value beyond that to which we ourselves lay claim. "I come down every day and check everything out. They send these things to me. Leave 'em on the beach. When the tide goes down I have to check 'em all. I don't like to get behind. Try to keep up with everything. See what's here."

10 THE PARALLAX EFFECT

REPRESENTATION AND INCORPORATION

I regularly recur to the memory of a conversation with my colleague, Kathy Mundell, in a fieldwork project over twenty years ago—we agreed that as the project came to a close our notions of "folklore" had changed significantly, and that in an ideal world we'd write novels about our experiences rather than ethnographic reports. Our "informants" had emerged for us as fully dimensional personal and social beings fully embedded in the lifeworld we shared with them, people for whom "folk" practice was at best a limited and self-conscious personal initiative, informed often by a sense of "tradition" or of the past or of history or of family or community not appreciably distinct for our own more formalized views, and often flowing from very personal, economic, social, or other crises or occasions in their lives: a divorce or separation, retirement, catastrophic personal loss, or simply as recreation, diversion, leisure activity. Whatever it was, improvisation, amateur, traditional, "vernacular," it was motivated at the point at which their lives articulated with the "official" or disciplinary world, as indeed most, or all, of our own interests and enterprises were. We called it "folk"; they might call it something else. But whatever we called it, it seemed to belong for us to a narrative we had been consciously or unconsciously piecing together out of our lives and our own modes of understanding that we needed to make sense of them—and the novel, I suspect, was for us the principal model for that process of sense-making that would somehow bridge the gap between their world and ours.

No doubt these impressions arose because our informants were in many ways people like ourselves living roughly in the same region, in the same general economy and polity, with the same technologies and much of the same history as our own. Nevertheless, the impulse to novelize our experiences seems to me indicative in many respects of what folklore or "vernacular culture"—what we identify as such, how we transfigure it for our own purposes, how we mediate, diffuse, disseminate, and represent it—is as an idea, as a discipline, and as a cultural resource.

I like to think of folklore as a historically contingent and relative concept, a kind of perspectival or parallax effect where epochs, technologies, polities, and the outlooks attached to them produce, by their mingling, frames of reference that expose one to the other in their full historical and social dimensionality. The very term "folk," which referred originally to a small phalanx or division of an army, and spoke primarily to feudal customs and beliefs, whether survivals or revivals, in the historical field of muscle-flexing nation-states, embodies such an effect. The effect is evident in such oxymoronic but familiar phrases as "oral literature" or "preindustrial production" or even "face-to-face interaction," each of which enshrines what may be a residual cultural practice within a dominant or hegemonic framework, as if, for example, the oral-formulaic epic were an extraordinary form of literary inscription, or the blacksmith's shop a kind of miniature precursor to the steel mill, or the ordinary social occasion somehow an illicit withdrawal from electronically mediated state and commercial networks, secure against government and corporate surveillance.

As it happens, developed literacy, as a frame of reference, *does* shed light upon the oral-formulaic process—indeed it is literacy that makes oral-formulism apparent in its differential character, as, in fact, the discovery of oral-formulaic practice concomitantly sheds light upon the nature of literary inscription. Something similar might be said about craftwork in an industrial age, as well as embodied face-to-face social interactions in a specularized information and commercial marketplace. But just as convincingly "folklore" may be what emergent cultural forms—e-prose and Weblore and cyberpunkadelia—look like to eyes still peering through postromantic spectacles (pun intended). Folklore may or may not be about quilts, sweetgrass baskets, and British ballads, or global-warming and carcinogen horror stories and hip-hop rhymes—but these are surely about people making contact with one another for contact's sake.

That the idea of folklore may be perspectival or relational, however, does not make it delusional. What all these perspectives disclose is that human knowledge in whatever form, however mediated over time in certain settled or at least more-than-transient human ecologies or milieus, always establishes itself as a body of habituated understandings or practices, Bourdieu's "durably installed generative principle of regulated improvisations" or *habitus,* the immediate environment of "thoughts, perceptions, expressions, actions" that produces us as social beings thence to reproduce the material and social conditions or the "ecology" of its own generation. Folklore may I think be understood as that organic and vital phase—I mean this in the sense that a communicable disease like the West Nile Virus has phases—of human knowledge that is capable of being retained by and communicated in and through the body, in its mutually defining individual and corporate senses, even if through some institutional or technological vector that intervenes between bodies. This would seem to suggest that in some sense *all* knowledge is folklore, or at least folkloric: well, yes. I don't think there's any other intellectually responsible way to understand it.

The tendency of folklorists to favor mimetic and aural forms of communication, and "face-to-face" interactions is well known; but this only indicates that what we call "folklore" is for certain historical, social, economic, and political reasons an *apparently* special instance of a far more general and one would hope universal productive power. There is no corporeal or mechanical apparatus for the storage, retrieval, and transmission of knowledge, including practical knowledge, that does not *in some sense and in some degree* admit of incorporation with the body and that indeed would be useless if it did not. It is that "some sense and some degree" that is the interest and the problem: folklore is among other things about the boundaries and the interactions between ourselves, individually and collectively, and our own technical and institutional extensions—how those extensions awaken us to what has been extended (and at the same moment transformed or lost), and to the personal and social milieu from which they derive and into which, in the moment of transformation, they carry us, and hence ultimately about how the human lifeworld in a given environment of bodies, as well as of supplements, extensions, and abridgments of the body, emerges, grows, and changes.

Hence, to offer a convenient example, from music. "Classical music" isn't "folklore" or "vernacular culture" in any useful sense, though there are certainly deposits of the traditional and the vernacular in it, as well as influences upon and deposits from it into vernacular and popular culture. Absent the mediation of a musical text, or, in another tradition, sophisticated training regimens and practical exercises, or both, a "classical" music can neither be incorporated with the body, nor performed, nor communicated by the body or among bodies. But *some* aspects of a classical symphony and of classical practice generally *may* and indeed must be—a motif or theme or melody or other idea; a manner or mode of approach; a style—and these elements ("memes," if you will, or "mentifacts") may become part of what certain communities, including the community of classical musicians, share with one another musically and continually reproduce and disseminate, and further contributing to the appreciation, the creation, and the performance of new musical compositions. Insofar as the community of classical musicians shares—and it certainly does share—an embodied knowledge continually refreshed and transformed through their mediated and immediate interactions with on another, they can be said to have a "folklore," not always or necessarily something that can be thoroughly disentangled from their disciplinary knowledge. You can bet, however, that if that community were suddenly to be permanently deprived of the whole machinery of texts, textual reproduction, recorded sound, training disciplines, and all the rest (which would imply a shift in its social valuation, its prestige) the classical tradition in music would shortly revert to a "folklore." In any case, learning a classical music is, in the end, incorporating it—by means of discipline, study, training, and practice, with the body.

Which brings us to literature.

"Folklore and literature" usually means the ways in which folktales or ballads become "literature" or return through literature into oral circulation; how folk motifs or themes become the subject matter of literature; or how literature itself depicts folk language and folklife. Fredric Jameson, in his essay "The Realist Floor-Plan,"[1] about Flaubert's literature of empty rooms and absent presences, suggests how the pioneer realist "decodes" and desacralizes the old libidinal world of the *ancien régime,* a world of beliefs, through a calculatedly reifying and quantifying prose, to create a world of uniform continuous space and hard materiality that is the staging area for bourgeois life, which is above all, from the literary viewpoint at least, a life individually and privately processed, a world of "subjectivities" and "daily life." Jameson allows that an older "modernist" symbolic or mythic reading of the text, in which a mantle clock in Flaubert's story "*Une Coeur Simple"* designed as a Temple of Vesta speaks to the virgin sacrifice of the story's two opposed principal characters, may coexist with his own "postmodernist" one, suggesting that the interest of the story lies in the fact that different communities of discourse and interpretative practices may coalesce around it. Fair enough. And it's interesting. Maybe the "historical overlap" Jameson describes is somehow akin to what I've called the parallax effect, an intellectual-cultural space that, in spite of its loftier stratum, is the same space in which folklore occurs, but closer to the ground.

Those of us who have been teaching literature to undergraduates over the last thirty-five years understand all too well that there is no literature as such without what might be called a folklore of literature—a whole range of embodied habits, practices, ideas, and understandings, a kind of literary *habitus* flowing from literary experience (in this case, from a particular elitist/nationalist/modernist tradition) into language and the responsivity to language and back into reading to transform, by a positive, creative intellectual labor, a semiotics into a semantics, a semantics into an embodied action (our own)—not a decoding (that is what the current crop of undergraduates, for many of whom reading is a toilsome second-order activity) but a kind of redemptive transaction by which we surrender our own vital resources, intellectual, moral, social, and so on to give body (literally) to disembodied text.

To illustrate, briefly:

ON FIRST LOOKING INTO CHAPMAN'S HOMER
Much have I travell'd in the realms of gold,
And many goodly states and kingdoms seen;
Round many western islands have I been
Which bards in fealty to Apollo hold.
Oft of one wide expanse had I been told
That deep-browed Homer ruled as his demesne;
Yet never did I breathe its pure serene
Till I heard Chapman speak out loud and bold:
Then felt I like some watcher of the skies
When a new planet swims into his ken;
Or like stout Cortez when with eagle eyes
He star'd at the Pacific—and all his men
Look'd at each other with a wild surmise—
Silent, upon a peak in Darien.[2]

The literal sense of the poem is easy enough. The poet wants to tell us that his sense of discovery on reading the Elizabethan translator Chapman's Homer, probably *The Odyssey*, was for him comparable to Cortez's (actually it was Balboa) discovery of something both wholly unexpected and inconceivably vast, the Pacific Ocean. And he touches this discovery with the memorable image of a group of men reduced to silence by their own amazement.

But from the literary viewpoint what "happens" in the poem, what Keats dramatizes there, is the process that first invests the poet's voice with the pomposity (itself a parallax effect) and rhetorical formality of the translation he has just been reading, as indicated by his various borrowings from the archaic Elizabethan imagery and diction ("Oft have I traveled," "realms of gold," "goodly states," "bards in fealty to Apollo") and then sends him, by line nine, into a tentative rumination upon his own on the process of discovery: when suddenly he is overtaken by the onrush of an image apparently not his own, but one that seems to have discovered him—the pace of the poem picking up as an extra syllable in line nine trips him up at the top of a stairway of syllables down which he plummets in a decisively non-literary language through line ten, all the syllables clumping together and landing in a heap at the end of the next line, the caesura (and "allhismen / lookedateachotherwithawildsurmise") recklessly abandoned in the urgency of the speech, until he finally recovers himself in the repose of a recovered caesura after "silent" (as prolonged as if Louis Armstrong were playing it), until he finally comes to rest in a euphonious and exotic place-name, "Darien."

A poem about discovery, then, Keats's own, a dramatized discovery that occurs, or seems to occur, in the midst of the poem's composition, and one that might testify to Keats's originality, were it not for the likelihood, certainly an element of the story that Keats means to tell, that the outstanding image of a band of mariners under a heroic captain with which the poem concludes must have been suggested to the young poet, as surely as the opening lines, by his reading, where a story of another well-known sailor and his crew consumes thirteen thousand some odd lines of verse. A poem about discovery, then—chiefly the discovery of the poet's own voice, in the midst of conspicuously derivative language and ideas. And so it is really a poem about an effect: a literary effect in this case, whose most salient aspect is that it is not really literary, though it is trying to be.

Yet it is just that much more interesting, and amusing, to recall that Keats was a Cockney, so that the posturing of the poet in the opening lines can be read, too, as that of a young man who knows that his social credentials don't match those of the high-flown literary fraternity into which he would like to gain entry. Perhaps the Tourette's-like rush of words that overtakes him in lines twelve and thirteen, not inconceivably haplessly delivered in Keats's piping Cockney voice, he might have wished to put back in their place. Perhaps the silence in the concluding line is the silence of mortification, a sort of joke on himself.

Very little of what is distinctively "literary" about "On First Looking into Chapman's Homer" has to do with writing or text, but about the embodiment of texts as sounds and as ideas, as well as a kind of sudden emancipation from texts into an urgent, idiomatic, spontaneous speech that indecorously violates the conventions of the sonnet in which the poem is framed. To "read" this poem, then, demands a verbal imagination already thoroughly habituated to, among other things, iambic pentameter, Elizabethan rhetorics, and industrial-age working-class speech, the fictionality of the poetic voice itself, the content of Homer's poems, the story of the Spanish voyages, and so on. None of this, of course, is "folklore" in the sense that folklorists intend the term—but it is all in the nature of embodied knowledge and practice in a milieu of books and letters, and it is the very essence of the literary effect. Classrooms attempt to foster it. Remove it, and you have mere text, indeterminacy, deconstruction as a pedagogical necessity even more than a critical practice, Jameson's realist floor-plan and a roomful of first-year undergraduates weaned on iPods and the World Wide Web.

All this is a complicated way of saying what professors of literature have always known, that "literariness" inheres in the sounds, more precisely the music of the language, which as Adam Phillips suggests is the condition of speech in the earliest period of our lives, when we hear unintelligible vocal sounds, especially those of a parent, still more the sing-songing of a mother's voice, as music. Hence the music of language like music itself is bound up with the primary drives: erotic, limbic, libidinal, perhaps at some level complicated by Oedipal rivalries, at once a seduction and a resistance. Sound, moreover, is the indicator of particular modifications of the vocal stream, achieved with the lips, the mouth, teeth, throat, and tongue, that we call phonemes or particles, the significant building blocks of words. That's why speech is intelligible even given immense variations among individuals making speech sounds: the sounds merely indicate definite physiological configurations that as configurations do not vary significantly from individual to individual. Hence vocalization is tied to definite configurations of the body and to recognition of them—suggesting that "literariness" is the embodied form of literary knowledge, what can be carried away from and towards the medium of writing in and through the body and what returns to the body through its traffic in the medium of the written word.

And it seems there is no form of knowledge that does not also traffic in some form of that materiality, whether of instruments or tools or even the materiality of the body itself, both in itself and in relation to other bodies.

Where, then, is "folklore?"

Folklore finds its opportunity at the boundary between knowledge and power, where it plays and with which it is also at play. Often folklore is self-evidently about the relationship of knowledge and power, sometimes in such intimate contact with the face of power that it can be said to play provocatively at the boundary of power and the privation of it, of force and counterforce, putting the official and authorized to unofficial and unauthorized uses, shifting disciplinary practices into adisciplinary spaces—that is why we can have an e-mail folklore, or a medical or a political or a workplace folklore. Folklore is inherently political because it is upon the body that power, from one point of view at least, is ultimately exercised and from which it does or does not extend; embodied knowledge is or is not melded to the sustaining technical and institutional apparatus of culture, whose densities and diffusions are roughly the densities and diffusions of power. Where history, or society, or politics or temperament, or simply an idle moment or a transient opportunity, has placed us in some degree outside the consensus at which power and prestige accumulates, and at which the prerogatives of power in institutions and establishments and technologies accumulate, there we find folklore; unburdened by what is fixed, formulated, worked and reworked, what by its very nature reproduced by power, folklore springs immediately from the imagination in its own character and speaks immediately to it. Hence like Keats's poem it is both a discovery and a thing discovered, both present and re-presented. In Keats's poem a vernacular poet struggles somewhat disingenuously to throw off his vernacularity only to find it sweeping back to secure the literary triumph in an unexpected way. The poem—flowing, culturally, towards elite culture instead of away from it—belongs to the same cultural zone as folklore, where the creations, explanations, responses, expedients, performances, stories, and expressions have (to borrow Whitman's phrase) the "indescribable freshness and candor" of inventions that are in immediate contact with the moments and the conditions of its necessities and exigencies—the perpetual newness of discovery, which is always the discovery of ourselves.

11 FOLKLORE'S PATHETIC FALLACY

THE CULTURE POWER

Ruskin asks: What is "the difference between the ordinary, proper, and true appearances of things to us; and the extraordinary, or false appearances, when we are under the influence of an emotion, or contemplative fancy; false appearances, I say, as being entirely unconnected with any real power or character in the object, and only imputed to it by us.

> For instance, in Alton Locke,—
> "They rowed her in across the rolling foam—
> The cruel, crawling foam."

"The foam is not cruel, neither does it crawl," Ruskin writes. "The state of mind which attributes to it these characters of a living creature is one in which the reason is unhinged by grief. All violent feelings produce in us a falseness in all our impressions of external things, which I would generally characterize as the 'pathetic fallacy.'"

The pathetic fallacy, Ruskin goes on, is "eminently characteristic of the modern mind. For instance, Keats, describing a wave breaking out at sea, says of it—

"Down whose green back the short-lived foam, all hoar,
Bursts gradual, with a wayward indolence."

"Homer would never have written, never have thought of, such words. He could not by any possibility have lost sight of the great fact that the wave, from the beginning to the end of it, do what it might, was still nothing else than salt water; and that salt water was neither wayward or indolent." But "Homer has some feeling about the sea; a faith in the animation of it much stronger than Keats's. But all this sense of something living in it, he separates in his mind into a great abstract image of a Sea Power. He never says the waves rage, or the waves are idle. But he says there is somewhat in, and greater than, the waves, which rages, and is idle, and that he calls a god."

> With us, observe, the idea of the Divinity is apt to get separated from the life of nature; and imagining our God upon a cloudy throne, far above the earth, and not in the flowers or the waters, we approach those vis-

> ible things with a theory that they are governed by physical laws. But coming to them, we find the theory fail, that, say what we choose about them, the instinctive sense of their being alive is too strong for us; and in scorn of all physical law, the willful fountain sings, and the kindly flowers rejoice. We fall necessarily into the curious web of hesitating sentiment, pathetic fallacy, and wandering fancy, which form a great part of our modern view of nature. But the Greek never removed his god out of nature at all; never attempted for a moment to contradict his instinctive sense that God was everywhere. But in thus clearly defining his belief, observe, he threw it entirely into a human form, and gave his faith to nothing but the image of his own humanity.[1]

This curious snare of hesitating sentiment and "contemplative fancy," Ruskin's "pathetic fallacy," is precisely the epistemological predicament of the folklorist, who, more than either anthropologist or sociologist, finds herself caught in a participatory indeterminacy rooted in folklore's ontological relativity; neither objectively discoverable nor altogether "constituted," seldom present to investigation independent of any a priori representation, virtually impossible to perceive much less analyze absent a background radiation of anxiety, nostalgia, interest, advocacy, even personal identification, its derivative "theory" rarely more than an extrapolated and rationalized justification of "practice" (often itself an opportunistic adjustment to an ever-shifting configuration of political, economic, and historical contingencies) folklore is never anything other than, as the late Alan Dundes said, "what the folklorist says it is," and this in a nontrivial sense.

For the library scholar of the folkloric—ballads and tales, myths and legends, ritual observances, music and dance, and the like, essentially textual and archeological materials—the "pathetic fallacy" is already so embedded in the character of the materials themselves that it scarcely can rise to the level of interrogation, much less critical consciousness. It could be said of them that a "hesitating sentiment" and "contemplative fancy" are precisely their reasons for being. But the contemporary "public folklorist," typically connected with an arts agency, a museum, a library, a university, a state or municipality, or some other official or quasi-official institution whose office is in some sense the maintenance of public or historical culture and collective memory, confronts the pathetic fallacy in the form of direct contestation among the several groups and interests her office is constituted to serve, none of whom will happily submit either to fancy or to sentiment. Heritage tourism, local history and historic preservation, the prestige and visibility of ethnic, minority, religious, occupational, and other cultural communities, the conservation and protection of space and place, natural environment, resources, animal and plant species, and even of economic viability—whether through exhibitions, museum collections, local festivals, educational initiatives, material preservation, mapping and documentation, economic revitalization, or even direct political intervention, all call in some sense upon the identification and representation of the "folkloric" from viewpoints favorable on the one hand to established powers such as the state, as in heritage tourism, or to voluntary movements, environmental, political, and cultural, set against the depredations of capitalism and state power.[2] What, under these conditions, can be the cultural "divinity" to which all of these interests might pay obeisance, mysteriously implicated in a range of otherwise contrary enterprises?

The public folklorist, though richly equipped with ideas that originate in library scholarship, of necessity performs, with the ethnographer, the better part of her work where folklore's pathetic fallacy is most radically challenged—the very heart of the "ethnographic trauma"—in the "field"; that is, in the community. The irresistible social-psychological force of ethnomimesis shapes the fieldworker's adjustment to new and often strange social, political, and material conditions, and compels an imaginative shift in her social and ultimately her cognitive orientation that at some point in the process can no longer anchor itself securely in the tokens and remembrances of or the symbolic and actual lifelines to the familiar habitual culture. The old and complacent relation between theory and practice is profoundly, usually permanently, disrupted or destabilized; "theory" as such vanishes, not because it has been exposed as inadequate (often quite the contrary) but because it reveals itself as a pure product of the folklorist's own material and social immunity—what Bourdieu calls "distance from necessity"—and hence as a thing interesting or useful only in a setting of already achieved and transmuted ethnographic representations and discourses.

"Practice," in turn, is radically recontextualized, materially, socially, psychologically, and politically, paralyzed by the contrary impulses of, on the one hand, rejection or repulsion, and on the other of sympathy, affinity, or identification, a kind of ethnographic transference. And the folk "arts," finally, in the broadest sense—artifacts, performances, practices—reappear as complex intersections or nodes ("zones of the exchange of information," to use Robert St. George's phrase)[3] in a vast web of relations that extends from minutely particularized local situations to unexpectedly remote influences and agents that is the salient characteristic of folk culture: a symbolic and actual cultural improvisation in an ever-shifting milieu of impinging necessities (i.e., "sites of resistance to concentrations of power").[4]

Hence "folk culture" as such simply disappears into the very system of class and other power relations that the idea of the folk occultizes and depoliticizes at the same time as it refreshes and rehabilitates. A worker community, an ethnic enclave, a life-cycle cohort, an institutionally grounded scene of reiterated social relations, a regulated pattern of occasional or variable momentary interactions: folklore's "constructedness," its "constituted" character, manifests itself precisely as such at the same time as its real political relations—and with them, therefore, the self-deceiving social-political sleight-of-hand that lies at the heart of the idea of the folk. A god, like Homer's Neptune, has been revealed: the Culture God, her face visible behind the momentarily disenchanted phantasmagoria of her manifestations.

"Folklore" is a catalytic reaction of the political imagination to the conjunction of two affiliated but distinctive historical forces: the cultural process, on the one hand, and the cultural product, performance, text, idea, or artifact on the other. The cultural process we identify by instinct, by experience, by detection, having been somehow distanced from it and perhaps ambivalently set against the "collective misrecognitions" that sustain the normal alignments of culture and power—ideologically distanced perhaps, or distanced perhaps on account of our own social dislocation, displacement, or destabilization. By the "cultural product," we mean all that can be said to have been "achieved," culturally, which we identify by tradition, training, and sometimes by inference or extrapolation from the former—or with equally compelling effect, from the latter, moving by inference from text or performance to process. It is this intellectual catalysis, perpetually rooted in the social distances, mostly but not exclusively of class, whose variations form the psychological climate of the discipline's historical evolution, academic and applied, that in the epistemological sense produces folklore, in the Wildean sense that Turner's paintings produce the fogs on the Thames.

That the cultural process and the cultural product, however conceived, can never be finally disentangled from one another—for surely the "cultural process" is ethnomimetic, involving in some form the communication of its achieved and accumulated products—I readily concede: hence the requirement, in Ruskin's sense, for a conceptual third term, the emancipated God, the Culture Power itself, that permits us to distinguish what cannot actually be divided, and to address it as a Power that like a god among other gods is autonomous within its own sphere, however deeply implicated other gods may be in the conduct and constitution of its divinity.

That we have already implicitly affirmed the existence of this divinity, without, however, ever having named or acknowledged Her as a force independent either of the processes in which she is manifestly active or the products and practices in which She is immanent, is more than indicated by the varied roles of "interest"—aesthetic, social, political, and personal—that distinguish our discipline. No sociology is free, of course, of "interest." But we consistently highlight our interest, magnify and valorize it, thence to diffuse, memorialize, celebrate, and enshrine it as "culture," "art," "performance," "memory," and "knowledge"; it is typically both our entrance into and our exit from the discipline, as well as its end and aim, whether academic or not, in more than an accidental sense. Under its influence we have already formed, whether as mediator, scholar, broker, advocate, or producer, a compelling idea of it, one that is never far from the powerful original impact of a work of material, musical, verbal, dramatic, or other embodiment of the folk imagination—its "folk" character already a function of the fact that we have mixed ourselves up in it, created an impure product so lovely in its impurities that we could never wish to purify it even if we could: notwithstanding the fact that the quest for purity, which is simply the quest to lodge our faith in "nothing but the image of our own humanity," is just that motive that has both divided the academic and applied disciplines as well as intermittently allied them, depending, usually, on the state of the political atmosphere.

This is not a quibble or a mystification. My own experience with the word, the concept, and the quality or characteristic (I do not say the fact) of folklore, in academic, popular, and vernacular contexts, is not simply that people mean different things by it or that they evaluate it differently; it is that for better or worse some think of folklore as in some fundamental ways directly or indirectly connected to their lives, however this is understood, and some do not. Where the connection is absent, folklore is something either archaic, fanciful (and therefore trivial), politically suspect, or contemptible; where it obtains, folklore is immediate, actual, intensely personal, inherently and powerfully oppositional or revolutionary, and passionately defended, protected, and loved. The same I suppose could be said in some sense about any category of learning, even as to the objective existence of the category itself. What is important is that those us who have made, or have been influenced to make, such a connection, naturally want to act upon it, to prove it out, in the most convincing and significant ways, and not be continually reduced to the condition of mere enthusiasts or cranks, "folkies," a relatively tiny cult of scholars, collectors, curators, concert and festival promoters, and arts agents engaged in a lively conversation mainly with themselves and only politely tolerated, if they are noticed at all, not only by the rest of the academic world much less of the public sector, but by the capricious and powerful riverine gods (I mean, of course, the Corporations and the State) whose repeated innundations of the "cultural watershed" (to use Steve Zeitlin's provocative phrase)[5] are precisely what, since the beginnings of industrial capitalism and earlier, have both exposed culture in the anthropological sense to view and have compelled over the twentieth century the various salvage-and-rescue operations mounted in its behalf.

The office of the public folklorist is, first, to make for others the connection she has already made for herself; to demonstrate not only that it is tragic to lose a mountaintop (I am thinking of Mary Hufford's disturbing paper on mountaintop removal in West Virginia presented at our 1999 professional meeting)[6] and all the knowledges, meanings, practices, rituals, and skills dependent upon it, not to mention an entire historical and cultural community, and that it is imperative to take steps to mitigate or actually to prevent this from happening—but that the loss is collective in more than a sentimental, pragmatic, political, or even a moral sense (I hate arguments that ancient herbal lores may someday provide a cure for cancer, valid as they may be—they are like arguments that the space program exists to provide new kitchen conveniences). It is to demonstrate to the managers, administrators, and owners, and to their various political operatives and shills that the loss is directly and immediately to them and to their clients, customers, and constituencies, whose very existence as such springs from the one resource in which all other resources have their value, and that is human membership, or more precisely, the enabling conditions of human membership from which humans manufacture their one species-specific product, culture, at every and all levels.

But to go further. Even should such a demonstration be made (and it can, and has been, but not necessarily by folklorists), it would leave us still where we are now, mere petitioners knocking at the gate. The interests and forces it seeks to direct or disperse, of technology, capital, and the rest, are in a sense irresistible. Indeed in some ways it is misleading to regard these forces as antagonists at all—they are simply the naked face of the capitalist Second Nature in which all of us have our economic, social, and cultural lives, including those lives that will be improvised where capital, symbolic or actual, is shallow, spurious, or scarce. The office of the folklorist, then, is to do (and I realize there is nothing new here—I am just crusading) what over the last two generations biologists, ecologists, zoologists, climatologists, and finally environmental activists have done: to model, first, at the sociological level, what (to borrow from Mary Hufford again) "human ecology" is and how it works.[7] This will be a multidisciplinary project that should bring folklore's existing but hitherto isolated insights together with the insights of a range of social sciences to define so far as possible what are the enabling conditions of culture. Second, it will be to show not simply that this or that species of culture is under threat—least of all by enshrining its archaic or ephemeral products—but that the human ecology itself is sweepingly imperiled by what is called "postmodernity" or "globalization," at the same time as these forces are creating environments for the growth of new human ecologies that it would be our business to identify; and third, to create a human ecology movement whose ultimate aim will be to produce definitions, limits, and standards for human ecological "health." Ideally such a movement would develop a cultural reading of existing law that would prepare the way for litigation to protect the *enabling conditions* of culture and ultimately a body of case law as well as cultural policy legislation, not conservationist or preservationist but constitutional in character, on the model of the National Environmental Policy Act, capable of subjecting any technical, political, and commercial encroachment upon human ecologies to legal scrutiny. The aim would be neither a pre- nor proscriptive cultural Bill of Rights, itself constrainedly "cultural," but a body of opinion and precedent that would form the basis for legal challenges to such encroachments or violations, and finally soliciting (as the Environmental Protection Agency does with its public and private stakeholders) "creative solutions" to problems of sustaining and improving the human ecology: and there is an occupation for folklorists!

"What may look like a simple catalogue of disparate measures," writes Pierre Bourdieu about the apparently passive neo-liberal acceptance of the inevitability of globalization and the obsolescence of the nation-state, "is in fact inspired by the will to break out of the fatalism of neo-liberal thinking, to 'defatalize' by politicizing, by replacing the naturalized economy of neo-liberalism with an economy of happiness, based on human initiatives and human will, making allowance in its calculations for the costs in suffering and the profits in fulfillment that are ignored by the strictly economistic cult of productivity and profitability."[8]

What am I dreaming of? First, of course, what we already have: a professional discipline of cultural scholars and practitioners in several affiliated fields. And the human ecology equivalent of environmental defense leagues, clubs, councils, federations, foundations, and funds; a legal subdiscipline with advocacy centers, service nonprofits (by analogy to the Legal Services Foundation), and think tanks; a human ecology lobby; and state and federal agencies or commissions, perhaps, allied to Health and Human Services, dedicated, perhaps, to "Memory, Livability, and Quality of Life."

One does not need to be a folklorist, or even know of the existence of folklore or folklorists, to feel the shock and the pain and the disorientation when a settled way of life is disrupted or undermined by corporate-driven development or by some State Department of Transportation with its thirty-year-old initiatives or by industrial outsourcing or downsizing, much less the laws that favor and promote such initiatives that consistently fly in the face of the lived localities and habitable spaces that are utterly defenseless against them. Collectively speaking, we are no better off than Rip Van Winkle, zonked out on his mountaintop, sleeping through the various technical and commercial revolutions we scarcely know have occurred until we wake to our own unconscious complicity in them and return to the home-place only to find ourselves strangers, the great spreading beech tree of custom cut down to make way for a flagpole, or, as the case may be, a cell-phone tower.

These are not the kinds of problems with which folklorists officially engage, except in their off-hours; but they are directly pertinent to the work of folklore, not only because they structurally reduplicate the violent incursions of capital, at another economic level, into working class, minority, poor, and outsider ways of life but because they are the untapped reservoir of anger and frustration from which a new rill of cultural progressivism might conceivably spring, not simply as the idyll of a middle class urgently trying to reproduce itself in Disneyized pictures of life but in a broader political campaign dedicated to protecting and constituting the conditions of cultural possibility for everyone.

Distasteful and even self-defeating as it will seem to any of us schooled in the humanities or the social sciences, the human ecology movement must learn what environmentalists, faced with increasing legislative pressure to subject environmental regulation to cost-benefit analysis, have learned to do—to speak to power in the language of money. Only in economic terms will any cultural counterforce prove effective ultimately against the narrowly economic reasoning that governs most political decision making. The profound social and psychological costs of cultural dislocation, disruption, and degradation will, I submit, admit of expression, albeit creatively, in economic terms; indeed, many such costs I suspect are directly and unequivocally economic. That workers, their families, and their communities all suffer grievously when a manufacturing plant shuts down is obvious enough; but *all* development involves hidden subsidies and hidden costs paid to commerce and to the developer himself at the expense not only of people directly removed or displaced but to those whom development is supposed to benefit. The same may be said of developments in transportation, education, health care, tax policy, and dozens of other areas in which the commonweal and the community intersect through constituted institutional power. And it happens that customary ways of life, embodying decades or centuries of economic as well as cultural evolution under particular conditions and circumstances, is often the cheapest, the most efficient, and the most rewarding way of life for those who live it. Human ecologists must cast the widest possible economic net, one that will capture the microeconomic impacts upon individual mental health and well-being, family and community function and dysfunction, employment and employability, education and educability and other dimensions of cultural life where the immense scales of capitalist investment and disinvestment, public and private, work like hurricanes and floods upon evolved cultural landscapes.

We are, it seems to me, essentially in the situation of the abolitionist movement before the annexation of the western territories made it imperative that the question of slavery be brought to the legislative table. Our "western territories"—by which I mean the new territory of global capitalism over which the issue of cultural ownership is currently raging—are in fact all around us, in our own communities and on our own streets, even in our parlors and bedrooms, subject to an incremental annexation by corporate power so subtle as to be virtually imperceptible except to historical memory: as if historical memory could be the sole preserve of history departments, elite preservation agencies, and struggling local museums and libraries, and not a primary obligation of our own priests and praise-singers.

And it is not immaterial, I think, that disciplinarily speaking we are in many ways the heirs of the abolitionists. They were radicals. They collected slave songs and established various schools, missions, and relief organizations; but they left their most powerful and lasting legacy in an interpretation of the law: in this case of the Constitution itself. If nothing else, we must become champions of the real, as against the commercially mediated life, lest we find ourselves (if we have not already) in a refeudalized society, divided between those for whom the whole of cultural and economic existence is conducted though networks of privatized information and access, and others—not improbably including the selfsame people—for whom social life remains grounded in palpable human interactions: in a society, in other words, that divides both people and communities against themselves.

There is no need to argue again the point that Barbara Kirschenblatt-Gimblett's "Mistaken Dichotomies" are mistaken, even as they are palpably reflected in ideological, disciplinary, and institutional arrangements and hence quite real existentially and practically, even personally, if not theoretically or essentially. But in our lingering preoccupation with these acknowledged "mistaken dichotomies" we are, I think, willfully and I suspect deliberately—because the political challenge is so daunting—blinding ourselves to the deeper dichotomy in our outlook that I am calling folklore's "pathetic fallacy," between the cultural manifestation, through which, and on behalf of which, and in relation to which, we have mostly carried out our various analytic, custodial, and advocacy projects, and the Culture Power, the very recognition of which is implicated in the "identification" or "discovery" or "invention" of the cultural manifestation to begin with.

Certainly the prerogative of representation opens a social and political channel for a cultural voice and the cultural image, even if it is within the very institutional and material structures originally responsible for the silencing of that voice and the effacement of that image, and it is necessarily preliminary to any authentic political participation. One or another version of this argument is a continuing strain in the various uses of folklore in traditions of social ameliorization, extending from Jane Addams's folk festivals and industrial crafts museum to Sarah Gertrude Knott's National Folk Festival to the Lomax song collections, radio programs, and folk concerts to the Smithsonian Folklife Festival to the National Heritage Awards and all the arts agencies, museums, schools, and other venues in which public folklorists work. This cultural situation is, I think, in many ways comparable to the ideological debate in pre-revolutionary America, which was invisibly underwritten by uneven distributions of access to the capital and technical resources of opinion making, that is, the printing press, allowing a gentocracy of prosperous tradesmen, merchants, and planters to redirect the mounting antagonism of the poor, the unskilled, deskilled, and disenfranchised against emergent native elites towards a demonized and distant king, when the real enemy, as would become evident a generation later, was the concentrations of wealth in whose interests the Revolution had actually been fought. It may be said at least, however, that in theory the constitutional government that ensued attempted to guarantee the right of political expression, even if it could not guarantee access to the resources of it; and it is indicative of the precise reversal of our political orientation that the Supreme Court should strictly identify, in the media age, and under corporate influence, money with free speech, in effect revoking the former guarantee on behalf of the latter. As Hendrick Hertzberg opines, our garrulous and short-lived populist agitations tend to be "an expression of disgust with a political system whose workings are obscure, whose mechanisms are subject to manipulation by unaccountable forces, and whose outcomes, seemingly, are more and more distantly related to any semblance of purposeful democratic choice."[9]

Substitute "cultural system" for "political system" in Hertzberg's lament and one discovers the arena in which a politics of human ecology must be worked out. As the Revolution carried colonial America beyond ideological contestation and moved class warfare into a historical play-zone where for the first time in history a political philosophy grounded, ironically enough, in the cultural innovation of the contract-bound mercantile trading company, found itself in the real world, enlisted in the genesis of the world's first actual social contract—so are we called upon, as cultural scholars, theorists, advocates, and activists to frame a discourse of cultural rights, obligations, and principles of governance in the new post-national, even post-cultural milieu of instantaneous global communications, virtually unrestricted capital mobility, almost infinitely flexible protocols of production, and among other alarming developments, the rise of computer modeling, whose predictive power exponentially outstrips that of any ideologically grounded theory or policy necessarily derived from deliberative processes, essentially eviscerating the role of ideas.

Whether the new challenges to cultural life represent differences of degree or of kind I leave aside for the moment; suffice it to say, perhaps, that we seem to have moved even beyond that point described only a decade ago as one of cultural exhaustion or expiration, the simultaneous death both of the subject and of the metanarratives in which subjectivity had historically located itself, into one in which the formerly receding cultural horizon has begun to come again into view, and something like the shape of the human ecology to come may be visible on it. It is a kind of apotheosis—the Culture Power rising, Triton-like, in its own shape out of the very waves that have swallowed it up.

What is that shape, and what are the principles of the cultural processes whose guarantees we must learn to make explicit? I'm only guessing; but thanks to the computer the idea of webs and networks, what Hardt and

Negri call "rhizomic" relations,[10] have already replaced the idea of groups and communities as the principal model of human social organization; that claims of authenticity will no longer flow from anthropological schemes of embeddedness but from the nodal points, virtual and actual, at which the flows of cultural information are concentrated and redistributed (themselves constantly changing); and that actual social affiliation, already bewilderingly multiple, shifting, and often, in a field of infinitely dispersed identities, protean and symbolic, scarcely real at all except as a sign in a total field of commercially and technically mobilized signs, will (or has already) acquire a revolutionary complexion, perhaps providing an impetus in the struggle against the corporation and the state for control of those "zones of the exchange of information" at which in postmodernity we are compelled to stage our humanity.

And here, perhaps, lies a clue to where our own cultural commitments, and our agitation for redress, ought to lie. Called alienation, or atomization, or fragmentation—in our own day epitomized by proliferations of markets, channels, and the codes that identify them—the strategy of capital has always been to isolate; it is really the cellular structure of the prison, more than the power of surveillance (the data barn is the perfect figure for the corporate totality), or their conjunction, that makes it such a powerful metaphor for culture in modernity. Isolation extirpates the human being from her entanglement in history and society, time, place, and association, and hence from the shaping forces of practice, habit, and custom, and makes her available for an economic role as producer, consumer, or client. Thrusts against the social and cultural erosions of capital always begin, even before ideology, with affiliation; and it is on this fundamental level that we must begin to stake out the area of the cultural, and equip it for the genesis, and not merely the conservation of, fertile human ecologies.

There are at least three self-evident and inalienable cultural rights, it seems, upon which sociality, social affiliation, and its fruits in practical and imaginative life materially depend: continuity in time and in temporal structures, contiguity in space and in spatial arrangements, virtual or actual, and what for lack of a better word I'll call neither time nor space but "breathing room": that field of intellectual and personal freedom and privacy, as well as the imaginative, practical, and communal liberty that ought to follow from them, in which, out of the free play of imagination upon the surfaces of practical, social, and spiritual necessity, and in the interplay of social influence, human beings accumulate ethnomimetically—developmentally, socially, and, in the broadest sense, artistically—that reservoir of structuring structures, *habitus,* the underwriting of which it should be the aim of any cultural policy to provide for and protect.

Just what "breathing room" might be, instrumentally speaking, is difficult to say: but among its clear enemies are corporate and political totalitarianism, "privatization," which, paradoxically, seems to accompany the eradication of the private sphere, and social-economic isolation, accomplished, for example, through such strategies as thematized (read commodified) or socially stratified environments or technical extensions of the social such as the Internet, a radically new cultural field whose enormous potential gifts and equally grave liabilities must be understood entirely apart from the immense corporate and political initiatives that support and promote them. In any case, it is certain that our breathing room has been stolen from us when we haven't a place to sit down and talk or a moment to think—because commercial communications (which is nearly all of the electronic field of communications) have accelerated (in whose interest?) the whole of life to an insupportable tempo, and saturated every public and private space with their message.

What the Interstate Highway Act of 1948 did not have—cultural consultants to try to project the coming world of an auto-dependent, deurbanized, socially, racially, and economically segregated society—the Information Superhighway conceivably could have, given the present state of our knowledge.

Let us, then, borrow a term from economist Amartya Sen, "capability," by which he means, for individual men and women, "the substantive freedoms he or she enjoys to lead the kind of life he or she *has reason to value*" (my emphasis)—a formulation in which a political concept of *cultural* rights is, I think, implicit.[11] Such freedoms might in legal or political discourse be regarded as rights—to secure our right to food, shelter, and clothing, for instance, is to guarantee our freedom from hunger and cold—since both rights and freedoms imply a context of superior power from which they derive, as immunities, exemptions, endowments, prerogatives, or privileges. But whereas "rights" describe relations of justice, fitness, appropriateness, and the like, with reference to some standard or norm, natural, moral, political, civil, legal, or otherwise, "freedoms" describe an original autonomy or agency, not derived from a superior power but distinct and independent of it, except insofar as that power may have limited, restrained, or controlled it. In this sense the Culture Power is a human productive power or "capability," the natural right to determine "the kind of life we have reason to value," whose exercise demands the imaginative and practical "breathing room" that such exercise necessarily opens and in which it occurs—freedom from corporeal, intellectual, or imaginative violence, for example, freedom from social isolation and exclusion, and freedom, perhaps, from freedom itself—freedom, that is, from the legal, illegal, and extralegal immunities that permit the caprice, the self-interest, or the mere expedients of private or public power not only to abridge "the substantive freedoms he or she enjoys to lead the kind of life he or she has reason to value," but arbitrarily to influence, shape or even determine what will be "the kind of life he or she has reason to value."

Continuity, contiguity, capability: I am not naïve enough to suppose that the formulation of a workable cultural policy grounded in such principles can or even should arrest the forward advance of capital. But at the very least, perhaps, we should not have in today's forms the catastrophic collapse of whole sectors of the economy, the sudden disappearance of the workplace or the gross devaluation of the resources upon which it depends, the violent upheavals in settled landscapes, the physical bifurcation and dismantling of neighborhoods, massive internal migrations, or any of the other assaults of pure capitalism upon human ecology without laws to prevent or at least mitigate them and public resources to sustain or to create the social fields in which new ecologies may evolve.

. . . .

As Homer at once acknowledges divine power and conceives of it independently of the matter in which it is immanent, so must we, having acknowledged the constituted or invented character of folklore, embrace its invented and collaborative character freely and openly, lending ourselves to it not only as brokers or agents but, in effect, as creators and shapers of a human manifestation in which we are already deeply implicated. Standards of scientific dispassion and objectivity, even insofar as they represent a methodological consensus that must underwrite any substantive one, and certainly belong to any purely scholarly or scientific discourse, have little place in the complex negotiations between folklorists and their various audiences and constituencies. Here the cultural message, and especially the truths we offer to embody in what we call "folklore"—truths that belong to, but are not identical with, their manifestations, from which indeed they must be continually disentangled lest our work only kill with kindness—is poetic and philosophical more than historical or scientific. Only in such a discourse can we move from a merely reactive ameliorist or preservationist to a genuinely constitutional stance in the struggle with capital for control over human desire.

As we become defenders of the Culture Power, so where culture itself is concerned must we move candidly beyond documentation, memorialization, and preservation towards active creation, forging a poetics of cultural transformation that frankly acknowledges and incorporates as an active element the migration we ourselves regularly facilitate, of vernacular expression into the public sphere: do, in effect, what our commercial culture already does so effectively (and has done even with folklore), not to reify or commodify—and I do not say these are always unmitigated evils—but to mobilize, reanimate, liberate. For beyond the cultural inventory lie the conditions that fostered it; beyond achieved culture in all its elements lies the range of capabilities of which it is the expression; beyond cultural rights lie the material and imaginative fields in which it is possible to exercise those rights. The poetics of public folklore, like any poetics, should aspire to the condition of music, affirming its rootedness in time, place, people, and experience, but also capturing essences, inventing unrealized histories, redrawing boundaries, absorbing influences, playing with new possibilities. To put this all another way: it is important to preserve a tradition, with apprenticeship programs, museum exhibits, recordings, and the like, and to protect it if possible from harm by political and legal means. But, emancipated from folklore's pathetic fallacy, we are free to protect, too, the conditions of its possibility, in whatever direction it may take and in whatever form; and free ourselves to participate, collaborate in, even initiate and originate its making new.

12 *HABITUS*, ETHNOMIMESIS

A NOTE ON *THE LOGIC OF PRACTICE*

Money can't buy me love.—the Beatles

A natural radiance transforms the base matter of human flesh into the sublimer element of our sociality, an occult but vital process through which people as such, independently of every form of social identity other than that of social membership itself, in various purposeful and accidental ways originate, communicate, circulate, and sustain such aspects of personhood that are the *sine qua non* of every other form of social participation. Ethnomimesis[1] is indicated, but not disclosed, in family, clan, and "community," in the pub or café life, and the myriad varieties of the town pump; but it lives a vaporous, phantasmal life as well, with an etiology that mostly eludes detection, though it spreads its influences everywhere. Like any circulatory system, ethnomimesis is a web of processes, many-centered, diffuse, and far-reaching, in essence more social alchemy than social mechanics, recognizable by its products and outcomes and at best only fleetingly perceptible—but less to sense than to understanding.

"Social alchemy" is Bourdieu's phrase—and like so much of his incidental or figurative language, it is not obviously constitutive of his social theory; and yet it is rhetorically and conceptually integral to it, and points to an only partially disclosed and half-formed notion, very like "ethnomimesis," that both undergirds and destabilizes the "systems of durable, transposable dispositions, structured structures predisposed to function as structuring structures,"[2] the "durably installed generative principle of regulated improvisations"[3] now famously called *habitus.*

Habitus, like folklore, is everywhere and nowhere, haunting the social scene like the memory of an old war, the sum of all that goes without saying, that we take for granted, that we consider natural and inevitable—precisely what we have somewhat casually taken "habitus" to mean—so long as generative "structuring structures" may be adduced from practice; but such structures, being necessarily hypothetical, do not necessarily lead to "dispositions," even as they intimate them, but, on the contrary, leave us perpetually behind the game, tied to already residual objects, performances, and forms whose very interest *is* that they seem to have resisted the transposability that is the essence of *habitus*, having allowed the stream of time, and the "objective conditions" ("possibilities and impossibilities, freedoms and necessities, opportunities and prohibitions")[4] to which *habitus* is a collective accommodation, to flow around and beyond them. That has always been the problem with the science of folklore, has it not, that its objects, texts, and practices, however powerfully indicative of originary and fundamental social processes, precisely for that reason remain elusive, unable to disclose the magic that produced them—processes that can never be understood except as it were alchemically, as essentially impenetrable even while under observation, perhaps illicit, at once a concretion and a negation and, paradoxically, only thinkable as paradox.

What is the social locale of *habitus*? Maybe an orthographical sleight of hand, an apparently innocent but strategic comma, that links, without explanation, dispositions to structures and structures to structuring, tendencies, and qualities to ideas and forms. In this respect it is a purely tactical idea, designed to mediate between the poles of what Bourdieu calls "objectivism" and "subjectivism"—a means not of exposing, but merely of isolating, the "prelogical" logic of practice in its prelogicality. Despite its evident utility in accounting for the limitless exfoliation of possible actions within equally evident systems of structures, *habitus* would seem to belong, really, not in the social dimension, but outside of it, with the other products of theoretical reason—not an engine of agency but a sump for indefinite deferral, a kind of necessary fiction into which we project what theoretical reason can neither locate in practice nor install in rules, systems, and syntaxes, neither freedom nor necessity but a kind of minor god, presiding over the delicate equilibrium in human motives of imagination and desire.

As *habitus* is rooted in practice, it is for Bourdieu inaccessible to objectivist accounts, which though airily speculative and specular nevertheless have a certain determinist logic lingering about them, utterly unresponsive either to history or to particular situations. Neither is it accessible to "subjectivism," which posits an entirely free self-interested agent in possession of a potentially infinite inventory of practical maneuvers by which to negotiate the ever-unfolding universe of happenstance. "Universal mental structures," finally, beg the question of culture and in any case cannot address the distinctive adaptation or evolution of structured social practices to or within "possibilities and impossibilities, freedoms and necessities, opportunities and prohibitions." If *habitus* is embedded in practice, Bourdieu seems to say, it cannot be accessible to theoretical discovery; it is an immediate existential resource, not, to its carriers, an obviously self-consistent system, even though an observer may readily detect consistency, regularity, and rule in it. *Habitus* is not a rational structure, says Bourdieu, adopting an image from Descartes, like a city that has been planned and executed by fiat; it is the work of many hands, an accumulation over time of many expedients, artifices, and contrivances whose origins are mostly forgotten, ways and byways in which persistent usages and slow adaptations, erosion and accumulation, maintain its identity through time and change.

Habitus thus releases the social agent from the rigidities of objectivist rule without altogether unfastening the tracery of regulation; the agent is disposed, but not constrained, capable of origination within the range of individual imagination, a horizon of social possibility, and the immediacy of situation—like mild-mannered Bartleby, who "*prefers* not to" because he hasn't any choice but to prefer.

Habitus, as William James says of habit, is "the enormous flywheel of society, its most precious conservative agent."[5] It subsists, with habit, in the plastic medium of the neural system, always returning, however compressed or distended, to its own form, a shape at once material and mental that impedes and facilitates, a force both for social inertia and for social momentum—or a kind of plasma that, like the soul or the ghost, retains, even as a disembodied idea, the intellectual form of the social body. What remains obscured in it, except to agents to whom ethnomimesis has disclosed it, is the capillary exchange in which such plasticity consists—what brings the agent into the embrace of "structuring structures" adjusted to the objective world of things and of persons and at the same time providing a medium for the "transposition" of dispositions; that incorporates habits with systems, communicates systems as structures, installs structures in practice.

Ethnomimesis, at one level, is a triangulation of persons to one another and in turn to the social world that transfigures the reflexes, reactions, expedients, and inventions arising from, recalled, and originated in situations, into the signs, indications, orientations, insinuations, and representations whose activation, in relation to "objective conditions," discloses *to the agent* a structured relation, and hence a structure: a "structuring structure." Its not-so-secret domain—an intimate and evanescent discourse of voluntary and involuntary movements, actions, expressions, postures, gestures, and inflections, as well as various physiological textures, tones, colorations and conditions, orientations and proximities—is the transient but sensible activity through which social intelligence communicates itself in and through agents, or to be more precise, in and through their bodies. Though not a "practice," ethnomimesis is nevertheless concrete, practical, and interactive, like language, a program of articulations that aligns signification to significances, only apparently arbitrary until actually enlisted, in practice and over time, as a system of shared adjustments to "objective conditions," especially the conditions of social relations themselves. Such adjustments, both in themselves and together, become the characteristic and indispensable forms of sociality, intelligible as forms and transposable as such; they produce a range of social performances that elaborate themselves redundantly in culture, becoming the tacit "structuring structures" of *habitus* and as such generating the regular practices of social life as well as the dialectic of representations that is the engine of social change.

Ethnomimesis, then, is both "objective" and "subjective." Indeed, we daily observe and experience it. It is a field of social activity, even of social action—but one as invisible either to "objectivism," which must objectify, or "subjectivism," which must subjectivize, either to the universal or to the particular, as the incalculably calculated punctualities, the vanishingly vanquishing glances and looks, the precisely measured but immeasurable angularities of heads, ineffable trepidations of shoulders, the exquisitely meaningful meaninglessness of movements and utterances that by what is both will and fate transform antagonists into intimates, strangers into lovers—and with equally unprepossessing prepossession dismantle the structures of amity to which they have devoted such ingenuity and patience.

Only a subjective objectivity, or an objective subjectivity, will expose the simultaneously liminal and subliminal, intersubjective, and objective character of ethnomimesis. We might, on its behalf, reclaim the eighteenth-century sentimentalist concept, associated with Shaftesbury and Rousseau, of *affection,* or recruit from clinical psychology the idea of "affect," ideas that together express a number of virtues and functions mingled together in ethnomimesis, including the subjective eruption of feeling ("affect"); the power of feeling to influence or establish, that is, to "affect" feeling transitively in others; the sense of spontaneous adhesion, coordination, or reflexivity between human beings (celebrated, for example, in improvisatory ensemble jazz) fundamental to ethnomimesis; and finally "affectation," or the power of setting forth in a social milieu, "theatrically," one's sense of identity or social place through inventories of "attitudes" that, as that term implies, are "transposable" configurations of ideas, feelings, beliefs, and the signs of every kind that embody and transmit them.

To conceive the social system ethnomimetically is in effect to think the power of affect laterally rather than vertically, not as something that springs out of some inferior mental stratum into consciousness but as an extensive field of interpersonal awareness originating in bodies and consistently and continuously communicated among agents' bodies whose "feelings" or "affections" are always in a sense seismographic "readings" of others' and hence continually learned and elaborated, reproduced and transmitted, as a total system of subtle "affections" that are the real, if invisible, ground of association, relation, affinity, and aversion, attachment and, as it were "affection." Ethnomimetically speaking, there is no "emotion" or motivation in isolation, nor strictly speaking do we produce either emotion or motive subjectively, autonomously, or individually, but interactively, responsorially, dynamically. Like jazz improvisation, or Bourdieu's "feel for the game," feeling and action erupt out of mimetically learned anticipations, predictions, transformations: which may explain why pathological "lack of affect" ("I can't feel anything") may be associated with social alienation, dislocation or disruption, and depression, or the retreat from action, with frustrated expectations—that is, with an incongruency of ethnomimesis and *habitus.*

Such a "practical *mimesis,*" Bourdieu writes,

> implies an overall relation of identification and has nothing in common with an *imitation* that would presuppose a conscious effort to reproduce a gesture, an utterance or an object explicitly constituted as a model—and the process of reproduction—a practical reactivation which is opposed to both memory and knowledge—tends to take place below the level of consciousness, expression and the reflexive distance which these presuppose. [The body] does not represent what it performs, it does not memorize the past, it *enacts* the past, bringing it back to life. What is "learned by the body" is not something one has, like knowledge that can be brandished, but something that one is. This is particularly clear in non-literate societies, where inherited knowledge can survive only in its incorporated state. It is never detached from the body that bears it and can be reconstituted only by means of a kind of gymnastics designed to evoke it, a *mimesis* which, as Plato observed, implies total investment and deep emotional identification.[6]

Mimesis certainly presupposes identification, and identification likely compels mimesis, even unconsciously. But whether or not "explicitly constituted as a model," the "practical reactivation" springing from bodily affinity presupposes both a consciousness of one's own body as well as of what is meaningful in its configurations—an awareness that is neither memory nor knowledge in the discursive sense but a "regulated improvisation," like that of a musician—as well as an imaginative sympathy that captures, even unconsciously, the meaningfulness in the attitudes, whether unconscious or not, of another's body. Even infants know this, and smile. In ethnomimesis the body reflects, impersonates, and represents its relation to other bodies *in relation* to the social world, even if and inasmuch as its meaningfulness may be an effect of, say, regular physical activity or the natural environment. While that relation is not necessarily a formal or informal "representation" in a fully motivated sense (i.e., "a sign in one system made to be a signifier in another")[7] it is nevertheless a *signification* that rescues symbolic action out of the mire of merely somatic motions, bestowing upon the body a social legibility that is the very definition of the body in society.

Bourdieu's insistence that "practical sense is a quasi-bodily involvement in the world which presupposes *no representation* [my emphasis] either of the body or of the world, still less of their relationship,"[8] then, is a vestigial form of the objectivist impulse to naturalize and in effect deny agency to the agent, where the unconscious character of "bodily involvement" re-registers the "automatic" character of practice *because* it is embodied. But while mimesis may be regarded as originating in involuntary reactions or reflexes as well as in intended or untended impersonation and formal or informal representation, whether or not visibly registered in the body and even if "below the level of consciousness," it is an act of discrimination between usable social meaning and a counter-realm of the repressed, the unthinkable, or the perverse, always a burst of *recognition.*

The mimetic activity of involuntary revealing, indicating, or purposeful pointing that are particular conditions of the body in relation to objective conditions, signifies a particular orientation of self to the world and to the other and perforce socially, between and among bodies. But mimesis, understood in this sense, is already at work in the genesis of perception; the reconciliation of the sensory message is already a structuring structure of the *habitus,* which like and in conjunction with language (but not exclusively through it) identifies, differentiates, organizes, and mobilizes the total structure of orientations whose accumulated message is the knowledge that constitutes *habitus,* the embodied adjustments and appropriated attitudes, physical and mental, to situations. Hence Bourdieu is right to insist that the "immediate self-evidence" of the "commonsense world" is "accompanied by the objectivity provided by consensus on the meaning of practices and the world, in other words the harmonization of the agents' experiences and *the constant reinforcement* each of them receives from expression individual or collective (in festivals, for example)."[9]

Ethnomimetically speaking, however, "expression" produces consensus, even more "harmonization," not merely by reinforcement through material demonstrations and objects, but though an *affective* influence running ethnomimetically through the social body apart from which there is no *habitus*. Representations are materially continuous with objective conditions (even if conventionally distinguished from "real life") and produce with them the mediation of responses that constitute the *habitus*—i.e., there is no world that is not represented in the very process of its making-real. "The ideality, the purity, the ingenuity, the glamour, the harmony, proportion, and form of the representation in its own phenomenality, all materially realized, have—even in the process of signification or mimesis—already transfigured what is signified or represented; to the extent that we can scarcely conceive of the object world apart from our representations of it, so is that world continually swept up in the ideality and glamour of representation. But at the same time that the representation detemporalizes and dematerializes what is represented, it is itself material and hence inevitably captured by time and change."[10] Which is to say: the materiality of the representation is touched in its materiality by its social meaning—"ideality, glamour, prestige"—so that objects or performances dissolve their own materiality as they acquire social meaning, becoming tokens in an ethnomimetic economy that objectifies and sustains objects and performances as such.

To locate Bourdieu's "structured structuring structures" within ethnomimesis, then, especially in the developmental phase, argues that the reconciliation of the sensory message can only evolve out of social accommodations to a shared lifeworld of habitual linguistic and other orientations. In this sense *habitus* is never static, but anticipates, resists, and adapts to change, not strictly speaking an "unconscious" resource but one diffused in social practice, a sensible, if subliminal, field of achieved significance, natural and conventional, that comprises a total system of orientations, or, to be precise, habits or "dispositions" of orientations. Because it is continually represented, sustained, and preserved in social interaction, *habitus* will of course be in some sense learned, remembered, and known; but its epistemological character, like that of language, cannot be understood apart from the fact that it is also continually modeled, reinforced, and incorporated, and like language may also be, when these influences cease, forgotten.

Understood this way, ethnomimesis, unlike *habitus*, is irresistibly imaginative at every point. There is no naturalizing of the *social* being in any phase of its activity or at any stage of its life, but always only the imagining body, caught up in the web of social life that it at once personifies and desires. All the revelations of and by the body—reflexes and reactions, impersonations and representations—belong to the "objective conditions" that are the sustaining environment of *habitus*. While enactments and performances, rituals and stories may "reinforce" what *habitus* has already made commonsensical, they also erect an imaginary milieu presumed to be part of the repertoire of unintended intentions: various gestural vocabularies and lores, formal and informal narratives, as well as ideologically grounded representations of family life, marriage, and gender roles, of ethnic, class, and racial others or stereotypes, of political/cultural heroes and counter-heroes whose social "styles," undefended by evaluations socially secured and sanctioned, enter the domain of tacit expectations, predictions, anticipations, what Bourdieu calls "closed doors," "limited prospects," and "dead ends." But these "things to be done and said," as Bourdieu calls them, or their contraries, may or may not answer to the dispositions of the *habitus,* even as they arise from them.

If, as Bourdieu writes, "a very close correlation is observed between the objective possibilities and agents' subjective aspirations," it is not because of conscious adjustment but, as he suggests, because "possibilities and impossibilities, freedoms and necessities, opportunities and prohibitions generate dispositions objectively compatible with these conditions"; these represent "a kind of immediate submission to order that inclines agents to make a virtue of necessity."[11] But if the ethnomimetic field of orientations, indications, cues, and so on both reflects objective conditions and perpetuates the expectations and aspirations compatible with them—e.g., "the culture of poverty"—then *habitus* may not only embody such adaptations but construe conditions ethnomimetically on its own behalf, altering both "objective conditions" and the adjustment to them. This is perhaps precisely the region of folklore, what Robert St. George calls a "zone of exchange of information,"[12] where enthnomimesis works not only within social formations but between and among them, the essentially stable "dispositions" of *habitus* producing consistent structures that while they perpetuate residual adaptations also in effect adapt the adaptations to new conditions—essentially the situation of diasporal cultures submitting unfamiliar practices to adaptive reuse at the same time as they apply old uses to new opportunities: precisely the condition of, say, African American music.

It is in the mystery of such correlations that Bourdieu identifies an "immanent law" that because he cannot locate it in the resonances and sympathies of ethnomimesis he must ascribe to the cold embrace of "history": "The practices of the members of the same group or, in a differentiated society, the same class, are always more and better harmonized than the agents know or wish, because, as Leibniz again says, 'following only (his) own laws,' each 'nonetheless agrees with the other.' The *habitus* is precisely this immanent law, *lex insita,* inscribed in bodies by identical histories, which is the precondition not only for the co-ordination of practices but also for practices of co-ordination."[13] This apparently ineradicable residue of objectivism strictly limits the concept of *habitus* to static traditional societies such as the Kabyle, where evidently unchanging objective conditions theoretically produce uniform histories. But ethnomimetic schemes for shaping and narrating "history," as well as, and more importantly, interpersonal mimesis ("orchestration") among legible bodies, tie practice to history through representations perpetuated in the social matrix itself. Within *habitus* there are no illegible bodies; outside the *habitus* there is only the ethnomimetic transfiguration of the body into new forms of intelligibility, of which the demonized or idealized "other" is the primary type.

The idea of ethnomimesis, then, relieves to some extent the hard empiricism as well as the incipient rationalism in the notion of practice as "the art of assessing likelihoods,"[14] or making virtues of necessities, even as it offers to anchor an otherwise purely speculative remark such as that "it is certain that each member of the same class is more likely than any member of another class to have been confronted with the situations most frequent for that class"—as if the harmonization of a class *habitus* reflected only some sort of statistical regularity. Surely it is not the *frequency* or the distribution of experiences, but the *consistency of association* that through ethnomimesis sustains *habitus*: such consistency of association may of course imply the persistence of the material conditions in which the community has its existence as such—but the community as such may also outlive the conditions that shaped its *habitus.* A collective "sense of future," or any other aspect of *habitus,* does not arise directly from those conditions, in any case, from conditions to experiences to individuals, but from communications—"community"—within a matrix of associations. This is not to say that Bourdieu's "identical histories," or the illusion of them, does not point to the embeddedness of "individual histories" in a collective "history" ethnomimetically distributed: but it is precisely the incongruence between "individual histories" and the collectively formulated messages of ethnomimesis that produces the content of subjectivity, flowing out of the gap between *habitus,* as a social inheritance, and the idiosyncratic messages of individual experience, or between one ethnomimetic field and another, such as, say, families or ethnic groups and institutional cultures, to which individuals may or may not be "adjusted."

It *is* nevertheless the case that *habitus* "ensures its own constancy"—not by choosing "a relatively constant universe of situations" (tautological because *habitus* summons situations and in a sense creates situations), but by keeping in effect its own company, especially in circumstances that imperil its cohesion. No human community can wholly control the circumstances in which it has its existence, however vigorously it may resist change, though it can sustain its own sociality, deliberately and often revivalistically, under new, perhaps alien conditions. Yet Bourdieu doggedly attributes "the tendency of groups to persist in their ways" to the "fact that they are composed of individuals with durable dispositions that can outlive the economic and social conditions in which they were produced."[15] No. Groups "persist in their ways" only insofar as they in some fashion persist *as groups* in consistent actual or symbolic association; individuals liberated or expelled from groups or classes to other groups or classes quickly adopt new ways, no matter how "durable" their dispositions, and moreover readily learn different repertoires of behavior for different social circumstances. The individual who adapts only with difficulty or not at all is perhaps one for whom, as in the case of certain subsistence tribal societies, or certain neurotic personalities, identity and society have been thoroughly absorbed into one another, where there is no "self" apart from its articulation with the activity of the group, to act as the agent of adjustment; hence the immediate environment of self, the incorporated *habitus,* has not in fact been incorporated but remains invested in the patterned associations of social life.

If shifts in objective conditions do not directly produce adjustments to *habitus,* then, but are mediated by the ethnomimetic field, *how* are changes in objective conditions eventually reflected in social expectations, especially as change seems mostly to occur between the generations? If, as Bourdieu writes, "the genesis of a system of works or practices cannot be described either as the self-development of a unique and always self-identical essence, or as a continuous creation of novelty," but rather arises "from the necessary but unpredictable confrontation between the *habitus* and an event that can exercise a pertinent incitement" upon it, how does *habitus* rescue such an event from the "contingency of the accidental," constituting it "as a problem by applying to it the very principles of its solution?"[16] As Bourdieu observes, *habitus,* as the "product of a particular class of objective regularities," tends "to generate all the 'reasonable,' 'common-sense' behaviors" compatible with those regularities, while excluding what is incompatible.[17]

As change can only occur within *habitus* itself, ethnomimetically, *habitus* cannot produce change until individual and idiosyncratic adaptations or maladaptations to new experiences have assumed through ethnomimesis a social character. Thus the irregular, the unthinkable, or insane becomes central, thinkable, natural. The social/cultural "pioneer" emerges not only as a simple reaction to new objective conditions but to the new patterns of association arising from that reaction, the nascent social style dilating into a nascent ethnomimetic field that gradually harmonizes and consolidates into a frangible mode of individuation in a context of social identity. Individuals adapt to new groups and groups to new conditions, as well as groups to individuals and conditions to both. But if new conditions summon new individuals, reformers, rebels, and pioneers, it is because those conditions have engendered new patterns of association through which the company both recognizes the individual as such and constructs him dialectically as a new social type, typically through conscientious representations of fictional heroes and models on the "social stage" as well as in drama and literature.

. . . .

With the concept of "symbolic capital," Bourdieu's science reaches beyond *habitus* to the interactions between and among society's constitutive groups, where through a dialectic of "distributions" and "distinctions," between a "material logic of rarity" and the "symbolic logic of distinction," society makes shift to maintain the alliance of reality and appearance, of power and representation, favorable to the *habitus* whose representations have become the touchstone of social power and material advantage.

This sociology, absent the idea of ethnomimesis, effaces the natural limits of the social, figuring a network of many ethnomimetic springs or centers linked to one another by complex technical systems as an internally differentiated but essentially unitary phenomenon, "society." In this phase of his theory, Bourdieu enters a purely semiotic world, where the central metaphor of "cultural capital"—limited social resources evaluated according to a "logic of scarcity" and distributed according to a "logic of distinction"—becomes a kind of reflective reflector, a symbolic system at once anterior and posterior to the social, in effect placing "capital" in the same relation to the social as in Derrida "writing" is to language: by a kind of metaphorical inversion the secondary becomes primary, the derivative the original, what wants explaining itself the explanatory scheme.[18]

That society should produce a ductile semiotic system that both organizes and accounts for itself, as if capital were the aim and end of the social, as writing for Derrida is the *telos* of language, suggests the possibility of a thoroughly self-consistent theory, as it turns the manifest content of the social or the literary text into complex schemes of "misrecognition" designed to efface the authentic operations of a latent content whose laws are the laws of the reified forms of value and of meaning. For capital is "always already" symbolic value. Bourdieu's sociology anticipates a postmodernity in which social prestige, puissance, power, knowledge, status, and charisma, ever and always what capital desires to be transformed into, may as readily be transformed into capital as property, goods, and provisions may be transformed into it—thus releasing capital as a theoretical third term in which essentially irrational relations of social value may be figured as the relations of rational economic exchange: a social alchemy becoming a social calculus.

Even so, Bourdieu explicitly rejects what he calls "economism," which applies to precapitalist societies the "categories, methods, or concepts which are the historical product of capitalism and which induce a radical transformation of their object, similar to the historical transformation from which they arose," capital being at once a cause and an effect of mobility, dislocation, atomization, and alienation, all of which it fosters for its own ends. "Economism" grounds its theory of society in a symbolic practice that, as Bourdieu points, out betrays the deterioration of the social as such, as more purely "economic" relations arise in proportion as people become strangers to one another. "As the relationship becomes more impersonal," he writes, "that is, as one moves out from the relation between brothers to that between virtual strangers, so a transaction is less and less likely to be established at all but it can, and does, become more purely 'economic,' that is, *closer to its economic truth*" (my emphasis).[19]

What economism cannot reckon is "symbolic labour"—the "work of reproducing established relations no less vital to the existence of the group than the reproduction of the economic bases of its existence, the labor required to conceal the function of the exchanges is as important as the labor needed to perform this function." For, in fact, Bourdieu says, "everything takes place as if the specificity of the 'archaic' economy lay in the fact that economic activity cannot explicitly recognize the economic ends in relation to which it is objectively oriented. The 'idolatry of nature' . . . combines with the systematic emphasis on the symbolic aspects of the acts and relations of production to prevent the economy from being grasped as an economy, that is, as a system governed by the laws of interested calculation, competition or exploitation."[20]

Economism "annihilates the specificity located precisely in the socially maintained discrepancy between the 'objective' reality and the social representation of production and exchange"; it "removes the conditions of possibility of the institutionally organized and guaranteed misrecognition that is the basis of all the symbolic labor aimed at transmuting the inevitable and inevitably interested relations imposed by kinship, neighborhood, or work, into elective relations of reciprocity, and, more profoundly, at transforming arbitrary relations of exploitation into durable relations, grounded in nature."[21]

It is not economism, then, that inspires Bourdieu's metaphor, but rather a trace of it, the "inevitable and inevitably interested relations" that capitalism exposes as an economy of "interested calculation, competition or exploitation." By winning this subtle exemption from economism, Bourdieu commutes the motive proper to one domain of symbolic exchange to another, placing the figure of "symbolic capital" at the heart of a society that as a consequence appears to be a displaced or sublimated form of the struggle for it, a relation of "interested calculation, competition, or exploitation" collectively misrecognized as an economy of deference, reciprocity, and ceremony. What is *habitus,* then, but the total body of "cultural capital," the "structuring structure" of a cultural marketplace organized by the "regulated improvisations" of collective misrecognition and driven by the perdurable "dispositions" of interested calculation, competition, or exploitation?

In Bourdieu's cultural capitalism, ethnomimesis is a welter of local and situational as well as systemic impersonations, his collective "make-believe," in which economic relations are continually figured as social relations and particular economic exchanges (as in advertising) symbolically situated in an imaginary social space. As capitalism more sweepingly and penetratingly achieves its economic ends, then, so does it increasingly figure itself in terms of imaginary social relations and social selves, with its own *habitus,* or extensions of *habitus,* that ethnomimesis generates in conformity with the imaginary (i.e., commercial) character of those relations.

Within ethnomimesis, then, under capitalism, there is an odd kind of recursion, where the society's representations of itself in politics, media, advertising, or news, and the like produce an *appearance* of particular social relations (families, groups, classes, and races), a kind of pseudopolitics, while in reality there are only economic relations, ethnomimetically dispersed through commercial and electronic narratives and images: a historical situation that Bourdieu's analysis extrapolates as theory, as if the state of capitalism in postmodernity were at once the *telos* and *ontos* of the social process. It is a world in which the "durable transposable dispositions" of the *habitus* have been expropriated, projected into a commercial form of what Bourdieu sees as the collective recognitions/misrecognitions of public ritual, the "officialization" strategies in effect returning, recursively, to generate a *habitus* of unconscious complicity:

> Because it does not offer the institutional conditions for the accumulation of economic or cultural capital (which it even expressly discourages through a censorship forcing agents to resort to euphemized forms of power and violence), this economic order is such that strategies oriented towards the accumulation of symbolic capital which are found in all social formations, are here the most rational ones, since they are the most effective strategies within the constraints of this universe. The principle of the pertinent differences between the modes of domination lies in the degree of the objectification of capital. Social formations in which relations of domination are made, unmade and remade in and through personal interactions contrast with those in which such relations are mediated by objective, institutionalized mechanisms such as the 'self-regulating market,' the educational system or the legal apparatus, where they have the permanence and opacity of things and lie beyond the reach of individual consciousness and power.[22]

Yes; but these institutionalized mechanisms become themselves fields of social relations, ethnomimetically extending, differentiating, and adapting the displaced cultural contributions of its participants (e.g., an office bureaucracy that perpetuates authoritarian and hierarchical cultural and religious structures). The social distinctions thus achieved, as through education or money,[23] are subjected to persistent tests, both in practice and in official procedures that are games of practice or practices of practice, to wrest legitimacy out of legitimization (e.g., "old" wealth as against *nouveau-riche*; learning as against certification)—in effect a *reinhabiting* or disalienation of the reified form of power.

"Interest" in Bourdieu, even as distilled from economism, carries a residuum both of Hobbesian self-interest and Marxian class struggle, a competition euphemized by the protocols, ceremonies, obligations, and policies of social life; all become an extensive ritual of "misrecognition" and "concealment" that, though Bourdieu identifies them with mimetic processes such as public ceremonies and demonstrations, are at bottom transfigurations of violence.

Ethnomimesis, by contrast, implies adhesion, compliance, conformity, membership, affiliation, affection, and love. Whereas Bourdieu wants to locate the basis of self-interest in the real economy, which symbolic capital perpetuates in the structures of social relations, as well as in what constitutes the "objective conditions" or the "limits of the possible" to which those structures are oriented and adjusted, ethnomimesis generates *habitus entirely* within the domain of actual and symbolic human affiliation, originating certainly in the family and elaborated ultimately in every form of the social relation where "interest" is not directly constituted by need (e.g., for nurture, comfort, protection, affection) but by the natural and learned behaviors that provide for them, as all needs are supplied by the human labor secured by social membership.

The primary *personal* interest, then, from the ethnomimetic viewpoint, is to be loved; but within that interest ethnomimesis pursues its own *social* end and aim, which, beyond imitation or impersonation, is identification, or the total surrender of the subject to the ethnomimetic influence, which is to say, *to love.* Love is the answer that ethnomimetic sympathy makes to the primary personal need to be loved; it is the altruistic tendency of ethnomimesis itself, which both in its origins and its ends absorbs self into other, assimilates subject and object. *Habitus,* in these senses, is a work of love, ethnomimesis its necessary and perpetual condition of becoming, the ever-interiorizing processes of human experience tending toward but never achieving the condition of objective knowledge its own practice embodies. "Money can't buy me love"—love admits of symbolic displacement to capital, but cannot be supplanted by it. Affection in this broad sense is the social engine of developmental learning, of all its differentiations and elaborations, and ultimately of all deference to authority or counter-authority of whatever kind that may issue in the officialization strategies Bourdieu describes—which is simply to feel, within particular social formations, that worthiness to be loved guarantees actual or symbolic inclusion.

"Ethnomimesis" captures this relation; it implies the priority of likeness, identification, affiliation, and loyalty in which community consists to the differentiation and difference, distinction, competition, and violence that are negations of them, and further, that a sociology of violence derives its analytical power from the specific social negations of capital: precisely where Hobbes and Marx derive it. Popular concepts of self-esteem go awry by radically subjectifying a function of personality where personality has incorporated and continually reproduces the social learning of the *habitus* (i.e., worthiness and esteem can arise only from what is socially marked as worthy and esteemed). *Actual wealth* is worthiness achieved through sociality, and in this sense "symbolic capital" is not a collective misrecognition/recognition of a "real" economy but the very thing itself, what "actual capital" wants, but most often fails, to produce.

When the conditions of ethnomimesis break down—as, say, when traditional societies move into cash economies—sociality itself breaks down, as agents imagine themselves to have become economically independent and autonomous. But the material and psychological interdependency fundamental to society will eventually reassert itself: for survival is not, ultimately, assured by the acquisition of capital, symbolic or actual. It is assured by the securing of membership, necessarily implying deference to all forms of social authority as well as enactment, demonstration, and representation of that deference (this is the "labor" that Bourdieu figures as misrecognition), even as these foster the acquisition of "capital." For the reduction of social relations to "callous cash payment" is never thorough and complete except in the special domains of capital exchange (nor, I would suspect, even there). Rather it tends to recur to underlying social relations: a fact that explains why racial and other kinds of discrimination bar access to capital, while "privilege," socially understood, opens access to it (i.e., why even within capitalism social discriminations tend to reproduce themselves in economic terms), and why even the *appearance* of privilege or the absence of it can be deployed to manipulate access to capital. (It may be that the myth of the free market is simply a description of the operation of capital in a milieu of social privilege—i.e., access to capital—taken for granted and hence in effect bracketed out; which is why the myth of the free market is always positioned in relation to privilege.)

Between *habitus* and "ethnomimesis," then, lies this crucial distinction, though not, in modern society, a division, between *social* practice as such and the articulations of ethnomimetic communities to the larger society in which a dialectic of distributions and distinctions produces economic relations as such. "In fact, the institutionalization of distinction, inscribing it in the hard, durable reality of things or institutions, goes hand in hand with its incorporation, the surest path towards naturalization," Bourdieu writes. That "distinction that is called natural . . . only exists in the distinctive relationship with more 'common,' that is statistically more frequent, dispositions."[24] Ethnomimesis, however, would suggest not a "statistically more frequent" effect, but the exhaustion at the outer limit of ethnomimesis, where dispersal of the social group and consequent weakening of the social message forms the ethnomimetic frontier of the group as such, which only technical extensions of its social images may cross. The "legitimizing theatricalization" thus secures its own power by reintroducing through ethnomimesis elements of *habitus* into what are at bottom economic, and not, except accidentally and technically, actual social relations.

Though the metaphor is of course prejudicial to his argument, Bourdieu nevertheless injects "social alchemy" into his brilliant analysis of distinction in *The Logic of Practice,* the germ of his later magisterial book on the subject, "a permanent struggle between those who, because of the position they occupy within the distributions, have an interest in subverting them by modifying the classifications in which they are expressed and legitimated, and those who have an interest in perpetuating misrecognition, an alienated cognition that looks at the world through the categories the world imposes, and apprehends the social world as a natural world. This mis-cognition, unaware that it produces what it recognizes, does not want to know that what makes the most intrinsic charm of its object, its charisma, is merely the product of the countless crediting operations through which agents attribute to the object the powers to which they submit."[25]

But such "crediting operations" are precisely "the representations that agents have of their own and other agents' positions in social space (and also the representations they give of them, consciously or unconsciously, through their practices or their properties)." They "are the product of a system of schemes of perception and appreciation which is itself the incorporated product of a class condition (that is, a particular position in the distributions of material properties and symbolic capital)."[26] They are, in other words, at once the means and the ends of "keeping up with the Joneses," the impetus behind ever-finer distinctions drawn within a race, a class, or religion (as hair-splitting distinctions of skin color, spiritual doctrine, "lifestyles"). "The very life-style of the holders of power," Bourdieu writes, "contributes to the power that makes it possible, because its true conditions of possibility remain unrecognized, so that it can be perceived not only as the legitimate manifestation of power but as the foundation of its legitimacy. 'Status groups' based on 'lifestyle' . . . are not, as Weber thought, a different kind of group from classes, but dominant classes that have denied, or, so to speak sublimated themselves and so legitimated themselves."[27]

And yet while the struggle for distinction is certainly "the perfect antithesis and the most effective negation of the struggle against another class, in which the class itself is constituted," it is not the case that "status groups" are simply a sublimated form of symbolic dominance. All the forms of symbolic distinction are themselves enunciations of membership in some actual or imaginary community, and entail subjective identification with that community as well as "theatrical" projections (i.e., representations) of such membership in it on behalf of adjacent communities. Social groups as such are formed ethnomimetically out of real association (incidental phrases such as "social neighborhood" suggest Bourdieu's sense of this) that may or may not conform at different times and places to the objective distributions that are the material basis of social class ("the material logic of rarity") or with the symbolic identifications ("the symbolic logic of distinction") through which agents assert and/or achieve or do not achieve symbolic membership in the (to them) distinctive group.

At different historical moments a social class (i.e., "working class") may, say, under industrial conditions arise ethnomimetically out of association at the same time as it becomes discernible on the social landscape *as* a class; at other times dispersal of the class (as understood in terms of objective distributions, as when an urban industrial working class rises into the suburban middle class) may weaken ethnomimesis, and consequently the formation of *habitus,* to the extent that consistent identification, which is to say, assertion of affiliation, cannot be anything but symbolic—that is, "lifestyle." This is certainly the case in the "consumer class," discernible as an effect of distributions but ethnomimetically diversified into multiple real memberships and symbolic assertions of membership. Where ethnomimesis carries symbolic assertions of identity outside the range of actual social interaction—when it becomes "common" and hence no longer registers the coherence or continuity of the ethnomimetic group—a "struggle for distinction" arises again as an effort to bring into congruency the incongruency between *habitus* and ethnomimesis that ethnomimesis has *itself brought about.* In the former case (the industrial "working class"), multiple enunciations of affiliation (e.g., "ethnic-American," "working man," "taxpayer," "citizen," "white man") reflect a "symbolic logic of distinction" underwritten by an assertion of larger imaginary memberships in which the ethnomimetic membership has its legitimacy; in the latter case (e.g., the consumer class, especially today's mobile executive-managerial class), mobility and dispersal generate a kind of spurious, standardized "*habitus,*" a sort of life-style *Esperanza* of standardized tract "homes," stereotyped church membership and deracinated religious "faiths," recreations (golf), "conservative" ideas and values that reflect the almost total subordination of *habitus* to the economic expedients of the corporation.

Ethnomimesis is a vital human need, the lifeblood of the social process. The "economic truth" of social interaction lies in the affectionate ties, affiliations, and interdependencies in which wealth in the deepest sense consists;

the deterioration of such ties inevitably produce, against a background of the psychodynamics of isolation, exclusion, and exclusivity, vigorous assertions, actual and symbolic, of ideological, economic, cultural, and other forms of social affiliation. Bourdieu's struggle for distinction is the mark of a bourgeois society atomized by the pervasiveness of capital relations, torn not by competition for cultural capital but for the symbolic affiliation, with its promise of actual membership, that cultural capital signifies and in which its power and value consists. It is the "material logic" of distributions set against the "symbolic logic" of distinction that underwrites the political embrace of race, class, sex, ethnic, occupational, or other actual or symbolic affiliations, however invidious in themselves, to declare or define one's social "place" in a milieu of displacement and alienation. Far from a "collective misrecognition," such affiliations, or declarations of them, reflect precisely an awakening from the hegemonically enforced "misrecognition" Bourdieu describes. Ethnomimesis mitigates the rule of capital at the same time as it facilitates its integration with the social body; but where capital has eroded or washed away, where its forward march has been breached or fractured, ethnomimesis rediscovers itself, new-minting the tender of human value in the flame of our social being.

With the everywhere acknowledged penetration of capital into the originary areas of the cultural, to nurture the social medium of culture would seem to be the proper aim of cultural work in postmodernity—not in any sense to capture and fix but rather to foster a social environment in which the power of culturality may work a transforming influence on the maniacal energy of capital. In a society divided by the struggle to reconcile the irreconcilable logics of invidious distributions and spurious distinctions, the material with the symbolic, and actual with the imaginary, one in which we are both petitioners to the larger imagined community, dominated by its meretricious spectacles, and participants in relations of affection, affiliation, and identification, a story of actual social relations of which we ourselves are the outcome, ethnomimesis—which is simply the God-given instrument of human sociality—works to supply the need for acceptance, to define the conditions of inclusion, and to bestow the gift of belonging.

NOTES

INTRODUCTION

1 See Robert Cantwell, *Ethnomimesis: Folklife and the Representation of Culture* (Chapel Hill: University of North Carolina Press, 1993).

2 Pierre Bourdieu, *The Logic of Practice*, trans. Richard Nice (Stanford, Calif.: Stanford University Press, 1980), 53.

3 Eric A. Havelock, *Preface to Plato* (Cambridge, Mass.: Harvard University Press, 1963).

4 Ibid., 152.

5 "Cells That Read Minds: A New Look at Mirror Neurons," *New York Times*, January 10, 2006.

6 See Ron Susskind, "Without a Doubt," *New York Times Magazine*, October 17, 2004.

CHAPTER I: IF BEALE STREET COULD TALK

1 Leon Botstein, "Damaged Literacy: Illiteracies and American Democracy," *Daedalus* 119 (1990): 55–84.

2 Robert Cantwell, *Bluegrass Breakdown: The Making of the Old Southern Sound* (Urbana: University of Illinois Press, 1984), 200.

3 Peter Rutkoff, "Two-Base Hit: Baseball and New York, 1945–1960," *Prospects* 20 (1995): 235–328.

4 *King Oliver and His Creole Jazz Band*. VJM 49 (London). Brian Rust, sleeve notes.

5 Nolan Porterfield, *Jimmie Rodgers: The Life and Times of America's Blue Yodeler* (Urbana: University of Illinois Press, 1979).

6 Nicholas Lemann, *The Promised Land: The Great Black Migration and How It Changed America* (New York: Alfred A. Knopf, 1991).

7 Robert Palmer, *Deep Blues* (New York: Viking Press, 1981), 130–32.

8 Martin Williams, *Cuttin' the Boogie: Piano Blues and Boogie Woogie, 1926–1941*. [Sleeve notes] New World Records 259, Recorded Anthology of American Music, Inc., New York, 1977.

9 Meade "Lux" Lewis, "Honky Tonk Train." Chicago, November 21, 1935. Parlophone R-2187. New World Records 259: *Cuttin' the Boogie: Piano Blues and Boogie Woogie, 1926–1941*.

10 Walter Roland, "House Lady Blues." New York, July 19, 1933. Banner 32832, Melotone M-12762, Oriole 8257, Perfect 0252, Romeo 5257. New World Records 290: *Let's Get Loose: Folk and Popular Blues Styles from the Beginnings to the Early*

1940s. See also Magpie PY4406 (Bexhill-on-Sea, East Sussex, UK), "Take Your Big Legs Off" The Piano Blues, Vol. 6: Walter Roland, 1933–35.

11 Albert Ammons and his Rhythm Kings, "Midnight Express." Chicago, February 13, 1936. Decca 749. NWR 259.

12 Bill Doggett, "Honky Tonk." Cincinnati, August 14, 1956. King 5444.

13 Howlin' Wolf, "Smokestack Lightnin'." Chicago, 1956. Chess LP 1434: *Howlin' Wolf: Moanin' in the Moonlight.*

CHAPTER 2: DARKLING I LISTEN

1 I've borrowed "goofy trail-crazed cowboy" from my own *When We Were Good: The Folk Revival* (Cambridge: Harvard University Press, 1996), 211–12, 218.

2 All citations of "Ode to a Nightingale" from H. W. Garrod, ed., *Keats: Poetical Works* (London: Oxford University Press, 1956).

3 Allen Ginsburg, *Howl* (San Francisco: City Lights Books, 1956), 9.

4 Samuel Taylor Coleridge, *Biographia Literaria: Or Biographical Sketches of My Literary Life and Opinions,* George Watson, ed. (London: J. M. Dent & Sons, Ltd., 1962), 167.

5 Ibid.

6 Michel Foucault, *The Order of Things: An Archeology of the Human Sciences* (New York: Vintage Books, 1970), 62.

7 In conversation with the author.

8 Conversation with the author.

9 Robert Conot, *A Streak of Luck: The Life and Legend of Thomas Alva Edison* (New York: Seaview Books, 1979), 107.

10 Quoted in Constance Rourke, *American Humor.*

11 William Wordsworth, *Preface to Lyrical Ballads.* In Abrams et al., eds., *The Norton Anthology of English Literature,* Vol. 2 (New York: W. W. Norton, 1968), 102.

12 See Greil Marcus, *Invisible Republic: Bob Dylan's Basement Tapes* (New York: Henry Holt, 1997).

CHAPTER 3: THE MAGIC 8 BALL

1 Greil Marcus, *Invisible Republic: Bob Dylan's Basement Tapes* (New York: Henry Holt, 1997).

2 John Cohen, "A Rare Interview with Harry Smith," *Sing Out!* 9 (April-May 1969).

3 Fredric Jameson, "Postmodernism, or the Cultural Logic of Late Capitalism." *New Left Review* 146 (July-August 1984): 92.

4 Michel Foucault, *The Order of Things: An Archeology of the Human Sciences* (New York: Vintage Books, 1970), 62.

5 Robert Cantwell, *Bluegrass Breakdown* (Urbana: University of Illinois Press, 1984), 192.
6 Cohen, "Rare Interview," 42.
7 See Harry's mural, now destroyed, at Jimbo's Bop City, pictured on pp. 24–25 of Paola Igliori, ed., *American Magus: Harry Smith, A Modern Alchemist* (New York: Inanout Press, 1996).

CHAPTER 4: THE INVISIBLE SCIENCE

1 René Descartes, *Discourse on Method and Meditations,* trans. Laurence J. Lafleur (New York: Bobbs-Merrill Library of Liberal Arts, 1960), 11.
2 Lewis Mumford, *Technics and Civilization* (New York: Harcourt, Brace and World, 1963), 88–89.
3 Walter Ong, *Ramus, Method, and the Decay of Dialogue* (Cambridge, Mass.: Harvard University Press, 1958).
4 Frances A. Yates, *The Art of Memory* (Chicago: University of Chicago Press, 1966).
5 Ibid., 373.
6 Descartes, *Discourse,* 11.
7 Julie Kristeva, *Desire in Language: A Semiotic Approach to Literature and Art* (New York: Columbia University Press, 1980), 69–70.
8 Michel Foucault, *The Order of Things: An Archeology of the Human Sciences* (New York: Random House, 1970), 62.
9 Jane Brody, "Brain Yields Clues to its Visual Maps," *New York Times,* March 25, 1993.

CHAPTER 5: FEASTS OF UNNAMING

1 Alan Lomax, public speech, Festival of American Folklife, July 7, 1968.
2 Richard Bauman, Inta Gale Carpenter, Richard Anderson, Garry Barrow, Patricia Sawin, William Wheeler, and Jongsung Yang, *The 1987 Smithsonian Festival of American Folklife: An Ethnography of Participant Experience* (Bloomington: Folklore Institute, Indiana University, 1988).
3 Ibid., 9.
4 See Carolyn Schiller Johnson, "The 'Culture' in Cultural Festivals." Paper delivered at the meeting of the American Anthropological Society, San Jose, California, December 1, 2006. "Participants to a large extent managed and represented themselves," Johnson writes, "and clearly had their own agendas and messages to bring to the US National Mall and Festival. Finally, after four years at Smithsonian Folklife Festivals, I am recognizing the interesting empowerment that other academics have noted in writing about this particular national-level festival.

It often is *in fact and practice* empowering for many participants. While being invited to participate in the SFF is often considered to be an honor by participants, I would argue that their ability to successfully and professionally pull off the many demanding performances, interviews, and conversations in this now historically ritual space often becomes significant, life-changing practice that affects not only their actions as 'culture-bearers' or artists, but also as members of their communities at home."

5 Debora Kodish, *Good Friends and Bad Enemies: Robert Winslow Gordon and the Study of American Folksong* (Urbana: University of Illinois Press, 1986), 134.

6 Annabel Morris Buchanan, "The Function of a Folk Festival," *Southern Folklore Quarterly* 1, no. 1 (March 1937): 30.

7 Ibid., 34.

8 Loyal Jones, *Minstrel of the Appalachians: The Story of Bascom Lamar Lunsford* (Boone, N.C.: Appalachian Consortium Press, 1984).

9 Don Yoder, "25 Years of the Folk Festival," *Pennsylvania Folklife* 23 (1974).

10 Alan Trachtenberg, *The Incorporation of America: American Culture and Society in the Gilded Age* (New York: Hill and Wang, 1982).

11 Howard L. Sacks and Judith Rose Sacks, *Way Up North in Dixie: A Black Family's Claim to the Confederate Anthem* (Washington, D.C.: Smithsonian Institution Press, 1993).

12 Paul Zweig, *Walt Whitman: The Making of the Poet* (New York: Viking Press, 1984), 209.

13 Werner Sollors, *Beyond Ethnicity: Consent and Descent in American Culture* (New York: Oxford University Press, 1986).

14 Martha Banta, ed., "Part Three, 1865–1910," in *The Columbia Literary History of the United States,* ed. Emory Elliott (New York: Columbia University Press, 1988).

15 T. J. Jackson Lears, *No Place of Grace: Antimodernism and the Transformation of American Culture, 1880–1920* (New York: Pantheon Books, 1981).

16 Ann Douglas, *The Feminization of American Culture* (New York: Alfred A. Knopf, 1977).

17 David E. Whisnant, *All That Is Native and Fine: The Politics of Culture in an American Region* (Chapel Hill: University of North Carolina Press, 1983), 6.

18 Archie Green, "The National Folk Festival Association," *John Edwards Memorial Foundation Newsletter* 11, no. 37 (Spring 1975).

19 Sarah Gertrude Knott, "The National Folk Festival after Twelve Years," *California Folklore Quarterly* 5, no. 1 (January 1946): 85.

20 Fred Danker, "Regionalism and the Uses of Folklife: The Carolina Playmakers."

Paper delivered at the annual convention of the American Folklore Society, Philadelphia, October 21, 1989.

21 Knott, "National Folk Festival," 93.

22 Sarah Gertrude Knott, "Folksongs and Dances, U.S.A.: The Changing Scene," *Southern Folklore Quarterly* 25 (1961): 189.

23 Joe Wilson, "Welcome," in *51st National Folk Festival: Lowell, Massachusetts, July 28–30, 1989. Program Book* (Lowell, Mass.: National Council for the Traditional Arts).

24 Robert W. Rydell, *All the World's a Fair: Visions of Empire at American International Expositions, 1876–1916* (Chicago: University of Chicago Press, 1984).

25 See Donna Haraway, "Teddy Bear Patriarchy: Taxidermy in the Garden of Eden, New York City, 1908–1936," *Social Text* 2 (Winter 1984–85).

26 Rydell, *All the World's a Fair,* 60.

27 Stewart Culin, "Retrospect of the Folk-Lore of the Columbian Exposition," *Journal of American Folklore* 7–8: 54.

28 Ibid., 59.

29 Rydell, *All the World's a Fair,* 65.

30 Ibid., 62.

31 Roger Abrahams, "The Winking Gods of the Marketplace," manuscript (n.d.). See also Abrahams, "Zones and Borders," chapter 8 in *Everyday Life: A Poetics of Vernacular Practices* (Philadelphia: University of Pennsylvania Press, 2005).

32 See Ormond Loomis, ed., *Cultural Conservation: The Protection of Cultural Heritage in the United States* (Washington, D.C.: American Folklife Center, Library of Congress, 1983); Marjorie Hunt and Peter Seitel, "Cultural Conservation," in *Smithsonian Festival of American Folklife Program Book,* ed. Thomas Vennum Jr. (Washington, D.C.: Office of Folklife Programs, Smithsonian Institution, 1985); and Richard Kurin, "Why We Do the Festival," in *Smithsonian Festival of American Folklife Program Book,* ed. Arlene Liebenau (Washington, D.C.: Office of Folklife Programs, Smithsonian Institution, 1989). See also Mary Hufford, ed., *Conserving Culture: A New Discourse on Heritage* (Urbana: University of Illinois Press, 1994).

33 Robert Cantwell, "On Stereotype," *New England Review* 13, no. 2 (Winter 1999).

CHAPTER 6: WHITE CITY ELEGY

1 Herbert Howe Bancroft, *The Book of the Fair: An Historical and Descriptive Presentation of the World's Science, Art, and Industry, as Viewed through the Columbian Exposition at Chicago in 1893,* 5 vols. (Chicago: Bancroft Co., 1893), 136.

2 James Fullarton Muirhead, *The Land of Contrasts: A Briton's View of His American Kin* (Boston: Lamson, Wolffe, 1898), 205.

3 Paul Bourget, "A Farewell to the White City," trans. Walter Learned, *The Cosmopolitan* 16, no. 2, 133–40.

4 Quoted in Daniel F. Burg, *Chicago's White City of 1893* (Lexington: University of Kentucky Press, 1976), 99.

5 Quoted in Alan Trachtenberg, *The Incorporation of America: Culture and Society in the Gilded Age* (New York: Hill and Wang, 1982), 229–30.

6 Bancroft, *Book of the Fair,* 131.

7 W. Lewis Fraser, "At the Fair: Decorative Painting at the World's Fair," *The Century Magazine* 46, no. 1 (May 1893): 15.

8 F. Hopkinton Smith, "A White Umbrella at the Fair,"*The Cosmopolitan* 16, no. 2, 154.

9 Muirhead, *Land of Contrasts,* 206.

10 Bancroft, *Book of the Fair,* 49.

11 H. C. Bunner, "The Making of the White City," *Scribner's Magazine* 12, no. 4 (October 1892): 406–8.

12 Thomas Cole, "The Course of Empire," *American Monthly Magazine,* new series 2 (November 1836): 513; and *The Knickerbocker* 8 (November 1836): 159, 168, 180.

13 Walter Pater, from *The Renaissance,* "Conclusion," in *Prose of the Victorian Period,* ed. William E. Buckler (New York: Houghton Mifflin, 1958), 551.

14 Teresa Dean, *White City Chips* (Chicago: Warren Publishing, 1895), 41. Originally published serially in the *Chicago Daily Inter-Ocean,* Spring-Fall 1893. It "is so sacred to the American public," Dean wrote, "that it is guarded in this journey by sheriffs, police, and soldiers of two cities; that it was escorted today by the mayors of both—the crowd saw the bell come down the avenue decorated with flowers drawn by some magnificent black horses and resting on a white truck that told you in gilt letters all around its sides what kind of soap to use. Alack and alas that liberty should come to this . . ."

15 Dean MacCannell, *The Tourist: A New Theory of the Leisure Class* (Berkeley: University of California Press, 1999), 13.

16 See Robert Cantwell, *Ethnomimesis: Folklife and the Representation of Culture* (Chapel Hill: University of North Carolina Press, 1993), 276–88.

17 Horace Herbert Markley, "Amateur Photography at the World's Fair," *The Cosmopolitan* 16, no. 2, 170.

18 Smith, "White Umbrella," 154.

19 Ibid., 150–56.

20 Dean, *White City Chips,* 30.

21 Walter Besant, "A First Impression," *Scribner's Magazine* 14, no. 4 (October 1893): 532.

22 Muirhead, *Land of Contrasts,* 205.

23 Will H. Low, "The Art of the White City," *Scribner's Magazine* 14, no. 4 (October 1893): 504.

24 M. G. Van Rensselaer, "At the Fair," *The Century Magazine* 46, no. 1 (May 1893): 11.

25 Besant, "First Impression," 534.

26 Dean, *White City Chips,* 417–18.

27 Mary Catharine Crowley, *The City of Wonders: A Souvenir of the World's Fair* (Detroit: William Graham, 1894), 55–58.

28 John J. Ingalls, "Lessons of the Fair," *The Cosmopolitan* 16, no. 2, 144.

29 Hjalimar Hjorth Boyesen, "A New World Fable," *The Cosmopolitan* 16, no.2, 178.

30 Dean, *White City Chips,* iv.

31 Robert Grant, "People Who Did Not Go to the Fair," *The Cosmopolitan* 16, no. 2, 163.

32 Besant, "First Impression," 36.

33 Quoted in Trachtenberg, *Incorporation of America,* 220.

34 Hamlin Garland, in *A Son of the Middle Border* (1928), quoted in Lawrence Levine, *Highbrow/Lowbrow: The Emergence of Cultural Hierarchy in America* (Cambridge: Harvard University Press, 1988), 213.

35 Clara Louise Burnham, *Sweet Clover: A Romance of the White City* (Boston: Houghton, Mifflin, 1894), 180–81.

36 Bancroft, *Book of the Fair,* 136.

37 James Gilbert, *Perfect Cities: Chicago's Utopias of 1893* (Chicago: University of Chicago Press, 1991), 224.

38 Will Payne, *Mr. Salt* (Boston: Houghton, Mifflin, 1904), 55–57.

39 Robert Herrick, *Waste* (New York: Harcourt, Brace, 1924), 112.

40 Ibid., 107–8.

41 Besant, "First Impression," 531.

42 Clarence Clough Bird, "Preliminary Glimpses of the Fair," *The Century Magazine* 45, no. 4 (February 1893): 617.

43 Burg, *Chicago's White City of 1893,* 106.

44 Bird, "Preliminary Glimpses of the Fair," 617.

45 F. D. Millet, "The Decoration of the Exhibition," *Scribner's Magazine* 12, no. 6 (December 1892): 606.

46 Quoted in Burg, *Chicago's White City of 1893*, 107.
47 Daniel C. Gilman, "The Eye and the Ear at Chicago," *The Century Magazine* 15, no. 3 (January 1893): 477.
48 E. C. Shankland, "The Construction of Buildings, Bridges, etc. at the World's Columbian Exposition," *Inland Architect and News Record* (Chicago: Inland Publishing, 1887–1908), no. 22 (August 1893): 8–9.
49 William Truettner and J. Alan Wallach, eds., *Thomas Cole: Landscape into History* (New Haven: Yale University Press, 1994), 219.
50 Crowley, *City of Wonders*, 100.
51 Ben C. Truman et al., *History of the World's Fair* (Philadelphia: H. W. Kelley, 1893), 451.
52 Bancroft, *Book of the Fair*, 97–198.
53 Ibid., 137.
54 Crowley, *City of Wonders*, 102.
55 Ibid., 102, 109.
56 Fredric Jameson, *Postmodernism: Or, the Cultural Logic of Late Capitalism* (Durham, N.C.: Duke University Press, 1991), 51.
57 Ibid., 44, 40.
58 Bancroft, *Book of the Fair*, 960.
59 Dean, *White City Chips*, 82–83.
60 Michel Foucault, *Discipline and Punish: The Birth of the Prison*, trans. Alan Sheridan (New York: Random House, 1979), 217.
61 See William Cronon, *Nature's Metropolis: Chicago and the Great West* (New York: W. W. Norton, 1991), 23–44; and Gilbert, *Perfect Cities*, 23–44.
62 Dean, *White City Chips*, 424.
63 Reid Badger, *The Great American Fair: The World's Columbian Exposition and American Culture* (Chicago: N. Hill, 1979), 130.
64 Ibid.
65 Bancroft, *Book of the Fair*, 960–61.
66 Herrick, *Waste*, 117.

CHAPTER 7: THE ANNUAL DANCE

1 All quotations from "The Dead" by James Joyce, *Dubliners* (New York: Penguin Books, 1967).
2 See Donald T. Torchiana, *Backgrounds for Joyce's Dubliners* (Boston: Allen and Unwin, 1986); Florence L. Walzl, "Gabriel and Michael: The Conclusion of 'The Dead,' *James Joyce Quarterly* 4 (Fall 1966); and Craig Hansen Werner, *Dubliners: A Pluralistic World* (Boston: Twayne, 1988).

3 Richard Ellmann, *James Joyce* (Oxford: Oxford University Press, 1959, 1982), 245.

4 John V. Kelleher, "Irish History and Mythology in James Joyce's 'The Dead,'" *Review of Politics* 27 (July 1965): 417.

5 Zo Za-Yong, "Folk Painting," in *Survey of Korean Arts: Folk Arts* (Seoul: National Academy of Arts, 1974). In Fredric Lieberman, "Defining Korean Folk Traditions," in *Festival of American Folklife Program Book,* ed. Thomas Vennum (Washington, D.C.: Smithsonian Institution, 1982).

6 Walzl, "Gabriel and Michael."

7 For an interesting discussion of Joyce's narrators in "The Dead," that distinguishes among them by means of prosodic analysis, see Janet Egleston Dunleavy, "The Ectoplasmic Truthtellers of 'The Dead,'" *James Joyce Quarterly* 21, no. 4 (Summer 1984).

8 Ellmann, *James Joyce,* 247.

9 Torchiana, *Backgrounds,* 227.

10 In a diabolically clever psychoanalytic reading of the story, Adrienne Auslander Munich, in "Form and Subtext in Joyce's 'The Dead,'" *Modern Philology* 82, no. 2 (Summer 1984), identifies Browne himself, "tall, brown and wrinkled," as a phallic symbol and notes a variety of masturbatory and digestive motifs in the story, principally associated with Freddy and Mr. Browne.

11 Kelleher, "Irish History and Mythology," 424.

12 Ibid., 430.

13 Torchiana, *Backgrounds,* 231.

14 Kelleher, "Irish History and Mythology," 427.

15 Torchiana, *Backgrounds,* 230.

16 Kelleher, "Irish History and Mythology," 425–26.

17 Roger L. Cox, "Johnny the Horse in Joyce's 'The Dead,'" *James Joyce Quarterly* 4 (Fall 1966).

18 Ellmann, *James Joyce,* 135.

19 Ibid., 245.

20 Ibid., 230–31.

21 Torchiana, *Backgrounds,* 233.

22 In an intriguing note, Richard Cronin suggests that Gabriel's allusion is actually to the three talented, beautiful, and well-married granddaughters of Richard Brinsley Sheridan, the "three graces" of the London musical and social world, whose successes are in melancholy contrast to the more modest successes of the maiden aunts. Richard Cronin, "Gabriel Conroy's Three Graces," *Notes and Queries* 36, no. 234 (June 1989): 200.

23 See Northrop Frye, *Secular Scripture* (Cambridge, Mass.: Harvard University Press, 1976), 121–26.

24 Hugh Kenner, *Joyce's Voices* (Berkeley: University of California Press, 1978).

25 Torchiana, *Backgrounds*, 242.

26 Walzl, "Gabriel and Michael," 27.

27 Tilly Eggers, "What Is a Woman . . . a Symbol Of?" in *James Joyce Quarterly* 18, no. 4 (Summer 1988): 28.

28 Ellmann, *James Joyce*, 248.

29 Through various clues in the narrative, beginning with Lily's three-syllable pronunciation of Gabriel's name, John Kelleher has suggested links with an Old Irish saga, Togail Bruidhne Da' Derga, "The Destruction of Da Derga's Hostel," which Joyce knew and made use of in *Finnegans Wake*. The saga tells the story of the Irish king Conaire who, returning to his kingdom from the south, is killed by his own kin in the Celtic otherworld embodied in the wayfarer's hostel. It seems at least plausible that if nothing else the saga has contributed the quality of the uncanny to these sections of the story.

30 Ellmann, *James Joyce*, 287.

31 Vincent Pecora, "'The Dead' and the Generosity of the Word," *PMLA* 101, no. 2 (March 1986): 241.

32 Torchiana, *Backgrounds*, 242.

33 Ibid., 230.

34 Ibid., 231.

35 Pecora, "'The Dead,'" 241.

36 Walzl, "Gabriel and Michael," 28.

37 As, in fact, Pecora brilliantly argues in "'The Dead' and the Generosity of the Word." In the final paragraph, Pecora writes, Gabriel "attempts what he had longed to do in the previous one . . . to 'pass boldly into that other world.'" He has "reproduced in himself . . . the most fundamental structuring device for heroism, generosity, self-knowledge, and spiritual transcendence in his culture: the story of Christ." As for reading the story in the way we have, Pecora remarks that as Gabriel "only reimplicates himself blindly in the cultural conditions he longs to transcend, then we may simply be doing the same thing, in our reading, in our lives" (243). This is powerful; but I suggest that while Joyce has used the linguistic and symbolic resources of his culture to communicate his meaning, and even in a sense commits himself to the significance of the cultural construction, he has at the same time defamiliarized and in a sense recreated, and hence in a sense mastered and transcended it, at once sustaining it as an element of culture and releasing it from the networks of social power.

38 Ellmann, *James Joyce,* 249.

39 Joanna Higgins, "A Reading of the Last Sentence of 'The Dead,'" *English Language Notes* 17 (March 1980).

40 Warren Beck, *Joyce's Dubliners: Substance, Vision, and Art* (Durham, N.C.: Duke University Press, 1969), 359.

41 James Joyce, *Portrait of the Artist as a Young Man* (New York: Viking Press, 1964), 172.

42 Nathaniel Hawthorne, *The Blithedale Romance* (New York: Penguin Books, 1985), 38.

43 Torchiana, *Backgrounds,* 253.

44 Joyce, *Portrait,* 214–15.

CHAPTER 8: FANFARE FOR THE LITTLE GUY

1 I am indebted to my colleague, Professor Philip Gura, for this suggestion.

2 Quoted in Joe Klein, *Woody Guthrie: A Life* (New York, 1980), 141.

3 See his *All That Is Solid Melts into Air* (New York, 1988), parts 3 and 4, 131–284.

4 Quoted in James Surowiecki, "The Care of the Audience," *Lingua Franca* 7, no. 7 (September 1997): 23; Michel Foucault had used this passage from Marx in a lecture.

CHAPTER 9: A HARVEST OF ILLTH

Hurston's remark to Franz Boas was cited by Marybeth Hamilton at the "Tangled Roots" conference, Princeton, New Jersey, November 22, 2002.

1 My thanks to Michael Kramer for helping me to think out the economic theme of this essay.

2 Dale Cockrell, *Demons of Disorder: Early Blackface Minstrels and Their World* (Cambridge, UK: Cambridge University Press, 1997), chap. 2, "Blackface in the Streets."

3 John Ruskin, "Ad Valorum," from *Unto This Last,* in John D. Rosenberg, *The Genius of John Ruskin: Selections from His Writings* (Boston: Houghton Mifflin, 1963), 258.

CHAPTER 10: THE PARALLAX EFFECT

1 Fredric Jameson, "The Realist Floor-Plan," in Marshall Blonsky, ed., *On Signs* (Baltimore: Johns Hopkins University Press, 1985).

2 H. W. Garrod, ed., *Keats Poetical Works* (London: Oxford University Press, 1966).

CHAPTER 11: FOLKLORE'S PATHETIC FALLACY

1 John D. Rosenberg, ed., *The Genius of John Ruskin: Selections from His Writings* (Boston: Houghton Mifflin, 1963).

2 See Mary Hufford, ed., *Conserving Culture: A New Discourse on Heritage* (Urbana: University of Illinois Press), 1994.

3 Robert St. George, internal document, University of Pennsylvania Department of Folklore (January 1997), n.p.

4 Barbara Kirschenblatt-Gimblett, "Mistaken Dictotomies," *Journal of American Folklore* 101, no. 400 (April-June 1988): 155.

5 Steve Zeitlin, "The Land of Stories and Memories," *New York Times*, Op-Ed page, August 1997.

6 Mary Hufford, "Dismantling the Social Body: The Cultural Economy of Mountaintop Removal," paper presented at the meeting of the American Folklore Society, Memphis, Tennessee, October 1999.

7 "I think of cultural conservation as a reform ecology approach, not a 'deep' one," Mary Hufford writes in an e-mail to me on August 16, 2000, "which is I think where a cultural bill of rights would take us." See Hufford, *Conserving Culture*, especially Laurie Kay Sommers, Yvonne R. Lockwood, Marsha MacDowell, and Richard W. Stoffle, "Folklife Assessment in the Michigan Low-Level Radioactive Waste Siting Process." I am indebted to Mary for this reference, for a number of specific ideas in this essay, and in a more general way to her for the inspiration, the impetus, and the occasion for it.

8 Pierre Bourdieu, *Acts of Resistance: Against the Tyranny of the Market* (New York: New Press, 1998), 68.

9 Hendrick Hertzberg, "Comment," *New Yorker*, October 18 and 25, 1999.

10 Michael Hardt and Antonio Negri, *Empire* (Cambridge, Mass.: Harvard University Press, 2001).

11 See also Sens's *Commodities and Capabilities* (New Delhi: Oxford University Press, 1987, 1999); *Resources, Values and Human Development* (Cambridge: Harvard University Press, 1984); and *Inequality Reexamined* (Cambridge, Mass.: Harvard University Press, 1992), as well as Martha Nussbaum's *Sex and Social Justice* (New York: Oxford University Press, 1999) and *Women and Human Development* (Cambridge, UK: Cambridge University Press, 2000).

CHAPTER 12: *HABITUS*, ETHNOMIMESIS

1 See Robert Cantwell, *Ethnomimesis: Folklife and the Representation of Culture* (Chapel Hill: University of North Carolina Press, 1993), 4–7, 80–84.

2 Pierre Bourdieu, *The Logic of Practice*, trans. Richard Nice (Stanford, Calif.: Stanford University Press, 1980), 53.

3 Ibid., 57.
4 Ibid., 54.
5 William James, *The Principles of Psychology* (Cambridge, Mass.: Harvard University Press, 1981), 121.
6 Bourdieu, *Logic of Practice,* 72–73
7 See Roland Barthes, *Mythologies,* trans. Annette Lavers (New York: Hill and Wang, 1972), 135.
8 Bourdieu, *Logic of Practice,* 66.
9 Ibid., 58.
10 Cantwell, *Ethnomimesis,* 286–87.
11 Bourdieu, *Logic of Practice,* 54.
12 Internal document, University of Pennsylvania Department of Folklore and Folklife (January 1997), p. 21.
13 Bourdieu, *Logic of Practice,* 59.
14 Ibid., 60.
15 Ibid., 62.
16 Ibid., 55.
17 Ibid., 55–56.
18 Jacques Derrida, *Of Grammatalogy,* trans. Gayatri Chakravorty Spivak (Baltimore: Johns Hopkins University Press, 1976), 7–9.
19 Bourdieu, *Logic of Practice,* 115.
20 Ibid., 113.
21 Ibid., 112–13.
22 Ibid., 113.
23 Ibid., 131–32.
24 Ibid., 139.
25 Ibid., 141.
26 Ibid., 140.
27 Ibid., 139.

INDEX

ROBERT CANTWELL is Townsend Ludington Professor of American studies at the University of North Carolina. His books include *When We Were Good: The Folk Revival; Ethnomimesis: Folklife and the Representation of Culture;* and *Bluegrass Breakdown: The Making of the Old Southern Sound.*

The University of Illinois Press
is a founding member of the
Association of American University Presses.
Composed in Scala and The Serif types
by Jim Proefrock
at the University of Illinois Press
Designed by Richard Hendel
Manufactured by Thomson-Shore, Inc.

University of Illinois Press
1325 South Oak Street
Champaign, IL 61820-6903
www.press.uillinois.edu